April 2021

Melissa Matthes

When Sorrow Comes

When Sorrow Comes

THE POWER OF SERMONS
FROM PEARL HARBOR TO
BLACK LIVES MATTER

Melissa M. Matthes

Harvard University Press

CAMBRIDGE, MASSACHUSETTS | LONDON, ENGLAND   2021

Publication of this book has been supported through the generous
provisions of the Maurice and Lula Bradley Smith Memorial Fund

First printing

Library of Congress Cataloging-in-Publication Data

Names: Matthes, Melissa M., 1964- author.
Title: When sorrow comes : the power of sermons from Pearl Harbor
    to Black Lives Matter / Melissa M. Matthes.
Description: Cambridge, Massachusetts : Harvard University Press,
    2021. | Includes bibliographical references and index.
Identifiers: LCCN 2020039167 | ISBN 9780674988194 (cloth)
Subjects: LCSH: Topical preaching—United States—History—20th
    century. | Topical preaching—United States—History—21st century. |
    Crisis management—United States—Religious aspects—Christianity. |
    Religion and civil society—United States—History—20th century. |
    Religion and civil society—United States—History—21st century. |
    Church and state—United States—History—20th century. |
    Church and state—United States—History—21st century.
Classification: LCC BV4235.T65 M38 2021 | DDC 251—dc23
LC record available at https://lccn.loc.gov/2020039167

For Olivia, Sophia, Renny, and Colin

Contents

When Sorrow Comes

Introduction

The Power of the Pulpit

"Southern California never awoke to a less warlike day."[1] On December 7, 1941, American journalists across the country noted the dissonance between the beautiful weather, the relaxed, familial weekend atmosphere, and the horrible news of the bombing of Pearl Harbor. This juxtaposition foreshadowed how Americans for decades to come would frame their national crises: the assassination of President John F. Kennedy on an unseasonably warm and sunny November day; the collapse of the Alfred P. Murrah Federal Building against the clear, big Oklahoma sky; the destruction of the Twin Towers on a perfect autumn Tuesday; and the slaughter of schoolchildren in Newtown, Connecticut, during the innocence of the winter holidays.

There is something theological about this reporting of catastrophe. It reveals a belief and a consequent expectation that in a created order, there should be a correspondence between nature and human history. A beautiful day should not usher in bloody violence. At least not for White America. When Black Americans die, the natural order itself seems to convulse with grief. There are the thunderstorms that foreshadow Martin Luther King's death during his last address. And the rainy night when Trayvon Martin is killed. In the hegemonic American

1

imagination, even the natural order responds differently to the deaths of those imagined as *its own* and those cast as *its others*. Embedded in this narration is a complicated political theology: a messy relationship between mourning and responsibility, between patriotism and religion, and between human history and the providential order.

At each of these historical junctures, Americans have turned to their clergy in an attempt to understand the dissonance, to reconcile their faith and their citizenship, and to find a way forward. Historically, American churches have been full in the immediate aftermath of crises. The pulpit, then, has unusual influence, and the clergy a large and vulnerable audience.

This book is an exploration of the sermons that American clergy, primarily Protestant ministers, have given in the first weeks after national crises, beginning with Pearl Harbor and including the assassinations of John F. Kennedy and Martin Luther King Jr.; the uprisings following the Rodney King verdict; the Oklahoma City bombing; September 11, 2001; the Sandy Hook Elementary School shooting; and the death of Trayvon Martin.

This exploration focuses on three analytic questions: (1) Who or what is mourned in the sermons? How do the sermons identify the tragedy and recommend that listeners process their grief? (2) What are the theopolitical meanings of the deaths, according to American clergy? How does this meaning inform the clergy's narratives of the relation between church and state during the crisis? (3) How is patriotism conceived? That is, what is the meaning ascribed to being both a Christian and an American during each emergency?

This research is further animated by three theoretical claims. The first is that who and how we mourn is not only of theological importance but of political significance. Mourning is a theopolitical act. Stretching back to Sophocles's *Antigone*, the polis (and now the state) has had an interest in how and for whom its citizens mourn. Just in the last half century, the AIDS quilt, the Vietnam MIA flag, and the activism of the Mothers of the Disappeared have focused attention on the intersection of mourning and politics. And recently, Claudia Rankine has named the condition of American Black life as one of mourning.[2]

At its center, mourning is a ritual of memory—who remembers, who and what are remembered, and the converse—who and what are forgotten and by whom. American sermons during periods of crisis demonstrate how deeply entwined theological and political understandings are with American conceptions of national identity, as well as with American narratives of the past.

In revisiting these sermons, it is striking to note both the continuities and discontinuities in the ways American clergy have interpreted biblical stories and historical events to address a contemporary crisis. Immediately after Pearl Harbor, the majority of sermons had a very long sense of the past. Many refer to ancient Greece and republican Rome to frame understandings of American democracy and humanity more generally. But Pearl Harbor was the last recent American crisis for which Protestant clergy made such references. By September 11, 2001, the past was a foreign country, and most historical examples were biblical rather than political. Mention was made of resonances between America and ancient Israel, but few clergy traced the 9/11 wreckage to a historical, political past.

It is revealing to note which biblical stories had currency during various crises and which were rather surprisingly occluded. After the assassination of John F. Kennedy, for example, there were numerous sermons comparing the assassination to the crucifixion of Jesus. The president's death and American suffering were perceived as being in service to some future, greater good; the suffering was redemptive. The sermons after the bombing of Pearl Harbor made no such claims. In 1941, the biblical stories invoked centered on human sinfulness; the deaths were not theologized. Men did not die "like Christ." Rather, "Scripture teaches that bloodshed is provoked by sin."[3] Quite different theopolitical possibilities were being enacted in these different crises.

This is the second theoretical claim. These sermons are not simply theological texts but civic liturgies. Like ancient Greek theater, sermons during periods of crisis serve as a form of civic education. They are ritual narratives, retelling religious and political stories in ways designed to reassure, renew, or realign their listeners. The sermons are theopolitical gestures enacted during an unstable period. It matters what stories we tell ourselves about who we are, where we are from, and who and what are important during a crisis. It is noteworthy that in a sample of over three hundred sermons given after September 11, only a half dozen mentioned specific people who died that day. The majority did not mourn individuals, but rather the loss of security, "a way of life" that had been irrevocably and unaccountably taken away.

Although sermons might be understood traditionally as a way for a denomination to detail its particularity to its congregants, in these American crises ministers seemed to understand the challenge less as one of denominational inscription and more as one of civic service: How are Americans to understand this event as Christian citizens? What is the relation between Christianity and citizenship in this crisis? How might Christianity configure American understandings of citizenship? How might conceptions of American-ness illuminate Christianity? Even after the assassination of President Kennedy, when many ministers remarked on his Catholicism, very few sermons made denominational differences the focus. Kennedy's Catholicism was embraced as part of "our" collective Christianity. The crisis distilled Christianity to its commonalities. Those differences would return, of course. Usually within several months, the diverse strands of a denomination would reemerge, arguing for their distinctions. But during those first weeks after a crisis, there was a collective, if tentatively constructed, "we."

One of the constraints of civic education, as Sheldon Wolin noted, has been that "the identity given to the collectivity by those who exercise power reflect[s] the needs of power rather than the political possibility of a complex collectivity."[4] In other words, as Ibram X. Kendi argues throughout *Stamped from the Beginning: The Definitive History of Racist Ideas in America,* ideas protect interests, and specifically ideas about race protect the status quo and its racial inequities.[5] Thus, some of what one finds in these sermons is that the church did indeed use these crises, in part, to assert its own authority and to criticize the power of the state. But the church also reconsidered and reimagined itself—its own responsibilities, failures, and possible contributions to each crisis.

The church also simultaneously rehearsed, and only in a few instances challenged, embedded American racial identities. In the sermons after the Oklahoma bombing, for example, everyone—the victims, the first responders, the children in day care—were all rendered White in the dominant ministerial discourse because the tragedy had "wiped away color. Everyone was American."[6] But during the violence after the verdict regarding the Rodney King beating, racial difference was the primary analytic the majority of White ministers used to interpret the event.[7] In that context, the violence was not perceived as American but criminal. Somehow, in the court of White public opinion, Timothy McVeigh escaped both his Whiteness and his American identity, whereas neither Rodney King nor the protesters could discharge their race or their citizenship status.

In none of the crises this project explores do the majority of sermons reduce a crisis to a failure of the state. Rather, the tendency was to use each crisis as an opportunity to reconsider church-state relations. As Aristotle detailed in *The Politics,* a good citizen must know both how to rule and how to obey. The civic education offered in the majority of these sermons confirms this recommendation—ministers urge their congregants to learn how to rule and how to obey. The challenge remains: Over whom should they rule? And whom should they obey? Perhaps even more pointedly, when should they obey and when should they disobey? These are not simply political questions. They are theological ones as well, perhaps framed by *Antigone* but explored fully from a Christian perspective by Augustine. When does one give to Caesar and when to God? What exactly is owed to each?

Hence the final theoretical claim of this project. These sermons display the historical variety and continuity of American conceptions of "crisis." With political theorists' renewed attention in the last decade to Carl Schmitt's and others' formulations of the power of the exception, these sermons are a reminder of how American emergencies have been understood as claims both about state power and about theological authority.[8] Many of the sermons adjudicate the distinctions between a political crisis and theodicy, between an "exception" and divine revelation. In other words, a critical reading of these sermons illuminates more than the "religious sensibilities" of the time; it tells us something about the evolution of American politics and society. For example, if a crisis is understood as raising questions of theodicy, as September 11 was understood by both church and state, how the state responds and how that response is judged by its citizens will matter significantly for framing church and state power. If the crisis is not understood as a theological conundrum, as neither Pearl Harbor nor the killing of Trayvon Martin were, then a different relationship between church and state is created. The spectacle of state and church power is articulated, negotiated, and occasionally realigned in many of these crisis sermons. It is Schmitt's sometimes mistaken assumption that in modernity there is only loss for church authority and only concurrent aggrandizement of governmental power that the historical analysis and trajectory of this book attempts to nuance and begin to revise.

Schmitt's interpretation has tended to configure the sphere of analysis about crisis, and thus some important features have been obscured. Interpretations have foregrounded how the state uses its power to exercise sovereignty, primarily through the regulation of the law. My argument seeks to revive an alternate understanding of what constitutes a crisis. Echoing Norman Jacobson's definition of a crisis as a broken paradigm, crisis sermons allow us to read a crisis as an epistemological failure—a moment when the reigning theoretical banisters can no longer support a ruptured reality.[9] Echoing Jacobsen, Peter Euben makes a similar claim about how suffering propels a renegotiation with one's own self-understanding.[10]

These crises of death and violence are not crises in which the durability of the state is really challenged; they are crises in which Americans struggle for meaning and understanding. Filled with epistemological and emotional trauma, they change and challenge more than the banisters of state power. They reconfigure American citizenry. They are transformative. The question "Who am I?" in a classically Greek sense is collectively revisited.

Each crisis becomes part of the collective memory of the United States. It destabilizes and potentially reimagines the previous collective memory, and the concurrent identity that memory created. In the face of Rev. Dr. Martin Luther King's assassination, Americans had to reinterpret their understanding of JFK's assassination. How did they integrate King's assassination into their sense of America? Of racial identity? Of trauma and tragedy? Trayvon Martin was killed on February 26, 2012. Fewer than ten months later, twenty students and six teachers at Sandy Hook Elementary School were murdered. How—or did—Americans reconcile their God, Country, Family identity with their perceived inability to keep their own children safe?

This is why mourning is a signature feature of my interpretations of each of these crises. How we mourn and for whom creates a collective identity. As other thinkers have noted,[11] American resistance to mourning in the post-9/11 era made possible some of the violence that was understood as the "answer" to the tragedy. In mourning, there can be transformation. Without mourning, the trauma of the crisis risks haunting all future possibilities. It is these elements of crisis that a Schmittian analysis leaves cold and untheorized. This book provides a remedy by exploring pivotal moments from the perspective of those who sought to counsel and console Americans about what it meant to be a Christian citizen during each crisis moment.

With these theoretical underpinnings in mind, a new, more robust understanding of church and state becomes possible. A more complete topography of the evolution of American political and religious cultures is revealed. This project shifts the frame just a bit. Rather than assuming that sermons tell us primarily about religion, I show how sermons tell us something fundamental about American political culture. Concurrently, this research demonstrates that signature features of American political culture (citizenship, patriotism, authority) are influenced by lessons offered from the pulpit, particularly during a crisis.

The State and the Church

Throughout this book, two terms will be used repeatedly: state and church. "The state" refers, first, to a political organization with a centralized government established to maintain a monopoly on the legitimate use of force. Often I have used "the state" and "government" interchangeably, although sometimes "government" refers more pointedly to a specific administrative bureaucracy, such as the Clinton administration or the Nixon administration. In such cases, "government" is a means through which state power is employed. Governments change, but the state endures.

"The state" will also be used in a more theoretically layered way in this analysis. "The state" refers to that apparatus through which power is exercised over and through citizens. The state is the location and method through which dominant powers are maintained. It includes the institutions through which American hegemony is maintained domestically and internationally. Using an Althusserian formulation, "the state" is a set of material practices through which the recognition of "necessity," "obviousness," and the "natural character" of given forms of social relations are enacted and sustained.[12]

The state produces the conditions and discourses that ensure the maintenance of its own existence. The state's construction of an American civil religion is a practice as well as an ideology that assigns transcendence to nationalist fervor, which produces patriotic chauvinism and which calculates military sacrifice as a moral good. Michel Foucault developed the most compelling articulation of this discursive power—power that is not only juridical and legislative but that concerns itself with the fostering of life itself.

The state has moved well beyond control of sovereign borders to a fastidious regulation of many elements of human life. Alexander Rustow (as quoted by Foucault) notes that the state of the last one hundred years is not primarily oriented any longer to the earnings and work hours of its citizens but is now dedicated to human beings' whole vital situation. This is Foucault's "biopolitics." The state is interested and invested in addressing "all the factors on which the happiness, well-being and contentment of man truly depend."[13]

How the state maintains its power over the arc of the historical period detailed in this research varies, of course. Part of the interest of this book is to explore the mechanics and technologies of those changes. How do the discourses and practices of the state modulate during crises of identity, of values, of existential confrontation with life's meaning? I argue that state power moves from defense of sovereignty to defense of society. The military response to the bombing of Pearl Harbor is primarily a defense of sovereignty, but the internment of Japanese Americans is cast as a defense of society.

By the time President George W. Bush has the bullhorn at Ground Zero, state power is almost solely constructed as being in service to the defense of society—"our way of life." The war on terrorism is not about preserving the integrity of a sovereign nation but about ridding the world of something more elusive and metaphysical: evil, a perceived universal feature of the human condition. By 2001, the exercise of the state's prerogatives has moved beyond political power to existential power. It is Sophocles's Creon on steroids. Indeed, some of the state's furious commitment to the arguably unnecessary wars that accompanied 9/11 was in response to the terrorists' usurpation of the power to dictate who may live and who must die. The terrorists had seized what the state declared belonged only to itself.

FOR THE PURPOSES of this book, "the church" refers most frequently to mainline Protestant Christian denominations—Baptist, Methodist, Lutheran, Presbyterian, and Episcopalian. Also considered are evangelical and fundamentalist denominations, especially as they become politically more significant and active in the early 1970s. These include the Southern Baptist Convention, Assemblies of God, Church of Christ, Lutheran Church–Missouri Synod, and Presbyterian Church in America.

During the eighty-plus years studied in this book, the majority of Americans were Protestant. In 1948, Gallup began asking Americans about their religious preferences using a question that seemed to cover all the major faiths in the United States at the time: "What is your religious preference—is it Protestant, Roman Catholic, or Jewish?" Sixty-nine percent identified as Protestant, 22 percent identified as Catholic, and 4 percent identified as Jewish.[14] To this day, the largest religious segment in the United States is Protestant.[15] Fifty-one percent of Americans still identify this way. Twenty percent identify as Catholic, and fewer than 6 percent identify with non-Christian faiths, according to current Pew Forum survey categories (i.e., Jewish, Muslim, Buddhist, Hindu). Increasingly, the unaffiliated, or the category known as "none," has also grown,[16] although the majority still remain Protestant. In fact, among African Americans, 80 percent still identify as Protestant.

But this project is not about religious self-identification or church attendance, or even the religious beliefs of Americans; rather it is about what Americans do in a crisis—and for the majority of Americans, including "none's," they still go to church. Of course, the meaning of that attendance has changed, as this book will explore, but gathering in grief at a worship space after violence seems to be a quintessentially American practice, perhaps even a democratic practice, as this project will also argue.

It is Protestants' cultural dominance that guides the focus of this study. The Protestant Church has functioned as a discursive power during American political crises. Through the pulpit, the church has played a role in American self-understanding, in conceptions of patriotism, and in adjudicating the so-called boundary between church and state. What kind of civic education has the church offered? How has each political crisis influenced the church's conception of its own role in politics? Toward this end, I draw on sermons by ordinary ministers from rather unremarkable congregations. So what constitutes "ordinary" or "unremarkable"? Since this is a qualitative study, those categories are achieved by the reading of the sermons themselves. For each crisis researched, I read several hundred Protestant sermons from a range of churches around the country. The churches were of various sizes and covered as wide a range of socioeconomic and racial demographics as possible. My conceptions of "ordinary" and "unremarkable" were derived from aggregating that research.

My analysis is less concerned with denominational differences than with the normative loosely Protestant view in each period. Although denominational differences were sometimes significant in everyday life, those differences became less prominent during a crisis, when ministers tended to focus on foundational Christian beliefs—understood, of course, through their own denominational lens but without the usual fastidious adherence to doctrinal principles. In some ways, this is not surprising. During all of the crises detailed here, Americans sought unity with one another. It is a signature feature that during tumult, some differences are no longer perceived as pertinent. Because a crisis unsettles what one had previously imagined was secure, the average American is most often looking for foundational certainties rather than theological nuances.

Some readers may be unsettled by this decision to collapse the denominations. Why aren't the sermons organized by denomination or region? I chose otherwise because this is a book about the construction of what becomes the dominant American political theology in each crisis. Of course, it is interesting to examine the Presbyterian view or the Baptist view of the assassination of the Catholic John F. Kennedy. And I did spend some time immersed in those distinctions. But that analytical lens would have produced another book. In this one, politics, not theology, drives the analysis—the antagonism between the church and state, the struggle for authority, and the claim to priority in allegiance. Denominational details are not sufficiently large to construct what became the theopolitical pulse for Americans during each crisis.

In addition, denominational differences were not foundational for this analysis because many of the people who crowded into the pews during the crisis were not regular churchgoers. They may have been unaffiliated with a denomination and perhaps lacked awareness of the nuances separating one from another. That is part of what makes this study so fascinating. Despite the known decline in religiosity in the United States over the last sixty years or so, Americans still flocked to churches in the same numbers during these crises. It didn't seem to matter that in 2001 the percentage of Americans who attended church regularly had been dropping for a decade.[17] Post-9/11 churches were as full as they were in the days following Kennedy's assassination—another period during which there had been a noted decline in religious commitment.

Occasionally, a Catholic, Jewish, or Muslim perspective became particularly influential during a specific crisis. When that is the case, the analysis will explore it. During the early 1940s, for example, the Office of Civilian Defense sent religious leaders around the country a "recommended sermon" that the government believed would promote the yet-undeclared war effort. The Catholic response was visceral and widespread. Catholic priests publicly denounced the proposal and argued vehemently for the necessity of religious freedom, exempt from state intervention. The priests were quickly joined by their Protestant brethren. So in this case, the homilies and other reactions of Catholic priests are examined as constructing the dominant theopolitical discourse after Pearl Harbor.

Much has been written about the lost influence of the Protestant Church and religion more generally over the last half century. In broad strokes, increased scientific understanding, accelerating religious pluralism, and more widespread prosperity have meant that Americans attend church less frequently, follow religious rules and commitments less conscientiously, and otherwise think of their denominational affiliations as loose threads that can be cut at will according to other preferences and priorities. There are several excellent histories that review these developments in detail.[18]

This book is more application driven: How do ministers use the opportunity of a church full of people during a political crisis to reassert their authority and religious authority more generally? How do ministers renegotiate the boundary between the church and state? How do ministers articulate their distinctive version of what it means for a Christian to be patriotic during the turmoil? During a crisis, the mechanisms and movements of these constituent questions are laid bare.

The development of each is more apparent. The sermons showcase how ministers mourn the loss of their power, seek to retrieve its influence, and work to persuade their congregations and others back into the sacred conclave. Revealed over the course of these chapters are not only the theological and political arguments ministers make but the ramifications—sometimes successful, sometimes bitter failures—of these lines of exhortation.

Preaching and Sermons

In grief, there is need for community. Among the most available and recognizable shared public spaces in America are churches. During a crisis, the space for grief is usually either the site of the tragedy, if nearby, or the neighborhood church. Churches are local, plentiful, and visible to most citizens. Bishop Paul Moore of the Diocese of New York remarked in January 2002: "During a crisis like this, the church, clergy and laity, have different vocations at different times. First, the vocation of prayer, trying to sift out our feelings in the presence of God. Then the pastoral vocation—one to one—of comforting the wounded people. We meet the Lord both in prayer and in finding his presence in the suffering of his people. And, finally, the prophetic vocations of preaching and action. These different vocations come and go in a crisis, but each one is necessary."[19]

When ministers preach from their pulpits during a crisis, they are doing multiple things: (1) they are doing theology of some variety; (2) they are doing politics by engaging in the civic education of their congregation, offering ways to understand the crisis and to manage suffering; (3) they are mourning the violence and death in the tragedy and, in many instances, the loss of their own influence through the diminution of religious authority; and (4) they are trying to reclaim some of that authority and influence. Throughout the crises studied here, the state and the church struggle to define the boundary between them, to insist that various elements belong to one or the other alone. This book will endeavor to reveal the processes by which that now seemingly settled border between the church and the state was achieved.

Among those practices is preaching the Sunday sermon. "Preaching is the most distinctive institution in Christianity. With preaching, Christianity stands or falls because it is the declaration of the Gospel."[20] Americans go to church for the prayers, the community, and the opportunity to reflect, but it is the sermon that frames each Sunday. The lectionary dictates the Bible readings, and the minister chooses whether to preach about one or all of the readings. Sometimes the minister can cull a theme from the readings. Mostly sermons reflect ministers' vocational training and what they are inspired to preach.

Preaching has long been entwined with American political life. Historians have written extensively on the impact that sermons had on the founding of the United States.[21] Of the several vehicles of political theology available to American ministers during that era, the most venerable were the election sermons preached for 256 years in Massachusetts and 156 years in Connecticut. The practice began in Vermont in 1778 and in New Hampshire in 1784. The Election Day sermon, second only to the Easter sermon, was preached annually to the governor and legislature after the election of officers. To be chosen for the task was an honor. The sermons were published and distributed to each official, with extra copies for the ministers of the official's home district.[22] Election sermons were sometimes repeated for different audiences.

Besides the election sermon, the artillery sermon was an annual affair in Massachusetts and dealt with civic and military matters. The Thursday or Fifth-day Lecture was begun by the Reverend John Cotton in Boston in 1633 and was practiced for two hundred years. It was combined with market day for gathering and discussing matters of social and political interest.

Early in the republic, days of prayer, fasting, and thanksgiving were proclaimed for particular occasions. Such times were nationally proclaimed ("recommended") at least sixteen times by the Continental Congress during the Revolutionary War. The entire community went to their various churches on such days to repent of sins, seek forgiveness, and implore God to lift their suffering—the jeremiad form so central to American consciousness.[23]

Days of thanksgiving were likewise proclaimed when divine favor was experienced. The end of war brought a great outpouring of praise and gratitude. Such proclamations became rarer under the Constitution but did not disappear; the Fourth of July regularly occasioned political sermons as well as orations. The death of George Washington evoked universal grief and countless sermons extolling the character of "the American Moses."[24] The Boston Massacre sermons commemorated the events of March 5, 1770, and the Patriots' Day observances, as they are now called, marked the battles of Lexington and Concord in New England each year on April 19. Such preaching was widely attended, repeated, and published as tracts, and was often reprinted in newspapers as well.

Similarly, during the Civil War and notably after the assassination of President Abraham Lincoln, sermons were quite influential. As religious historian Harry Stout has detailed in his magisterial work *Upon the Altar of the Nation,* ministers in the United States helped to frame the nation's understanding of what constituted a "just war" from an Augustinian Christian perspective, with specific attention to how the abolition of slavery was or was not mandated by Scripture.[25] During the prolonged mourning of Lincoln over the course of three weeks, with the funeral train stopping at over 180 cities across the United States, ministers were again influential in creating a public theology.[26] The funeral was part of the re-creation of a national identity that had been torn apart by the violence of four years of war.

How the ministers used their sermons to address church authority, church-state relations, and American Christian patriotism changed, of course, over time. Although it is beyond the scope of this book to detail this history, the braiding together of American political life and the sermons from the Christian pulpit has been well established by other scholars.[27] The point is that the relationship between the pulpit and politics has been significant and enduring.

Antigone as an Analytic Touchstone

One of the most well-known examinations of the politics of mourning is the fifth-century play *Antigone* by the Greek playwright Sophocles. Antigone, forlorn daughter of Oedipus, decides that her obligations to the gods exceed her duties to reigning authority. For her defiance, she is buried alive. The tragedy highlights how the disenfranchised (both literally and metaphorically) have used rituals of mourning to contest the power of the state. It demonstrates the investment the state has in seemingly private practices of mourning. Who we mourn and how, as well as who we do not mourn and why not, are acts of nation building.

Lest this seem irrelevant so many years later, it is noteworthy that *Antigone* was among the first plays whose performance Adolf Hitler banned in both France and Germany. Clearly, the Nazi regime recognized that civil disobedience staged around acts of mourning and burial would cut to the heart of the Final Solution. The state understood that mourning practices can be a democratic form of resistance to regimes that seek not only to obliterate races and peoples, but memory itself.

Since Sophocles's *Antigone* will serve as an analytic touchstone throughout, the following quickly summarizes the play and highlights its most relevant elements. The play opens with Antigone and her sister Ismene discussing King Creon's edict that he will give a proper burial to one of their brothers, Eteocles, who fought for the polis, but not the other, Polyneices, who Creon believed was a traitor. So the dispute begins: Who should be mourned after a political battle? By whom—the state or the family? Who decides? Is mourning a religious ritual or a political practice?

Choosing familial loyalty and religious obligation over political obedience, Antigone announces that she will "dare the crime of piety" and bury Polyneices despite Creon's edict that if anyone defies his order, that person shall be stoned to death (line 75).[28] For Creon, the corpse is without any relation to him, to others, or even to the gods; it is merely the remains of a traitor. He imagines the dead only in political terms.

Before Creon discovers that it is his niece who has buried Polyneices, the Chorus recites the now well-known and much celebrated, "Choral Ode to Man." The Ode begins as an homage to the talents and abilities of human beings, but ends with a warning: "There's only death that he cannot find an escape from. . . . Clever beyond all dreams the inventive craft that he has which may drive him one time or another to well or ill. When he honors the laws of the land and the gods' sworn right, high indeed is his city; but stateless the man who dares to dwell with dishonor" (pp. 170–171, lines 359–379).

The Ode foreshadows the tragic flaw that will haunt the play—the human desire to control everything and the concurrent refusal to recognize boundaries. The Ode foretells that human beings are unraveled not only by outside forces but by their own repudiation of anything other than their own powers and perspectives. Thus, the Ode offers both psychological and epistemological insight. As Bonnie Honig has argued about the play as a whole, the Ode is a reminder of the necessity of the cacophony of multiple (and thus democratic) epistemologies.[29] When Creon listens only to himself, he risks not only the legitimacy of his own reign but the stability of the polis itself. Legitimate power requires dissent, necessitates listening to others, and does more than impose its authority; it is responsive to the demands of the ruled.

Finally, after a prophetic warning, Creon reluctantly concedes to the burial of Polyneices, whose body has already been torn to pieces by dogs. Creon then hurries to the cave where Antigone has been entombed. He finds her dead, hanging with a noose of linens around her neck. Both his son and wife subsequently kill themselves. As a result, Creon is, as had been predicted, now consumed with grief and becomes a "breathing corpse" (line 1290). His punishment is to outlive everyone he loved. But he does not mourn the loss of Antigone or seemingly take responsibility for her death. Creon denies that the outcomes are the result of his own actions and thus seeks to lessen his responsibility for the dire results.

The Chorus reminds the audience in the concluding lines of the play, "The gods must have their due" (line 1350). This is Antigone's wisdom throughout regarding the importance of mourning the dead to maintain just political power as well as the balance between religious and political authority. As Judith Butler argues in *Antigone's Claim*, Antigone and Creon are mirror images of one another. First, literally because of Antigone's incestuous lineage, her kinship with Creon is muddled. Second and more analytically, their mirroring illuminates, contests, and attempts to reconcile the relationship between divine mandate and political authority.[30] It is a mirror that American Protestant ministers will hold up to their congregations during many political crises, detailing again this confounding relationship between church and state prerogatives.

Finally, Creon's reduction to perpetual mourning serves as a profound warning of the disasters that await if either the ministers or the state fails to give the dead their due. As African American thinkers from W. E. B. Du Bois to Toni Morrison have made manifest, progress—

racial and otherwise—is only possible when Americans collectively come to terms with the suffering and violence of the past, "a better world, a more generous world involves being more receptive to those dissonant, uncomfortable dimensions of life and history that threaten our sense of stability, coherence and achievement."[31] A democratic and just United States is one in which Americans remember and mourn.

Mourning: Religion and Politics

At least since the classical period, then, mourning has been understood as a universal human experience. The human capacity to grieve the loss of a loved one is believed to unite us all in a shared, if reluctant, community. And yet, as W. E. B. Du Bois tells the story of mourning his first born, one becomes acutely aware of how the very experience of grief is still saturated with American political and racial history. When his baby son dies, Du Bois first details the universality of his family's grief: "Only in the chamber of death writhed the world's most piteous thing—a childless mother."[32] But when he describes how he and his family were walking on the street to the cemetery to bury his son, passersby indifferent to the mourning of the funeral procession yell out racist slurs. With that Du Bois is recalled not only to his race and its double consciousness but to a double kind of mourning—one for the son he has lost and another for the racial inequities that his son might have had to endure had he lived. And Du Bois, like Sethe in Toni Morrison's *Beloved*, wonders if his young son's freedom might actually lie in his demise: "My soul whispers ever to me saying, 'Not dead, not dead, but escaped; not bond, but free.'"[33]

Judith Butler has recently proposed that who we *choose* to mourn has the potential to create new kinship networks. By conscientiously mourning those beyond our familiar cohort, we can establish new bonds and thus reconfigure whose sorrow counts, whose life matters, and whose loss reverberates.[34] Claudia Rankine, too, hopes that national mourning might align us with one another.[35] As Chapter 6 of this book will address, this is the foundational claim of Black Lives Matter. It echoes Antigone's claim that her brother's death is important, is worthy. Through her defiant burial of Polyneices, Antigone values his life and marks their relationship. Similarly, in the summer of 2020, many Americans are claiming the deaths of African Americans such as George Floyd, Breonna Taylor, and Ahmaud Arbery as part of their mourning circle.

Rites of mourning are critical to every culture and to every religion. "For blessed are they who mourn, they shall be comforted" (Matt. 5:4). In Christianity, as in other religious traditions, mourning is a manifestation of a relationship, of simultaneous bereavement and consolation. It is an act attentive to absence but with a commitment to hope. As political theologian Johann Metz details, mourning for Christians is "hope in resistance."[36] It is also dependent on a belief in God's consolation.

Just as in the play, there are contemporary political powers that seek to thwart, to confiscate the power of mourning and its concomitant obligations, and to claim it as their own. This is the most meaningful element of Sophocles's play for understanding contemporary political crises. Who are the contemporary Creons who seek to appropriate mourning as solely political? How do the contemporary Antigones defy them? How do the defiant mourn the dead in meaningful and intentionally religious ways? How often does Antigone succeed? How and when does she fail? More broadly, does mourning interpolate mourners into political life, or does it suggest an alternative to political life and thus serve as a critique of the status quo? Today, the organized mourning of the death of George Floyd is a tragic reminder of the young, passionate Antigone as Black Lives Matter activists defiantly lament against the strictures of their riot-clad law-enforcing Creon counterparts.

Over the course of the historical period addressed in this book, Protestant ministers increasingly mourn the loss of their religious authority and of religious influence more generally. In each crisis, ministers are attentive to the specifics of the event, but increasingly they rue the secularization of American public culture and the dismissal of what are considered church values. For liberal and conservative ministers, what defines this loss might differ, as will be detailed throughout. But on the whole, they lament the loss of ministerial influence and the simultaneous aggrandizement of government authority. Ministers grieve the secularization of American life, the stiffening of the boundary between the church and state, in which the church's role is diminished and allegiance to the flag dominates. What begins in the sermons of Pearl Harbor as a recognition of the limitations of the state becomes an obituary for the lost independence of the church in the sermons of the Black Lives Matter movement. The modern church has ceded much of its former power and now often finds itself dependent on the intercession of the state to make a meaningful impact on American life.

Leading a community in mourning is traditionally assigned to religious leaders. Even in the military, chaplains lead servicemen and women in rituals of mourning. This is not to deny that there are state funerals for political leaders and that the state has a role in community mourning. Nothing, perhaps, makes that more manifest in the United States than Arlington National Cemetery. Over six hundred acres are dedicated as a burial ground for the men and women who have served in the United States' armed conflicts. Arlington is a testament to the power of the state to secure a final resting place for its own.

In some ways, the cemetery is an appropriation of religious power, a feature of secularization and of the state's uncontested prerogative. Why should the state have any control over the dead? What good can the state do the dead? This is one of the mistakes that Creon makes in *Antigone*— he assumes he has jurisdiction over the living *and* the dead. Yet burial in Arlington is perceived as a way for the state to acknowledge the sacrifice and service of its military members. Since military service is the only way to be awarded space at Arlington, it is also a spectacular way to exhibit the awesome authority of the state. At Arlington, the state is proclaiming that it takes care of both the living and the dead.

Occluded, ironically, is that the state often precipitated the deaths of those buried there. Many did not die of natural causes. They died in service, sacrificing themselves in a profound pledge of loyalty. This is an expression of Foucault's biopolitics—the power of the state to "let live" or "let die." Many in Arlington are casualties of the state's policy of "let die." In return, they are given dignity in death, "this special benefit" that will be denied to those who did not serve. Again, the state reaches into life processes—rituals of mourning—to claim them as part of the state's purview.

Mourning is an ideal site to think through the relationship between the church and state, because in American political culture it has been a site of contest. Political and religious discourses have been staged through rituals of mourning. Some historians have argued that since the Civil War and the assassination of Abraham Lincoln, death, sacrifice, and rebirth have been signature features of American public culture.[37]

Americans have had to explain to themselves their slaying of one another as well as the relationship of that violence to their democratic republican ideals. They have done so after each of the crises discussed in the chapters that follow, and perhaps nothing makes that ongoing challenge more manifest and more urgent than the national mourning of murdered unarmed Black Americans in the summer of 2020.

What Defines a Crisis?

It is a cliché of contemporary American life that nearly everything is a crisis—there's a financial crisis, an opioid crisis, a climate crisis, and multiple political crises nearly every week. We are continually in a state of emergency. Time is compressed and micromanaged; everything must be done immediately, if not sooner. Our thinking is truncated. Details are compressed into tweets, and layered emotions are reduced to emojis.

Yet over the last eighty years or so, while the circumstances and historical contexts are quite different from one another, it has still been possible to focus the United States' collective national attention—as Pearl Harbor, the assassinations of both President Kennedy and Dr. Martin Luther King Jr., the Newtown school shooting, and the death of Trayvon Martin all powerfully did. These were each crises not of urgency and governmental destabilization but of identity. They were foundational quandaries, like the riddle of the sphinx, which provoked Oedipus's existential question, "Who am I?"

They were crises that cut to the core of American identity, power, and conceptions of justice. Did American patriotism demand the internment of Japanese American citizens as part of the war effort? How could Americans assassinate their own president? Was the United States in the 1990s a godless country with its domestic terrorism and police brutality? Or was the United States still a Christian nation? Had it ever been? For some Americans, as Langston Hughes noted in 1932, it was easier to assess American blindness: "That justice is a blind goddess / Is a thing to which we black are wise / Her bandage hides two festering sores / That once perhaps were eyes."[38]

The crises explored in this book—Pearl Harbor, the assassinations of President John F. Kennedy and Dr. Martin Luther King Jr., the so-called

Rodney King Los Angeles "race riots," the Oklahoma City bombing, 9/11, the Sandy Hook school shooting, and the murder of Trayvon Martin—compelled Americans to look at the violence foundational to American power. Americans asked themselves whether theirs was a country built on noble sacrifice or constructed from "blessed brutalities."[39] Perhaps it was some nebulous confluence of both.

As Americans waded through these turbid waters, they either mourned the loss of certain accounts of themselves or tried to reconcile the conflicting versions of the American ethos. Why did Americans act as heroic first responders in Oklahoma City but as angry, violent bullies in Los Angeles? Were the police a force for good or for malice in American civil society?

During each crisis, a paradigmatic feature of American political identity was disrupted. As Norman Jacobson describes, there is an absence of animating vision during a crisis. Overarching, collective assumptions have been shattered—or exposed as never having been shared. Hannah Arendt (citing Alexis de Tocqueville) notes in her essay "The Crisis Character of Modern Society," "When the past ceases to throw its light upon the future, the mind of man wanders in obscurity."[40] When over three thousand were dead at the financial center of the United States, had God abandoned America? Was religion now the root of violence in the twenty-first century?

Of course, there were other crises happening and other questions being asked during the periods addressed in this book. But the ones detailed here seem most powerfully to crystalize around conceptions of identity, power, and justice. They also had mourning at their centers. These tragedies were what Paul Ricoeur names "limit experiences."[41] They gestured to human limits and simultaneously opened up the possibility of a transcendent or divine meaning. They potentially redefined or adjusted human understanding of the boundaries of human capacities. From these kinds of events, Ricoeur optimistically believed, creative possibilities could develop. Some of these crises definitely had elements of creativity and celebration. But just as often they demonstrated the perspective taken by Reverend M. Craig Barnes: "It's the one you spent most of your life avoiding, dreading, defending yourself against, like death and separation."[42] These were the tragedies one prays never to experience. So while tragedy can open up possibilities, it can just as easily cultivate paralysis, fear, and defensiveness. Which response is showcased is frequently the result of how participants mourn.

In mourning, Americans gathered in community. Some differences were set aside and grief was given its due (partially). Theological and political questions were central. For whom and how did Americans mourn? How did they acknowledge unexpected loss? Did they believe that the living could redeem the violent deaths of others? How? When was it considered appropriate to transition from mourning to action? Was mourning itself understood as an activity? What kind of activity? A religious one? A political one?

The American crises explored in this book are challenges to American identity, to American self-understanding. They are violent, unexpected events that necessitate a review of "Who are we?" They do not fit the expected order; they seem unnatural, extraordinary. They are challenges to the status quo. They unsettle routines and shake human complacencies.[43] Yet these American crises were not solely psychological. They were also epistemological. They were in some respect watersheds, necessitating that Americans examine how they know what they know. These crises demanded that Americans reflect on their history and their legacy. Americans had to look around themselves and assess their relationships, their communities. Crises expose the United States' myopia, its blind spots, and in some instances its arrogant presumptions of being in control and knowing everything.

These crises were also understood in relation to one another. They were entwined—sometimes accidentally, sometimes in the popular imagination, and sometimes by political history. September 11 was initially understood as the new Pearl Harbor. The assassination and mourning of Dr. King were comprehended and (de)valued in contrast to the assassination of President Kennedy. The bombing of the Alfred P. Murrah Federal Building and the heroics of the first responders was held up against (and over) the beating of Rodney King and the mayhem of the Los Angeles uprisings. Violence against children was incomprehensible to many, yet ordered in a racially hierarchical way, with the shooting deaths of predominantly White Connecticut children grieved more fully than the deaths of young Black boys.

Where Do Americans Go during a Crisis? Renegotiating Church-State Relations

> So religion, which among Americans never directly takes part in
> the government of society, must be considered as the first of their
> political institutions, for if it does not give them the taste for liberty,
> it singularly facilitates their use of it.
> —ALEXIS DE TOCQUEVILLE, *DEMOCRACY IN AMERICA*[44]

During each crisis addressed, many Americans, Protestant and otherwise, have crowded into churches. Even nonreligious Americans went to church in the days after each tragedy, particularly after the assassination of President Kennedy and September 11, 2001. Of course, Americans went to church after the bombing of Pearl Harbor, but this in large part was their usual habit. A considerably larger number of Americans went to church in the 1940s than in the 1960s, although often in the 1940s their attendance was more a manifestation of community belonging than of religiosity.

After September 11, 2001, many ministers noted that although their churches were full, those who attended were not all regulars. Reverend John Huffman observed that his colleagues frequently said to him, "Many of these people I don't remember ever seeing before."[45] He hypothesized, "We all were there seeking perspective and even answers to the mystery of terrorism and the apparent random nature of life and death."[46]

This is precisely what I analyze: how Protestant ministers offered solace to Americans in the first few weeks after a crisis event. This book considers the sermons that ministers preached during these chaotic periods as a form of political theory—as a way for Americans to reconstruct their understanding of the political as well as the religious order.

Norman Jacobson, in his well-known book *Pride and Solace: The Limits and Function of Political Theory,* argued that "political theory begins precisely at the moment things become, so to speak, unglued."[47] Jacobson used the long lens of history and demonstrated how canonical political theorists such as Machiavelli, Hobbes, and Rousseau meet their own historically disorienting moments by providing solace and attempting to fasten principles in the midst of uncertainty.

Taking up this conception of political theory, I contend that during contemporary crises, Protestant ministers were for many Americans the political theorists of the crises. Churches were crammed with expectant and downcast mourners. The sermons were the texts and the ministers the theorists seeking to create a shared public theology to console those in the pews.

In those first Sunday sermons, the ministers used an alternate vocabulary to describe America's past, the present moment, and what it meant to be a grieving citizen. Ministers were engaged in what Richard Rorty named "redescriptions."[48] Protestant ministers developed alternative narratives; they offered a competing lens through which Americans could comprehend the tragedy. Their sermons were a form of civic education that opened or closed different avenues of possibility. Sermons were not merely theoretical or theological. They were a kind of political theory that attempted to offer answers to practical questions, such as "What is to be done?"

The sermons had theological elements, of course, but their purpose was primarily twofold: (1) to offer solace, to allow mourning, and to renew a shattered community; and (2) to attempt to reassert church authority—to use the aporia provided by the crisis to influence their congregants' understanding of the importance of theology, of the transcendent, and of religious convictions. Many of the sermons sought to renegotiate the boundary between the church and state, primarily through a reclamation of the church's standing.

Nonetheless, over the last many decades, the jurisdiction between the two has been decided mostly in favor of the state. The state has assumed many of the elements of church authority, including even rituals of mourning. But sometimes in a crisis, political power is vulnerable. Americans revisit their religious commitments, asking collectively: "Have we lost our equilibrium? Have we conceded too much to secular values and not enough to religious ones?"

These concerns are always in tension with other foundational American beliefs and identities. Americans are God's chosen people; they have a special covenant with God; God speaks to Americans through the events of political history. Thus, political tragedies challenge identity for Christian Americans. Has God abandoned that exceptional relationship? Has American behavior forfeited the privileges of God's blessings?

Thus, in a crisis, Americans wonder aloud whether they have maintained the appropriate symmetry between church authority and political prerogatives. Over the last hundred years, the state has tried in various ways to insist that the balance is correct. More power to the government is better for the majority of Americans, it insists, offering more security, less violence, and enhanced possibilities. And American civil religion is so entwined with American conceptions of patriotism that for some, the flag and the national anthem are not symbols of the government but of the *Christian* nation. Claims that Jews and Muslims are Americans sometimes have to be rehearsed—some Americans have to be reminded that non-Christians are equally American.[49]

During a crisis there is often a human need to assign a higher purpose to the suffering, some meaning to that which appears merely random. This impulse is particularly acute in the United States, where the dominant religious narrative is of Christian suffering and redemption. The Christian story explains suffering as the price of a future heavenly reward. It assigns existential significance to what might otherwise be misunderstood as the aimless violence of human life. Implicitly, the church stands as both an empirical and a transcendent challenge to man-made institutions. This is Antigone's claim as well: there is something else, something more important than human law. Churches are a source of solace for those who are mourning; a place to relieve the disorientation that results from unexpected tragedy.

So what kind of answers are Americans seeking? Political answers? Or do Americans decide that there are no political answers to tragedy? Is that an element of American exceptionalism—that when bad things happen to America, there must be a larger, more metaphysical explanation? Americans don't just fight violent enemies; they take on the forces of evil. Miraculously, they even confront the metaphysics of sin. American adversities—so the narrative details—transcend history.

Yet historically, American nationalism has given assurance to its citizens that they belong to a protected, purposeful, and meaningful community. When all is well, there is the illusion that the state "guarantees some kind of salvation to the individual by virtue of his membership and participation in that community."[50] When tragedy strikes, that promise is jeopardized. Perhaps it needs to be reevaluated. It is ironic that Americans go to church or synagogue or temple during a crisis, because for nearly a century they have seemingly conceded most of the authority once enjoyed by the church to the state. Nevertheless, Americans still go to religious services to seek answers to their questions. How does one endure the misery of life? How does a community interpret and adjust to a shared tragedy that the state could not prevent?

During ordinary times, Americans spend their energy and leisure seeking fulfillment of their individual desires, freely pursuing whatever it is they imagine will make them happy. Modern Americans use the community primarily as an instrument in service to their efforts to enhance themselves. This is the neoliberal order. But when tragedy strikes, they are recalled to the community—its obligations and its implications for the islands of self and family. Americans regain a sense that they belong to something larger than themselves. They become, in the words of sociologist Sidney Mead, "a nation with the soul of a Church."[51]

In a strange way, tragedies have become for many Americans the primer for their civic education. Tragedies join disparate parts of the republic together in mourning, in solace, and in fearful recognition of mortal fragility. In the Oklahoma City bombing, catastrophe became its own kind of church. The bombing prompted the question, "Who are we?" And the response became, "We are people who survive."

The historical arc of this book reveals that at midcentury, after the bombing of Pearl Harbor, American clergy took full advantage of the power of the Christian moral demand system. They understood immediately the role and importance of the church in helping to steer not only American Christians but the state itself through the crisis. The Protestant ministers of the 1940s deployed the authority of the church to draw a political line between just and unjust state actions, between permitted and forbidden policies, and between virtuous and sinful approaches to war.

At that point, the state still sought the church's validation of its activities. President Roosevelt sent a letter to the Catholic archbishop of Detroit, Edward Mooney, outlining the reasons for his response to the Pearl Harbor bombing and implicitly asking for the church's validation. Roosevelt promised that his goal was "the establishment of an international order in which the spirit of Christ shall rule the hearts of men and nations." Mooney answered with the promise that "with a patriotism that is guided and sustained by the Christian virtues of faith, hope, and charity," the bishops would "marshall the spiritual forces at our command to render secure our God-given blessings of freedom."[52] The archbishop promised to support the state using the theological resources at his command. This was the nature of the relationship between the church and the state in the 1940s. Not only Catholics but Protestants had sufficient political standing that the enlistment of their support was deemed important to the success of a political proposal, particularly one as important as going to war.

In contrast, by the time we examine the Black Lives Matter sermons that begin with the killing of Trayvon Martin and continue through the killing of Michael Brown and the Ferguson protests, and galvanize the nation again after the killing of George Floyd in 2020, clergy have lost their clout as well as the authority of the Christian moral demand system. A racist ethos of tolerance among White clergy made them reluctant to engage fully with the ideas of the movement. A kind of universal detachment, disguised as tolerance, made the church largely effete during the outrage of the 2013 acquittal of George Zimmerman for the murder of Trayvon Martin. Clergy did not seem to have decisive insight into what justice demanded in response or what was required of American Christians throughout the escalating public focus on state violence against unarmed Black teenagers. There was no MLK to articulate Christian principles of nonviolence or rehearse the power of agape. Although Black clergy had a different perspective from their White counterparts, they too primarily chose to focus on the goodness of individuals rather than on the structural racism embedded in American law enforcement. Police officers as well as victims were reduced to their personal biographies and assessed on a case-by-case basis.

What Clergy Do during a Crisis: Negotiate Christian Patriotism

In much American scholarship of the last fifty years or so, "religion" has been separated from other domains of community life, such as "politics" and "economics." In many ways, this divide between the religious and the secular, between private worship and public civil society, and between the church and state more broadly has assumed the status of a static binary. This analytic promotes an essential distinction between the domains, such that "politics" is conceived as secular and nonreligious, whereas "religion" must remain apolitical to be considered truly "religious."[53] A common mistake made in American media analysis and political discussion is that of assuming that religion and politics are analytically distinct, if sometimes combative categories. They are imagined as mutually exclusive categories rather than as mutually constitutive ones.

Among the conceptions that are negotiated between the two spheres during a crisis is that of patriotism. Defining a patriot becomes urgent, foundational. What counts as a patriotic act assumes the status of a security matter. For ministers, sometimes defining patriotism requires the construction of an enemy as they try to make sense of the loss of human life. Sometimes the enemy is an idea or abstraction, and sometimes a group of people. Often, ministers were trying to answer existential questions such as "Why did this happen?" to construct a conception of "Christian patriotism."

Contesting interpretations around patriotism have a long history in American political and religious life. One of the earliest and most well-known political and moral meditations on patriotism is Frederick Douglass's "What to the Negro Is the Fourth of July?" As the title suggests, the freed slave Douglass challenges whether Negroes can celebrate a freedom from which they are excluded. The debate continues in contemporary debates about NFL players, led by Colin Kaepernick, taking a knee during the national anthem to protest police brutality against unarmed Black men. Although questions of patriotism are often part of the national dialogue, during a crisis the focus on patriotism is laser sharp. Many Protestant ministers feel compelled during such times to think through the interrelation between patriotism and Christianity.

Being a Christian patriot is often a challenge for the faithful. Even during a crisis, the identity can feel like an oxymoron. The principles of Christianity are universal, intended for all peoples. The premise of patriotism is to be partisan, loyal, and concerned with a specific set of people. Christianity is about being in the world but not of the world. The values and rewards are elsewhere. One's future is as one of God's people—a universal community, exempt from borders. Patriotism is about the authority of the nation-state. One's future is as a citizen, dedicated to fulfilling political policies.

Thus, over the course of the historical period traced here, ministers will sometimes claim that patriotism is irrelevant—"our citizenship is in heaven" (Phil. 3:20). Universal values are at stake, and the church will not choose one side over another. The glimpse of this future with God is described in Revelation: "There before me was a great multitude that no one could count, from every nation, tribe, people and language, standing before the throne and before the Lamb. . . . And they cried out in a loud voice: Salvation belongs to our God" (Rev. 7:9, 10).

Other times, ministers declare that a good Christian is de facto a loyal American patriot—the values are similar, if not identical. Evangelist Billy Sunday stated: "*Christianity* and *Patriotism* are synonymous terms, and *hell* and *traitors* are synonymous. God's goals and the country's goals are one and the same. It is not just a civic duty to love and support America, it is also a Christian duty."[54] On these occasions, ministers insist that the church is the most patriotic institution in America. This was particularly true after the assassination of President Kennedy. The majority of ministers named themselves guilty, in part, because as leaders of a powerful institution, they had not done enough to protect a beloved president from the vicissitudes of sin in a fallen world. Ministers boldly asserted that the best security for the state was provided by the church.

In contrast, after the bombing of Pearl Harbor, ministers primarily offered a political assessment and were quite clear that the violence had nothing to do with God and very little to do with the church. The ministers were secure in their authority and had a rather "tsk, tsk" attitude toward the follies of the government. During the 1940s, most American ministers maintained clear distinctions between love of country and Christianity.

After the tragedy of September 11, 2001, ministers framed the event as all about God: His relation to the United States, His suffering in tandem with victims in the United States, and His signaling of both pleasure and displeasure with American political and cultural practices. Following the lead carved out in the 1970s by Reverend Billy Graham, ministers in 2001 claimed that patriotism could be a vehicle that fulfilled God's purposes on earth. Discipleship became not spiritual but national. Although some of the denominational and political differences were manifest in what the ministers believed God was actually communicating, very few seemed to doubt that God was using the tragedy to address all Americans, not only Christians. They were also confident that the American government and its people constituted a wing of God's celestial army.

When recent crises have been inflected by racial categories and interpretations, patriotism has again been animated by the conundrums posed by Frederick Douglass. After the murder of Trayvon Martin, during the summer of Michael Brown's killing, and again during the mourning protests for George Floyd in the summer of 2020, some Protestant ministers (although not the majority) felt called to stand up to the government. They declared that the church must show its autonomy and theological insights by detailing its criticism of the state. This was true for both conservative and liberal ministers; the primary distinction depended on whether the preacher was White or Black.

During these crises, patriotism was framed less in terms of what loyalty one owed the state and more on whether the state had been part of the protection and preservation of one's community. Black ministers especially detailed the fallibility of an American patriotism that seemed to require that African Americans accept the state's account of the traitorous behavior of its own congregants. Nonetheless, the ultimate resolution for the majority of ministers, both Black and White, was that solutions depended on government action rather than on church agency to resolve the injustices. For the majority of Protestant ministers, patriotism rested on the foundational assumption that the state could always resolve whatever issues confronted and confounded it, because the state was fundamentally virtuous. It's a rather strange and tangled path that results in a sometimes-shortsighted concession of church authority by ministers themselves to the mechanisms and agency of the state. It is the work of this book to travel this path, exploring the convolutions, highlighting the negotiations, and detailing the ways of mourning and the conceptions of American identity preached by Protestant ministers during American political crises of the last century.

CHAPTER ONE

"Necessary Injustice"

Pearl Harbor and the Internment of Japanese Americans

SUNDAY MORNING, DECEMBER 7, 1941

The unexpected Japanese naval attack on Pearl Harbor changed most Americans' opinion about US commitments in World War II. They were ready for war. But for Japanese Americans, the news was met with stunned horror. Some quickly tried to "burn, bury or otherwise destroy items from Japan: Buddhist shrines, statues, language textbooks, Japanese flags, kimonos, photographs . . . anything that linked their owners to Japan."[1] Japanese Christians gathered in their churches, nervously waiting to learn what would happen next.

Within hours, reporters and "man on the street" accounts were attesting to what the *Boston Post* reported: "The attack in one instant has destroyed the disunity which has been disturbing America."[2] Much of the presumed disunity had centered on whether Americans should remain out of the war or whether their moral responsibilities mandated intervention. A Gallup poll in February 1941 indicated that 85 percent of Americans wanted the United States to remain out of the war.[3] For those clergy who were "neutralists," the argument centered on maintaining the United States' uncompromised ability to broker a future peace and provide humanitarian assistance by remaining out of the fray.

There were additional hesitations motivated by the failures of World War I and a reluctance to partner with Russia, given Stalin's nonaggression pact with Hitler. Among neutralist clergy, there was a presumption that the most effective force against Hitler was God, not militarism. "This is a time for sackcloth and ashes. Our first line of defense is God, and without him, all else is useless."[4]

For interventionists, especially among ministers, there was concern that German domination of Europe would result in worldwide loss of religious freedom without American intervention. Furthermore, there was the expectation that Christian moral responsibility, most powerfully articulated by Reinhold Niebuhr, required engagement with the difficult choices of a broken moral universe. Christians must be willing, in Niebuhr's terms, "to risk becoming morally soiled in the dirty business of serving God in a fallen world."[5] Christian principles required a "just peace," not simply a negotiated peace as the neutralists wanted. Finally, interventionists insisted that there was something worse than war: tyranny. Tyranny denied humanity its freedom to love and seek justice, as Christianity required.

Despite these ongoing arguments, the United States' policy of neutrality technically ended with the Lend-Lease Act of 1941. The act allowed the United States to sell, lend, or give war materials to allied nations. After repeated attacks by German submarines on US ships, Roosevelt announced on September 11, 1941, that he had ordered the navy to attack German and Italian war vessels in the "waters that we deem necessary for our defense."[6] In many ways, arguments about neutrality and intervention were becoming moot prior to the bombing of Pearl Harbor.

Nonetheless, there was little doubt that, while not unexpected, the attack caught Americans by surprise. Most learned the news via radio. "The point must be made that the radio was the Paul Revere in the picture. After the immediate facts of the assault were broadcast, it was radio that saddled the ether waves and gave the door to door call to arms."[7] Most descriptions of those first hours and days described a resigned and "unexcited" citizenry: "Washington tonight is a city stunned, not afraid, not excited, but like a boxer, who after three rounds of sparring, catches a fast hook to the jaw, rocks back, rolls with the punch. Tonight, Washington is rolling back from the clout but in the rolling, set itself grimly, solidly for the counterpunch."[8]

From the vantage point of a post-9/11 world, this kind of resignation may seem incredible. Weren't Americans terrified that they had been attacked? Didn't they gather to mourn collectively in public places? Wasn't there an outcry against the Japanese?

Most Americans did not express fear. They were confident in the initial weeks that the war would be primarily a naval battle in which the homeland would not be involved. Furthermore, there was relatively little public mourning for the nearly 2,500 people (including 68 civilians) who had died. The initial focus was on war-readiness, not grief. Because of the massive fires and destruction of Pearl Harbor, most of the military men were buried in mass graves or left interred in the sunken ships. It was not until after the end of the war that the bodies of many "unknowns" were buried in the National Memorial Cemetery of the Pacific in Honolulu.[9]

Unlike the aftermath of crises that would confront Americans in the coming decades, most Americans would not see photos of Pearl Harbor for nearly a month. The navy and the War Department were not eager to release photos that showed the damage. It was not until the first anniversary of Pearl Harbor that *Life* did an extensive photo spread.[10] Nonetheless, the motto "Remember Pearl Harbor" animated American commitments to the war.

While there was no public mourning, there was, within hours, an unfortunate governmental response. By Sunday nightfall, Japanese Americans were being detained, arrested, and collected for eventual internment.

From the Pulpit: Who Were the 1940s Clergy?

The most politically and socially powerful American denominations in the 1940s and 1950s were the nine White, mainline Protestant denominations: Congregationalists, Episcopalians, Methodists, Disciples of Christ, United Lutherans, Evangelical Lutherans, American Baptists, and Northern and Southern Presbyterians. Southern Baptists had a separate convention. Black Baptists and Black Methodists were on the margins of a then-deeply segregated society.

A Roper poll conducted in 1942 ranked the clergy third among the groups "doing the most good" according to the American public. By 1947, ministers ranked first. Roper indicated that no other group came close to matching the prestige and "pulling power" of ministers.[11] One rather odd event confirmed the perceived influence of the clergy in this period: the debacle led by the Civilian Defense League, which outlined a sermon for clergy to preach across the nation.

More than six months before Pearl Harbor, President Franklin Roosevelt set up the Civilian Defense League (CDL) to coordinate state and federal measures to protect civilians in a war-related emergency. Over the course of the war, the CDL organized approximately ten million volunteers, training them to fight fires, decontaminate areas after chemical weapon attacks, provide first aid, implement emergency utility repairs, and so forth.[12] With his wife Eleanor's encouragement, President Roosevelt had also set the CDL the task of maintaining morale and creating national unity.[13]

Thus, in November 1941, as part of the CDL's "Defense Week," the director of the CDL, Fiorello La Guardia (also mayor of New York City), sent a letter to influential American clergy with the outline of a recommended sermon. "During this designated week," La Guardia's letter stated, "everyone will be asked to share a great effort to make a demonstration of national unity and devotion to the ideals of freedom. . . . Sunday, November 16, has been designated as Freedom Day on which all our people will reaffirm their faith in and devotion to liberty. We need your help to make this day one of rededication to the ideals of our country." The letter reminded the clergy that the defense of the United States "calls for more than guns and ships and airplanes. It demands also a purging of the heart and a strengthening of the moral convictions of our people."[14]

La Guardia then launched a directive: "We are suggesting that in every church and synagogue the morning sermon on November 16 center on the themes of religious freedom, with particular emphasis on what a powerful part religion played in the formation of the nation, its cleansing influence throughout our history and its importance in the present crisis.

Following this letter is a sermon outline which exemplifies the kind of message we are thinking about and which might be used effectively." The letter included a recommendation for clergy attendance at interfaith meetings hosted by the CDL that Sunday night, and concluded with a final assertion: "In a profound sense, the present world struggle is a spiritual one." In what sense the struggle was spiritual was not detailed, only that the main emphasis of Freedom Day would be "upon a re-examination of and rededication to these ideas of freedom which are the might and power of the American spirit."[15]

The enclosed sermon began, "The miracle of America is the miracle of the mingling of many peoples. . . . Out of diversity our unity is born."[16] American religious freedom has been developed and safeguarded "not [as] the result of indifference to religion but [as] a profound realization of the value and importance of it."[17]

The sermon was divided into three sections. The first was "Religion is the source of democracy"; the second, "Just as religion is the source of democracy, so democracy gives religion its most satisfactory opportunity"; and the third, "Democracy and religion can together build the good society." As a whole, the sermon detailed the entwined genesis of religion and democracy. Since all human beings were children of God, all were equal in His sight. This became the original idea for democracy. According to the CDL sermon, "the Judeo-Christian revelation in due time brought forth the political philosophy of democracy."[18] Democracy was a Judeo-Christian creation. And because democracy rests on religious faith, "religion flourishes and bears its fruit only where freedom reigns."[19] The two were mutually interdependent. La Guardia was basically enjoining American clergy to preach the state's version of civil religion.

After quoting the Episcopalian Book of Common Prayer, the sermon urged "the believers in the truth of religion . . . to take a firm part in the maintenance of our democracy in America and in the world."[20] The sermon proclaimed that in the countries where tyrants have enslaved their own people, the "boldest voices opposing them have been those of bishops and pastors and rabbis."[21] This was the CDL's call to American religious leaders to use their traditional role as preachers to fight dictators and thus both implicitly and explicitly support the necessity of armed struggle against them.

The sermon's closing contained the claim: "We have had no place here for racial intolerance or religious bigotry. We have demonstrated that freedom for all can work. Protestant, Catholic and Jew, we have joined hands and built a good society under God." It was unclear whether the CDL believed there had been no racial intolerance or religious bigotry in the United States, or if it imagined that would be the position of most American ministers. There followed a long quotation from Thomas Jefferson's first inaugural address about the freedoms achieved through the Protestant Reformation and during the American Revolution. The sermon concluded with a bid to remember the gift of freedom: "We can go forward not only to create a nation dedicated to liberty but to build a world of brotherhood fit to be called the Kingdom of God."[22]

The story of the sermon and the resulting scandal landed on the front page of the Sunday *New York Times* on November 9, 1941. Ministers were outraged. Reverend Charles Clayton Morrison, editor of the *Christian Century,* called the letter "an unspeakable insult to the clergy of the United States."[23] Rather bombastically, he continued: "Hitler and Goebbels never went further. Totalitarianism is already here. Mayor La-Guardia's 'request' will soon grow into a demand." A spokesman from the Office of Civilian Defense responded only, "Nobody's forcing them to use it."[24]

This tempest demonstrated how influential sermons were perceived to be by the state in prewar American culture. The CDL was encouraging ministers to preach the United States' civil religion. Not surprisingly, ministers would have none of it. Or at least, most did not seem willing to abide the attempt. Several ministers went out of their way to say that they were not arguing with the content of the sermon; they were just disturbed by the recommendation that they should do the government's bidding from the pulpit. They did not want to be accused of being "unpatriotic," but they did not want to become a conduit for the messages of the state.[25]

La Guardia's sermon revealed, albeit in a clumsy way, how civil religion was constructed and how it could fail when there was still powerful church authority. As Robert Bellah detailed in his seminal article "Civil Religion in America," civil religion is a vehicle for national religious self-understanding.[26] American civil religion aims to establish the meaning of the United States for the whole world—as the CDL sermon likewise attempted to do. Oddly, the "canned sermon" (as the clergy derisively called it) was more akin to the type of sermon ministers would give post-9/11 than the ones they gave after the bombing of Pearl Harbor.

La Guardia's sermon acknowledged what Tocqueville knew was a pivotal part of the role of religious institutions in early America: the church was a political institution that powerfully contributed to the maintenance of a democratic republic. "Nothing shows better how useful and natural religion is to man, since the country where today it exercises the most dominion is at the same time the most enlightened and most free."[27]

What the canned sermon neglected, which 1940s ministers were acutely aware of, was the second part of Tocqueville's observation: "But when religion wants to rely on the interests of this world, it becomes almost as fragile as all the powers of the earth. Alone, religion can hope for immortality; tied to ephemeral power, it follows their fortune, and often falls with the passion of the day that sustains those powers."[28] In other words, civil religion might be quite good for the state, but it was decidedly less good for the church if it necessitated that the church forfeit its autonomy. The civil religion promoted by the CDL was the kind of heresy (from the minister's perspective) that sought to boost the health of a limitless state, not a state devoutly aspiring to keep the peace and preserve civil society.[29]

The canned sermon was not the only rather didactic attempt by the US government to create national unity prior to the bombing of Pearl Harbor. In the 1940 Supreme Court case *Minersville School District vs. Gobitis,* the court ruled that public schools could compel a student—in this case a Jehovah Witness—to salute the American flag and recite the pledge of allegiance, despite the student's religious objections.

Writing for the majority, Justice Felix Frankfurter argued: "The ultimate foundation of a free society is the binding tie of cohesive sentiment. . . . We live by symbols. The flag is the symbol of our national unity."[30] The court reasoned that since the pledge and the salute did not promote or prevent a particular religion, their compulsion was permissible under a compelling state interest in creating national harmony.[31] From the Supreme Court's perspective, the state mandate for manifestations of national unity actually created the possibility of religious freedom.

The legal and political construction of a civil religion made clear to the clergy that politics was a symbolic realm as much as religion was. Politics was not solely the sphere of rationality, decision making, and logic. Martin Marty has noted, "Political leaders are priests and prophets who invoke symbols and use rituals to highlight a particular set of beliefs to mobilize constituents for or against a specific policy or change effort."[32]

That was also what La Guardia's sermon aimed to do: recruit congregants to the necessity of the United States' engagement with the war. Not only politics was at stake, La Guardia's sermon argued, but religious freedom itself. The United States had to preserve democracy around the world so that religious freedom could flourish. The CDL's shrewd but historically suspect genesis story of democracy was intended to demonstrate the mutuality of the church-state relationship. Each needed the other to flourish. Because the United States was a nation dedicated to liberty, it must simultaneously be dedicated to building a world "fit to be called the Kingdom of God."

It is worth contrasting this sermon with the position that German theologian Karl Barth was taking at about this time. During the 1930s, Barth was among the most influential Christian theologians and a staunch resister to the appropriation of the German Church by the Nazis. He was the primary author of the Barmen Declaration of 1934 that condemned German Christians who had aligned with the German state. The Declaration roundly "rejects the false doctrine, as though there were areas of our life in which we would not belong to Jesus Christ, but to other lords."[33] The Barmen Declaration also rejected the "false doctrine, as though the Church apart from this ministry, could and were permitted to give itself, or allow to be given to it, special leaders vested with ruling powers."[34]

Barth's work was a radical articulation of the sovereignty of God, as well as of the otherness of Christian revelation. Neither could be reduced to human reason, natural law, or politics. For Barth, Nazism was not a political problem with theological implications. It was a theological problem with political implications. God always set the terms of any issue, Barth insisted, not the secular ruling order. Theology was not applied to the world; rather, theology constituted the world.

Barth's analysis was, as theologian Alan Torrance argues, "a theologically driven approach to the state rather than a political approach to God."[35] No political situation could prescribe the agenda for theology. It was God's freedom that initiated all activities. The church's role was to serve as a reminder to the humans around it of the justice of the kingdom of God, already established on earth through Jesus Christ. The church offered the promise of that kingdom's future manifestation.

Barth's recommendation was not that the church should withdraw from political life but that the church must remain the church to recall the human world to the activity of God. "The kingly rule of Christ extends not merely over the Church . . . it also confronts and overrules with sovereign dignity the principalities and power and evil spirit of the world."[36] In all areas of human life, Christians needed justification and sanctification through Jesus.

During the 1930s and 1940s, this political theology was an urgent call to resist Hitler's domination of the church's autonomy and to recognize the falsity of the claim that one could divide one's spheres of loyalty. It was a powerful political theology and one with which many American Protestant ministers, especially Presbyterian and Lutheran ones, would have been familiar in 1941.[37]

Despite the power ascribed to the pulpit and the esteem in which ministers were evidently held, during the 1940s most of the Protestant clergy had had no exposure to a theological education. One study found that fewer than half of them had even graduated from college. Only after the US military upgraded their role as chaplains during World War II did most ministers receive a college as well as a seminary education. For example, during the war more than eight thousand American clergy received additional training at the Chaplain School of Harvard.[38]

This initial lack of educational background is relevant because in the 1940s as in generations past, the printed sermons of influential and well-educated ministers remained the way the majority of clergy learned their denominations' theology. Printed sermons set the terms for local, less educated ministers.[39] Thus, it is reasonable to assume that the printed sermons available from this period reflect what many clergy were preaching from their pulpits as well.

Who or What Is Mourned in the
Pearl Harbor Sermons?

To understand how clergy responded to the bombing of Pearl Harbor, it is important to understand first how in 1941, with the benefit of hindsight, they understood their role in World War I. Many American ministers were ashamed of the ways they had participated in that war. Although they believed they had been misled by state propaganda and the secular press, they still held themselves responsible for having contributed to what was called "a nation drunk with hate."[40]

It is not an exaggeration to say that American clergy did contribute to a culture that made the complete subordination of Germany feel like a divine mandate. At the end of that war, the editor of *The Churchmen* declared: "We are not called upon by our religion to love these people. They are the enemies of God."[41] Others, including Presbyterian chaplain Howard Duffield of the Ninth Coast Artillery, announced that war could not come to an end until "the black eagles of the Hapsburgs and the Hohenzollerns have their necks wrung. There must be no peace without victory and without penalties against those who began hostilities."[42]

For many clergy, at the end of World War I Christianity and patriotism were collapsed: the righteous anger of Christianity, offended by the atrocities of the Kaiser and his regime, demanded the patriotic response of unconditional surrender of the enemy. Victory was theologized as a confirmation of God's partisanship. Even the liberal editor of the *Christian Century* thought it appropriate to thank God for the outcome of the war, since "it was God who had aroused the conscience of the world against our enemies . . . and brought us into the conflict . . . [and] helped preserve the most wonderful morals in our soldiers and . . . [kept] them fit for their duties."[43] The National Lutheran Council, representing most of the Lutheran bodies in America, issued a statement: "Thanks unto Almighty God who has given our just cause such magnificent victory."[44] Clearly, during World War I there was plenty of rhetorical sentiment that God was on America's side.

"America's interests" were promoted as being in "God's interests" as well. "America's interests" were not selfish, parochial, or partial, but transcendent. Methodists announced after the Treaty of Versailles, "The published notes exchanged between the Allies, the speeches of America's great men—all made clear to the world that we were engaged in a righteous war, in which greed and national aggrandizement never figured."[45] The United States had been fighting not on its own account but for something greater than itself. American victory was a victory for the whole civilized world and for God as well.

While there were, of course, ministers who had been pacifists throughout the war and who condemned bloodthirsty vendettas against one's enemies, by and large the Protestant clergy in 1941 felt that they had not been true to the mission of the Christian Church in their nationalist support of the war. As a demonstration of repentance, many denominations passed resolutions declaring war a "sin." Thousands of clergy pledged never to endorse or have anything to do with another war. In a 1931 questionnaire of 53,000 clergy (of approximately 100,000 clergy in the entire United States), 53 percent stated that it was "their present purpose not to sanction any future war or participate as an armed combatant."[46] Gradually, disillusionment with war filled the pulpits:

> Our people—government and all—were shouting wonderful things that were going to come to pass as the result of this war. It was a war to end war. It was to make the world safe for democracy. It was to make a new world order where Christian principles were to reign among nations. There is no denying that we are in a disappointed world—a world that looks back upon the men who were at Paris as betrayers of their words and promises. We got no world safe for democracy, no new world order, no Christian era of international good-will.[47]

The Chicago Federation of Churches, representing 650 churches and 15 denominations, went on record: "In humble penitence for past mistakes and sincere repentance for our want of faith and devotion to the ideals of the Kingdom of God . . . we declare ourselves as unalterably opposed to war."[48] In June 1930, the General Synod of the Reformed Church in America adopted a statement that "war is contrary to the spirit of Jesus Christ," and adopted a resolution expressing the "conviction that American citizens should be free and unhampered to follow the dictates of conscience in determining their course of action relative to bearing arms for the nation."[49]

Among the most well-known penitents were those who would be influential in framing the ministerial response to World War II, especially Reinhold Niebuhr and Harry Emerson Fosdick. Niebuhr confessed: "Every solider fighting for his country in simplicity of heart without asking many questions, was superior to those of us who served no better purpose than to increase or perpetuate the moral obfuscation of the nation. . . . I am done with this [war] business."[50]

Fosdick made a similar pledge: "I do not propose to bless war, again, or support it, or expect from it any valuable thing."[51] Powerfully, Charles Clayton Morrison, who as editor of the *Christian Century* had pronounced his previous blessing on the war, called on the churches to renounce war forever and advised that "the preachers repentantly resolve that they will never again put Christ in khaki or serve as recruiting officers or advisory enforcers of conscription laws!"[52]

While the trajectory of the rhetoric changed dramatically, from nearly anointing World War I as a holy war to rebuking all war as a sin, in some respects the approach remained the same. Theology was central to understanding the war. Although there were a few ministers who recast World War I as a "political war" about the "deep rooted economic competition to control the raw material and markets of the world," the majority thought that they had misunderstood the relationship between war and religion. Rather than God having ordained military victory, most clergy now argued that war and the religion of Jesus Christ were incompatible. "There is no such thing as a Christian military procedure. . . . Is there any reasonable hope that cruel military methods will solve any human problem? Are we not, then, driven to the higher ground that evil can never be overcome by another evil but only by good, good will, right reason and a minimum of violence and coercion? I think this would be the mind of Christ facing a threatened modern war."[53]

Ministers insisted that World War I had not achieved any of its promised ends: "Justice was not achieved. Liberty was not secured. The rights and liberties of small nations were not guaranteed. Brute force was not banished from international affairs. The world was not made safe for democracy or for morality or for Christianity or for anything else that decent men care for and would be glad to die for."[54]

Postwar ministers argued that it was the responsibility of the Christian Church to end war—both its necessity and the justifications used to promote it. Religious values could no longer be confirmed by waging war. Morrison noted in his sermon "On Saving Civilization" (May 8, 1940), "It is the nature of war to clothe itself with grandiose moral aims. . . . The idea that we can preserve civilization by modern war is logically absurd and empirically false. There can be no destruction of civilization comparable to the destruction, which this war, if continued, will accomplish."[55]

Hitler himself was an object lesson of collective human sinfulness:

> The very weapons that Hitler has developed so formidably and used so fearfully have come from other nations—the tank from Britain, the bomber from America and France, the machine gun and submarine from America. This man, so cruel, so ruthless, so revengeful, is not alien to ourselves. He is the perversion of *our* lusts, the poisoned distillation of *our* crimes.[56]

Finally, as more World War I veterans recounted their experiences of being on the battlefield, the perception of war as a noble calling deteriorated. One of the most famous chaplains who had served with US troops was Father Francis Duffy of the Rainbow Division.[57] Five years after the armistice, he pronounced, "As I look back, I see no occasion for the ordinary man to have had religious experiences while in the service. War is something so opposed to God! It is so full of the Satanic. . . . Most men have seen in war-experience nothing but evil in its nakedness. . . . Forever stand these words over war which Dante placed over the entrance to Hell—'All hope abandon, ye who enter here!'"[58] During the interwar years, war experience was decried as traumatic and hellish rather than sacralized.

With this context in mind, one can understand why the sermons given in the days, weeks, and months after Pearl Harbor seemed to mourn the failure of World War I more than the loss of American lives in the Pacific. "This is the saddest war in history. We are not jubilant, but infinitely dejected. . . . We expect nothing from this war except that everything sweet and precious will be crushed out of life for most of us. Nevertheless, we could do no other. This is not a just war; it is just war. We are in the war and none of us can get out. We shall have to see it through in a spirit of inexpressible grief."[59]

Mourned also in many early sermons was the lost opportunity to have prevented this precipitating event: "It is a truism now that we won the last war and lost the peace—lost the peace because we had learned what sacrifices we had to make to win the war, but had not learned what we must give up to make peace secure."[60]

It is difficult to imagine clergy saying a similar thing during another American national crisis and being confirmed rather than chastised for it. We know now, for example, the outraged reaction to Reverend Jeremiah Wright's similar analysis after the collapse of the Twin Towers. Would it have been possible for clergy to critique American culture and foreign policy after the assassination of John F. Kennedy? After the demolition of the Alfred P. Murrah Federal Building? What kind of clerical authority is required for ministers to feel empowered to make these kinds of observations?

It is noteworthy that as late as June 1942, a third of Americans were still telling pollsters they did not know what their country was fighting for. Some polls found that many Americans did not trust the Allies. Nearly a third said they were willing to negotiate a separate peace with Germany in the summer of 1942.[61] So worried was the Roosevelt administration that Americans would misread the war as only about self-defense and avenging the Japanese attack that FDR established the Office of War Information (OWI) to ensure that the American people understood the status and progress of the war effort.[62] Roosevelt wanted it to be clear that the war was not primarily about the Japanese but about destroying fascism.

There was even an ill-conceived and unsuccessful appeal aimed at African Americans that described the war as "a fight between a slave world and a free world." In a pamphlet entitled *Negroes and the War* published in the spring of 1942, the Roosevelt administration specifically encouraged African Americans to support the war. Many Americans, including many African American leaders, advised the OWI that the attempt to link Nazi Germany to slavery would only highlight African American grievances in the United States, which were quite substantial in the 1940s. Among them were the segregated military, the navy's refusal to enlist Blacks except as messmen, the nearly all-White US Marine Corps, the regular and persistent defense industry discrimination, the Red Cross's segregated blood bank policy, and all of the other malicious features of Jim Crow generally.[63] Yet the OWI was so captivated by the analogy that they refused to alter it.

The aim in these early months was to create a sense of national unity. This unity relied on a conception of American tolerance, even in the face of contrary historical evidence. The political desire was to shift the debate from Jews versus Nazis to *civilization* versus Nazis.[64] Accordingly, Nazis had an ethos of "divide and conquer," whereas Americans had an ethos of "tolerance and unity."

Roosevelt was careful to distinguish American unity from Nazi uniformity. Uniformity was intolerant, a precursor to fascism, whereas unity fostered acceptance, especially religious liberty. Nazi ideology aimed to turn one group against another. American unity aimed to foster unanimity of purpose. What exactly united Americans remained vague, but it included some formulation of "American values" or "the American way of life."[65]

The National Conference of Christians and Jews (NCCJ) created "tolerance trios" that exemplified this ambition and its paradox. Tolerance trios were traveling theater troupes composed of a rabbi, a priest, and a minister. They visited cities and military camps, demonstrating a version of religious tolerance. The shows were part comedy and part didactic education. Over the course of the war, it is estimated the trios visited nearly eight million enlistees. On average, each year they traveled 9,000 miles and performed across the United States for 130 audiences.[66]

This kind of performative tolerance was possible because in the United States in the 1940s, religion and other "social differences" could be readily imagined as relegated to the private sphere. "Tolerance" meant simply "live and let live." The trios were cultivating "faith in faith" and demonstrating what Catholics, Jews, and Protestants had in common: their *American* commitment to the value of the individual and to democracy generally.

One of the trio scripts used a Booker T. Washington metaphor without irony.[67] It asserted, "In all things religious, we Catholics, Jews and Protestants can be as separate as the fingers of a man's outstretched hand, in all things civic and American we can be as united as a man's clenched fist."[68] Religious differences, unlike racial or ethnic ones, were not imagined to genuinely divide Americans. Religion was not perceived as challenging anything significant to the war effort. What united Catholics, Jews, and Protestants was being American; what differentiated them was rendered irrelevant.

Civic beliefs (i.e., American patriotism, American values, democracy) in contrast were public and thus were perceived as serving a unifying function. In the post–Pearl Harbor months, tolerance meant primarily American religious pluralism, as opposed to Nazi ideological control. The tolerance campaigns were not attempting to promote American tolerance at home, but to highlight how *our* religious pluralism was a bulwark against *their* Nazi fascism.

President Roosevelt, in his well-known State of the Union address in January 1941, outlined the four freedoms that distinguished the United States and that he claimed were essential to humanity generally—among them, freedom of worship.[69] These four freedoms would form the foundation for the Roosevelt administration's justification for going to war. The United States had a mandated responsibility for bringing democracy and freedom to other peoples. Roosevelt was so enamored of the tolerance trios that throughout the war, he declared the last week of February to be "Brotherhood Week."

Yet ironically, when the tolerance trios visited military bases they spoke to troops segregated by race. Race was a challenge to this version of American tolerance because, unlike religious difference, race could not be privatized or sequestered and rendered invisible in the private sphere. Nonetheless, the tolerance trios carried on, seemingly oblivious to the paradox.

Furthermore, the internment of Japanese Americans the following year was integrated into this conception of tolerance, as will be further explored below. "Tolerance" in this context meant not that native-born Americans trusted their Japanese American neighbors, but that Japanese Americans "tolerated" their own internment as part of their commitment to national unity and forbearance. Being an American meant sharing the sacrifice, like a mother sending her son to die in the war. In 1942, what the United States required of its citizens of Japanese ancestry was their acceptance—their compliant "tolerance"—of their temporary internment.

The Pearl Harbor Sermons

Many of the initial Pearl Harbor sermons expressed a tragic resignation: the nation was again at war. The ministers exhibited little surprise, either politically or theologically. Emotions were surprisingly held in check, especially around expressions of animosity toward the "Japanese enemy." As Reverend Homer Yinger said, "Let us remind ourselves that it is no cruel fate that has brought the world to this terrible travail, but our own foolishness and stupidity and pride."[70] Echoing this sense of responsibility, Reverend Kenneth Morgan Edwards said: "Ours is a starkly, bitterly tragic world. We have ourselves to thank for the tragedy."[71]

Neither God nor the Japanese were held fully accountable for the bombing. Rather, Americans themselves had helped to create the conditions that made the calamity possible. Reverend Edwards included a long economic analysis of American policies that had strangled Germany and Japan: "No matter how we feel about the outrageous assault of the Japanese upon Pearl Harbor, there are certain causes which must be understood."[72] Reverend Walter Arthur Maier of the International Lutheran Hour asserted in his radio address on January 23, 1942: "We did not send enough missionaries to convert the Japanese; now, we must send soldiers to destroy them. We have not trained our youth for the Savior, now we must train them for the slaughter."[73]

One of the most powerful reiterations of this theme was written by Reverend Charles Clayton Morrison in his first *Christian Century* editorial after Pearl Harbor: "America is no longer free. You and I are no longer free. We are bound. We have been bound by our own acts, by our own blindness, by our national selfishness, by our statesmen's lack of imagination, by our unwillingness to trust in God. . . . It is fate, inexorable fate, whose web has been woven chiefly by human hands."[74]

Many ministers reminded their congregations that now was not the time for hatred but for Christian love. In a collection of the abstracts of 454 sermons preached on Sunday, December 14, 1941, gathered by the Information Service of the Federal Council of Churches, nearly one-third reminded listeners to "love thy enemies."[75] Reverend Kenneth Edwards asserted, "Japan has been treacherous . . . and for that she will be punished, but after she has been punished there still remains . . . Japanese men and women with children . . . those children must be fed . . .

the real test of American honor is when the fight is over."[76] As Reverend E. Stanley Jones proclaimed, "I did not have one code of morals on Saturday the 6th and another code on Sunday the 7th of December. What Christ meant to me Saturday, he meant to me Sunday. Since my code is the same, my conduct will have to be the same. . . . It was my business as a Christian to reconcile men . . . before the war; it is still my business."[77]

On the National Day of Prayer on January 1, 1942, with President Roosevelt and Winston Churchill in attendance, the Episcopal priest Reverend Edward Randolph Welles prayed that Americans would "drive out of our minds and heart every bit of bitterness and hatred."[78] He went further, comparing "the sins of our nation" to those of King David when the king arranged for his mistress Bathsheba's husband, Uriah, to be killed: "We ought to be ashamed of the treatment of Indians, of Yankee imperialism and exploitation abroad." Patriotism is a dedication to the truth, "however unpalatable it may sometimes be." This was a rather astonishing prayer to be given not only to an executive audience but on a formal occasion. It demonstrated the autonomy and confidence that the 1942 church had in itself and its prerogative to assert its authority in the face of perceived government overstep and mismanagement.

Still, the National Day of Prayer ended with Reverend Welles's reminder that there was a "vast difference between Americans and the Nazis." The democratic way of life in the United States encouraged the Christian way of life. The two had a symbiotic relationship. Reverend Welles proclaimed, "The spirit of Christ alone stands in the way of successful Nazi world domination." This was why, Welles said, the Nazis sought to crush Christianity: they recognized the threat Christianity posed to fascism.

Here at last was the civil religion that Roosevelt's unsuccessful "canned sermon" had tried to inculcate. Entwined Christianity and democracy, these Protestant ministers proclaimed, provided the best bulwarks against fascism.

There was another thread among some of the sermons—that part of the cause for the Japanese bombing was the fault of American churches. "[Churches] spent lots of time and money making religion soft and powerless and intellectual, and scientific and colorless as the desert sands."[79] This was a gendered echo of what ministers had been saying in the early

1930s about German Christians: the church had grown effete. Reverend Norman Schenck, general secretary of the Board of the Hawaiian Evangelical Association, argued (including a rare mention of the Pearl Harbor dead), "It is the church's business to send our citizens into this realm with disciplined and controlled bodies, and minds, and spirits. . . . If the cruel bombings of December 7, 1941 were needed to jolt us out of the lethargy of ease, comfort and self-centered living, then they who died shall not have died in vain."[80] The fervor and adamancy of the sentiment suggested that perhaps the reverend was preaching to himself and his fellow clergy as much as to his congregants.

Tellingly, there was nothing in this sermon that would have precluded it from being delivered in 1918. Perhaps that was the point. Many clergy were reacting to the tragedy at Pearl Harbor as they wished they had responded to World War I, or at least to the Armistice of 1918. It was as if the church was reminding itself that it needed to be a powerful presence in American political and cultural life. When it neglected this role, growing "soft and intellectual and colorless," disaster arrived. As Reverend Peter Marshall asked: "What right have we to expect peace? What did we do with peace when we had it? How did we use the 21 years of peace after the first World War? What if war has come because we were not fit for peace?"[81]

When one focuses on the reality that these sermons were written and delivered only a few weeks, at most, after the bombing of Pearl Harbor, it is surprising that they primarily speak of Christian responsibility for the tragedy rather than of what Christian Americans might owe the dead. The contrast with the sermons that will be given sixty years later, after 9/11, is striking. Of course, the Americans killed at Pearl Harbor were mostly enlisted military men, whereas those killed September 11, 2001, were civilians. Perhaps the 1940s clergy assumed that military deaths required no such justification—the men had died in the purposeful service to their country.

Another reason the clergy avoided naming the individuals lost at Pearl Harbor and declined to grieve with those families publicly was because the clergy wanted to resist any attempt to make violent death in battle redemptive. Ministers did not want to promote an ethos that offered military sacrifice as a pathway to Christian salvation. A narrative that made the Pearl Harbor dead into heroes or elevated the grief of survivors would have risked affirming that these losses had theological significance rather than simply political consequences. Instead, clergy repeatedly refocused congregants on the cause of their grief rather than the grief itself: "Why, if the wave of the future belongs to God, is there this suffering? Why does God not destroy the tyrant? *Because in part we have made these tyrants.* We have created the conditions under which they flourish. . . . We have justified racial inequality . . . we have coined nationalist slogans which reveal an indifference to other people."[82] Mourning was not considered. The focus was on why American Christians might be responsible for the grief they were experiencing.

The Pearl Harbor sermons did parallel the 9/11 sermons in one way: both confirmed the ready-made category of "enemy." Neither challenged the assumed necessity for violence against that enemy. But there was an important difference. The Pearl Harbor sermons were much more careful about detailing what the enemy deserved. Sermon writers contended that although the Japanese were now the enemy, they were not a permanent or eternal enemy. Americans must still conduct themselves with the "plume of decency, tolerance, and self-respect creaseless and without stain."[83] More significantly, in contrast to the 9/11 sermons, 1941 ministers considered how peace would be achieved after the violence.

Still, the great majority of Protestant clergy, who in 1942 were White, would abandon this seemingly generous formulation when they were confronted by the alleged threat from "the enemy within"—Japanese American citizens living primarily on the California coast.[84]

What Is the Relation between Church and State in the Pearl Harbor Sermons?

In the year before Pearl Harbor, the debate among clergy about the desired relation between the church and the state was primarily framed by two issues: (1) the advent of peacetime conscription, and (2) President Roosevelt's decision to open diplomatic relations with the Vatican to try to negotiate peace in Europe. A third issue, Reinhold Niebuhr's formulation of "Christian realism," was part of the debate, and I have addressed his conception of the relation between history and Christian principles through the lens of "Christian patriotism" in the final section of this chapter.

In early September 1940, Congress passed the Burke-Wadsworth Bill, enacting the first peacetime conscription in US history. Also known as the Selective Service Act, it required that men between the ages of twenty-one and thirty register with local draft boards. The government then selected men for active service through a lottery system. If drafted, a man served for twelve months.

Prior to the bill's passage, religious leaders across the spectrum protested. Only one religious group, Reverend Carl McIntire's recently founded American Council of Christian Churches, went on record endorsing conscription.[85] Religious bodies worried, correctly, that peacetime conscription would change the balance of power between the church's moral authority and the presumptive military dominance of the state. Reverend Raphael Harwood Miller of the *Christian Evangelist* predicted that military conscription would inevitably lead to a "military minded government with all the restraints which are inseparable from militarism."[86] Even conservatives such as Ned Stonehouse, a leader of the Orthodox Presbyterian Church, protested that conscription would engender "statism . . . service to the state as an end in itself."[87]

Initially, the bill made little provision for conscientious objectors (CO). It merely maintained the World War I ordinance that stipulated exemption from combatant service would be allowed solely to members of "any well recognized religious sect whose creed . . . forbids members to participate in war in any form."[88]

Yet because of the spiritual transformation of American clergy initiated by the debacle of World War I, many religious figures successfully contested the CO aspect of the bill and testified against it. Among those who helped reformulate the bill were Dorothy Day of the *Catholic Worker*, Harold Evans for the Quakers, Paul Bowman for the Church of the Brethren, James Crain for the Disciples of Christ, Charles Longacre for the Seventh Day Adventists, Amos Horst for the Mennonites, Harry Emerson Fosdick of Riverside Church in New York City, Roswell P. Barnes for the Federal Council of the Churches of Christ in America, and Charles Boss for the Methodist Commission on World Peace.[89] The final version of the bill contained a provision (section 5g) for conscientious objectors that exempted anyone "who by reason of religious training and belief is conscientiously opposed to participation in war in any form. Any such person claiming such exemption . . . shall be assigned to noncombatant service as defined by the President . . . or assigned to work of national importance under civilian direction."

The controversial portions of the bill lay in determining what counted as "religious training and belief" and "noncombatant service." The challenges can be gleaned from a brief overview of "typical questions" that those seeking exemption were asked:

· To what church do you belong?
· Do you attend regularly?
· How do you explain God's command in the Old Testament to smite the enemy?
· You have received benefits from your country—why shouldn't you defend it?
· Why should other men fight for you?
· Was the United States justified in fighting the Revolutionary War?
· Why should you oppose noncombatant service, especially helping the wounded?
· What would you do if your sister, mother, wife was attacked?[90]
· Would it be all right if the "Japs" just came here and took over?
· Do you really think nonviolence can work against people such as the Germans and "Japs"?
· Do you think we can trust Hitler?[91]

Although a full historical exploration of this fascinating contest between state authority and church theology as exemplified in the tensions between the state and American churches is beyond the scope of this chapter, several aspects of the debate are significant for understanding church and state relations in the Pearl Harbor sermons.[92]

First, since many Protestant clergy insisted that the conscription bill include a provision for conscientious objectors who were not members of the historic "peace churches," they were implicitly highlighting that their churches too had theological commitments that challenged the war ethos. With this expansion came a rigorous discussion about what qualified as "religious training" and "belief." What counted as belief and how did one prove such belief even if it was not constitutive of a denomination?

It is noteworthy that as African Americans sought CO status, various churches also advanced issues of racial equality. The most well-known example concerned a Black professor from Fisk University who was granted CO status and then requested placement in a Civilian Public Service program camp in Tennessee. He was denied this request since there was an "unwritten law" that "did not tolerate Negroes overnight in the county."[93] The story outraged many churches, which argued that the state was overreaching its authority and violating religious freedom by seeking to apply a law (especially an unjust one) to those who had already been granted legal immunity from its authority, at least in this circumstance.

Second, although the bill excluded all ministers from the draft, there was significant concern and disagreement about the drafting of students slated for seminary and theological education. Some denominations felt that they were particularly vulnerable, since their seminarians attended college before entering seminary. Government policy seemed to favor those denominations that ordained ministers before they entered seminary, or that started training students for ministry before college. Other denominations were concerned that the draft would limit the number of men who would or could enter the ministry.

Third, there was a contentious discussion about what counted as "noncombatant work" in a war economy. Clergy worried that what the president deemed "work of national importance" would privilege the state's political ambitions and not the church's theological commitments. To attempt to address this issue, the churches independently financed the Civilian Public Service program. Legally, COs were required to work for the government, although initially they received no pay or medical insurance. Often when they were compensated, their checks were impounded. Their dependents too received nothing. The state was reluctant to compensate those who were not "fighting in the war effort." Consequently, the churches paid COs' bills and supported their families. "For the sake of protecting their men, the churches suffered throughout the war the frustrations and humiliations of this bastard system."[94]

Finally, additional tension between church and state focused on nonaligned conceptions of what constituted "tolerance." From the perspective of the Selective Service, "tolerance" for the conscientious objector meant that accommodating them should never hamper the overriding task—recruitment of manpower for national defense. "Tolerance" required above all else that the CO faithfully perform "work of national importance" in return for the "privilege" of exemption from fighting. Furthermore, the conditions of the exemption should be as nearly equivalent as possible to the conditions of military service (i.e., as demanding and as inconvenient), yet meet the legal requirement of civilian direction.

American churches had a different understanding. To them, preserving the integrity of the individual's faith was paramount. In a society that accepted war as an essential instrument of its security, a line would inevitably separate the actions of a conscientious objector from the community. Yet it was obvious to the churches that work could be military even if the supervisor was wearing civilian clothes. "Erecting an airplane spotting tower, building a road as part of a strategic communications system, and cutting wood for use in naval shipbuilding were all projects which entailed a military purpose."[95] Most churches agreed with the position taken by the so-called peace churches that the work of COs should be used to maximum social advantage and include service with religious and social welfare organizations as well as relief efforts and reconstruction abroad. During the war years, COs spent much of their time fighting forest fires and doing agricultural work to ameliorate the effects of the food shortage. According to polls from the period, although initially COs suffered from a low approval rating, by the end of the war their services were recognized and appreciated by most Americans.[96]

While the number of conscientious objectors was statistically small (only twelve thousand men over the course of the war), the number was triple those who had sought exemptions during World War I. And the perceived importance of COs to churches across the political and theological spectrum exceeded their numbers. Resistance to peacetime conscription and cultivation of an ethos of exemption from the state's increased military power were important religious commitments.

Despite the unity regarding COs among many Protestant denominations as well as Roman Catholics, when Roosevelt appointed Myron Taylor as unofficial ambassador to the Vatican, Protestant resentment toward Catholic power was foregrounded. Ever since 1867, when an act of Congress terminated diplomatic relations between the American republic and the world's oldest diplomatic entity, the United States had been unrepresented at Vatican City. Roosevelt's short-lived attempt to reconstitute some form of permanent and effective diplomatic presence was born in controversy and lasted only from 1940 to 1950.[97]

In polite society, resistance to the envoy was voiced on constitutional grounds—the necessary separation of church and state. No act of the administration, they argued, should be undertaken that gave support to any religious body, however numerous its adherents. The relation between the Vatican and its bishops and priests in the United States would jeopardize this separation, giving the pope undue influence in American affairs.

In less polite society, suspicions centered on what some perceived as the growing hordes of semiliterate Catholic immigrants from Ireland and Italy, who posed a threat to a Protestant sense of "property and propriety."[98] These recent proletariats were perceived as "un-American" because of their presumed obedience to the hierarchical Vatican. Catholic groups, not surprisingly, argued that they were "the best Americans" because their religion was the one best positioned to win world peace through the influence and authority of the pope, which spanned the globe.[99]

Roosevelt's decision to work with newly elected Pope Pius XII was intended, as he said in his Christmas 1939 address to Protestant and Jewish leaders, "so that no effort would be spared to seek ways and means to restore peace to the world."[100] Even when the state was ostensibly working to solve an issue to which ministers were theologically committed (in this case, peace), American clergy were reluctant to trust that the state was the best vehicle to do so. The controversy suggested that during the interwar years, American clergy remained generally suspicious of the state's exercise of power.

With these antagonisms in mind, one appreciates why so many of the first sermons after the bombing of Pearl Harbor restrained expectations about the state's ability to resolve the conflict. "This is crucially important for us to see plainly because the 1940's are conspicuously a decade in which people and nations of the world—these United States included—are making a little god of the nation."[101] Many sermons argued, like this one, that Christianity offered a challenge not only of message but of method.

For many clergy, the bombing of Pearl Harbor marked the failure of the state.[102] That failure now had to be solved by the church. Unlike the 9/11 sermons that theologized the violence, in 1941 American clergy stated: "War is not in the program of God. It is one of the problems of men to God."[103] Pearl Harbor was not understood as a fulcrum event; there were no pre– and post–Pearl Harbor conditions in the theological vernacular in the way there would be for 9/11. Rather, Pearl Harbor was part of a political trajectory. In his sermon of January 1942, "Can Human Beings Be Made Over?," Reverend Ernest Fremont Tittle asserted: "The disaster which has come upon us was not, I feel bound to suppose, deliberately willed by any man or group of men, living or dead. Total war is the result of innumerable decisions and acts of innumerable individuals, who did not set out to create hell on earth but only to realize a selfish ambition."[104]

Of course, there were dispensationalists who did interpret the bombing and the war as precursors to the apocalypse. Similar believers had interpreted World War I in the same way. In 1941, some believed that "war and rumors of war" were among many signs that marked the Second Coming. Mussolini was interpreted by some as the White Horseman from Revelation who would revive the Roman Empire, while Hitler was understood as the Red Horseman.[105]

But generally, the tragedy was not theologized or understood as part of salvation history. Rather, the bombing was part of human history, enacting in some odd way the church-state divide. "The disaster which has come upon us . . . is the result of innumerable decisions and acts of innumerable individuals."[106] More theologically conservative clergy such as Peter Marshall and Walter Maier also saw war as a mark of the failure of the state.[107] For neither Marshall nor Maier does the bombing raise questions about God's goodness; it only invokes questions about humankind's sinfulness. "Scripture teaches that bloodshed is provoked by sin," says Maier, while Marshall asks, "What if war comes because we are not fit for peace?"[108]

Yet neither Marshall nor Maier was arguing that the violence, death, and grief of Pearl Harbor were divine punishment. God did not cause the tragedy because of American sinfulness. Instead, the violence was the result of human brokenness. The violence was the result of Americans having chosen actions that had awful consequences, like all sinful actions. This was a subtle but significant theological distinction. For example, George Buttrick, in his January 1942 sermon "Good and Bad Alike?," says that God did not speak through the elements of the tragedy but only through the good man's response to it. Buttrick referenced the ways men responded to the sinking of the *Titanic*—a few saved themselves while some saved others. "Goodness can make the dark bright, and redeeming love can turn the worse [*sic*] into the coming of God on the earth."[109]

Rehearsing Christian suspicion of, if not antagonism toward, the state, many early World War II sermons reminded listeners that Christianity was a worldwide movement, not bound by the parameters of national interest. "The Church is the only institution in the world that by its very nature transcends all nations, races and physical limitations of man."[110] In contrast, in 9/11 sermons, Christianity became so entwined with American nationalism that 2001 clergy rarely spoke of Christianity as transcending the boundaries of the nation-state; Christianity and the United States were mutually defined. From 1941 to 1942, clergy did not conceive of Christianity as either contained or hampered by national borders. Christianity had a robust, even transcendent, autonomy from the state.

There was, however, a powerful if minority ministerial influence arguing that the state could potentially be a vehicle for the fulfillment of Christian purposes. Embedded in these sermons addressing church-state relations was often an implicit critique of Reinhold Niebuhr's Christian realism. At stake in Niebuhr's formulation was the church's moral authority. If the church accommodated "political reality" (i.e., the state), it conceded that secular principles were "first order," almost ontological. Christian principles were then "second order," responsive and accommodating to the first.

Those who supported Niebuhr claimed that the church's moral authority would be enhanced by its alignment with the state in its struggles to preserve democracy. Some clergy argued that the church must support the violence, because without it, religious freedom would be impossible. Like Niebuhr, they came to believe that there was something worse than war, and that was tyranny. Few, however, seemed initially to have been persuaded by Niebuhr's distinction between the kingdom of God and the kingdom of human possibilities, and its implication that

human beings had to make their moral assessment in the universe of
"good and better" versus "bad and worse," rather than in the absolute
moral terms of good versus evil.

Christian Patriotism: A Theopolitical Conundrum

Early World War II conceptions of patriotism from the pulpit echoed
Edwin Errett's assertion in the *Christian Standard* that the United States
needed a vital Christianity and church more than Christianity and the
church needed a vital United States. "Many of us believe that the greatest
service that citizens of the United States can render is to preserve a representative government at peace even if all else collapses. But Christians need to be taught that is not identical with Christianity. Even if
the United States goes down, the kingdom of God will still live. And,
despite handicaps it can still conquer."[111] For both liberal and conservative clergy, being a better Christian made you a better American. Christianity set the parameters for patriotism.

Most of the religious rhetoric around patriotism was centered on
values stemming from concepts that were cherished—democracy,
freedom, and liberty. In contrast, during World War I, the clergy had
participated in nationalist rhetoric: what it meant to be "patriotic" was
to be against anything "not American." The World War I period was
not unlike 2001, when sauerkraut was called "liberty cabbage" and
frankfurters were renamed "hot dogs." Anything remotely recalling
the Germany enemy had to be cast aside.

By the time of Pearl Harbor, the rhetoric of patriotism had been re-
fined, at least by American clergy, to address primarily the *values* of democracy versus those of totalitarianism. Because of this, American
clergy were out in front early, if largely ineffectually, in protest against
the internment of Japanese Americans.

The morning of December 7, 1941, before the news of the bombing
had reached the East Coast, Harry Emerson Fosdick preached on the
similarities between Christianity and democracy. For both, he argued,
there was a profound commitment and longing for liberty, but "liberty
without loyalty" was a useless virtue. Liberty without loyalty was only
half the story. In the hands of a more conservative minister, this theme
might have been developed into one about patriotism. Fosdick concluded

his sermon, "Loyalty, the Basic Condition of Liberty," with the proclamation that genuine liberty can only be achieved by a committed loyalty to Christ.[112]

Unmentioned in the sermon was the loyalty one might be expected to give to the state. Fosdick did not draw parallels to the liberties Americans enjoyed and the ways those liberties required one's loyalty. Only briefly did he remind his listeners that democracy demanded recognition of interdependence and cooperation. One could not think only of one's narrow self-interest, he chided. Nonetheless, there was nothing about national loyalty or American patriotism in this sermon.

The following week, Fosdick preached "The Church of Christ in a Warring World." He asserted that the church could not be separated from either the people or the nation but must serve as the "leaven" in this evil world for decency, brotherhood, and peace.[113] In other words, Christianity had a role to play politically; it would be the agent (the leaven) by which democracy would be maintained.

Fosdick was reluctant about but resigned to the United States' entrance into the war. He spoke realistically about how difficult it would be to maintain his oppositional stance. On the Monday after the bombing, he reportedly said to the church secretaries, "Well, I thought you girls would be down in the Navy yard signing up."[114] Even those who were against the war recognized the powerful contagion of war fever.

Even so, the majority of ministers were stern in their criticisms of patriotic war fever. Reverend Howard C. Scharfe of First Presbyterian and Trinity Church began his Sunday sermon after Pearl Harbor with the assertion, "Now that war has come, there are probably some who would feel relief if they could convince themselves that we are in a holy war and that God is on our side, but I cannot preach that kind of sermon."[115] The remainder of Scharfe's sermon examined how God was dependent on Christians to make peace their primary focus. "The biggest job for both our country and Japan will come after this war is over. . . . Amidst the fighting of a war can we keep room in our souls for a little humanity that we may have some moral stamina left for the post-war job?"[116]

Even the conservative Reverend Peter Marshall challenged claims that "God is on our side," reminding his listeners: "We must not permit ourselves to identify the success of the Kingdom of God with the success of the allied nations in this present world conflict. God will win, even if we are defeated."[117] Others, less subtle than Marshall, mockingly asked: "The case of the Civil War is particularly confusing. Americans, as we know, are always on God's side. . . . Did this mean that God was warring against God?"[118]

Challenging the nationalist rhetoric, many ministers agreed that the cause was righteous but insisted that Christians must keep the war separate from God's intervention. "We shall not be treating [God] any more as if he were a vest pocket edition of our own desires, called in to run our errands, or to bless our willful and peevish brutalities. . . . Wanting God to do as we want is wanting him to quit being God!"[119]

From a contemporary perspective, it is difficult to imagine that ministers did not equate either victory or loss with God's reward or punishment. Nor did they seem preoccupied (as they would be in the post-Auschwitz church) with questions of theodicy. Rather, in the early months of 1942, clergy resisted the question "Where is God in the conflict?" and replaced it with "What are you doing to please God?"

Thoughtfully, many ministers did not exempt themselves from the temptations that the war offered. As much to themselves as to their congregants, ministers asserted: "It is not the function of the Church to help win the war. A church that becomes an adjunct to a war department has denied its ministry."[120] Reverend Scharfe was even more specific, citing three ministerial temptations: first, a minister can make himself "an amateur news commentator, dressing up those comments with a text and a few verses of Scripture." Second, he can become a propaganda agent for the government and preach sermons that encourage young men to join the army, the navy, or the air force. Third, he can ignore the war entirely and keep on preaching as if there were no war at all. Scharfe asserted that the "only task" for the minister in war is "to minister to the inner needs of people, to keep alight the spirit of man . . . to keep men's eyes turning to their Christian faith."[121]

As tempting as it would be to claim that the clergy remained stalwart about not collapsing "Christianity" and "patriotism," there was a radio personality, Lutheran minister Walter Maier, who makes that position historically difficult to maintain. Maier was one of the most popular radio figures of his time. His Sunday sermon program *The*

Lutheran Hour was carried by 1,200 outlets and reached an audience of five million weekly. Over the course of 1942, he received 260,000 letters, primarily from within the United States, but also from around the world. His program was described as "the soapbox delivery of a Harvard script."[122] So popular was Maier's program that there is an anecdote repeated in multiple sources that radio station KFEL in Denver received a phone call from an irate listener who wanted to know why *The Lutheran Hour* was canceled on December 7, 1941. When told that schedules had been upset by the war news, he snorted, "Do you think the war news is more important than the Gospel?"[123]

Prior to the bombing of Pearl Harbor, Maier, who had served as a chaplain in World War I, wrote editorials urging American neutrality. He reiterated the ghastly effect of war on humanity and the work of the church, and suggested that only communism would benefit from another war.[124] Yet, once the United States had been attacked, he announced that "our task is to defend ourselves and to defeat our enemies. 'V' indeed must stand for victory, but if it is to be a God-pleasing triumph, it will be a victory based on justice, righteousness, equity with no room for personal profit, class advantage, or national aggrandizement."[125]

After Pearl Harbor, Maier was concerned that his program would be dropped as a peacetime luxury, so he and his team worked diligently to expand the number of outlets carrying his programs, particularly focusing on stations that could be heard by men and women in the armed forces. Maier's son, Paul Maier, claimed in his biography of his father, "This was the first time in history that the church's message, aside from the chaplaincy, was delivered to troops fighting on many fronts by one of the most effective means possible under the circumstances. Radio could penetrate sea-lanes and air lanes, reaching soldiers, sailors, marines, airmen in navy vehicles from jeeps to bombers, in every shelter from foxholes to hospitals, in most encampments from barracks to shipboard, and in every condition from 'just scared' to dying."[126]

Excerpts from the thousands of letters *The Lutheran Hour* received confirmed that the troops found Maier's weekly sermons an important source of solace. He received letters from the start, including from men who had been listening to his December 7 sermon before the bombing began. One pastor wrote to Maier: "Our sailor friend, by the grace of

God, came through unscathed. He cannot help but feel that the Lutheran Hour which he had just heard gave him the strength in those dangerous moments when life was hanging by a thin thread."[127]

Maier's influence extended beyond the military. From 1941 to 1945, attendance at *The Lutheran Hour* rallies ranged up to twenty-seven thousand (the largest-capacity auditorium at the time). At these rallies, attendees took what was called the double pledge: "I ask you, standing in spirit with me beneath the flag of our glorious nation and beneath the cross of our Savior, to repeat this declaration of loyalty; I pledge allegiance to the flag of the United States of America and to the Republic for which it stands, one nation indivisible, with liberty and justice for all. I also pledge allegiance to the Cross of Jesus Christ and to the faith for which it stands, one Savior King eternal, with grace and mercy for all. So, help me God!"[128]

The pledge was reproduced in newspapers and magazines and recited on public occasions. Because of the demand, great quantities of small cards were imprinted with the double pledge and distributed on request. *The Lutheran Hour* also developed a lapel pin with miniature American and Christian flags creating a *V* for victory, beneath which was a scroll embossed with the motto, "For Christ and Country." These were so popular that a factory was dedicated to making them through the war years.

All of this suggests that for many Americans, Christianity and patriotism were entwined. But there was a historical difference from what would develop over the next fifty years that needs marking here. First, unlike later in the century, the wartime church did not imagine itself as under siege. Maier and others were working from the presumption of strength—not only theologically but socially. Maier knew that the church could and did exercise political power. His was a demand that the state answer to God's theological claims, not that the United States was chosen by God. Maier's "Christian patriotism" was not an appeal to covenantal theology (i.e., the United States was founded and chosen by God) or American exceptionalism (i.e., because of its chosen-ness, the United States was exempt from some principles). Maier's appeal was that "followers of Christ are true patriots" and "the number one enemy of the United States is unbelief, and rebellion against God." The best way to defend America was by accepting Christ: "Every man, woman, and child in the US who acclaims Jesus Savior and Sovereign can help bring divine protection on this land through personal prayer."[129]

This 1940s Christian patriotism was of a different order than the one promoted after 9/11. In 1942, there was still an articulated sense of obligation to Christian principles; the United States was not owed anything by God. The United States would earn its relationship, its "divine protection," by the way Americans worshipped, prayed, and adhered to Christianity. There was a robust sense that being a "patriot" meant being a witness to Christ.

After 9/11, the terms were reversed. Being Christian required being a patriot. Tellingly, 9/11 lapel pins had only the American flag; there was nothing invoking Christianity or any other religious commitment. The state defined the terms of the debate, with Christianity merely a welcome addendum. There were decidedly fewer sermons that asked Americans to behave as Christians to make sense of the violence. Rather, Americans were encouraged to rally and unite as Americans in response to what had been done to them. "Christian patriotism" in 2001 focused more on what the United States had suffered than on what Christian witness required in the face of that suffering. This will be more fully explored in Chapter 5.

Japanese Americans, Christianity, and Citizenship

Within hours of the bombing of Pearl Harbor, the US government had arrested nearly every Buddhist priest in Hawaii, California, and Washington State. The FBI had classified Buddhist priests as among the most dangerous Japanese aliens living in the United States, despite the lack of evidence that any of the priests were functioning as a "fifth column" (spies) for the Japanese government. Indeed, historical records reveal only one incident in which a Buddhist priest was even potentially engaged in espionage.[130]

But the internment was not about evidence, as California representative John Tolan clearly articulated while debating the internment before the House Select Committee Investigating National Defense Migration (aka the Tolan Committee). "So far, there are no cases of sabotage; that is, generally speaking. Well, there weren't any in Pearl Harbor, either, were there, until the attack came. There wasn't any sabotage; it all happened at once. In other words, Miss Peet, if the Pacific Coast is attacked, that is when the sabotage would come, with the attack, wouldn't it?"[131] Thus, Tolan's committee felt justified in assuming all Japanese Americans and Japanese immigrants were saboteurs until proven otherwise.

This presumption of Japanese subterfuge echoed other racist conceptions of Asian Americans common in 1940s America. As Emily Roxworthy details in her cogently argued book, *The Spectacle of Japanese American Trauma:* "In the Euro-American imagination, the rapidity of (Japanese) Western inspired modernization (during the Meiji Era 1868–1912) was interpreted as symptomatic of the uncommon *imitativeness* of Japanese people, with the concomitant implication that their Westernization was only a *surface imitation* that was not truly assimilated into Japan's feudal soul. Japanese American claims to American citizenship were merely surface imitations of Americanization that disguised their deep-seated loyalty to the Japanese empire."[132]

J. Edgar Hoover's FBI was wary of Japanese Americans for this very reason; he insisted that "Americanization projects" were merely disingenuous facsimiles by Japanese Americans to "seem American." The FBI was also distrustful of attempts by various organizations to preserve Japanese cultural traditions (i.e., Buddhist churches and Japanese language schools) in the United States.[133] Little space existed for Japanese Americans to be patriotic Americans—they were either already traitors or about to be revealed as traitors. As Tennessee senator Arthur Thomas Stewart roared from the Senate floor, "I say that where there is one drop of Japanese blood there is absolute Japanese treachery."[134]

Some of the fear of Buddhist priests was based on a misunderstanding of the difference between Buddhism and what was called in the 1940s "State Shintoism." Throughout the war (including prior to the bombing of Pearl Harbor), the Japanese government exerted considerable influence on their homeland citizens to worship in Shinto shrines to demonstrate their nationalism. State Shintoism emphasized the worship of the emperor as a deity and required loyalty to the Japanese imperial empire.

Buddhism was not part of this coercion and had little affiliation with imperial ambitions. American Buddhists were decidedly not aligned with the nationalist push. In fact, as soon as Executive Order 9066 went into effect, the Buddhist Mission of North America sent a notice to its members urging them "to register for civilian defense. . . . Your loyalty and devotion to the cause of the United States of America in her war against the aggressor nations of the Axis, must be translated into action. Do your part unflinchingly in the defense of the STARS AND STRIPES."[135]

From a contemporary American perspective, this is a remarkable recommendation. Yet it aptly captures the paradoxical situation in which Japanese Americans found themselves. Accused of being insufficiently "American," they were advised to demonstrate their "American loyalty." But in being expected to manifest loyalty by *not* resisting internment, they simultaneously jeopardized their futures as American citizens. Most of those interned lost their businesses, farms, and homes as well as substantial portions of their personal and household effects.

The authorization of Executive Order 9066 by President Roosevelt on February 19, 1942, allowed local military commanders to designate "military areas" as "exclusion zones" from which "any or all persons may be excluded." This power was used to declare that all people of Japanese ancestry were excluded from the entire Pacific Coast, including all of California and much of Oregon, Washington, and Arizona. Of the 127,000 Japanese Americans living in the continental United States at the time of the attack, 112,000 lived on the West Coast. About 80,000 (nearly two-thirds of those eventually interned) were nisei (second generation, or Japanese American people born in the United States and holding American citizenship). The rest were issei (first generation, or immigrants born in Japan who were ineligible for US citizenship). Approximately 14,500 people of German and Italian ancestry and 2,200 ethnic Japanese deported from Latin American countries were also subject to wartime confinement. In full, nearly 110,000 Japanese Americans were interned in relocation centers sited primarily in Western states.

As suggested by polls, newspaper editorials, and minutes from the Tolan Committee meetings held throughout the Northwest within weeks of the bombing, the majority of Americans supported the internment.[136] Characteristic of the support was this observation by a Tolan Committee citizen-advocate: "This is not the time for namby-pamby pussyfooting, fear of hurting the feelings of our enemies; this is not the time for consideration of minute constitutional rights of those enemies but this is the time for vigorous, whole-hearted, and concerted action."[137]

Nothing confirmed that Japanese Americans had reason to be nervous more than the alacrity with which Executive Order 9066 was created and the relative ease with which it was implemented. In addition to the detention of Buddhist priests, Japanese American bank accounts were frozen and some homes raided. By February 1942, the order for internment was in place, locations had been selected, and Japanese Americans notified of their removal.

There was some early, although largely ineffective, opposition to the internment. The Portland Council of Churches made suggestions about how to make removal as humane as possible, although it did not directly question the need for evacuation. On December 9, the Foreign Missions Conference issued a statement that "called upon the church people of this country to maintain a Christian composure and charity in the dealing with the Japanese among us."[138] Reinhold Niebuhr's editorial, "A Blot on Our Record," was a more direct critique, comparing Executive Order 9066 to Germany's Nuremberg Laws, but it was not published until the spring of 1942.[139]

Many mainline Protestant churches skirted condemnation of the incarceration during the first months. A group of ministers in Southern California publicly expressed their regret in April 1942 but "did not criticize the policy . . . contented with deploring its apparent necessity and wishing well its victims."[140] Reverend Galen Fisher wrote a long essay, "Our Japanese Refugees," in which he offered American Christians cover by claiming it was ignorance, not malice, that had led Christians to quietly condone the internment. His was an attempt to thread the needle between remaining patriotic and arguing against the Executive Order. Other clergy maintained that opposing government policy was not good church policy—or, more pointedly, not good for the church's long-term interests.

Influential opposition was primarily led by individuals affiliated with the University of California, Berkeley, in an organization initially named the Northern California Committee for Fair Play for Citizens and Aliens of Japanese Ancestry.[141] This committee was composed of university presidents, faculty, several rabbis, and some Christian clergy. Rabbi Irving Reichert was a founding member. The Methodist minister

Reverend Fran Herron was a member who testified that the over-whelming majority of Christian issei were loyal to America. The nisei he had "known for 15 years, boys whom I married to their wives are as truly American as your son, Congressman Tolan."[142]

Members of the committee expressed concern that the internment jeopardized American values and opened the floodgates for many other ethnicities, including Germans, Italians, and Austrians, to be interned. Louis Goldblatt, who was also secretary of the California State Indus-trial Union Council of San Francisco, urged, "And, Mr. Tolan, if we follow such a procedure, we can land in only one place. We will do a perfect job for those who want to sabotage the war effort. We will have the American people at each other's throats."[143]

Several Christian clergy submitted written statements to the Tolan Committee opposing the internment, reminding members: "We here on the coast must live with the Japanese after the war is over and we are anxious that nothing be done that would make us ashamed of the manner in which they are treated now. . . . The manner in which minority groups are handled is a final criterion of the standard of national civilization."[144] Several pointed out that many of the Japanese had only remained "aliens" because US law forbade their naturalization. One clergyman noted that while American methods were kinder than Hitler's, the injustice was the same, and that the internment would mean that Americans had been conquered by Hitler's spirit and methods, if not by his military machine. "We cannot fight for democracy by such methods."[145]

What was most poignant about the internment was captured in the photographs taken by Dorothea Lange. Lange had been commissioned by the War Relocation Department to take the photographs, but the government confiscated her work because her images were too revealing of the injustice of the internment. Lange showed the loss of privacy en-dured by the "evacuees" (the 1942 term for those interned in the camps), the horse stalls that had been incompletely converted into living quar-ters in some of the camps, and lines of women with parasols waiting for group meals outside the mess hall. She depicted the "classrooms" where young children, who looked like "every day American school children," knelt on dirty floors to do their schoolwork. She afforded the Japanese Americans their dignity while simultaneously illumi-nating their suffering.

Subsequently, Ansel Adams was asked to photograph the Manzanar War Relocation Center, an internment camp located in Owens Valley, California. He too was given free access to the camp but instructed not to photograph barbed wire, armed guards, or the guard towers.[146] With only one exception, Adams complied. He also took no photographs of elderly Japanese inmates. The US government did not want to be perceived as being so heartless as to intern the clearly nonthreatening. Dorothea Lange's photographs had been full of the old and feeble, interned as potential spies.

Ansel Adams's photographs were eventually displayed at the Museum of Modern Art in 1943. There was mild controversy surrounding the exhibit, since anti-Japanese sentiment was still high, but Adams's photographs were largely interpreted as revealing the beauty of the American West as well as the peaceful and orderly life of the camps. He said that he wanted to showcase how "loyal" Japanese Americans had adjusted to camp life, and to demonstrate their patriotism and Americanism.[147] Toward that end, Adams depicted Japanese Americans attending Christian churches,[148] playing baseball,[149] and men and women returning to the camps to visit family members while proudly wearing their US military uniforms.[150]

A complete analysis of life in the internment camps is beyond the scope of this chapter.[151] But a few signature features of camp life help illuminate the sermons that Christian ministers gave in the weeks after the bombing and just before removal.

First, the War Department actively encouraged church services to be held at all the camps. Services for all religions, including Buddhism, were permitted. In fact, Buddhism gained strength in the camps because the War Relocation Authority's parameters necessitated that Buddhist sects cooperate with each other. For the duration of the internment, doctrinal differences were often ignored in favor of a shared, pluralist Buddhism. For example, all sects chanted *namu butsu* (homage to the Buddha) rather than each sect's unique incantation. They even composed a new hymn, "Onward Buddhist Soldiers." Consolidation, rather than diminishing Buddhism, increased its membership in the camps.

The only religious prohibition was against Shinto practices, with the added caveat that "religious activities were not to be used as vehicles to propagandize or incite the members of the center."[152] In other words, services were supposed to offer solace, not solutions to confinement.

Furthermore, and without a trace of irony, the War Department believed that the camps could be training grounds for the interned to learn about democracy. The War Department sought ways the interned Japanese Americans could have "self-government." For example, when internees protested, accommodations were made, such as that more Japanese cuisine would be served in the mess hall and that some supervisors would be internees.[153] Somehow the US government imagined that improved prison conditions would teach incarcerated Japanese Americans the value of democracy in a way that living freely in American society had not. That the majority of those interned were American citizens seems to have been completely disregarded in this zealous quest for so-called Americanization.

After a year of internment, in January 1943, it became mandatory for Japanese Americans to declare themselves loyal to the United States. Each was required to answer the question, "Will you swear unqualified allegiance to the United States of America . . . and forswear any form of allegiance or obedience to the Japanese emperor?" When the program ended, thirty-one thousand Japanese American citizens had answered "yes."

On the other hand, more than six thousand had answered "no," and three thousand others had qualified their answers, refused to answer, or neglected to register at all.[154] Among the reasons many answered "no" was first, and perhaps most obviously, to register their protest against internment. Some of those who marked "no" wrote on the questionnaire, "If we are citizens, how come we are in these camps? I answer 'NO' because of resentment and because of how they treated us." As Morton Grodzins rightly points out in his compelling essay, "Making Un-Americans," some citizens answered no because they believed that the United States had violated itself and its own principles through the internment.[155]

Others answered no because they were worried that if they answered yes, they would be drafted, and if they were killed in the war, their parents would be left impoverished and stateless, without even a country to protect them. National disloyalty was in direct tension with family loyalty, especially Japanese and Buddhist conceptions of respect and responsibility for one's elders.

Some of those who answered no did so because they were afraid that if they answered yes, they would be forced to leave the camps and would be exposed to the hatred of their fellow Americans. Since countless internees had lost their businesses, household effects, and prospects for employment, many believed that until the war was over, it was better to suffer in the security of the camp than risk social and economic violence at liberty in the American homeland.[156] Others answered no because issei had been barred from obtaining US citizenship on the basis of race since 1922 (*Ozawa v. U.S.*, 260 U.S. 178); if they renounced allegiance to Japan, they would be stateless. Issei who answered yes were swearing allegiance to a country that did not allow them to be citizens. The questionnaire was a facile and brutal attempt to measure what historical and political realities in many instances explicitly prohibited.[157]

Although loyalty questions would not be asked until a year after the bombing of Pearl Harbor, they demonstrate the racial context of the internment and the grim backdrop that Christian ministers, many of Japanese descent, faced as they preached to their congregants in the week or so before internment began.

Sermons before Internment: "Ours Is a Strange Exodus"

Late in the spring of 1942, Japanese American ministers collected the sermons they had preached to their largely issei and nisei congregations in the weeks before internment.[158] The dozen sermons gathered were from Methodist, Congregationalist, Episcopalian, and Presbyterian churches, primarily along the West Coast. Two years later, the collection was edited and self-published by a Quaker missionary in Japan, Gurney Binford.[159]

These sermons overwhelmingly agreed that the internment was as much about theological issues as political ones—indeed, they argued that the internment was probably decidedly more theological than political. These sermons were a near-perfect counter to those given by largely White Christian clergy, who had framed the attack on Pearl Harbor as decidedly more political than theological.

The collection's foreword asserted that it was "a continuation of the eleventh chapter of Hebrews showing the victory of faith by those who went out not knowing whither they went nor why they were required to go; and secondly, this witness brings to Christians the knowledge and understanding which will help American churches to welcome Japanese Christians into their church fellowship."[160] The internment was an opportunity offered by God for Japanese Americans to lead others to faith. "Never has the Church had a finer opportunity to display the meaning of Christianity and never have we had finer material to work with than these Japanese Americans."[161]

Solemnly echoing the New Testament, the ministers described those about to be interned as like Jesus bearing the cross. The meaning and power of the internment rested on the shoulders of Japanese Americans and their ability to make this "strange exodus," this "Abrahamic migration," into a clarion call, not only of their American patriotism but of their Christian faith and God's redemptive power. Perhaps oddly from today's perspective, Japanese American ministers took ownership of the internment as being as much a result of their own violation of God's law as of American intolerance.

Several minsters advised their congregations to "give God a chance. Since we are bound to God by this tie of Christian love, let us give God a chance to reveal his will for us and to work in us and through us."[162] Further invoking the biblical tradition, other ministers reminded their listeners that "the Love of God turns the misfortunes of a chosen people into their own good, using both the chosen and the foreign races as instruments in His Divine Plan."[163]

There were multiple references to Abraham in these sermons; the issei and nisei Christians, like Abraham, were "the new pilgrims."[164] They had to "leave many worldly possessions behind. We, too, have had to receive God's hard lesson. . . . It is good, because it is God's plan. Let us learn of Abraham in this faith and walk like him."[165] There were references as well to the suffering and exile of the Jews, the destruction of Jerusalem, and the unwarranted but restorative suffering of Jesus. "In a sense, this is our Calvary, and we must be willing to say: 'Father, forgive them, they know not what they do.'"[166] One minister, Reverend Hashimoto, noted that Japanese American suffering, like the suffering of Americans writ large after the bombing at Pearl Harbor, was the result of

human sinfulness. God did not cause suffering; human beings cultivated it themselves. "God does not purposefully give suffering to man.
Suffering comes from the result of man's sin. Yet, God uses even the
consequence of sin to the end that man should see aright and turn to
Him."[167]

There were no theodicy questions among the Christian Japanese
American faithful, no worries about how a good and loving God could
permit such misery. Reverend Hideo Hashimoto, pastor of the Japanese
Methodist Church in Fresno, California, asserted, "From the standpoint
of American democracy, this evacuation is a shame, a dangerous attack
upon the fundamental principle upon which our nation is built. But from
the standpoint of a Christian Nisei, it is a well-deserved punishment for
our indifference, our falling down on the job, our self-centeredness, our
sin."[168] The internment in this interpretation was political *and* theological; it was a political violation but a theological opportunity for reconciliation with God. Hashimoto drew an elaborate analogy to the destruction of Jerusalem in BC 597 and the Babylonian exile. Compared
to those trials, he said, "Ours is nothing."[169]

It is noteworthy and disturbing that neither he nor the other ministers drew an analogy to the condition of contemporary Jews in Europe.
But there were references to the plight of African Americans. One minister said, "You would think that Negroes would jump at the opportunity of crying 'Japs' and joining the nation in oppressing us, but they
have not done it. They understand how it hurts to be segregated and denied civil rights."[170] There was an astute political analysis embedded in
this ministerial observation. In the Jim Crow South of the 1940s, White
southerners were worried that relocated Japanese Americans would make
common cause with southern Blacks. In fact, southern White leaders
insisted that Japanese Americans must sit in the front of the bus, drink
from the White man's fountain, and use the White man's restrooms.[171]
Southerners wanted Japanese Americans to think of themselves as
White.

Most of the Japanese American ministers, like their Black counterparts in the South, detailed the ways Japanese Americans had been
model citizens: they were patriotic, high achieving, obedient, rarely
criminal or violent. They agreed with their White Christian counterparts that Pearl Harbor was primarily a political act, but one ripe with

redemptive possibilities. White Protestant ministers did not imagine that they had in any way earned the punishment and suffering of the war. Japanese American ministers, on the other hand, despite their conception of their congregants as "model American citizens," did not laud themselves as model Christians or as inoculated from punishment. They were more inclined than their White mainstream counterparts to claim that it was their failure as Christians that had created the gap into which this denigrating internment had slid.

Several ministers addressed directly why they had chosen Abraham as their biblical counterpart rather than Moses. Reverend Sokei Kowta, pastor of the Japanese Presbyterian Church in Wintersberg, California, referred to an article in the magazine *Christian Century* in which the unnamed author apparently praised Japanese Americans but noted, "Among them, however, no Moses has yet appeared." Reverend Kowta then detailed why Moses would not be the ideal leader for the contemporary crisis. He described how there was no pharaoh to whom Japanese Americans could appeal: "We Japanese are not expected to make demands of the Army that is in control of our affairs. We are simply asked to obey and cooperate with whatever the Army commands us to do. Under such circumstances, even Moses would not be able to show his God-given talents to the fullest extent."[172]

Kowta's sermon was paradigmatic of the collection in that he offered not only a theological frame through which to understand the internment but a role for Japanese Americans who answered God's demands, not the requirements of the US government. Indeed, the reverend did not mention the US government once in his ten-page sermon. References to the US government were largely absent from the collection as a whole.

Although it might seem that Japanese Americans were complying with internment from a sense of loyalty and a concomitant patriotic dedication to the United States, what they were really doing, according to Reverend Kowta and many others, was complying with God's demands. Their obedience was not submission to injustice, but faith in the Judeo-Christian call to exile, suffering, and submission to the unknown.

Later in the same sermon, Reverend Kowta explicitly named Abraham's three "outstanding characteristics." First, Abraham was a man of faith, and specifically a man who was justified before God "not through

his good works . . . but through his faith." Second, Abraham was praised
for his obedience: "One's faith is most well proven when he trusts in and
obeys God without any reservation. . . . Abraham went out not knowing
whither he went. What a faith, what a trust, what an obedience it was!"[173]
Here Kowta, like many of the other ministers, gave a theological explanation that did not require Japanese Americans to resist internment.
Through the internment, Japanese Americans were becoming Jewish
wanderers ("the Babylonian exile"[174]), Hebrew prophets in exile
("Abraham, the Migration Leader"[175]), and Christian pilgrims ("new pilgrims"[176]) witnessing for their faith. Their compliance was a manifestation of Christian faithfulness, not a banal mark of American patriotism.

Reverend John M. Yamazaki compared the book of Exodus to the
evacuation, calling the "Nisei of the Exodus" to cross the river and enter
the Promised Land as the Hebrews did. "Those of the older generations
among us, even if they perish in the wilderness . . . the Nisei will find a
way to a better and newer world. I know they will reach the promised
land if they prove to be like Joshua and his followers in their faith and
loyalty."[177]

Abraham's second virtuous quality, Reverend Kowta said, was hope.
Even though Abraham's life was filled with challenges, "he was always
conscious that he was a pilgrim in this world and that he was constantly
looking for a city whose builder and maker was God."[178] Quoting Paul's
epistle to the Romans, Reverend Kowta noted, "In hope, Abraham
believed against hope." Again, the virtue recounted was one of internal
reconciliation with external realities. There was no call for protest, for
overturning the tables, or for becoming an outcast. Christian faithfulness, in this rendition, was optimistic, although politically passive.

This was a typical rendition of Christian salvation: through suffering,
there was liberation and redemption. Although this was not the radical
liberation theology of 1960s Latin America, it did begin to suggest that
there was wisdom, insight, even chosen-ness in suffering. God did have
a preferential option for the poor and suffering.

These internment sermons showcase what will become a standard
homiletic argument over the next sixty years of American crises; those
without power assign their suffering redemptive power, while those with
power can make the cause of their suffering political. The powerful are
confident in their own capacity to reconfigure the world toward good.

White ministers in 1942 claimed such power for themselves. Those without power fear that without God's intercession, their suffering will remain meaningless—overlooked by the majority and random in its execution. By making their suffering part of God's salvation history, Japanese American ministers retrieved their suffering from the waste bin of American history and strove to counter American imperial power with the certainty of God's redemption.

Abraham's last outstanding characteristic was that he was a man of love. Reverend Kowta repeated the biblical story of the conflict between Abraham's herdsmen and Lot's herdsmen. Abraham resolved the conflict by agreeing to split the land, even though Abraham's seniority meant that Lot legally should have conceded to Abraham. Abraham was a conciliator; he did not insist on what was rightfully his, choosing to avoid conflict.

Although it might be possible (and generous) to interpret this sermonic repetition as an incipient claim to the power of nonviolence, there was nothing in the sermon that detailed how politically unjust the internment was or how Christian faithfulness might be a way to resist that injustice. Rather, the sermon was a Protestant meditation on how individual faithfulness would result in a deeper relationship with God.

Kowta's sermon noted, "Every crisis is a testing time of one's character." The reverend scolded Japanese Americans who might be worrying too much about their troubles and thus not demonstrating their best character. He prayed on their behalf that they would "have faith in Almighty God, cultivate hope in the future of our people, and increase love for our fellow men. Fully equipped with these virtues, we shall then have nothing to be afraid of. Give us a desert, we shall make it a beautiful garden; give us a wasted land, we shall change it into a productive field; give us a wilderness, we shall convert it into a fruitful orchard."[179]

The sermon concluded with a profoundly poignant turn. Kowta spent the last two pages describing the challenges and mental anguish of disposing of one's property and the concomitant anxieties about deciding what to take to the camps. "Within a very short time, we shall have to move out from this fair city of Los Angeles, leaving 'Little Tokyo' behind us. And this dear church, too—this church where we have played together and prayed together, this church where we have talked together and worked together. . . . And this very sacred place where many young hearts were joined together in marriage, and where we uttered our final farewell to our departed ones."[180]

The sermon finished:

> And no man can justly blame the Japanese people for feeling a deep sense of attachment to what they are soon to leave behind. But we Japanese shall not be like the thoughtless wife of Lot. We shall not foolishly look back and weep and mourn and turn ourselves into pillars of salt. Rather, we shall be like Abraham, the mighty migration leader; filled, not with hatred or bitterness, but with faith, hope and love; we shall go wherever God wants us to go, and as we go along, we shall bless the people everywhere, as did Abraham of old.[181]

From today's perspective, these ministers seem to be reiterating a 1940s racial stereotype in theological terms. Japanese immigrants are perceived as being accommodating; in theological terms, the ministers are reminding their flock: "We are a people of faith, not works. Our faith will be the sign, not our actions." Perhaps unintentionally, or perhaps with pragmatic deliberation, the ministers were insinuating to those about to be interned that quiescence could be a demonstration of faith as much as an act of resistance could be. Moses acted by leading the Jews into the desert for forty years. Abraham, these ministers argued, did something infinitely more powerful—he trusted in God. Abraham, not Moses, was the role model for the Christian Japanese American community.

Some ministers made the point that unlike Moses escaping Pharaoh, Japanese Americans did not have a specific tyrant to overcome. Apparently, the US government was not to be cast as a tyrant. Rather, several of the ministers insisted counterintuitively that the internment was *not* the result of American decisions but the tragic consequence of the "war system." "In the final analysis, it is not the army, nor the federal government, nor the people, who are sending us to a temporary exile. It is the war system and the present world society which is built on the war system, which is doing to us this unwelcome deed."[182]

Japanese Americans were then framed as reformers. The nisei minister Reverend Royden Susu-Mago said: "God cannot mend the nation except through those who work from inside it. God needs us just as much as America does."[183] The interned were actually on a mission from God for the United States.

The sermons Japanese American ministers gave between Pearl Harbor and the internment set the parameters of the struggle for authority that would animate the Protestant Church for the next sixty years. On the one hand, White Protestant ministers were confident in their authority, concisely naming Pearl Harbor as a political issue, not a theological one. They demanded respect, chiding the government when it imagined it could tell them what to preach, even if those messages were in support of the nation.

But there was simultaneously an early manifestation of the fraying of that certainty and the eclipse of church authority. First, the ministers did not mourn the dead at Pearl Harbor, believing that their deaths were too monumental for a mere church service. The deaths of military servicemen required something heroic, oversized. Eventually, that would become the massive USS *Arizona* Memorial at Pearl Harbor, operated by the National Park Service. This marked the transfer of a significant religious ritual to the state. The injustice at the internment centers, meanwhile, would wait close to fifty years to be acknowledged by any kind of memorial.

More important, when confronted with the suffering of Jews in Europe and the internment of Japanese Americans, the church faltered. It was without institutional mechanisms to implement its theological vision for a just world. Instead, it relied ineffectively on statements criticizing the policy, but still deferring to the fears and insecurities that propelled Roosevelt's administration to Executive Order 9066. Individual ministers were sent on missions to persuade Hitler or to offer solace in the internment camps, but there was no coordinated movement against American neglect of justice.

Lost was Barth's vision of a radically other divine order. Instead, there was Niebuhr's practical accommodation, the "dirty hands of politics," which he mistakenly believed would accelerate church influence but instead rendered it meaningless. The state had no reason to listen to the church or negotiate with it when what religious authority seemed to be offering was coordination with the state's chosen positions. The church had significantly more influence when it refused to pragmatically adjust its message to political realities—when it was perceived as a viable alternative. It was a lesson that the Protestant ministry would come to regret not having fully internalized.

Still, in the post–World War II United States, ministers remained admired and respected as opinion makers, helping to frame the American narrative of valor and virtue during the war. This influence was helped in part by "GI Jesus"—the military chaplains who served admirably with the troops during the war. Yet the postwar period was also a time during which state power was accruing. The United States had assumed its role as a world power and was learning how to conduct itself at center stage. Britain and France had been humbled by the Germans, although they had fought heroically according to the standard narrative. The United States had not been chastened in the same way, and had emerged triumphant. The annihilation of Nagasaki and Hiroshima had literally and metaphorically destroyed any doubts of the United States' dominion. And with that kind of power, the United States could afford to be gracious.

The war economy lifted many American families, especially veterans, into a prosperous middle class. Church attendance surged through the 1950s and early 1960s. Yet the double consciousness of the United States remained. Irreconcilable notions of who was a "true American" would continue with McCarthyism and the Red Scare as well as the 1954 *Brown v. Board of Education* decision and efforts to integrate public schools. With the assassination of President John F. Kennedy, Protestant ministers would be challenged to give an account of who embodied the real United States. Was it the handsome, charming JFK, or the disheveled and violent Lee Harvey Oswald? How could Americans have murdered one of their own? Especially their own esteemed leader? It was one thing to be assaulted by a foreign enemy, but another thing entirely to discover that the worst treachery lurked within.

Protestant ministers during the bombing of Pearl Harbor and the internment of Japanese American citizens had insisted on two things: First, that the destruction of Pearl Harbor was not a referendum from God; God was not involved or interested in the violence; rather, the bombing was the effect of political decisions and the failures of government. God had nothing to do with it. Second, in slight tension with the first, American patriotism could be reconciled rather easily with Christian principles. The internment of Japanese Americans was an occasion to highlight how easily American patriotism and loyalty could be exemplified through the Christian suffering of Japanese Americans willingly accepting the cross of their internment. Christian redemption could be achieved by an ennobling sacrifice for the good of the state. Although God might not have inaugurated the violence against the United States, He would accept the violence that the United States did in His name as redemptive. It was not the first time, nor would it be the last, that Protestant ministers would make Christianity do some of the theopolitical work of maintaining racial hierarchies and inequities.

Twenty years later, when American violence resulted in the murder of President Kennedy, ministers would have to consider whether they had done enough to ensure that Christian principles were still foundational to American life. They would have to address whether those principles were sufficiently robust to protect the state from its own worst impulses. In 1963, ministers fastidiously interrogated their own culpability in the death of a beloved American. Although they would not consider the violence of Kennedy's death as a question of theodicy, they were less confident than they had been after Pearl Harbor that individually and institutionally, the church had done enough to confirm that Christianity was at the vital center of American political and cultural life.

CHAPTER TWO

We All Killed Kennedy

The Assassination of President John F. Kennedy

In the days after the assassination of President John F. Kennedy, "it was almost as if the whole people bowed their head and America, for a time became a church," declared George Cornell, Associated Press religion writer.[1] American churches were indeed full the weekend after the Kennedy assassination. Regular services were held on Sunday morning, November 24, 1963, often to standing room–only crowds. According to estimates at the time, more Americans attended church on the Sunday after Kennedy's assassination than any other day in American history.[2]

Then, on Monday, November 25, the designated national day of mourning, there were denominationally specific memorial services that were also well attended. In many cases, both Sunday and Monday services were broadcast on local radio stations, and bulletins were distributed with reprints of the minister's sermons. But George Cornell's image of the nation as a church meant more in 1963 than simply filling pews.

A church-like silence fell over most of the United States on Friday, November 22, 1963. The profane was disdained and silenced, and conceptions of the holy were collectively constructed. By midafternoon, movie theaters, restaurants, and many stores were closed. Broadway shows were halted and college football games canceled.[3] Even Jack Ruby, we now know, closed his strip club that night.

Some ministers celebrated this silencing of popular culture, declaring that the crisis had restored God to the center of American life. Americans were remembering what was important: "I'm so glad that many of the entertainment features were cancelled. . . . I'm glad also that the doors of God's house stayed open, for when sorrow comes, God's house is the place to come."[4] "It sometimes takes tragedy to bring people . . . to the realization of God's purpose for the world . . . and to set aside peripheral matters in their lives for the sake of really getting at the all-important tasks of carrying out God's plan for the world."[5] The suspension of "the marketplaces of our nation" had given Americans a "brief vision of Ultimate Reality. . . . We have seen and know that there is a Mystery beyond."[6]

Television networks suspended regular programming and began what would be the longest continuous coverage of a single event prior to September 11, 2001. AC Nielsen's figures show that 96 percent of US home televisions were tuned to assassination coverage for an average of thirty-two hours over the four-day period.[7] Again, ministers applauded this turn of events—evidently without anticipating how eyewitness journalists would one day erode their own ecclesial authority for truth telling and meaning-making. Various ministers noted that television had reversed its frivolity and violence and was now serving the American people as a source of solace and unity.[8] Reverend Billy Graham, in his radio sermon "Fleeting Lives," said, "The immediate sense of personal loss is much greater for the American people than it was at the deaths of McKinley, Garfield or even Lincoln, because by means of television the president was almost a daily visitor in our homes."[9] The living room television set had become a new altar around which community was formed and the narrative of the tragedy shaped.[10]

It was too early that weekend for a critique of the violent role the media might have played in Oswald's assassination. Corporate media and the American public were initially quite proud of the dignity with which the president was being memorialized and the assassination and funeral televised.[11] Although some Americans gathered in the streets,

especially in front of store windows with televisions, there were none of
the temporary memorials that were to mark later events of collective
mourning, such as September 11. As Mohammed Bamyeh has argued
in another context, "transforming the sad scene of the ruins into tragic
beauty" is a way to acknowledge the decay embedded in the human condition.[12] Yet the site of Kennedy's death was not an inspiration for
mourning America's vulnerability. Although some flowers were placed
at Dealey Plaza, where the president was shot, formal memorials were
still the preferred venue for expressions of American and Christian grief.
Within hours of the assassination, however, Americans from across the
country were sending letters of condolence to the White House. On
Monday, November 25, 45,000 letters were delivered. Within seven
weeks, Jacqueline Kennedy had received 800,000 letters.[13]

The death of the president was understood as a heroic event, requiring
something monumental to mark its end. Kennedy's death was observed
as a continuation of the epic tradition of the world wars. Kennedy was
celebrated in his own words: "He has become the greatest chapter in his
Profiles in Courage."[14] His death was perceived to transcend what could
be signified by a transient, impromptu memorial. The event was too co-
lossal for such a puny shrine. This elevation meant that ordinary Americans felt insufficient in the face of their gigantic loss.

In part because of this church-like ambience, ministers played an
important role in framing how Americans might make sense of the
tragedy. Who and how Americans mourned was not only of theological
importance but of political significance as well. In 1963, according to
Gallup polls, 69 percent of Americans identified as Protestants and
24 percent as Catholics; only 2 percent said they had no religious affiliation.[15] Also, over 55 percent of ministers in the United States were under
the age of forty-five in 1963,[16] adding to their likely sense of identification with the assassinated forty-six-year-old president.

But the Kennedy assassination was not a crisis in which the durability
of the United States itself was understood as genuinely at risk, although
there were deep suspicions about the threat that Soviet and Cuban Communism posed to American stability. Many Americans envisaged that
a bulwark against this insidious infestation had to be secured. Thus, this
tragic event compelled Americans to reassess the meaning of their collective life.

This was also a particularly modern crisis, because in modernity human beings feel themselves abandoned in the eye of the hurricane, out of which each believes they must somehow conceive meaning anew.[17] Without secure foundations, elements of life that once seemed settled, even natural, are reinterpreted and contested. In 1963, Americans were more likely to experience anything unexpected or startling as a crisis, in part because there was precious little they collectively took for granted. It was relatively easy to shake their epistemological foundations—foundations that many acknowledged rested insecurely on sheer force of will rather than on a tradition of irrefutable conviction.

Thus, Kennedy's assassination raised questions about American identity. Protestant ministers wrestled in their sermons with the question of whether Americans were more aptly symbolized by the vigor, style, and charm of John F. Kennedy or the lost, angry violence of Lee Harvey Oswald. Both were Americans. Who was *more* American? How could Americans account for the disparity? How could Christians?

The United States became a church, as Cornell notes, because so many Americans gave the church another opportunity to provide meaning and to detail the Truth during the crisis. That's a signature feature of a crisis—society readjudicates what has previously been taken for granted and reevaluates its priorities. Part of the disorientation of a crisis is that it is unanticipated. One questions how one might have or should have known of this tragic possibility and thus, what one might have done to prevent it. During the tumult of a crisis, blind spots are revealed and focus is redirected. It's a time of civic education and often a time when individuals turn to public political action.

It is also, as Norman Jacobson reminds us, during a crisis that we look for solace. And historically, the American Church has been a place to offer both reorientation and comfort. From pews filled with tear-stained faces, Americans asked, "Can the Church do what the State has demonstrated it cannot?" The state had shown that it could not protect its citizens from random violence, not even its most important citizen, the president. In mourning Kennedy, Americans explored again what ought to be their conception of the ideal relation between church and state authority—it was both a personal and political query.

The Kennedy sermons were not simply texts, then, but civic liturgies. Like ancient Greek theater, they served as a form of civic education. They were ritual narratives, retelling both religious and political stories in ways designed to reassure, renew, and realign their listeners. The sermons were theopolitical gestures enacted during an unstable period. What stories Americans told themselves about who they were, where they were from, and who and what was important during this crisis became a constitutive element of American political history.

Although sermons might be understood traditionally as a way for a denomination to detail its particularity to its congregants, ministers seem to have understood the challenge less as one of denominational inscription and more as civic service. How are Americans to understand a crisis event as Christian citizens? What is the relation between Christianity and citizenship in this crisis? How might American Christianity configure its concurrent understanding of citizenship? Conversely, how might so-called American-ness illuminate Christianity?

After the assassination of President John F. Kennedy, although many ministers remarked on Kennedy's Catholicism, very few sermons made denominational difference the focus. Rather, Kennedy's Catholicism was embraced as part of "our" collective Christianity. The crisis distilled Christianity to its commonalities. Differences would return, of course, and rather quickly. Within months, the diverse strands of Christianity would again argue for distinctions, but during those first weeks, there was a collective "we."

This crisis of death and violence was not one in which the durability of the state was realistically challenged. It was primarily a crisis in which Americans struggled for meaning and understanding. Echoing Norman Jacobson's definition of a crisis as a broken paradigm,[18] the Kennedy sermons allowed Americans to read the crisis as an epistemological failure—a moment when the reigning theoretical banisters could no longer support a ruptured reality. It reconfigured conceptions of American citizenry. The crisis was a transformative event. Specifically, American Christians changed in part because their understanding of themselves was challenged. The question "Who am I?" in a classically Greek sense, was collectively revisited in many of the sermons.

The death of the president revealed the vulnerability of the state. It disrupted American notions of national superiority, particularly around issues of law and order. Many Americans were ashamed that "it could happen here." Challenged was a sense of American superiority in comparison to developing countries, where political assassinations were imagined as the order of the day. The United States' borders no longer protected its citizens from what others had long endured.

During this American crisis, there was a contest between church and state authority. Why were the churches full? Because implicitly, the tragedy had called into question the certainty, if not the power, of the state's ability to protect its own. The crisis reanimated the specter—if not necessarily the validity—of alternatives to the City of Man. Perhaps Americans were mistaken in their reliance and confidence in American hegemony. Had American power been shown vulnerable? Had her supremacy been damaged by her own flaws rather than by that of a foreign enemy? This was partially why the suspicions about a conspiracy were so compelling. It was easier for 1960s Americans initially to believe that they had been undermined by a hostile foreign power rather than that their own indigenous violence had spun out of control. Where else could citizens look for answers? For conviction? For certitude? Norman Jacobson argues that "political theory begins precisely at the moment when things become, so to speak, unglued."[19] Perhaps, in American political history of the twentieth century, it might be more apt to say that *political theology* begins at that moment.

This chapter explores what Protestant ministers preached to try to resolve the crisis provoked by mourning Kennedy. Although the majority of ministers praised Kennedy for having been more judicious about the separation of church and state than they had anticipated, most cast the crisis in theological rather than legal terms. To restore the proper balance between religious and governmental authority, they made three important points. First, they told their congregants that Kennedy had died a martyr. He was not merely murdered, he was sacrificed. Kennedy's death reinscribed the value of the United States rather than degraded it. If one so valuable, so worthy, was sacrificed, the nation must be truly great. Kennedy was the quintessential American Christian patriot. Indeed, many ministers compared Kennedy to Christ.

Second, ministers laid responsibility for the tragedy at their own doorsteps. What had killed Kennedy, they lamented, was not the state's deficiency but the church's failure to be the church. In an era of waning social and cultural authority for the church, Protestant ministers sought to showcase what happens when the church hesitates. The ministers did not blame the state for limiting church authority. They blamed themselves and their congregants, suggesting, "We are responsible for the death of Kennedy."

Third, most White Protestant ministers tried to solve the crisis of violence provoked by Kennedy's death without mentioning race or racial difference. They clearly failed, as continued violence throughout the decade revealed. Race was a large lacuna in the hundreds of sermons read for this chapter. Remarkably, the predominant explanatory Christian model regarding the American "culture of hate" did not address White racism; the ministers focused on an anemic, decontextualized "failure to love." They reasoned that since both Kennedy and Oswald were White, violence must have an origin other than race. The silence and limits of the White ministerial version of "the culture of hate" came to a painful conclusion when Rev. Dr. Martin Luther King Jr. was assassinated four and a half years later, in April 1968. In 1963, White Protestant ministers did not recognize the racial inequality and violence that would propel the decade.

JFK: A Martyr for the United States

The majority of sermons given in the first weeks after his assassination referred not to Kennedy's murder but to his martyrdom. "John F. Kennedy has become one in a long, long line of martyrs."[20] His trip to Dallas was revered as one in service to his ideals, rather than as an early campaign visit, as most analysts now agree it was. In reality, Kennedy was not doing a civil rights action or anything specific that would warrant the label of martyrdom. Yet many ministers claimed his visit was a reconciliation mission for which he gave up his life.

Kennedy was not perceived as having been murdered like a dog in the street, as some later said Dr. Martin Luther King was. The manner of Kennedy's death was cast as a sign of glory, not degradation. His death was monumentalized; he *and* his death were exceptional. "Let us not think of him as a vanquished leader lying dead on the frontiers of the earth, but as a victorious hero, alive in the presence of Christ on the ever-widening frontier of eternity."[21] "More than a man has been assassinated. A principle of freedom—of love—of religion—of speech—has also been wounded."[22]

For the ministers, Kennedy's martyrdom was a testament to the legitimacy of the state for which he died. His sacrifice for the nation confirmed American greatness. If one so noble, so admirable, loved American ideals and was willing to die for us, then surely we were worthy. Exactly what those ideals were remained hazy. Nevertheless, Kennedy was imagined as having put himself literally in the line of fire for the United States.

Many of the sermons compared JFK's death to the crucifixion of Jesus Christ:

> John Kennedy died for us. He died as the symbol of freedom and justice and the dignity of man. . . . By his death we are redeemed.[23]

> Tonight three deaths engage our attention beyond all others. The first occurred almost twenty centuries ago. It came upon a cross, unjustly, at the hands of men who hated. . . . When shots rang out and when hammer clanged upon a bloody nail both were against the majesty of God.[24]

Some even suggested that Kennedy and Jesus were killed for parallel reasons: "Our Lord was crucified because he challenged and corrected the status quo of his generation."[25]

Many sermons noted how both Jesus and Kennedy were killed on a Friday; several referred to "that other Friday" (i.e., Good Friday), striving to establish a correspondence.[26] Some noted that Lincoln too was killed on Good Friday, thus creating a holy trinity among the three martyrs. They suffered "cruel assassination" so that others might live. "I am come that they may live and might have life abundantly. Enter thou and receive the reward of intensive service."[27]

An African American spiritual was recorded a few days after the assassination:

> *Well, they rushed him to a hospital. Only five minutes away.*
> *People standing in the lobby, and they didn't know what to say.*
> *Well, this is what I did, when I first heard the news:*
> *I said, Lord, God Almighty, what we poor peoples going to do?*
> *Well. Let me tell you people, what we'd better do,*
> *Keep our mind on Jesus, for he's a president, too.*[28]

A sermon given by the African American reverend Omie L. Holliday entitled "The Assassination of JFK and the Crucifixion of Jesus" had as its animating motif the question, "Why did they both have to die?"[29] The answer, in part, was that both JFK and Christ were part of God's plan for liberation. Reverend Holliday stated that the assassination of Kennedy was a sign of God's love for African Americans. Kennedy's death accomplished what Medgar Evers's death could not: it influenced the American people and the world, and thus advanced the African American cause for civil rights. God loved African Americans, Holliday averred, so he sacrificed Kennedy, as He had His own Son, for their redemption.[30]

Kennedy's sacrifice, a scapegoat in Girardian terms, thus unified the community.[31] If Kennedy was sacrificed rather than murdered (or sacrificed himself as a martyr), then faith in popular sovereignty, paradoxically, was renewed. Through the sacrificial witness of an innocent victim, the people and the nation were ennobled. Rather than jeopardizing American values, Kennedy's death confirmed them.

Meanwhile, his corpse became a testament to American Christian ideals. Because Kennedy was literally killed in the street, from a Christian perspective he simultaneously became part of the Christian ethos of privileging the dishonored. How he died preempted how he had lived. His dead body became a vehicle for articulating the sacred. As Paul Kahn has noted regarding the relationship between violence and the sacred, "The finite body is nothing and remains nothing until or unless it becomes the vehicle for the showing forth of the sacred."[32]

Yet Kennedy's death, unlike Jesus's, did not fully atone for the United States' sins. His death was not enough to rectify what had caused his murder. Atoning for his demise was left to the living: "You and I shall help determine whether or not he died in vain."[33] Although Christian citizens were reconstituted through Kennedy's sacrificial death, they had to carry through with their new responsibility to the dead. This was the secular version of Christ's recommendation to his disciples, "Do this in memory of me."[34]

American Grief

While Americans grieved for Jacqueline Kennedy and her fatherless children, they did not consider themselves her equal. Many of the consolation letters previously quoted began with the recognition that Jacqueline probably would never read the letter—and even if she did, it would have little effect: "I know that you are keenly aware of the great shock and sadness which the President's death brought to this nation; it can only be a pallid reflection of your own."[35] And then, poignantly, "I don't know whether you will ever see this letter but I feel that I must write it. Only in this way am I able to assuage my grief. I am one of the 'little' people."[36]

The presidential Kennedy family had been imagined in 1963 by the American public as belonging to a different realm. The Kennedys were embodied symbols, aspirations beyond the reach of most Americans. A week after the assassination, in an interview with Theodore White for *Life* magazine, Jacqueline Kennedy used words from a Broadway musical to describe the Kennedy presidency: "one brief shining moment that was known as Camelot."[37] She ossified what ministers had begun myth-making the weekend before: the surreal unreachability of the Kennedys. She repeated twice, "It will never be that way again."[38] Not only his death but his entire administration was now meant to be beyond the grasp of history. This was merely the beginning of putting JFK beyond the specificity of quotidian reality.[39]

Several ministers even imagined Kennedy's death as having destabilized sacred/profane hierarchies. With his assassination, "there [was] something very human about God; something very sacred about man."[40] Even more profoundly: "There is something in the heart of God that is dead. . . . As on a Friday almost 1930 years ago, a man of Nazareth was put to death after the mockery of a trial. . . . So as on this Friday last—something is dead in the heart of God."[41] Apparently, Kennedy's death had existential ramifications. So significant was Kennedy's death that, as with Christ's crucifixion, the future would reverberate with his loss. Speechwriter and special counsel Theodore Sorensen named Kennedy's death "an incalculable loss of the future."[42] Senator Patrick Moynihan offered a similar eulogy: "We may smile again, but we will never be young again."[43] With Kennedy's death, the future became nearly impossible. All future actions would be mere memorials to the tragedy.

Although this conception of the Kennedy administration as a hinge in history would become a staple of American political rhetoric, Christian ministers initially did not eulogize the Kennedys as Knights of the

Round Table. Rather, the ministers sought to put the Kennedys beyond the grasp of the secular and transient by creating a narrative of the First Family as the Holy Family. Jack's relationship with Jackie, specifically, was described as "of the highest, *holiest* and most noble kind."[44] Many ministers noted that because of his class privilege, Kennedy could have been a "playboy" (the most frequently used term and perhaps an unintended acknowledgment of the influence of Hugh Hefner's enterprise in the 1960s). Yet JFK chose to commit himself to his family and to government service: "He was born with a silver spoon or should we say a gold spoon, in his mouth. He never had to labor for the necessities of life. . . . He could have been a playboy . . . but this was not for the life of JFK."[45] With subsequent public revelations of JFK's multiple infidelities, these ministerial characterizations now seem both naive and overreaching.

In grief, Jacqueline Kennedy too was rendered holy. "We have seen clearly in the demeanor of Mrs. Kennedy the majesty and solace of a Christian commitment . . . this *holy witness* before the nation and the world."[46] Her grief transcended the profane: "A beautiful young widow has shown an uncertain world that, with faith in God's promises and in man's God-given destiny, mortals can walk victoriously through the valley of the shadow of death."[47]

Clergy focused on the family narrative in part because many were already drawing parallels between Kennedy's death and Jesus's crucifixion, and it was relatively easy to craft a narrative of JFK's life as paralleling the Christian story. "For us citizens of the United States of America, Kennedy represented the majesty of God."[48] Thus, in several sermons, Kennedy was cast as both Joseph (father) and Jesus (son), and his ability to assume these multiple roles added to the accumulated sense of his transcendence.

The family narrative also reflected many of the ministers' perception that the whole world was grieving with the United States. In this grief, the world had become a "family of humanity"; "this is not an American hour, but a human hour."[49] American sorrow became universal grief in recognition of human commonality: "we worship a God who created of one blood all nations."[50] This was a trope of the powerful, one that would be repeated with particular ramifications after 9/11. The trope declares that American sorrow affects all. "There was a brotherhood of humankind such as there has never been in man's history."[51] One of the most frequently cited pieces was from John Donne's Meditation XVII: "No Man is an Island. . . . Any man's death diminishes me because I am involved in mankind. . . . And therefore never send to know for whom the bell tolls; it tolls for thee."[52]

American clergy imagined the "family of grief" for the human condition, the United States' shared human vulnerability and fragility. The world grieved because it too loved Kennedy and with his assassination recognized how vulnerable we all are. The world's grief, according to the 1963 ministers, was less about the United States' sorrow than a shared recognition of humanity's existential exposure to death and the perils of sin.

Clearly, Kennedy's death was understood as gesturing beyond itself. Jacqueline Kennedy herself wanted the legacy of her husband to escape the bitter clutches of men who write history. "She did not want Jack left to the historians."[53] Bishop Cushing noted in his eulogy, "He (Kennedy) has written in unforgettable language his own epitaph."[54] Kennedy was able, with the obvious help of the ministerial class, to write his own ending, to decide what his death meant.

According to the ministers, his death was oddly exempt from history. Like Christ, JFK made meaning and gave meaning to others. "President Kennedy wrote history, made history and has become history."[55] "When we look back over the fateful moments of history, starting with the Cross on Calvary, and moving down through the wars and tribulations of Western civilization, to the bleakness of Nov. 22, 1963, we consistently find a man of God speaking to the times."[56]

Here the most politically important element of Kennedy's death started to take shape as a petition for political and spiritual change. Americans were called to make their lives have meaning in relation to Kennedy's death. It was a paradoxical gesture. Instead of relating the loss of Kennedy to one's own mortality and making one's life have meaning in relation to that, Americans were encouraged to make the meaning of their lives resonate with the death of another.

For the ministers, Kennedy's assassination became less about reconciliation with the existential dilemmas of unexpected and violent death and more about a claim for American political and spiritual renewal. Although the world family was grieving with the United States, ultimately Kennedy's death did not remind ordinary American Christians of their own future deaths. His death was not a confrontation with mortality but an acknowledgment of the United States' collective sin: "Our grief, as real as it is, cannot be our atonement for this crime."[57]

Citizens as Sinners: The Theology of Patriotism

The weapon that killed John F. Kennedy was not only in the hand of his murderer but was in the heart of every one of us who ever hated; whoever set brother against brother in his selfish spirit.[58]

Only one finger squeezed off those three shots. Only one eye peered down the barrel of the rifle. The seeds of destruction were planted in our city by only a few; but a million tongues and two million hands watered those seeds. We have reaped what we have sown.[59]

The grief was general for somehow the worst in the nation had prevailed over the best. The indictment extended beyond the assassin, for something in the nation itself, some strain of madness and violence had destroyed the highest symbol of law and order.[60]

The blood that splattered and stained the clothing of Jacqueline Kennedy has splattered and stained us as well, for we have made the world in which a Lee Harvey Oswald—or whoever the bloody man might be—could be born, grow, mature, and bear such an unholy fruit.[61]

For American clergy, President Kennedy's death was personal. Not only would Christians always remember this dreadful day, but American clergy called on their congregants to take responsibility for the president's death. According to the majority of clergy, Kennedy's assassination was not the tragic result of an action by a rogue madman. Oswald's act was the culmination of a long history of strife and divisiveness for which Christians in particular were culpable.

We must ask ourselves today, what have we done or failed to do, that we should be robbed of our president? What have we done or failed to do that we could produce a man so full of hate as the man who killed the president? . . . Where has the church of Jesus Christ failed? Is it because we have had our religion in the church and have not taken it into our society?[62]

This meditation is paradigmatic of the sermons that mention "collective guilt" (approximately 65 percent). Baptists in particular repeatedly mentioned a specific sense of shared guilt for the assassination. The president died in Texas—the state, as many ministers noted, with more Southern Baptists than any other. Dallas had the largest church in the world, First Baptist Church, with more than twelve thousand members and a yearly budget of more than half a million dollars. But Baptists failed in Dallas "to reach a heart of anger and hatred and malice and ill will."[63]

Or again in another sermon, "How is it possible for such a man [Lee Harvey Oswald] to go through childhood, adolescence, enter high school in such an area as the Dallas-Fort Worth area where there are more churches per square mile than any place on earth, where there is found one of the finest Baptist seminaries, a fine Christian University, and a greater concentration of church members than can be found anywhere else in the world?"[64]

The answer was that Texans, like Americans writ large, were guilty because of the climate of hatred they had fostered. Usually, ministers detailed a litany of events signifying this culture of hatred: calls for the impeachment of Supreme Court justices, Texans spitting on Ambassador Adlai Stevenson as well as Vice President Lyndon B. Johnson and his wife, and the bombing of children at a Birmingham church.

Also frequently cited was American violence in movies and on television. "We live in a society that feasts on violence for breakfast and dinner through the pages of the daily newspaper and we find the violent acts of the trivial there faithfully recorded in all their gory detail. . . . National games are games of violence . . . and we solve our personal problems with violent eating, violent drinking and violent smoking and violent driving."[65]

All of these were sins of the 1960s. This collective guilt was not inherited from one's parents. According to the ministers, it was a historically short tether that tied Americans together in collective responsibility for the assassination. None of the sermons mention, for example, how

Americans had shared guilt before or experienced similar periods of collective responsibility. The shared guilt of 1963 was cast as a singular and new phenomenon. That is, ministers did not say, "Just as the American culture of 1865 was culpable for the assassination of Lincoln . . ." or "Americans created a culture of hatred that enabled the internment of Japanese Americans." The collective guilt in 1963 was preached as if it were sui generis, the result of that moment and that particular configuration of social and political events. One Lutheran minister claimed that this "sickness born of our prosperity" was not present when "hardy pioneers hacked fields out of the wilderness and it was not there when the men of Concord stood up to the troops of Britain and it was not there when our republic fought within itself for its very life during the Civil War."[66]

"Collective responsibility" was in some ways a parallel to patriotism, functioning as a theological mirror for that secular discourse. Collective responsibility, like patriotism, required an identification with an abstract group—a compound of a few actual and many imaginary ingredients.[67] Although patriotism is most often conceived as love of country, what a country is remains quite abstract, even imagined. Of course, a country is a territory, a place, a geography with a specific distinctiveness, but as American political theorist George Kateb describes it, "[A country] is also constructed out of transmitted memories true and false; a history usually mostly falsely sanitized or falsely heroized; a sense of kinship of a largely invented purity; and social ties that are largely invisible or impersonal, indeed abstract, yet by an act of insistent or of dream-like imagination made visible and personal."[68]

In this instance, the 1963 collective was a rather unwieldy "Americans who hate"—clearly an imagined collectivity rather than a known association. This kinship depended as much on shared memories, true and false, as on social ties that were largely impersonal. For example, Americans shared memories of recent examples of hatred (i.e., Adlai Stevenson being spat upon, the bombing in Birmingham) to generate a group; the memory was understood to help craft an identity and sense of belonging.

Furthermore, this collectivity of Americans who hate was initiated by the simple act of self-examination. Ministers urged their congregants to inventory their consciences and behaviors for evidence of hate: "Have you ever gossiped about your neighbor? Are there people you dislike and will not speak to?"[69] What the inventory would reveal, according to this ministerial conception, was that each citizen was responsible for creating the culture in which it was possible to assassinate Kennedy.

Memory and conscience spawned collective responsibility. As a theological mirror of patriotism, this responsibility required giving oneself to the group and accepting the obligations of one's membership. With collective responsibility, one assumed both great agency (i.e., "eliminating my hatred can change the world") and profound, passive submission (i.e., "my failure may have cost my country its leader").

Here, Christianity, like patriotism, was a way of acquiescing to one's inferiority. The United States (Jesus) is great, but its individual citizens (believers) are small and flawed. What was heroic in this version of patriotism were the forces outside oneself. Ralph Waldo Emerson described it: "All the rest behold in the hero or poet their own green and crude being—ripened; yes, and are content to be less, so that they may attain to its full stature. . . . They sun themselves in the great man's light and feel it to be their own element."[70] In other words, the light cast from Kennedy's halo revealed to Americans their own dim sinfulness.

Kennedy's sacrificial death was thus observed as a mark of both his patriotism and Christian faithfulness. Patriotism, like Christianity, is a theology of love and sacrifice. Whereas patriotism is often understood as primarily love of self—or at least love of those like oneself—Christianity's ethos of "love thy neighbor" is more often intended as a discourse of obligation to the stranger, exemplified in the parable of the Good Samaritan.

In the 1963 sermons, the ministers successfully conflate the two. Kennedy died as a Christian patriot, for those like himself, "his fellow Americans." And he did so willingly, unnecessarily, like Jesus. While the claim is difficult to square with the historical record, many of the sermons insist that Kennedy knowingly died, perhaps chose his death, to redeem the nation. Frequently, ministers mention that he died to save his friends.

Fortuitously, this collective guilt was not paralyzing. Ministers had not lost confidence in Americans' ability to amend their ways. Rather, the crisis and its concurrent guilt augmented Christian citizens' power to change themselves and their culture. Acknowledgment of collective guilt was meant to ignite a sense of responsibility for the future, not fear or doubt. It was intended to spur strengths American Christians may not have realized they possessed.

Conservative and liberal ministers took a similar view, although they formulated the culture of hate slightly differently. For liberal ministers, the hatred had been brewed by individual intolerance for difference and the loss of respect for political authority. For conservative ministers, the hatred had been fomented by a decadent media and by families who had lost their moral compass, evidenced primarily by rising divorce rates. For both, the culture of hatred was the result of a continuous appeal to the United States' lowest emotional appetites.

Lee Harvey Oswald was a symptom of Americans' loss of relationships with one another. Americans had forfeited their ability to be in relationship with each other, as well as their sense of obligation to do so. "You can manipulate things to suit your own advantage; you don't have to worry about their feelings. It's much easier to make money and influence people than it is to make friends and love them. It's much less trouble to give a beggar a quarter than to ask how he got into this position or take any steps to remedy the situation."[71] This contemporary culture of hate defied the Christian imperative to love all humankind: "To envy and slander is to murder the Holy One; to kneel and adore is to confess before the Child our debt of love for all mankind."[72]

Consumed by this conception of collective guilt, scarcely any sermons raised issues of theodicy after the assassination. The overriding assumption, much as it was in the Pearl Harbor sermons, was that "man creates murderers while Christ creates miracles."[73] Also like the Pearl Harbor sermons, the Kennedy sermons were about human sin, not God's liabilities. Even in the post-Auschwitz world of the 1960s, American Protestant ministers were still secure that God had not caused this tragedy. Nor did they feel abandoned in their suffering. "God, although supplying the strength to the finger which pulls the trigger, is not to be held responsible for the sinful deeds of men. . . . Men are responsible for these guilty actions."[74]

Hatred was also not considered purely psychological or even political; the ministers argued that this hatred was beyond politics. "On Friday when the word had come to the church . . . we began immediately trying to lay the blame on the right wingers and the left wingers and the communists. Somehow, we all enjoy playing these little Adam and Eve games. We get a certain amount of relief out of it. You remember the game in which Adam said, 'Lord, it wasn't me, it was Eve.' And Eve responded in like manner, 'Lord, it wasn't me, it was that snake.'"[75] Hatred was theological; it was a manifestation of sin.

For the ministers, it was not about what one believed politically. The culture of hatred was found across the political spectrum: "Hate knows no political loyalty."[76] It was the result, in part, of American freedom as well as the mishandling of that freedom, specifically the freedom of speech. "We live in a country where you can voice your opinion. Sometimes, however, we become very rabid and violent in holding to certain opinions and before we know it, we are filled with hatred and prejudices which can lead to murder."[77] Many ministers noted that Americans mistakenly believed that "freedom of speech" meant they could say whatever they wanted, however and whenever they wanted. "Extreme words lead to extreme acts. . . . I recognize that freedom of speech is a commitment under our form of organization, but license in criticizing politicians is a national sin. . . . There has been too much violence, written, talked—too much toleration for speech that only leads to Cain's dastardly crime."[78]

Ministers were seeking to reveal the dark side of American democracy and how it still needed the moral compass of the church. "Democracy is of no value when sin rules in the heart of the land."[79] Several sermons detailed the risks of freedom and how, like the free will God gave humanity at creation, the freedoms Americans enjoyed could become a sin: "For there is no such thing as freedom without risk, no such thing as freedom that does not contain within itself the very seed of temptation and of evil."[80]

Tellingly, the risks of freedom did not require increased security, as many ministers would recommend after September 11, 2001. Instead, the risks necessitated learning to accept the costs of freedom and to cling more fully to Christian principles. Many ministers recommended that Americans be more disciplined with their freedom. "Somehow we have failed to discipline ourselves as a people. . . . We have come to think that right or wrong is determined by what I happen to want. . . . Since our service began I have been handed a note that some person has taken the law into his own hands and Oswald has been shot as he was being transferred in Dallas."[81] The issue was not that Americans needed greater state protection but that they needed greater Christian insight: "Rise up with Christian indignation to build new on that which is noble."[82]

DALLAS MINISTERS FACED a daunting challenge explaining the assassination in their city. As Presbyterian minister T. K. Mullendore noted in his sermon, "Our civic pride is hurt. . . . We ask, but why did it happen in Dallas? May I ask, 'Why should it not happen in Dallas?'"[83]

Dallas Methodist minister Rev. William Holmes created a national tempest with his sermon: "This is the hardest thing to say: there is no city in the United States which in recent months and years has been more acquiescent toward its extremists than Dallas Texas. We, the majority of citizens have gone quietly about our work and leisure, forfeiting the city's image to the hate-mongers and reactionaries in our midst. The spirit of assassination has been with us for some time, not manifest in bullets but in spitting mouths and political invectives."[84] While not exactly blaming Dallas for the assassination, he certainly charged that the climate in the city, with its political extremes, created the possibility.

Among the most inflammatory examples Holmes gave was a fourth-grade class of Dallas children who reportedly applauded when told the president had been killed. He also recounted how Vice President Johnson and his wife had been spat upon during a recent visit; Ambassador Adlai Stevenson, too, had been spat upon and had a sign thrown at him after a speech. Holmes noted that a handbill had been passed around Dallas on the day of the assassination charging the president with treason, and a full-page ad in the *Dallas Morning News* mockingly welcomed JFK with text bordered in black, as if it were an obituary.

Holmes's sermon, which was initially given to his seven hundred parishioners at Northaven United Methodist Church, was later read on television as part of the *CBS Evening News* with Walter Cronkite. Before the program went off the air, threats of violence were telephoned to the station as well as to Rev. Holmes's private residence and church. The minister and his family had to be moved and placed under police protection.[85] This simply confirmed the image of Dallas in critics' minds. Other Methodist ministers rallied to endorse Holmes's position, which was then debated across the country.

On November 26, 1963, Dallas mayor Earle Cabell made a statement to the city council (which was later adopted as its official stand) asking churches and synagogues to "speak to us with utmost candor both of the ideals of truth and the shortcomings of our community that we may be guided into the paths of right."[86] While this "official stand" seemed to acknowledge the possibility that "the shortcomings of our community" might be worthy of study, it is noteworthy that Dallas politicians asked for guidance from churches and synagogues. Ministers were clearly being invited to participate in the civic education of Dallas.

So what exactly was the guilt of Dallas? Of course, ministers did not imagine that Dallas had conspired in any substantial way with the assassin. Rather, Dallas stood accused, as did the rest of the Christian United States, for what it had failed to do. The editors of the *Christian Century* named it "original sin. . . . It is the sin of preoccupation with oneself that results in the sins of omission—it is what we did not do but should have done—that haunts the conscience of this city."[87]

Dallas was understood to be a metonym for the rest of the country. American historians have often noted the significance of place for constructions of American identity. Frederick Jackson Turner's "The Significance of the Frontier in American History" and Perry Miller's *Errand into the Wilderness* each argue that constructions of place have been a significant element of American self-understanding.[88] For each of the crises detailed in this book, place is a significant feature of the narrative understanding of what happened. The bombing at Pearl Harbor, for example, is known simply by its place name, "Pearl Harbor." The date is largely irrelevant, and many Americans would be hard pressed to recall the date as more than "a day that will live in infamy."

Although the assassination of John F. Kennedy was closely aligned with Dallas, it is noteworthy that the Kennedy administration itself sought to relocate the frontier from "out West" to a "new frontier." In fact, several ministers rebuked Dallas for being part of that "old frontier," with its cowboy violence, and recommended a focus on Kennedy's new frontier: "Though Fort Worth may be proud that it is the city where the West begins—let Dallas become the city where the West ends. . . . I, for one, am ready to let the so-called culture and glory of the West die and be buried in the history books. Let's have no more glorification of gun glory. Let us join civilization."[89]

The new frontier embodied not only Kennedy's forward-looking ambitions for American domestic and foreign policies but was also part of his bold program for space explorations. There was an existential element as well. Kennedy claimed: "We stand on the edge of a New Frontier—the frontier of unfulfilled hopes and dreams, a frontier of unknown opportunities and beliefs in peril. Beyond that frontier are uncharted areas of science and space, unsolved problems of peace and war, unconquered problems of ignorance and prejudice, unanswered questions of poverty and surplus."[90]

These elements of the new frontier made it ripe for theological inflection. Perhaps the assassination on the frontier (i.e., Dallas) meant that the United States had not yet conquered the wilderness. The violence and chaos of its not-yet-settled frontiers forestalled Kennedy's ambitious relocation of the border. Indeed, part of the hope of Kennedy's Peace Corps was that Americans would bring "civilization" to the "Third World." But the United States' own violence raised questions about its ability to do so. One minister asked prophetically: "It is said that he who lives by the sword shall perish by the sword. Could it also be true that we who live by violence shall perish in violence?"[91]

While the new frontier offered the promise of technologies that had civilized "nature," the "nature" that remained untamed was the United States' own. As Rev. Ewing Carroll preached: "The people of Israel were on a New Frontier. . . . And while the Bible tells us Moses was able to say, 'MISSION ACCOMPLISHED' the legacy of our New Frontier is a *great unfinished task*."[92] Nonetheless, at least one minister used the image of the frontier to eulogize the president. "Let us not think of him as a vanquished leader lying dead on the frontiers of the earth, but as a victorious hero, alive in the presence of Christ on the ever widening frontier of eternity."[93] So while the United States' own frontier murdered him, in death Kennedy was still able to create a new frontier—one with eternity. It was a frontier that transcended the United States' liabilities.

ONE OF THE earliest and frequently reprinted photographs taken after the assassination was that of two African American women crying outside Parkland Hospital in Dallas that afternoon.[94] Implicitly, the image erased differences between Whites and Blacks in grief. Everyone mourned Kennedy's death; he was a source of unity. "A colored minister [unnamed] in Chicago said, 'As a man of God, I felt the pain of the bullet in my neck, and shared the sorrow of his wife.'"[95] Many commentators referred to that photograph as testimony that African Americans loved Kennedy and that JFK was committed to civil rights. Many Black ministers confirmed this. African American pastor Rev. Maurice E. Dawkins called Kennedy "the new Lincoln" and said JFK "died for the freedom of all people of all races and creeds."[96] African American journalist Simeon Booker went even further in his essay in *Ebony* titled "How John F. Kennedy Surpassed Abraham Lincoln."[97] Booker argued that Kennedy, unlike Lincoln, treated Blacks with dignity and "stimulated them to stand up and fight for first class citizenship."[98]

Several other sermons referred to the story of an African American woman who held up her baby as Lincoln's casket passed by and said, "Take a long, long, look. . . . He died for you." In 1963, both Black and White ministers repeated this story with the recommendation, "It would behoove us to hold the hands of our sons and daughters and say of JFK, 'Take a long, long, look. . . . He died for you!'"[99]

This was a notable change in rhetoric, however, among African American ministers. When Kennedy first started campaigning for president, a 1959 *Jet* poll of Black ministers found that the majority opposed his candidacy on religious grounds.[100] Reverend Martin Luther King Sr. advised his congregation to vote for Nixon because he could not abide supporting a Catholic.[101] But while many members of the Black community, including Martin Luther King Jr., lamented the slow pace of many Kennedy reforms, by the time of Kennedy's death most were convinced that he was a "friend of the Negro," even if the claim itself was intended to exert "legacy" pressure on President Lyndon Johnson. After Kennedy's assassination, Julian Bond, founding member of the Student Nonviolent Coordinating Committee (SNCC), noted that the Kennedys "knew almost no black people and had few associations with them. This was alien territory to them. And, so the Birmingham movement was an eye-opener for John F. Kennedy."[102]

Two public opinion polls conducted shortly after the assassination suggested that African Americans believed themselves to be the most profoundly affected of all Americans by Kennedy's death. In one, people were asked to compare their own reaction against a perceived norm.

Overall, 30 percent of Americans believed that they were more upset than "most people," whereas 49 percent of African Americans thought they were more upset. Two-thirds of African Americans, versus 38 percent of all respondents, agreed with the statement that they were "so confused and upset, they didn't know what to feel." Furthermore, half of African Americans surveyed, compared with 20 percent of the total sample, "worried how this might affect my own life, job and future."[103]

Not surprisingly, when they first heard the news, nearly one-third of Blacks believed a segregationist was behind the killing. Whites, whether northerner or southerner, pro-Kennedy or anti-Kennedy, were much more likely to attribute the deed to a communist or Castro supporter.[104] One first-person account of a Black girl from Alabama described how, for her all-Black community, "the assassination was a calamity" and "we whispered, 'Please, God, don't let his murderer be black!'"[105] Blacks felt specifically vulnerable. Only 20 percent of White Americans expressed the fear "whether anybody could really be safe in this country these days, when the President himself can get shot," as compared with nearly 40 percent of Blacks.[106]

Yet occluded in almost every sermon was the issue of genuine differences shaping American Christian citizenry. The ministerial hope was that the assassination would make those differences go away, as the photograph of the grieving Black women seemed to suggest. Tellingly, the ministers did not name religion itself as a source of violence, despite evidence that it was among the elements creating a culture of hatred.

On the evening of November 20, 1963, for example, Reverend J. Sidlow Baxter told the fifty thousand delegates of the Baptist General Convention of Texas that the American electorate had made "one of the greatest blunders in its history when it put a Roman Catholic President in the White House." In the upcoming elections, he urged them "to vote not Democratic or Republican, but Protestant." Eyewitness reports confirmed that his audience rose in acclamation, cheering, "Amen."[107]

While most sermons were against violence, including the violence that killed both Medgar Evers and the four little girls in the Birmingham church bombing, it remained unclear what kind of support for civil rights was recommended in light of the assassination. As mentioned, only one of the several hundred sermons read for this chapter mentioned Martin Luther King Jr.: "Martin Luther King, the negro leader of the struggle for equality and justice for his people, who himself lives every day with the threat of violence or death, said something to this effect, 'We do not regard the white men who oppose us as enemies to be destroyed but as brothers to be won to a fellowship of love and understanding in the brotherhood of man under God.'"[108] Other than this, neither King's ideas nor his actions were referred to, nor were they recommended as a model for future nonviolence. Ministers seemed more interested in asking their parishioners to do a self-inventory of abstract and rather generalized hatred than a detailed collective and community focused diagnosis of structural racism. This partially reflected a Protestant ethos of prioritizing the individual as the most vibrant source of accountability and change, although even that would not have precluded a focus on individual racism.

While the trope of collective guilt held much promise, particularly as a way to account for a culture of segregation, discrimination, and so forth, nearly all of these sermons neglected to take that next step from "our culture of hatred created the possibility for the assassination" to "perhaps if we repair the culture of White racism, we can begin to heal at least one element of the violence." Only one or two sermons specifically mentioned the church's position on civil rights as a way to begin to ameliorate hatred: "It may seem harsh to say this on this particular day, yet I believe it is true and we must reckon with it. The stand which the Congress of the United States and the stand which we, the people, take in this difficult area of civil rights in the weeks and months just ahead will reflect the actual sincerity with which we mourn this assassination. One cannot weep over his death and turn and ignore the values for which he stood without being liable to the charge of hypocrisy."[109]

Although there was a recognition that racism led to violence, there was very little in these sermons that called for the elimination of racism and the promotion of civil rights. While one could argue that perhaps that seemed obvious to the ministers and could therefore be considered redundant, one suspects that civil rights were understood as "political," whereas "hatred" could remain a politically neutral, theological category, much like "sin." If racial hatred was a sin, then civil rights would become a virtue, but in November 1963 most White ministers were not quite prepared to make that leap. Rather, their recommendations remained more modest and less political: more prayer, greater generosity, more faith in God: "deeds of love and concern for fellow man such as feeding the hungry, giving drink to the thirsty, talking to the stranger, clothing the naked, visiting the sick and imprisoned."[110]

Of course, there were ministers and others who dissented from the collective guilt paradigm: "As to our all sharing in the responsibility, this is true to a certain extent, just as it is true that we all share in some degree in every aspect of crime and injustice and degeneracy in our land. But no more or no less. Human beings as individuals are at least as responsible as is society for what they do."[111] Those who disagreed with the collective guilt paradigm also argued that the grief that many Americans felt for the assassination was testimony that they would have done anything within their power to have prevented the death. That Americans were so affected by the death was demonstration that they were not an alienated, violent people. American mourning was evidence, rather, of collective goodness. "I wish to emphasize the other side of the picture which characterizes the citizens of this nation more accurately than do these crimes of violence . . . the churches filled everywhere to overflowing with reverent, penitent, sorrowing people; the silent and respectful thousands waiting patiently for hours in the cold to file silently by the bier; the halting of commercial activity and pursuits of amusements, all these things are evidence of qualities which are rooted deep and unconquerably in the hearts of our people."[112]

The *Wall Street Journal* likewise challenged the collective guilt paradigm, asking: "What society has ever been without it, what nation has ever been free of assassins? [Kennedy] would not make the mistake of imputing to our freest of all societies the sins of more primitive lusts for power. He would know, in his early won knowledge that no society and no bullet proof car can protect against the telescopic rifle of the deranged mind."[113]

Others, too, disagreed, blaming the moralizing style of American Protestantism. To reform meant to remedy the defects of character. Protestants were blind to the structural elements of public policies that created the climate for the assassination.[114] None of the sermons considered how Protestantism might have contributed to the violence; none considered the segregation of churches or the denominational resistance to creating a more inclusive theology. Most sermons were jeremiads:

American congregants had not been Protestant enough. They had fallen away from their own principles, which if adhered to would apparently have resulted in less racial injustice.

Perhaps this merely confirmed that the ministers largely represented the privileged safety of White Christendom. In contrast, the majority of 9/11 sermons mourned Americans' loss of security as well as of innocence. In 1963, however, American culpability was not that Americans were negligent or inadequately prepared from a security perspective. American culpability was that the United States itself was full of hate; the country had not been innocent at all.

Sin: A Theopolitical Category for the 1960s

Embedded in the notion of collective guilt was a significant theological category: sin. In many sermons, sin was imagined as a disease, often "the cancer of hate." Sin proliferated, spawning "seeds of hate."[115] Sin was not merely an individual failing but a collective threat.

This organic metaphor was particularly apt, the ministers insisted, because, like a cancer cell, sin multiplies rapidly, chaotically, creating the possibility of corporate liability. Sin is not individual; it reverberates throughout the community and cannot be contained. "We are all aware of the sickness out of which this grew and so we will pray in silence for the sickness of the world, the nation and our church."[116]

Many ministers noted how sin violated all borders, specifically the one between church and state. Part of the nefarious power of sin, they argued, was that it did not respect the wall dividing the two. Sin disrupted more than one's relationship with God; it disrupted the stability of the state, as Kennedy's assassination powerfully demonstrated. Americans' personal sins (i.e., hatred) disordered the state, confounding those who would insist that religion must remain privatized. No person or place was exempt from the reach of sin. Sin was a transgressor and would not be bound by man-made laws and taxonomies. The claws of sin snatched Kennedy, and neither secular security measures nor political power could protect him.

It is remarkable in light of the multiple conspiracy theories that would animate debates for decades to come that Christian ministers in those first days never once questioned whether there were sufficient Secret

Service agents on duty that day or whether the government should have done more to protect its president. After Pearl Harbor, ministers had been confident that the violence was the fault of the political world. Ministers were confident about what had killed Kennedy—sin—and it could not have been thwarted by secular forces.

By naming the cause of the assassination as sin, not only did the assassination become theological (as well as political) but it restored some of the church's authority. The church had the necessary tools to address the problem. Yet ministers were careful not to make the claim that this was simply about aggrandizing the church; rather, restoring the church was also good for democracy.

Christian Patriotism and Church-State Relations

For many Americans in the days after the Kennedy assassination, their understanding of the tragedy and themselves was framed by asking, "Who was more representative of the United States, John F. Kennedy or Lee Harvey Oswald?" The early sermons struggled to make sense of how both men could be features of the American landscape. On the one hand, many argued that "the sight of John F. Kennedy and Mrs. Jacqueline Kennedy was symbolic of the best America had to produce. There was pride and joy in the hearts of all seeing this young and beautiful couple representing this mighty land we call America."[117] Again, referring to President Kennedy, "There was something distinctly American about him. When you saw him or listened to him on most occasions you felt his strength and you sensed his courage."[118]

Oswald was also understood as quintessentially American; he was the incarnation of the United States' "culture of hate" and an object lesson of American moral laxity—a reminder of what "we" had failed to prevent. Most ministers were confident that if Christian men and women had intervened at any point in Oswald's life, he would not have assassinated Kennedy. "He grew up in our public schools; a person who was a misfit, bitter, friendless, loveless, a chip on his shoulder. I wonder if he was a member of a Sunday school. I wonder if anybody in Fort Worth showed any spiritual compassion for him. . . . I wonder if a Christian man ever gave him a strong hand of guidance."[119]

A dozen or more sermons also noted that there were more assassinations in the United States than in any other civilized nation. "Why have we assassinated more heads of State in the United States of America than any other civilized nation in the world? Why has there been a 114% increase in crime in our country in the last twelve years? . . . We need to face the fact that there is a strata of violence in the makeup of America."[120]

Several also added that England had not had a prime minister assassinated in over a hundred years. "Why and how this could happen in America is the subject of much soul searching. Our Canadian neighbors with whom we share a cultural heritage, have not had this experience with their public figures. No Prime Minister of England has been assassinated in recent times. There is scarcely a civilized nation in the world in which this has been true."[121]

The tension between Kennedy and Oswald as manifestations of the United States was further demonstrated in the rhetoric of collective guilt. For American Christians to share in Oswald's deed, they had to recognize him as part of their group. He had to be included as *one of us* for Americans to feel guilty. If he were cast primarily as "the other," then Americans were not responsible for his deeds. But since Americans—at least Christian Americans—were holding themselves responsible for Kennedy's death, Oswald had to be acknowledged as implicitly one of "us."

From a contemporary perspective, it is surprising that Oswald was not named by the majority of ministers as "un-American." Frequently, ministers referred to Oswald's service as a US marine, his status as a husband and father, and his residence in an ordinary American neighborhood. Most Americans would not learn of Oswald's complicated background until the Warren Commission submitted its 888-page report nearly a year later.[122]

Yet that "us" with which Oswald was identified was "American," not "Christian." The culpability of the Christian community was that it had not thwarted Oswald through the power of Christianity—whether through actions or ideas. It seemed that the United States produced Oswald, but Christianity was responsible for him. Because Christian Americans were not sufficiently Christian, Oswald's godless communism had damaged the state by killing Kennedy.

Conservative ministers argued that Christianity had failed because the state had overstepped its jurisdiction. Through various restrictions, primarily the recent prohibition of school prayer, the state had thwarted the church's ability to do its work. They viewed the assassination as the tragic result. "The idea was never that government was either evil or apart from God. . . . Public office is a sacred trust. . . . We have a religious responsibility to be good citizens."[123] "This assassination points to the need, also, it seems to me, for a deeper religious consciousness in our country. People who truly believe in God and who understand His will would never think of killing anyone."[124]

More liberal ministers argued that the wall of separation between church and state meant that the domain of "culture" belonged to the church. The church had abdicated this responsibility, conceding it to secular forces. "His death is on our hands. It rests with anemic churches that have fought and hated and held hands while men like Lee Oswald grew up without direction and purpose. It rests with churchmen that read: Love your neighbor and then held grudges deep within their hearts. It rests with communities calling themselves Christian that deny Negroes entrance to schools, churches, hearts and lives."[125]

Both these claims about what the relationship should be between state and church were made by the church, which in 1963 still believed in its ability to shape the political and social order. Not a single sermon said, "The cause of the assassination lies with the State." The church perceived itself as an influential element in American events writ large. "Good government does not simply feedback upon itself or live on its own resources. It is fed from depth; from the spiritual soil of a people whose first allegiance is to God and from which every other worthy loyalty is derived."[126]

What it meant to be patriotic was for American Christians to be "better Christians." Not because America and Christianity were understood as identical, as they had been for Father Coughlin during World War II, or because God had chosen America, as many ministers would argue in 2001. It was because Christianity protected the state. It was duty, not destiny, that called American Christians. Failure to be fully Christian put the state at risk. Christianity was a supplement to the state's insufficiency. Christianity was not incompatible with citizenship; rather, it was what made citizenship possible.

Most ministers argued that Kennedy and Oswald existed on parallel, yet unrelated tracks. That is, there was no relation between the Kennedys and the Oswalds in American culture; they did not give rise to each other. The ministers suggested that their congregants were responsible for the Oswalds, whereas the Kennedys gave birth to themselves.

The Kennedys were an oxymoron: they were symbolic of the United States, of American possibilities, particularly around wealth and style, but they were not then imagined as indebted to the United States. John F. Kennedy was the quintessential self-made man, a heroic figure of individualism, not reliant on anyone or anything for his success. Oswald, on the other hand, a failed solitary figure, was the result of the malfunction of the United States. According to the Protestant ministers of 1963, the successful were autogenerative while those who failed were the fault (and responsibility) of the rest of us.

This was an improvement from the formulation that posited failure as the result of the insufficiency of the individual. But it still occluded how the powerful benefited from the culture that enabled their success. Invisible in this formulation were the features of the 1963 American landscape—specifically racial and class privilege—that made possible the success of the Kennedy family.

Issues of patriotism in 1963 were referred to primarily as issues of identity. Just as the question of loyalty had been negotiated on the bodies of Japanese Americans through their internment in 1942, it was again raised during the 1960 presidential campaign with regard to Kennedy's Catholicism. Could an American have dual loyalties? The hybrid identity of Japanese American and Catholic American raised questions not only of who was American but what the qualities and characteristics were that defined an American.

As is well documented, Kennedy successfully resolved American doubts about his imagined dueling commitments to American principles and Vatican dictates. After his assassination, many Protestant ministers were effusive in their praise of his commitment to the separation of church and state. Several even claimed that he had done a better job of maintaining the separation than his recent predecessors. "I wish today from every Baptist pulpit, for Baptists hold very precious this principle of liberty, it could be acknowledged today that our late president stood firmly on the line against some of the most powerful princes of his church in America."[127] This sermon also went on to note that Kennedy did not appoint an ambassador to the Vatican and stood firmly against any direct aid to parochial schools.

One of the more striking features of how the sermons adjudicated between church and state issues was their insistence that God ordained positional authority; that is, many ministers repeated the biblical injunction to pray for those in authority. Many noted how the loss of respect for authority, specifically for the office of the presidency, was also a sign of the moral decay of the United States more generally: "Few presidents have been so disrespected as President John F. Kennedy. His family has been lampooned. Every simple event has been ridiculed. . . . We are no longer a nation under authority, but every man does as he pleases."[128] Reverend Newman Flanagan echoed the claim, declaring that "criticizing politicians is a national sin."[129] Governmental and divine authority were entwined, although most ministers did not develop a theopolitical argument that America was thus a chosen nation. Most simply emphasized that God had ordained governmental authority, not blind nationalism; this was a rather Lutheran position taken by nearly all the Protestant denominations after Kennedy's assassination. The acclamation of nationalism would come later, specifically in 9/11 sermons.

Although the tragedy of the assassination demanded a reexamination of American culture, American governance nonetheless remained hallowed ground. The state was still applauded by the ministers; the peaceful succession of Lyndon B. Johnson provided evidence of the "systematic immortality" of the American government. The transition from the violent death of the 35th president to the uneventful inauguration of the 36th confirmed for American citizens (and for Christians) that the death of the ruler was not concurrent with the death of the system; in this way, the state had conquered one pivotal element of morality—it had, in effect, made rulers substitutable for one another (at least in terms of the system of governance).

The tragedy was not perceived by ministers as the result of flawed American constitutional principles—these were eternal and sacred. Rather, Oswald's lawlessness was the collective responsibility of the culture. In the 1963 ministerial imagination, God was still autonomous and exempt from American political issues; the United States was responsible for its own liabilities. Many sermons repeated the reminder,

"Though our 35th president is dead, God still sits on his throne."[130] This was a theological cue that what happened in the United States did not destabilize the transcendent order; God was still big and the United States relatively small in the ecclesial establishment. In contrast, by September 11 there would be many sermons that claimed that what happened in the United States did affect the divine order.

Partially, the difference lay in American claims to empire in 1963 versus 2001. The Kennedy era, as James Patterson's book title demonstrates, was a period of "grand expectations," of anticipated American ascendency. Reinhold Niebuhr, in his sermon at St. George's Episcopal Church, named one of the reasons for "the immensity of the grief" as the loss of a "gifted president combined with the increasing world prestige and power of the American presidency, derived from the growing prestige of our nation as a leader of the non-Communist world."[131] The loss of a "gifted president" created what Niebuhr called "an anxious and prayerful attitude" about the United States' capacity to fulfill its world responsibilities. The United States was less secure in its role as a world power, and thus still striving to verify its worthiness.

This, in part, explains the rhetoric of humiliation and shame in 1963. The assassination was an embarrassment to a country trying to increase its power and standing in the world. "There has come also, if only briefly, a new humility. The loss of our President is shared by the world. The humiliation of his death belongs to us alone. We have been shamed that in this land, so evil a thing could come to pass."[132]

Mourning

While mourning is relentlessly specific—a particular person is dead—Christian rituals and processes of mourning are intended to move Christians beyond that specificity to the Gospel story, to the universal witness of the resurrection. "It is better to mourn, for in mourning we learn the ways of God. We come not to God with our puny little minds. We come to God with our great questions, we come to him in silent wonder, we come to him in contemplation, and we come to him in awe."[133] Mourning is transformative, according to Reverend Arnold. Through it, Christians escape their puniness and surrender in wonder and awe to God.

But throughout the 1960s, Americans had been unsettled by their grief. To cope, they had professionalized and anesthetized the process of mourning. Jessica Mitford's runaway best seller, *The American Way of Death*, argued that Americans had become consumers of death, urged by greedy funeral directors to buy elaborate and expensive caskets and embalming services to demonstrate the love and honor in which they held their dead beloved.[134] Mourning had become an economic enterprise.

But the loss of mourning, while perhaps related to the ascendency of funeral services and economic exploitation, had other, more philosophical features in the 1960s. What was lost in this "American way of death" was the capacity to be changed by grief. What the Kennedy sermons detail was how ministers were reluctant to dwell in sorrow, to explore the turbulence that grief provokes. Instead, they offered recommendations for how to move beyond grief to action.

Although there was nothing "wrong" with these recommendations, what was alarming was how quickly the ministers expected their congregants to mobilize. It was as if parishioners were expected to understand immediately the implications of Kennedy's violent death and respond accordingly. Americans were not afforded much time to process the assassination before being told what to do about it. What mattered was that Kennedy was dead; that was the change. How Americans could be changed through the process of mourning his death was not considered. His death, not their sorrow, told Americans what to do.

This acceleration was a feature not only of the 1960s but of the American relation to death for the next half century. Others have noted, for example, how quickly President Bush moved to memorialize the dead of September 11, 2001—even before the second plane had hit the towers. This desire to scar over the pain quickly means Americans rarely learn from their sorrow.

Thus in 1963, it was difficult for ministers to be silent in their grief. There was a surfeit of words. Their mourning was characterized by a kind of restlessness, a desire to move forward, to decide quickly what was to be done. "Let us not dwell too long upon ourselves, our hurt and our sorrow. May we see tasks left undone, jobs that are not finished, a community of man that is yet to be."[135]

Although many ministers began their sermons by citing the insufficiency of words, echoing Reverend Arnold's call for silence, most still said something. "Words are futile. Yet futile though words be, we rely on them (with the help of God)."[136] The tragic death of the president was not a trauma that had rendered the ministers silent, although they offered little hope or confidence that their words would make a difference.

The ministers wanted to overcome not only their grief but in some respect the process of mourning itself. Most did not seem to believe, as Reverend Arnold preached, that mourning put one into closer relationship with God. There seemed to be very little expectation that Americans would be transformed by the process of mourning. As Charles Stewart noted in his comparison of sermons after the Lincoln and Kennedy assassinations, "Clergymen developed lengthy portrayals of the grief and shock caused by Lincoln's assassination, but sermons on Kennedy's death contained only brief expressions of sorrow and amazement."[137]

Indeed, there was very little actual mourning in many sermons. There was a search for solace—the desire, in Norman Jacobson's terms, to regain mastery over a world that seemed out of control. "Going to church" was one of the rituals through which the American Christian community in crisis generated meaning and understanding. Hence the narrative quickness in the majority of sermons. The ministers tried to produce a coherent meaning for the assassination and to instruct their congregants on how to redeem it.

But in mourning, one expects to suffer. Suffering is part of what it means to grieve. Emmanuel Levinas, in "Time and the Other," argues: "In suffering there is an absence of all refuge. It is the fact of being directly exposed to being. It is made up of the impossibility of fleeing or retreating. The whole acuity of suffering lies in this impossibility of retreat."[138] In other words, suffering is what happens to us without our will and from which we cannot escape. In modernity, this is exactly what most Americans find anathema—the passivity of suffering, the loss of agency, and the impossibility of escape.

Neglected, however, because of American impatience with suffering was the ancient Greek conception that through suffering, one learns.

Mourning changes one's understanding of oneself and one's world. This was one of the most powerful epistemological lessons of Greek tragedies. Through tragedy, individuals become not only more fully themselves, but fully human. In suffering, humans reveal themselves to themselves as well as to others. *Antigone* details how Creon's failure to mourn hastened his undoing and the tragic consequences of this failure for his entire family. The play does not settle the question of whether Creon has learned from his suffering, because when he does mourn the consequences of his deeds, he neglects to name the death of Antigone among them. Her loss remains unmourned; that aspect of Creon's self remains undiscovered.

After Kennedy's assassination, most ministers insisted that mourning was not political. This was repeated usually after the minister announced that he and perhaps his congregants did not agree with everything that the president had been doing. Many denounced this period of mourning as inappropriate for politics, "Partisan speeches are profane in this atmosphere."[139] Congress, too, declared a month of mourning without partisanship. Indeed, the afternoon of the assassination, Senate Republicans adopted a measure describing "John F. Kennedy as a friend and a distinguished chief executive."[140] Many sermons paraphrased the Pauline scripture from Galatians 3:28 (There is neither Jew nor Greek, slave nor free, there is no male or female for you are all one in Christ Jesus) to some rendition of "We were no longer Republicans or Democrats Friday afternoon. We were no longer Negroes or White, no longer northerners or southerners, no longer labor or management, no longer Protestant or Roman Catholic or Jew. We were only Americans, and our President was dead."[141] Identity was crafted as a political (and therefore profane) category, irrelevant in this time of mourning.

The death of the president was no time for division: "If this tragic death does not bring the nation to its knees, there is something spiritually dead in us as a people."[142] Partisanship was anathema, but theology was required. A vast number of sermons, at least one hundred, referred to the story of the death of Uzziah, king of Judah in the Book of Isaiah. In that biblical story, Isaiah enters the temple, distraught over the death of the king, and sees the Lord, sitting on his throne (Isaiah 6:1). The sermons noted how the loss of political security in Isaiah became a prophetic revelation. There was also the rather obvious interpretation that even with the death of the political leader, God was still in charge. "God is alive, God is good; John F. Kennedy is dead, but God still lives. God still lives and God still rules America."[143] These ministers sought, perhaps, to reenchant the world. The state might have lapsed, but the holy remained secure.

Ministers did not argue that God was speaking through the tragedy but that the temporary dislocation of political power was a potent reminder of divine power. Although a few ministers, perhaps a half dozen or so of those read for this chapter, insisted that God was using the tragedy for His own ends or permitted it to happen to fulfill His purposes, most believed that God was not responsible for the tragedy. Rather, the tragedy was an opportunity for Christians to restore God to His dominion in their lives.

This formulation was significant because it marked the transition from the Pearl Harbor God who was personified by Protestant ministers as sufficient to defeat Hitler without the US military to the 9/11 sermons in which God would become rather effete and require the US military to realize His will in the world. For Pearl Harbor and Kennedy ministers, God and Christian principles were still a force to be reckoned with. If anything, the state was believed to be vulnerable, perhaps even insufficient. By September 11, however, God seemed to have lost His standing among ministers who now believed that the interests of the state were the umbrella under which God flourished. The 2001 state now protected God in a rather ironic inversion of theological superiority. By 9/11, much of the American Protestant Church appeared to have been convinced that the apparatus of the state offered the best option for the fulfillment of God's expectations. In 1963, Protestant ministers still had more ambivalence. While they conceded enormous positional authority to the executive office (even comparing its holder to Christ), they were reluctant to collapse the United States and Christianity.

A traditional Christian interpretation of Kennedy's death insisted that his death could only be redeemed by God; the meaning of the slain president's life was found in the resurrection of Christ and in Christ's union with the Father. At the same time, most of the sermons appropriated this task of redemption and said that for Kennedy not to have died in vain, the living had to ensure by their actions that this would be so.

Only one sermon made a distinction between the redemption offered by God and that offered by American Christians. Reverend Leroy C. Hodapp, pastor of the First Methodist Church, stated, "If the Christian faith is true, then John Kennedy has not died in vain."[144] But regarding JFK's public life, he added, "You and I shall help determine whether or not he died in vain."[145] Even here, God's redemption is not sufficient; the living have a necessary part to play. This was perhaps the genesis of the church's apprehension in later crises that God might not be enough on His own. This rhetoric marked a hesitation that history, rather than salvation, would determine the meaning of a man's life.

Ministers of 1963 urged American Christians to continue the ideas and ambitions that Kennedy had pursued. It was a strained tautology—Kennedy guaranteed his own redemption if Americans fulfilled his recommendations. This was in direct contrast, of course, to the ministers' insistence that God was still in charge and that American Christians should renew their dedication to their faith. Yet, at least as far as it concerned Kennedy, Americans, not God, would secure the meaning of Kennedy's death. Tellingly, many sermons used JFK's own words rather than Scripture to mandate the American response. The issue was not so much what God demanded but what JFK required.

Because Americans oversaw this redemption, they mourned less. They were not transformed by the trauma; instead, they moved quickly to action. President Johnson confirmed the necessity: "This is our challenge—not to hesitate, not pause, not to turn about and linger over this evil moment, but to continue on our course so that we may fulfill the destiny that history has set for us."[146] Grieving was not appreciated as giving birth to new insights and understandings. Americans were expected to overcome their grief quickly because they were charged with doing something that was readily named and understood. This was the inauguration of American twentieth-century commemoration. It stabilized an uncertain reality by putting meaning decisively in human hands.

Perhaps what was least addressed in the assassination sermons was how the violence of Kennedy's death disrupted signature features of American life. As sociologist Kai Erickson detailed, "One of the crucial tasks of culture is to help people camouflage the actual risks of the world around them; to help them edit reality in such a way that it seems manageable."[147] The president's violent death revealed the state's vulnerability.

Ministers used the opportunity of this destabilization to reenchant the world, ironically by giving their congregants something concrete to do. These acts presumably would inoculate the American populace from their own violence, which the ministers had already named as the cause of the assassination.

One could argue that the collective failure to mourn continued the violence that led to the assassinations of Martin Luther King Jr. and Robert F. Kennedy. Walter Benjamin, in his essays against consolation in the post–World War I era, argued that the anesthetization of violence and the glorification of the warrior featured in collective mourning after Auschwitz meant that the opportunity for "deeper understanding of the sources of the shocks which might ultimately lead to changing them" was lost. That is, in a collective yearning to overcome sorrow and find salvation, people reached for a false symbolic closure, in which the horror and violence were not fully mourned. Without mourning, according to Benjamin, there was no real experience. There was no long-term effect on one's thinking about one's relation to the world.[148]

Unlike the Pearl Harbor sermons, which were lamentations for the past (specifically the battlefield carnage of World War I) and the beginning of lamentations for what was to come, the Kennedy sermons sought to make grief itself into a spectacle of wonder and awe. This was the result most obviously of the ability of television to enter into the intimacy of American living rooms and "show repeatedly the blood-caked suit of the First Lady" and the funeral procession of the riderless horse with its stirrup turned backward. Americans did not simply grieve. They watched themselves grieving. Watching became what it meant to mourn, the activity of grieving.

A theater of suffering developed. "As the television cameras swept across the faces of shocked people in the nation, in the cities across the land, the faces most stunned, most grief stricken, most hurt and bewildered were the faces of the humble, the poor, the disenfranchised, the yellow faces, the brown faces, the black faces. Inarticulate, their crumpled countenances were stained with tears unashamed. In bewilderment they confront the fact that, of a surety, they had lost a beloved friend."[149]

While funerals have long been closely aligned with theater, with the Kennedy funeral the suffering became a spectacle. As Guy Debord argues, "The spectacle is not a collection of images, but rather it is a social relationship between people that is mediated by images."[150] Instead of grief being orchestrated through relationships, it was codified in images. As both Jackie Kennedy and Debord understood, a spectacle prevents individuals from realizing that the spectacle is only a moment in history.

In her brilliant creation of a spectacle of grief, Jackie Kennedy ensured that her image of the Kennedy administration would become its history. Using everything from the Lincoln draperies to line the room where Kennedy's body lay in state to her recommendation to her three-year-old son that he salute the passing coffin, she gave the United States a collective memory that sacralized the violence of Kennedy's death, consolidated the imagined power of the state to control the rhythms of death, and added elements of religious awe to the death of a secular figure.

Occluded from view, as Debord notes, were reminders that this moment could be overturned by the spectators once they took control of the narrative. By decade's end, with the assassinations of Martin Luther King Jr. and Robert F. Kennedy, as well as the wreckage of the war in Vietnam, most of the sacred spectacle of Kennedy's funeral parade had been unraveled.

It is a bitter irony that King's name was left off the invitation list for the JFK memorial. Although the oversight was repeatedly described as "inadvertent," King's absence was a reminder to some spectators that their grief, as well as their grievances, remained invisible. Ministers lamented that the assassination had shown that the United States was not more civilized than other nations, but they did not make the connection that this violence was linked to the murder of the country's Black citizens.

Most of the 1963 sermons insisted that mourning was apolitical. Yet clearly, who Americans mourned and who they did not was a political act. African Americans of the 1960s would have easily recognized this. Surely, that the nation mourned for Kennedy but did not similarly mourn for Medgar Evers was a political distinction. If the United States had observed national mourning in the wake of the bombing of the Birmingham Church in September 1963, would that not have been a political act? When, a week before the bombing, Governor George Wallace told the *New York Times,* "Alabama needs a few first-class funerals," wasn't he recognizing that death and mourning have a politics?

Yet Protestant ministers in 1963 avowed that mourning Kennedy rose above politics, whereas the deaths of Negro children could not transcend their Black bodies and thus provoke universal grief. Black children were not part of the family of humanity whose blood unites. Their Black bodies held them close to politics and history, while JFK, a White man of privilege, could be a martyr for all Americans. His dead body could gesture beyond itself to a promised future. Weren't the girls who died in Birmingham martyrs, too? Yet not a single sermon in 1963 named them so.

With Kennedy's assassination, Protestant ministers embraced a Roman Catholic as one of their own. While it might seem that this was an inaugural gesture of religious pluralism, the assassination of Martin Luther King Jr. a mere five years later would reveal that the embrace had been of Kennedy's paradigmatic Whiteness, not his Catholicism. After Dr. King's assassination, White ministers regretted the loss to the Black community but did not experience it as a loss to their own. Black ministers felt despair at the loss of a man who had seemingly done everything God could possibly ask, but who, like many other Black men and women before him, had paid the ultimate price. African American preachers lost their confidence—not only in the possibilities of political life to adjudicate racial inequities but in whether God was interested in American politics at all. It would be a turbulent time for the pulpit. The implicit racial divide among ministers led them on a journey that would ultimately ossify rather than diminish racial tensions.

CHAPTER THREE

Existential Despair

The Assassination of Rev. Dr. Martin Luther King Jr.

Perhaps the most well-known speech after Dr. King's assassination was that given by then-presidential candidate Robert F. Kennedy. Although Kennedy was not a minister, his speech that night helped to calibrate how Black Americans might mourn King with compassion and without rancor. As the brother of the recently slain American president, RFK carried a kind of moral authority weighted by both personal loss and perceived racial understanding. And because that night, RFK was speaking to a primarily African American audience in the heart of a predominantly Black neighborhood in Indianapolis, his words assumed a sermonic resonance for many Americans.

RFK had spoken earlier in the day at the University of Notre Dame and Ball State University. He had focused on domestic issues, the Vietnam War, and racial issues. At the end of his speech at Ball State, an African American student asked: "Your speech implies that you are placing a great deal of faith in white America. Is that faith justified?"

Kennedy answered, "Yes," and added, "Faith in Black America is justified, too."

While on a plane to Indianapolis, Kennedy told a reporter, "You know it grieves me . . . I just told that kid this and then walk out and find that some white man had just shot their spiritual leader." Kennedy did not learn that King had in fact died until his plane landed in Indianapolis. According to reporter John Lindsay, Kennedy "seemed to shrink back as though struck physically" and put his hands to his face, saying, "Oh, God, when is this violence going to stop?"[1]

Although the Indianapolis chief of police warned Kennedy that they could not provide adequate protection for him at a scheduled rally if the crowd rioted, Kennedy decided to speak regardless. He spoke for fewer than five minutes, focusing on what kind of nation the United States was and what direction Americans wanted to move in. He named potential Black responses to King's death:

> For those of you who are black—considering the evidence
> there evidently is that there were white people who were
> responsible—you can be filled with bitterness, with hatred,
> and desire for revenge. We can move in that direction as a
> country, in great polarization—black people amongst black.
> White people among white, filled with hatred toward one
> another. Or we can make an effort, as Martin Luther King
> did, to understand and to comprehend, and to replace that
> violence, that stain of bloodshed that has spread across our
> land, with an effort to understand with compassion and love.[2]

Kennedy validated Black anger—there were Whites who were responsible, you can be filled with the desire for revenge—but he deflated that legitimacy with the next sentence "we can be filled with hatred toward one another. Black people amongst black. White people among white, filled with hatred toward one another." The hatred is abstracted, removed from the death of King. Why would White people hate Black people? A peace-loving, nonviolent spiritual leader had just been killed. Why would White people be filled with hate for Blacks without the specter of racism?

Unaddressed in Kennedy's speech was why Black people would possibly be motivated to follow his advice in light of King's fate. What good were understanding and compassion when, as Kennedy had just said, those qualities were exactly what King had embodied, and he had "died because of that effort"?[3]

In the next two minutes of the speech, RFK, as Jackie Kennedy would also do a day later, equated King's and JFK's deaths:

> I can only say that I feel in my own heart the same kind of feeling. I had a member of my family killed, but he was killed by a white man. But we have to make an effort in the United States, we have to make an effort to understand, to go beyond these rather difficult times. . . . What we need in the United States is not division; what we need in the United States is not hatred; what we need in the United States is not violence or lawlessness; but love and wisdom, and compassion toward one another, and a feeling of justice toward those who still suffer within our country, whether they be white or black.[4]

This was the only known time that RFK referred publicly to his brother's death, and the pain in his voice was audible. Kennedy was attempting to persuade a largely African American audience to recognize that both assassinations had been unjust and that both Black and White men had suffered as a result. Kennedy was linking his suffering upon the death of his brother with Black suffering upon the death of Martin Luther King. The shared suffering, while not racial, was still intentionally linked to injustice. And powerfully, RFK recognized that the suffering was personal. RFK elevated Black grief—claiming it as equivalent not only to that of a White man but to the loss of an American president.

The speech ended with a spiritual solution, "So I shall ask you tonight to return home, to say a prayer for the family of Martin Luther King, that's true, but more importantly to say a prayer for our own country, which all of us love—a prayer for understanding and that compassion of which I spoke."[5] The speech was so successful that there was no rioting in Indianapolis after King's death.

RFK's words are returned to so often because they represent the road not taken in mourning King. The contrast between how King was ultimately mourned and not mourned by White America, how rage roared through Black communities in response to King's death, how the indifference to the death of another Black man compared to the profundity assigned to the death of a White man are all rebukes in hindsight of 1968 America. That the words of a powerful White man offered sufficient solace to Black Americans is a reminder of what might have been possible if more White Americans had adequately faced the devastation of the loss of King, in the ways they did after the assassination of JFK. The Landmark for Peace Memorial now marks the site where Kennedy spoke.

WHEN JOHN F. KENNEDY WAS assassinated, First Lady Jacqueline Kennedy received thousands of condolence letters from ordinary Americans. Many of these cards described how the writers couldn't sleep, or how Kennedy's loss reminded them of the deaths of their own fathers, husbands, or brothers.[6] When Martin Luther King Jr. was assassinated, Coretta Scott King too received condolence letters. Hers more pointedly revealed the racial divide of the United States in 1968.

Letters from White people acknowledged King's contribution to the Black community, without remarking on how his might be regarded as an "American loss." None claimed the tragedy as an intimate part of their own family history. The notes from Black Americans took King's death in stride, seemingly unsurprised, offering Coretta primarily recommendations for how the movement should continue. Only the letters from Black schoolchildren seemed to grieve King's loss personally, poignantly asking: "Are you okay, Mrs. King? How are your children?" "I wish Mr. King were alive. Don't be sad."[7]

In the sermons given by Black and White ministers, most, in marked contrast to their sermons after Kennedy's assassination, did not celebrate King's death as an opportunity to fulfill his dream. King's death was primarily understood as a sign of the unraveling of that dream. In the five-year period since Kennedy's death, ministerial optimism had diminished, and the rioting public spectacle of Black grief seemed to have convinced many that the church had failed. Whereas Kennedy was mourned as a Christ-like figure martyred for his beliefs, and for whom all Americans bore responsibility, Dr. King was primarily mourned as an apostle of Jesus now enjoying his eternal reward. His death, not its consequences, was the fulfillment of his work.

Unlike Kennedy's assassination, King's did not unite Americans in collective mourning. Nor did his death "prove" to dissenters the justice of his cause. Rather, King's assassination raised questions regarding the very possibility of agency when those who mourned were the disenfranchised. Because of the violent aftermath of King's death, it was difficult for either Black or White Americans to interpret his murder as in any way redemptive. King's death was yet another reminder of a long lineage of dead Black men who had an extensive and cultivated rapport with death and suffering. This was most profoundly made manifest by the eulogy that Dr. King wrote and spoke for himself as his own funeral.

The focus in this chapter will remain on the sermons preached after King's death, but it should be noted that this crisis (unlike any of the others explored in this book) puts at the center a religious figure doing theopolitical work that results in violence. While 9/11 will again put religion (and race) at the center of violence, the assassination of a Black man, a Protestant minister, showcases how the Black and White church struggled to resist the state, here manifested by the brutality of law enforcement, an injudicious legal system, and a politically astute and active clergy.

Very few sermons were preserved after King's death, so there is more in this chapter about how King was mourned beyond what was said from the pulpit. Because of the nature of the American civil rights movement— inaugurated as a church movement, frequently led by ministers and preached and managed by Black ones—in 1968, the street was a pulpit, as many Protestant ministers insisted.[8] There are, to the best of my current knowledge (and archival research), only two studies in the last fifty years that have examined exclusively the sermons of the 1960s. One is an unpublished dissertation thesis written by Brady B. Whitehead, "Preaching Response to the Death of Martin Luther King, Jr." (1972; cited in endnote 8), and the other an article entitled "The Negro Pulpit and Civil Rights," published by two communication professors, John H. Thurber and John L. Petelle, both of the University of Nebraska, Lincoln, in the *Journal of Communication Studies* (Spring 1968). In Thurber and Petelle's essay, they sought to answer the question, "What is the nature of the message offered in the cause of civil rights by Negro ministers from their pulpits?" Of the small number of ministers who responded to their queries, most insisted, "He did not consider his church alone as his pulpit." Others considered their most significant statements to have been delivered outside the church to civic groups, voters' leagues, social welfare groups, church assembly meetings, and the like. Perhaps more than illuminating elements of Black preaching, these responses indicated that Black ministers of the 1960s imagined their theological practices as extending beyond the pulpit. Although the pulpit was important, the statements and work ministers did with civic groups beyond the confines of the sanctuary were also considered a significant part of their ministerial work on civil rights.

Whitehead wrote his dissertation comparing the responses to the death of Dr. King by Black and White ministers in Atlanta and Memphis. He sent 620 requests (one to each Protestant church in both cities of the following ten denominations: African Methodist Episcopal Church, African Methodist Episcopal Zion Church, the Christian Methodist Episcopal Church, the Disciples of Christ Church, the Presbyterian Church in the US, the Protestant Episcopal Church, the United Church of Christ, the United Methodist Church, and the United Presbyterian Church in the USA, and the Baptist family of denominations). He asked the ministers both to fill out and return a questionnaire and to include any sermons mentioning Dr. King that they had preached either of the two Sundays after his death. Although Whitehead's dissertation did not include the exact dates the research was conducted, he sent the initial requests within several weeks of King's assassination. Whitehead received only 51 sermons (including some notes) and 148 completed questionnaires.

This low level of return was methodologically significant for this present chapter because as Whitehead detailed at length in his dissertation, it was obvious that those who viewed King favorably were more likely to respond than those who did not. Whitehead knew this in part because he conducted random interviews of those who did not respond to his second requests, and in the majority of those interviews, the minister indicated he did not respond because he did not think favorably of Dr. King. About a half dozen returned the questionnaire without a mark on it; three returned the stamped, self-addressed envelope but did not enclose the questionnaire. One person enclosed nothing but the first page of the cover letter in the envelope. This was on the second mailing. The cover letter for this mailing began, "I am betting $70.68 (the postage cost for the entire second mailing) that you will answer this second request to fill out and return to me the enclosed questionnaire!" This minister wrote across the top of the letter, "You lose!"

Six ministers communicated without filling out the questionnaire. One explained that the minister did not preach on King's death because "my people knew about it" and "because I preach Christ, first, last and always." Another said, "When the tragic news . . . was told in my church, I immediately rose up in the midst of the people and said, "You may kill the man, but you can't kill his spirit."

Also, there were three explicitly disapproving letters from Memphis (all without questionnaire or sermons): "Martin Luther King's death was no more significant than the death of thousands of Americans in Viet Nam. . . . I believe some of you ministers are chasing fleas." And another, "We have a Christ to preach; some of you fellows evidently don't." And finally, the third, "I'm fed up to the eyes on such bunk. Let King remain dead. There's too much of importance to attend to. Why don't you get with it?"

Nonetheless, the completed questionnaires tell another story. The results are quite positive: 64 percent thought King the most outstanding Black leader of the decade; 31 percent thought of King as a modern prophet; only 4 percent thought of King as a tool of the communists. Furthermore, only 3 percent thought King was wrong in the goals he sought, but 32 percent thought he was wrong in the methods he used. And finally, 9 percent thought King caused violence wherever he went.

THIS CHAPTER FOCUSES primarily on how the King assassination sermons understood and narrated the public spectacle of Black grief, from the funeral to the rioting. Although there were surprisingly few analogies drawn in the sermons between the Kennedy and King assassinations (except for some ugly racist remarks on the order of "Who does Coretta think she is, Jacqueline Kennedy?"), most sought to make Black grief a political concern, not a theological one. Apparently, most ministers (Black and White) no longer believed that comfort would be given to those who mourned.

Moreover, the decorum of White grief was cast as the only legitimately "American" form of mourning. White Americans tended to view Black grief as just that—Black, not American. White grief, like that featured in the spectacle of Kennedy's funeral, was perceived as uniting a nation. The King assassination sermons articulated a divide. They were not only a form of a racial civic education but delineated the tensions of the disinherited, who were both subjected to grief and subjects speaking grievance.

On the night of King's assassination, President Johnson addressed the nation: "Once again, the heart of America is heavy—the spirit of America weeps—for a tragedy that denies the very meaning of our land." Johnson issued a proclamation announcing a national day of mourning. "A leader of his people—a teacher of all people—has fallen. . . . Men of all races, all religions, all regions must join together in this hour to deny violence its victory—and to fulfill the vision of brotherhood that gave purpose to Martin Luther King's life and works."[9]

According to Johnson, King was a teacher for all, but not a leader of all. No Black man could do that. Only whiteness rose above color to represent everyone. Nonetheless, Johnson's response was an appropriate, if not particularly heartfelt, response. It was well-known that Johnson did not have any deep affection for King, especially after King's critique of Johnson's Vietnam policies. The significance of Johnson's words depended more on their juxtaposition to his words after Kennedy's assassination.

In his address to Congress several days after Kennedy's death, Johnson had noted: "Our American unity does not depend upon unanimity. We have differences; but now, as in the past, we can derive from those differences strength, not weakness, wisdom, not despair. Both as a people and a government, we can unite upon a program, a program which is wise and just, enlightened and constructive."[10]

After King's death, Johnson called for the opposite. "Men of all races, all religions, and all regions must join together in this hour to deny violence its victory—and to fulfill the vision of brotherhood that gave purpose to Martin Luther King's life and works." After Kennedy's death, American unity permitted differences—"we can derive from those differences strength"—but after King's death, "differences," particularly racial differences, required overcoming.

In 1968, Johnson's language shifted away from acceptance of difference within plurality to a call for unity without difference: "All must join together in this hour to deny violence its victory." Racial differences ignited violence—the rioting ten blocks from the White House—but other kinds of differences contained strength, wisdom, and constructive insight. Racial differences did not have any of these virtues. Racial difference was a problem, as W. E. B. Du Bois had so eloquently noted in 1903. For Johnson in 1968, there was no double consciousness, no second sight available through racial difference. There was only violence in his version of liberal "colorblindness."

Johnson should not be too roundly criticized, however. By the very next day, April 5, he had written a letter to the Speaker of the House urging the passage of what would become known as the Civil Rights Act of 1968.[11] After Kennedy's assassination, too, Johnson had immediately insisted that there "is no memorial oration or eulogy that could more eloquently honor President Kennedy's memory than the earliest possible passage of the civil rights bill for which he fought so long. We have talked long enough in this country about equal rights. We have talked for one hundred years or more. It is time now to write the next chapter, and to write it in the books of law."[12]

Although Johnson did not argue that the 1968 legislation was a *memorial* to King's work, it was King's death that provided the impetus for his action. "This tragedy has caused all good men to look deeply into their hearts. When the Nation so urgently needs the healing balm of unity, a brutal wound on our conscience forces upon us all this question: What more can I do to achieve brotherhood and equality among all Americans?"[13]

There was, however, one element of the legislation that revealed the association Johnson's administration (and many other White Americans) still made between blackness and violence. This was the rider attached to the legislation that made it a felony to travel across state lines with "the intent to incite, promote, encourage, participate in and/or carry on a riot."[14] The provision was widely understood as a response to the protests after King's death and to accusations that, during his lifetime, King himself had been an "outside agitator," specifically in his final work in Memphis. Southern Democrat Robert Byrd of West Virginia, in November 1967, criticized Dr. King on just this count: "Martin Luther King fled the scene. He took to his heels and disappeared leaving it to others to cope with the destructive forces he had helped to unleash."[15] This element of the legislation was hardly something that could be understood as a memorial to the man who, as Johnson had himself proclaimed, "devoted his life to the nonviolent achievement of rights that most Americans take for granted."

Although King had spent his entire life engaged in nonviolent resistance, the violent response to his murder persuaded Americans that any collection of Black protesters was imminently combustible.[16] In fact, a surprisingly large percentage of White Americans believed that King had brought his death upon himself.[17] This addendum to the Civil Rights Act of 1968 was a manifestation of an American tradition—that a Black man was, in some unfathomable way, always responsible for his own murder.

Obituary for Nonviolence: American Religion in Black and White

In 1957, a Gallup poll revealed that 69 percent of American adults felt that religion was increasing its influence on American life. By 1969, only 14 percent felt the same way.[18] Ministers noted this shift: "We tended to mix up the religious dimensions of American culture with the cultural dimensions of American religion. The passage of time may prove that an essentially alien social order has trapped and tamed the churches. Now when people are in trouble, they turn to the government, not to the churches. The role of the state is expanding, while that of the church seems to be becoming more and more marginal."[19]

Yet, as C. Eric Lincoln noted in his survey of Black clergy in the 1960s, "The civil rights movement at the grassroots level is largely in the hands of the minister and the ministers themselves have found a new dignity which lifts them above the stereotype of pompous behavior, fried chicken and expensive automobiles with which they were once identified."[20] While this was a painfully crude formulation, despite being articulated by one of the most respected scholars of African American religion, it was a reminder that any calculus regarding "church authority" and its influence had to be attentive to the 1968 racial divide.

For American Black men, a career in the church was a source of respect and authority. The ministry offered a way to support their community, be spared some of the grievances of a White-dominated workplace, and thus maintain a semblance of racial autonomy. As James Baldwin observed in his 1962 essay, "Letter from a Region in My Mind": "Every

Negro boy—in my situation during those years, at least—who reaches this point realizes, at once, profoundly, because he wants to live, that he stands in great peril and must find, with speed, a 'thing,' a gimmick, to lift him out, to start him on his way. *And it does not matter what the gimmick is.* It was this last realization that terrified me and—since it revealed that the door opened on so many dangers—helped to hurl me into the church. And, by an unforeseeable paradox, it was my career in the church that turned out, precisely, to be my gimmick."[21]

This is not to suggest that Black ministers were not "true believers" or that they did not consider their vocation as one dedicated to the Almighty. The point is to highlight that sociologically, the role of a Black minister was also an act of resistance to White racism, which humiliated Black men as being insufficiently human, inadequately masculine, and lacking in self-sufficiency.

With the assassination of Dr. King, the pastoral period of the civil rights movement was over.[22] If Black men had imagined that the ministry could inoculate them from White violence or that the practices of Christian love would coax White Americans to racial justice, those illusions were shattered with King's violent death. As Floyd Bixler McKissick, leader of the Congress for Racial Equality (CORE), said to a reporter a few hours after King's assassination: "Dr. Martin Luther King was the last prince of nonviolence. Nonviolence is a dead philosophy and it was not the black people that killed it. It was the whites that killed nonviolence, and white racists at that."[23]

A rioter a few days after the assassination echoed the sentiment to a *Jet* reporter: "Martin Luther King wasn't our leader, but he was black. If white people can't tolerate him when he tries to help the poor, they certainly can't tolerate us. We don't believe in conciliation and negotiation. You can scrap the NAACP and the Urban League; keep their leaders busy talking on the radio about how great King is—dead."[24]

The funeral of Dr. King and the sermons, eulogies, and Memphis memorial march five days after his assassination wrestled with this tension. On the one hand was a vulnerable hope that nonviolence and implicitly Christian principles could still redeem American White racism and offer salvation to Black Americans. On the other, the bloody evidence was that with King's death, nonviolence and the Christian principle of love had been shown to be woefully inadequate. After King's death,

Christianity itself was imagined by some American ministers to be at risk. Even the famous Trappist monk Thomas Merton asked, "Is the Christian message of love a pitiful delusion?"[25]

After Kennedy's assassination, ministers asserted that the moral lapses of individual Christians, in concert with the neglect of the institutional church, had created the possibility for the evil that led to Kennedy's death. In particular, the displacement of the church by the state and the government's growing power had created the possibility for the assassination. They included themselves as partially responsible. Ministers, they argued, had abdicated some of their Christian authority by trusting that the US government could succeed in ensuring, or even be sufficient to ensure, American virtue.

With King's death, the doubts were more profound. Perhaps God had abandoned the United States. Reverend Gardner Taylor, in a sermon entitled "Is God Dead? Can God Die?" delivered two Sundays after King's death, argued: "In the sense that He [God] disappears from among men for a time, God does die. There was an absence from the world the day Jesus died. The earth grew sick with lost equilibrium."[26] Although the sermon ended with the possibility of God's return, it was primarily a meditation on despair and hopelessness in God's absence. Reverend Taylor lamented that God had finally withdrawn from the United States, horror-struck by the American capacity to slaughter the most devout and the most dedicated to God's service.

Two sermons by White Lutheran pastors echoed this claim. Reverend Robert Koons argued in his compelling sermon, "The Church That Makes God Sick": "God is not dead. But He must get sick many times— sick at heart over the sins of men. . . . Their indifference to Him mak[es] it seem in the eyes of the world as though He were absent or dead, instead of the living, suffering, redeeming Presence in their midst which He shows Himself to be in Jesus Christ."[27] The sermon asked, "Is there racism in Lynchburg?" The answer was a resounding, "Yes!" Rev. Koons detailed elements of that racism, including "printing Negro obituaries in the classified section of the newspaper."[28] Another sermon by Reverend Herman Stuempfle, a chaplain at the Lutheran Theological Seminary at Gettysburg, noted: "We live in a scarred world. And a scarred world is not a place for an unscarred God. But whatever else He may be, our God is not unscarred."[29]

In these sermons, God was damaged by the acts of men. This was not a question of theodicy—a merciful God had not allowed tragedy to befall the innocent. Rather, the wicked have caused God to withdraw in sickened despair.

Dr. King had warned that the United States' failure to recognize the requirements of racial justice would ensure its apocalypse. "The Negro may be God's appeal to this age—an age drifting rapidly to its doom."[30] A sermon by Edler Hawkins from St. Augustine Presbyterian Church in the Bronx echoed this feeling of abandonment and creeping sickness that was overtaking the country: "Only a part of the nation recognized the sickness was deep . . . only a part of the nation saw that the sickness was deep when Medgar Evers was shot. A little larger part, but still only a part saw it when the little children of Birmingham were killed. And let's be honest a little further, many of those who mourn him now, were in the opposite corner to him before Thursday evening."[31]

Rev. Dr. William Truly Jr. asked in his poetic tribute to King:

> Death? Did I say death?
> But King is not dead,
> Evers is not dead. Malcolm is not dead.
> It is perhaps we who are dead.[32]

For some White pastors, the sense of abandonment was also tinged with fear. "But the tragedy is now there is none in power nearly so moderate as Martin Luther King to take his place, and his death leaves the terrifying possibility that all the Negro drive towards civil rights will be formed by the more radical elements of Negro leadership. No matter how much some people dislike him and his methods, he reflected the most moderate leadership that the Negro community would follow."[33] In an interview several weeks after King's death, James Baldwin remarked about the instantaneous canonization of King by White Americans, "It's the proof of their guilt, and the proof of their relief."[34]

It might be tempting to imagine with the long lens of hindsight that King's assassination was a tragic catalyst for White America's appreciation of his leadership and the significance of his work for racial justice. Unfortunately, there is very little evidence to support that conversion narrative. Instead, there were substantial indications that rendering King a tragic figure was yet another way to enervate the cause he championed.

As Kenneth Foote notes in *Shadowed Ground: America's Landscapes of Violence and Tragedy*, it was much easier to mourn the loss of a "fallen hero" than to address the violence, injustice, and brutalities of American life.[35] That was primarily how King was grieved by White Americans—as a fallen hero and not as a political activist pointing to American viciousness. The *Jet* editorial staff maintained: "Many of those who extend sympathy and heart-warming statements bemoaning his loss were his enemies in life. They plotted against him. They hurled epithets at him. They contended that he was foolish and way out. Only death has sainted Dr. King in the United States."[36] Reverend Gilbert Schroerlucke echoed the claim: "Many who fought him and resisted his movement in our city, now speak highly of his work. How sad it is that they 'did not know the times of his visitation' (Luke 19:44)."[37]

King's 1948 Morehouse classmate, Samuel Dubois Cook, in a May 2 memorial address to fellow alumni, reminded them what King himself might have said about the event:

> Now, my dear friends, I don't want to sound ungrateful. Please do not interpret my final remarks as ingratitude. I appreciate, so much, the proposed buildings, programs, scholarships, professorships, statues, streets, monuments and all the other fine and kind things in my honor. But, in the final analysis, these things are not of much significance. . . . The supreme task is the removal of the heavy yoke, the tall mountains and dreadful scars of oppression born of wretched racism, degrading poverty and terrifying militarism. What is ultimately needed is the beloved community, the creation of institutions and structures of justice and humanity, the reconciliation of blacks and whites.[38]

Reverend Jesse Jackson elaborated: "There was a total outpouring of people. My anger was, in part, because—how many people had been with us April 3, fighting for the garbage workers, the Poor People's Campaign? Then, on April 9, such an outpouring of love for Dr. King, as a memory. The outpouring of people was an expression of appreciation.

But when you're fighting, you need followers, not just admirers. It's cheap grace to admire a great sacrificial person. There were many who admired him but few who followed him."[39]

Milton Rokeach, a research psychologist, had been preparing a survey in April 1968 as part of the National Opinion Research Center at the University of Chicago when King was assassinated. The survey was intended to address differences among Christian denominations regarding life values (i.e., honesty, a comfortable life, world peace) as well as two theological issues concerning salvation and forgiveness. Before he mailed the surveys, he tacked on two more questions. First, "When you heard the news of the assassination of Dr. Martin Luther King, Jr., which one of these things was your strongest reaction: 1) anger 2) sadness 3) shame 4) fear or 5) he brought it on himself." Second, "After King's death, did you feel anger or did you think about the many tragic things that have happened to Negroes and that this was just another one of them?"[40]

In response to the first question, about a third of the one thousand respondents said that King had "brought it on himself" and another 10 percent reported that their primary response was fear. Rokeach found that on virtually all social issues, specifically those related to compassion and bigotry, "the frequency of church attendance did not make much difference—the regular churchgoers were no more compassionate than the less regular churchgoers."[41]

In response to the second question, a majority of churchgoers reported, "It never occurred to me," with regard to whether they had considered Negro history in their perception of King's death. There were some White Americans who appreciated King for who he was and what he had been trying to accomplish. A group that called itself "a group of young White Americans" took out a quarter-page ad in the *New York Times* on Monday, April 8, 1968, which read, "White Americans Demand Action: More than a Bowing of Heads Is needed." They, at least, were beginning to develop an implicit critique of the sanctification of King.

One minister, Reverend William Chase, urged parishioners "to transfer portions of their savings to Harlem banks as a means of expressing Christian concern for the plight of slum residents."[42] A New York bishop recognized immediately that King was a Christian exemplar: "We needed Martin Luther King not to prevent riots, not to stop black protest, not to control ghetto demonstrations, but we needed Martin Luther King rather to hold up for all of us the Christian ideal of reconciliation."[43]

But there were also a substantial number of White ministers (according to Rokeach's survey, about a third) who claimed that King had "brought it on himself." Several fundamentalist denominations, specifically Assemblies of God and Church of God, as well as some dissident Presbyterians, had long opposed King's practices of civil disobedience as lawless and disruptive to legitimate authority. "In our present situation and under our present laws and even in spite of the fact that they may at times be unjustly administered, it does not seem likely that any case of civil disobedience is justified."[44] Although these ministers acknowledged that civil disobedience was appropriate when "God's law" was in conflict with civil law, they did not believe the current situation, particularly regarding segregation, necessitated it. God's law was not in peril because of racial discrimination.

To further address the issue, the Southern Presbyterians developed a formal distinction between forced and voluntary segregation.[45] Their members contended that most segregation was voluntary and embraced by both races. The Church of God leadership stated: "The relationship between the races is respectful, dignified and brotherly in the Church of God. The colored work of the Church is a vital part of it, with equal rights and requirements. In our recent General Assembly (as in all of them) there were delegates of many races present, and participation by all on the program. Yet there is no untoward fraternization between our members of different races."[46] In other words, neither race wanted to interact with the other, so their denominational segregation was mutual and agreed upon.

After King's assassination, some of these conservative White ministers argued that the violence of the cities could best be solved by evangelization. "While we deplore the violence that racial unrest has brought to our land, we who know the Lord and his Word must recognize that the spreading revolution and lawlessness are part of a divine judgment. . . . Civil rights legislation cannot, I believe, meet the basic needs of the ghettos, but the gospel can." According to these ministers, racial unrest had prompted the violence, not demands for racial justice. The "basic needs of the ghettos"—housing, jobs, services—could not be met by legislation. Some even hypothesized that "race rising up against race" was a sign of the end times; thus, this violence could be interpreted and integrated as part of God's preordained plan.[47]

There were very few details about how the Gospel (rather than legislation) would resolve the conflict, especially given that King was himself a devout Christian preacher. If that particularity was noted, it was usually argued that although King had been a minister, his tactics of civil disobedience were "a problem" and "misguided." This was ironic, since civil disobedience is usually considered by many as foundational to the Christian experience of Jesus in the Gospel. The parallels between Dr. King's civil disobedience and Jesus's seemed ready made. King, like Jesus, mingled with the outsiders—tax collectors, lepers, prostitutes, sanitation workers, Blacks. King, like Jesus, went to prison and forgave his enemies. King, like Jesus, praised nonviolence and embraced a life without wealth. One Black minister, Reverend Reuben Henry, wrote a spiritual making the comparison:

> *like Paul and Silas, he went to jail*
> *That man might be free*
> *he paid a mighty bail*
> *Beaten, rebuked and often scorned*
> *He bore his racial cross and wore his crown of racial thorns.*[48]

The sanctification and the pleas for moderation cloaked the racism implicit in Whites' fear of Black grief. As someone yelled at one of the first memorial gatherings, "You have killed the last good nigger!"[49] An article in the *New York Review of Books* in April 1968 was more direct: "Here in Memphis it was not the killer, whoever he might be, that was feared, but the killed." In a disturbing reversal, there was more fear of Black folks and their grief than of Whites and the racist rage that killed King.

When King's funeral continued in Memphis with a scheduled march, the National Guard was on full display—not to honor Dr. King, but to protect the city from his mourners. "The National Guard, tense with gun and bayonet as if for some international battle, made the quiet, orderly march through the still streets appear a bit of a sell. The number of the National Guard, the sheer body count, spoke of a national psychosis. They were on every street, blocking every intersection, cutting off each highway."[50] It was troubling that only the violence of the rioters was mentioned in most accounts of the mourning, not the martial law of the state.

The Days Before

Several weeks before his death, King had led an unsuccessful march supporting Memphis sanitation workers. The march was "unsuccessful" because among the one hundred men and women who marched with him, a dozen or so, primarily teenagers at the back of the group, had broken windows and thrown bottles at police. Violence ensued, and police in riot gear attacked with tear gas and clubs. Sixteen-year-old Larry Payne, a suspected looter, was shot to death. Dozens of protesters were injured and nearly three hundred Black people arrested. King fled the violence, and the next day's newspapers printed unflattering photos of his exit, naming him "Chicken a la King." The *St. Louis Globe-Democrat* called Dr. King "one of the most menacing men in America today," and published a wild-eyed minstrel cartoon of him aiming a huge pistol from a cloud of gun smoke, with the caption, "I'm Not Firing It—I'm Only Pulling the Trigger."[51]

At the airport the next day, reporters hounded King about whether he could ensure that there would not be more violence at upcoming marches. Questions persisted about whether he still had the necessary authority to lead nonviolent demonstrations. There were concerns about his forthcoming Poor People's Campaign, planned for May 1968 in Washington, DC. Speculation hummed that the DC march would turn violent and should be canceled.

About a month into the Memphis garbage workers strike in 1968, one of the primary organizers, Reverend James Lawson, had invited King to Memphis. The strike had been largely organized by Black clergy and was considered to have both a political and spiritual agenda. The Memphis clergy had been mobilized when they had been maced by police during a peaceful protest earlier in the strike. One minister preached, "I am sick and tired of Negroes getting on their knees and begging the great white father for the crumbs that fall from his table."[52] The strike's clear focus on dignity and the psychic injury done to African Americans by systemic racism was the persistent thread line preached by Memphis ministers directly from the pulpit.

The signature mantra of the march, "I AM A MAN," was credited to the ministers. The mantra carried the weight of many meanings: from a human rights assertion that Blacks were humans created in the image of God (*imago dei*) to a deeply gendered formulation of how the exploitation of Black men's labor damaged the Black family; the poor wages "so emasculated our men that our wives and daughters have to go out and work in the white lady's kitchen, leaving us unable to be with our children and give them the time and attention that they need."[53]

On Monday, March 18, 1968, King addressed the largest audience in civil rights history. Over twenty-five thousand people crowded into Mason Temple: Church of God in Christ to listen. He began by noting the religious unity: "We have Baptists, Methodists, Presbyterians, Episcopalians, members of the Church of God in Christ, and members of the Church of Christ in God, we are all together."[54]

King returned to Memphis on March 28 for the strike and march. Then things began to unravel. Police blocked the march's way, and violence broke out behind. King was jostled and shoved, and eventually his friends insisted that he leave the area in a waiting car. The National Guard occupied the city and Memphis was put under martial law. The president of the Memphis Chamber of Commerce told the *New York Times* that they "would not have had the trouble if the Negro ministers had tended to their ministering."[55]

It was a devastating conclusion to an event that initially seemed to hold so much promise. As one newspaper headline aptly noted, "The Day Began as a Carnival and Ended as a Horror Show."[56] Even NAACP (National Association for the Advancement of Colored People) treasurer Alfred Baker Lewis told a membership rally in Virginia, "The Reverend Martin Luther King, Jr., must bear the blame for racial rioting in Memphis, Tennessee, because he exerts no discipline over his followers."[57]

After he left the march, King was blocked from returning to the Peabody Hotel where he was staying, so a patrolman rerouted him to the Rivermont. Previously, King had stayed at the Lorraine Motel, but he had been warned away by one of Memphis's Black officers, Lieutenant Jerry Williams, because of its exposed balconies. After the failure of the march, even this decision was decried in the press. King was reviled as a hypocrite since he was paying twenty-nine dollars a day for a select hotel rather than staying at a less expensive, Black-owned business. This media criticism would have dire consequences when King made the decision to return to Memphis two weeks later.

King was losing some of his influence for two competing reasons. First, because of his antiwar stance, many Americans, including the board of directors of the NAACP, had condemned him. The *New York Times* said, "King has diminished his usefulness to his cause, to his country, and to his people."[58] Many felt he had become too radical. For the first time in a decade, King's name was left off the January 1967 Gallup Poll list of the ten most admired Americans. Financial support for his organization had nearly dried up, and some public speaking engagements, including at universities and colleges, were withdrawn. No American publisher was eager to publish his work.

As others have described it: "King was already politically and socially dead before he was killed. Martyrdom saved him from becoming a pariah to the white mainstream."[59] Andrew Young was probably the most accurate, "King survived challenging the racial status quo, but was murdered when he began to address poverty and war and to challenge in an even more fundamental way the basic structure of the American economy."[60]

King was clearly at risk. Although his staff tried to dissuade him from returning to Memphis, he insisted, angry at the suggestion that he would permanently retreat. His flight to Memphis was delayed while American Airlines searched the plane because a threat had been made on King's life. King apparently joked to Ralph Abernathy, sitting in the seat next to him, "Well, it looks like they won't kill me this flight, not after telling me all that." "Nobody is going to kill you, Martin," Abernathy replied with assurance. American Airlines also reported to the Memphis police and the FBI additional threats against King. None of those were passed along to King when he arrived in Memphis.

As is well known, King was scheduled to speak again at Mason Temple on April 4. Abernathy was scheduled to speak the night before. But when Abernathy arrived, the crowd was noisily disappointed that King was not there. Abernathy called King and begged him to come speak. King drove through high winds and a storm and eventually stood before the crowd around 9:30 P.M. It was his last address.

When he introduced King, Abernathy joked: "Despite King's honors, he has not yet decided to be President of the United States. But he is the man who tells the President what to do." Other ministers joked, after Abernathy sat down, that he had just preached King's eulogy. King smiled. King named and thanked the clergy who had been leading the movement in Memphis. "So often, ministers aren't concerned about anything but themselves. . . . It's alright to talk about long white robes over 'yonder,' in all of its symbols. But ultimately people want some suits and dresses and shoes to wear down here."

King had returned to Memphis on April 3 to prove his leadership. That he was unceremoniously executed in the process of seeking to demonstrate the validity of his nonviolent principles made manifest not that King could not control his protesters but that White racism was so virulent that nonviolence was impossible. As one Memphis minister at the time noted: "It is not the nonviolent movement that is on trial in Memphis but—once more—American democracy. Not the leadership of some Negro ministers that is threatened, but the nation itself."[61]

Dead Black Bodies and Black Grief

The other side of the funeral, like an Act Two ready in the wings,
was the looting and anger of a black population inconsolable for all
its many losses.
—Elizabeth Hardwick

After Emmett Till's mutilated and decomposed body was found in the Tallahatchie River in 1955, his mother, Mamie Till Bradley, insisted on having an open-casket funeral so that "everyone can see what they did to my boy." Emmett's body, "his head . . . swollen and bashed in, his mouth twisted and broken—became a new kind of icon. Emmett Till showed the world exactly what white supremacy looked like."[62]

In contrast, White America's mourning had traditionally been sentimental and romantic. Mourning was about building consensus, not about political contestation. The universality of death was a call to put differences aside. In death there was unity, not division. Jackie Kennedy had created the myth of Camelot in part by suggesting to her three-year-old son that he salute the passing coffin of his dead father and by enveloping the rotunda with the Lincoln drapes. The Kennedy funeral was a romantic rebuilding of America.

The funeral for Dr. King could not help but remind Americans of racial disparities. Black grief had always been entwined with American
racial injustice. The violent death of an American Black man, even a
preacher, did not recall most Americans to their shared humanity; rather,
for African Americans it was a reminder of how entwined mortality had
always been with race.[63] The mule-drawn cart, the open casket upon
which King's preacher father fell, wracked with grief as he tried to hug
his son through the glass enclosure, and the violence that followed were
witness to the challenges of racial reconciliation rather than romantic
rebuilding. African Americans refused to cooperate in any mythmaking
around King's demise. Their violent response had something to say "to
every politician who had fed his constituents with the stale bread of hatred and the spoiled meat of racism."[64]

Americans were not allowed to see the dead body of John F. Kennedy. But when Martin Luther King died, Coretta decided that "those
who came from far-off places to honor him should be able to view his
body for the last time . . . that the multitude who loved him might see
him in death as they had seen him in life."[65] King's body, Coretta affirmed, was for those who loved him, whereas Kennedy's body was protected by Jackie for the preservation of future myth. Coretta believed
that King's body could provide what Elizabeth Hardwick called a "reunion of the family at the grave."[66] The multitude who loved him would
be reminded of what he died for. Coretta also knew that a photograph
of yet another dead Black man would become part of the chronicle of
American racism.

For by 1968, the United States had grown accustomed to seeing Black
men's dead bodies. From photographs of lynchings made into postcards
to media images of dead Black civil rights activists, displaying another
Black man in a coffin was a potent political gesture and part of what
Coretta had in mind when she talked in those first days of the necessity
of "resurrection." After King's murder, there was no "cult of the dead";[67]
that is, there was no sense that all the living were collectively united
through King's demise. In fact, in Atlanta most of the White-owned
businesses remained open and Governor Lester Maddox only sent state
employees home at 2 p.m. "for security reasons."[68] There was no shared
understanding that with the supreme sacrifice of Martin Luther King,
God's special destiny for the United States might have been lost.

In 1968, there was a continuing, if fragile, narrative of American exceptionalism. The sense that the United States was "chosen" for greatness was vulnerable. Not only was 1968 the year of fierce peace protests but also the Tet offensive. Johnson had announced just days before the assassination that he would not be seeking reelection. Two days after King's assassination, a ninety-minute police shoot-out with the Black Panthers in Oakland had killed seventeen-year-old Bobby Hutton while he was in his underwear, hands up, surrendering.[69] So how could Martin Luther King be mourned without acknowledging the violence at the heart of what had the gloss of unity?

KING'S FUNERAL WAS the largest ever staged for a private US citizen.[70] The televised events were viewed by more than 120 million people across the United States (over half the population in 1968) and made headlines in international newspapers.[71] The funeral was the subject of multiple magazine cover stories. The April 19 issue of *Life* magazine—the most widely circulated weekly in the United States—featured a portrait of King's widow accompanied by the cover line "America's Farewell in Anger and Grief." *Jet* magazine—one of the most influential media sources for African Americans—featured the widow and her children on its April 25 cover with the headline "King's Widow: Bereavement to Battlefield."

In the five days between the assassination and the funeral, riots broke out in more than one hundred cities across the United States. In Washington, DC, Chicago, and other cities, buildings were destroyed by arson. A firebomb was set off in Tallahassee. Violence escalated in Boston, Winston-Salem, New York, and Minneapolis. In Detroit, police officers sent to control rioting were shot. By the end of the week, some 57,500 National Guard troops had been dispatched around the country, the largest force mobilized for any domestic situation.[72] Over the course of that week, 39 people died, 2,600 were injured, and 21,000 were arrested. Thousands of buildings were burned, and contemporary estimates put the cost of the damage at close to $400 million. In Washington, DC, alone, the riots left 2,500 people jobless.

Describing the violence in the *Los Angeles Times*, Max Lerner evoked an image of destruction: "The skyline of urban America in the past week has been a desolating one—not only the landscape but the manscape:

fire-riddled blocks of houses and looted shops cordoned off in the Negro ghettos; at least a half dozen great cities turned into fortresses and watched over by guardsmen and soldiers; cities ravaged from within by their own dwellers and occupied by soldiers from without."[73]

At a news conference after King's death, as the rioting was beginning in Washington, DC, a reporter asked Stokely Carmichael, "Do you fear for your life?" Carmichael responded: "The hell with my life. You should fear for yours. I know I am going to die. . . . The black man can't do nothing in this country. Then, we're going to stand up on our feet and die like men. If that's our only act of manhood, then goddammit, we're going to die. We're tired of living on our stomachs."[74] A student at Howard University echoed the sentiment: "Martin Luther King compromised his life away. He had to avoid bloodshed. . . . If I'm nonviolent, I'll die. If I'm violent, I'll still die, but I'll take a honkie with me."[75]

With King's death, "I Am a Man" became "I Will Die like a Man." King's nonviolence was replaced with a warrior masculinity. There was still a claim for manhood, a resistance to the humiliation of racial subordination, but now resistance was accompanied by Black death. As Carmichael and the Howard student reminded the journalists, in some ways it had always been that way. "In Memphis, black people successfully asserted their manhood and dignity and won a point of justice—but at a terrible cost. If that is the end of the matter, what will really have been proved is that in Memphis, in America, justice costs too dear—and perhaps, that liberty is less likely than death."[76]

Coretta Scott King gave a press conference with Reverend Ralph Abernathy at the Ebenezer Baptist Church on the afternoon of Saturday, April 6. Abernathy began the conference with the proclamation, "You may have been able to stop the heartbeat of Dr. Martin Luther King, but you will not be able to stop the search for freedom, dignity, and equality in this country."[77] The "you" who might try to stop this liberation remained unspecified.

Coretta Scott King followed with a long acknowledgment of how important Ralph Abernathy had been to her husband and how often Dr. King made the recommendation "that if anything happened to him that Ralph should take his place as head of the Southern Christian Leadership Conference [SCLC]." She thanked all the friends and "people of good will" throughout the nation and the world whose condolences had lightened her grief. She then read a prepared statement: "I would have preferred to be alone at this time with my children, but we have always been willing to share Martin Luther King with the world because he was a symbol of the finest of which a human being is capable of being. . . . So, once again, I have put aside traditional family considerations . . . [for] the thousands who have asked how they can carry on his work."

Neither Coretta Scott King nor Ralph Abernathy mentioned the riots or the violence that was ripping across the United States in the wake of King's assassination. Coretta did not chide Black violence as contrary to her husband's love of peace or justify it as the inevitable outcome of justice deferred. Rather, she clearly put the onus where she believed it belonged—on the shoulders of the "society infested with racism" that "could attempt no way to solve problems except through violence." Coretta insisted that "nothing hurts more than this."

The following day, Sunday, April 7, Ralph Abernathy, in his new capacity as president of the Southern Christian Leadership Conference, released a "Statement Regarding the Death of Martin Luther King." Printed entirely in capital letters, the three-page statement began like a manifesto: "Be it known that our grief is deep, our anguish is intense, and as mortal men and women we are angry at the senseless, depraved act that snuffed out the life of our leader. Take heed, however, that we are pledged to continue our non-violent struggle for the liberation of all oppressed peoples—even more militantly than in the past."[78]

Presumably addressed to White people, the statement was partially an explanation of Black anger and its current manifestations in violence. "The existence of some unhappy outbreaks should not obscure the fact that a moral, social upheaval has erupted in our nation. Anger, anguish and a sense that the nation failed to hear Dr. King have gripped the minds of millions . . . black and white, Christian, Jew and unbeliever. They are demanding that we now do what should have been done."

Speaking of Dr. King in the present tense, Abernathy said: "Dr. King and I and all of SCLC abhor violence. Just as much as we abhor poverty, injustice and racial discrimination. Our prescription for ending the current violence and to avoid future violence is for Congress to enact legislation at once that guarantees a job to all and for those unable to work a guaranteed annual income to insure decent life." Abernathy implied that the rioting was "in one sense" the beginning of the Poor

People's Campaign. Congress needed to recognize that King's death had created a crisis and by enacting these measures, "the healing of the nation's wounds can begin immediately."

Abernathy declined using the power of King's death to call off Black violence or to ask the rioters to step down. Instead, he recommended that Congress step up, commit to racial justice, and resolve the crisis themselves, nonviolently, through legislation. He concluded the statement with what was perhaps the most eloquent articulation of the tragedy in those first days: "In losing Dr. King, the black people have made the greatest sacrifice in their history. Such a loss can only be redeemed by a social gain of the same magnitude." Black people had lost King to White racism. It was an enormous debt, perhaps one that could never be fully paid.

For forty-eight hours—from Saturday, April 6, through Sunday, April 7, King's body lay in state at the Sister's Chapel at Spelman College in Atlanta, Georgia.[79] Tens of thousands of mourners stood in line for hours to pay their respects. The city was overwhelmed with visitors as even more arrived for the funeral. After all the hotels were full, churches, colleges, and private homes were opened to accommodate the visitors. When local radio stations put out a call for help or food, people responded. A close friend of the King family, Xernona Clayton, recalled: "It was a marvelous thing, everyone coming together. I don't think anyone paid for food for two or three days."[80]

On Monday, April 8, Ralph Abernathy and Coretta Scott King led forty-two thousand silent marchers in Memphis to honor King and to support the Memphis sanitation workers. Eight days later, the city and its workers reached a settlement of the sixty-five-day strike.[81] Meanwhile, in Atlanta, City Hall was draped in black for the funeral on Tuesday, April 9. City schools were closed, ostensibly so that Black children could attend the service, and implicitly so that White children and their families could stay securely at home, afraid of the potential for violence.

Although Atlanta's mayor, Ivan Allen, was supportive and worked to coordinate with the SCLC, Georgia's governor, Lester Maddox, was barricaded inside the state capitol, surrounded by 160 state troopers, whom he notoriously instructed to "shoot them down and stack them up." He refused King a state funeral because he considered him an "enemy of the state."[82] He had also initially declined to hang the capitol flag at half-staff until he was notified that it was a federal mandate from the Johnson administration.

Governor of California Ronald Reagan described the assassination as "a great tragedy that began when we began compromising with law and order and people started choosing which laws they'd break." South Carolina senator Strom Thurmond wrote to his constituents, "We are now witnessing the whirlwind sowed years ago when some preachers and teachers began telling people that each man could be his own judge in his own case."[83] Politicians were not the only ones who dissented. Many pastors, particularly Southern Baptists, proclaimed that it was "scandalous" to fly the American flag at half-staff in memory of someone they considered a lawbreaker.[84]

Into this maelstrom, King's funeral began on Tuesday, April 9, in Atlanta, at the church where three generations of King men had been preachers—Ebenezer Baptist Church. Organized ostensibly by Coretta and her sister-in-law, Christine King Farris, the service featured the choir and congregation singing some of King's favorite hymns. His close associates said prayers, and King's college professor and mentor, Harold DeWolf, delivered a tribute.

The service opened with Reverend Ralph Abernathy repeating what he had said at the press conference: "We gather here this morning, in one of the darkest hours in the history of the black people of this nation and in one of the darkest hours in the history of all mankind."[85] Abernathy paraphrased the 1845 poem "The Present Crisis" by American abolitionist James Russell Lowell, saying that "to side with truth is novel." The poem was a favorite of the civil rights movement, and King had used it in the conclusion of his sermon at the National Cathedral on Sunday, March 31, 1968.[86]

Lowell had written the poem in response to the election of Democrat James Polk to the presidency, who supported slaveholders and their expansionist ambitions. Polk had only narrowly defeated Whig Henry Clay by a mere half of a percentage of the votes. It was an election in which the outcome for slaves went from bad to worse.

The parallels to the crisis of 1968 were palpable. Abernathy focused on the poem's elements of "God within the shadow, keeping watch above his own" and ended with the Gospel, John 11:25: "He that believeth in me, though he were dead, yet shall he live. And whosoever liveth and believeth in me, shall never die." Abernathy's prayer traced what would become the arc for many of the sermons in the following weeks: Where was God when King was slaughtered? *In the shadows.* What are we to do now that he is dead and so apparently are we? *Believe.* It was a formulaic answer that signaled that perhaps there was no better one possible.

Assistant pastor Reverend Ron English followed Abernathy with one of King's favorite hymns, "When I Survey the Wondrous Cross." The hymn ended with, "Were the whole realm of nature mine / That were a present far too small / Love so amazing, so divine / Demands my soul, my life, my all." And then Reverend English began, "In our finitude and limited vision we cannot begin to comprehend the full significance of this tragic occurrence. And so, we raise the perennial question of Job, "Why?"

Although English confidently stated that "in the total economy of the universe, good triumphs over evil," he did not attempt to find "a silver lining" or any potential good in King's death. Like many others, he avowed: "We need not weep for the deceased. For here was one man truly prepared to die." This refrain was repeated over and over again. The implication was that because King knew that his death was inevitable, it was somehow less tragic. Even Coretta repeated this sentiment in her press conference, when she detailed that King had prepared her and their children for the inevitability of his demise and that she was "surprised and pleased at the success of his teaching. For our children say calmly, 'Daddy is not dead. He may be physically dead, but his spirit will never die.'" This insistence strained credulity. King's children were only five (Bernice), seven (Dexter), eleven (Martin Luther III), and thirteen years old (Yolanda) when he died. So what was being demonstrated here? Perhaps Coretta, like the wives, mothers, and sisters of many other dead Black men, was refusing to perform her devastation for the White gaze—the journalists and the television cameras. Perhaps she was demonstrating that mourning was what Black people must do and had always done in the racist United States; it was part of the legacy of racial subordination. Black men and women woefully knew how to mourn; indeed, they prepared for it. That didn't mean it was easy, but it was part of the fabric of African American life.

But Coretta Scott King and Reverend Ralph Abernathy were also insisting that mourning was *not* all they did. They were not reduced to weeping or by weeping. Coretta said: "We intend to go on. . . . And we hope that you who loved and admired him will join us in fulfilling his dream."[87] Reverend Ron English continued, "Grant that the Congress and the President of this nation who have been so generous and gracious in their memorial tributes will be guided by the memory of this suffering servant, and return to the legislative halls to pass, without compromise or reservation, legislation so vitally needed to preserve domestic tranquility and quell social disruption." In this, Reverend English echoed the statement released two days earlier by Reverend Abernathy. He called on the politicians to do more than offer "gracious memorial tributes." They could stop the violence—"quell social disruption"—by passing legislation.[88]

There was also a probing Christian overlap between "this suffering servant" who was both Jesus and Martin Luther King. The elision was intentional. If politicians would not act in memory of Dr. King, perhaps they would act "in the memory" of Jesus, who at the end of his life had bid his apostles, "Do this in memory of me" (Luke 22:19). Reverend English was simultaneously speaking in two different registers to two separate audiences.

Reverend English ended with a prayer in which a question was embedded: "Oh, God our leader is dead. And so now the question that he posed during his life finds us in all its glaring proportions: *Where do we go from here? Chaos or community?* We pray, oh merciful Father that the removal of this man will not nullify the revelation given through him. . . . Deepen our commitment to nonviolence so that this country will not be run asunder by a frustrated segment of the black masses who would blaspheme the name of Martin Luther King by committing violence in that name."[89]

Reverend English was the only Black preacher who suggested that the violence "blasphemed" the memory of Dr. King. Abernathy, toward the end of the service, referred to the violence obliquely, but he implied that it was simply ineffective, not blasphemous: "And there are hard hearted and bitter individuals among us who would combat the opponent with physical violence and corroding hatred. Violence, by creating many more social problems than it solves, never brings permanent peace."[90]

What was most moving and created a gripping media spectacle was the homily delivered at the end of the service—a recording of "Drum Major Instinct," a sermon King had preached at Ebenezer two months earlier. In it, King envisioned his own funeral and provided recommendations for how he might be eulogized:

> Every now and then I think of my own death, and I think about my own funeral. And I don't think of it in a morbid sense. Even now and then I ask myself, "What is it that I would want said? . . . I'd like somebody to mention that day, that Martin Luther King Jr. tried to give his life serving others. I'd like for somebody to say that day, that Martin Luther King Jr. tried to love somebody. Yes, if you want to say that I was a drum major, say that I was a drum major for justice. Say that I was a drum major for peace. I was a drum major for righteousness. And all the other shallow things will not matter.[91]

The church mourners were visibly overcome. Andrew Yung openly wept, and King's younger children looked around in confusion.

The decision to use the "Drum Major" recording had been announced to the media before the funeral, and the text of the sermon ran as an op-ed in the *New York Times* the day of the funeral. That King gave his own eulogy was fascinating to the press, announced in headlines such as *Jet*'s "Rev. King Preached Own Funeral before Death" and the *Washington Post*'s "King Gave Outline for Eulogy."[92]

The message was twofold. First, so awesome was King that he was the best (and perhaps only) person able to eulogize him. Second, so familiar with death were Black men that they prepared their own eulogies and lived in readiness for their own deaths. King had made this point in his *Playboy* interview with Alex Haley: "If I were constantly worried about death, I couldn't function. After a while, if your life is more or less constantly in peril, you come to a point where you accept the possibility philosophically."[93]

But King and Abernathy had done more than accept it philosophically. They had role-played each other's demise. King and Abernathy frequently preached "mock funerals" for one another as a way to lessen the tension that accompanied everyday living. Once in 1963, before initiating the campaign in Birmingham, King was describing the risks to the members of the action. Sensing their fear, he broke the tension with a claim that if some of them did not make it back, he would preach a marvelous tribute for them. He turned to Andrew Young and proclaimed, "Andy, when the Klan finally gets you, here's what I'll preach: 'Lord, white folks made a big mistake today. They have sent home to glory your faithful servant, Andrew Young. Lord, have mercy on the white folks who did this terrible deed. They killed the wrong Negro. In Andrew Young, white folk had a friend so faithful, so enduring, they should never have harmed a hair on his head. Of all my associates, no one loved white folks as much as Andy.'"[94] The humor revealed both the ease and intimacy of these friendships and the stark reality of living with one's death figured daily before one's eyes.

Perhaps because King was quite candid about living with the reality of his own death, when he was assassinated, some of the coverage of his death, including in publications with a favorable view of King, seemed to minimize his death because he "knew it was coming." *Life* magazine's eulogy noted: "His own scorn for danger led him to his death, and it could not have really surprised him. The night before he died, he told a cheering crowd in Memphis, 'It really doesn't matter with me now, because I've been to the mountaintop.'"[95] There was a consistent repetition that King's death was not a surprise, to him or to anyone else, with the implication that Black men (and their families) should expect that in the United States in the 1960s, they would not live to old age. Yet rather than provoking outrage, this recognition seemed to be almost normalized.

Throughout his life, King maintained a belief that suffering could be redemptive, that it could result in good. At the funeral for the girls of the 16th Street Baptist Church in Birmingham, he preached: "And, so my friend, they did not die in vain. God still has a way of wringing good out of evil. And history has proven over and over again that unmerited suffering is redemptive. The innocent blood of these little girls may well serve as a redemptive force that will bring a new light to this dark city."[96] Belief in the power of suffering was part of King's theology—a way for him to reconcile Black suffering with a loving God.

Recently, Mika Edmonson has traced this intellectual debt to King's father, who argued that suffering was an active, purposeful transition to a better future rather than a passive submission to an undeserved fate.[97] This perspective did not seem to endure, at least among Black ministers, in the weeks after King's assassination. It was replaced with a lament that the suffering was pointless, redundant, and without God's redemptive mercy. For most Black ministers, Black grief was a wrenching consequence of White racism. God's grace felt painfully absent.

On Sunday, April 7, Reverend Ralph Abernathy held a memorial service for King at his own church, the West Hunter Street Baptist Church. He read what he called "A Short Letter to My Dearest Friend, Martin Luther King, Jr." The eulogy was addressed to King, much like the eulogies they had playacted for each other in previous years. He asked King "to look up those black friends and talk to the ones you and I talked about and the ones that you and I left, and the ones who so gallantly followed our leadership."[98] Without explicitly naming it, Abernathy was recalling for all the mourners in the church the legacy of the many anonymous others who had died along with King, doing the work of racial justice.

Abernathy reminded King to thank the prophets, to say hello to Peter, and to mention Abernathy somehow in conversation with Gandhi. Finally, he said, "Above all, I want you to see Jesus, go to the throne and tell how thankful we are. . . . Tell him about us down here—all of us and all of our families—and how we have sustained ourselves in many battles all of our lives."[99]

It was a powerful piece, not only because of the intimacy of Abernathy's requests but because he showed that even while enjoying heaven, Dr. King would still be working for racial equality and social justice. For Abernathy, King was not dead. He was just functioning in another realm.

After the official funeral, King's casket was placed on a mule-drawn wagon, which pulled his body through the streets of Atlanta for four miles to his alma mater, Morehouse College. The mules were a reminder of Jesus, who rode a mule into Jerusalem. King would be delivered with the same humility to his resting place. The rather shoddy wagon was in stark contrast to the shining horse-drawn caisson that rolled through the streets of Washington, DC, with President Kennedy's body on its way to Arlington. The wagon reminded the mourners that King was of and for the people, and recalled the persistent economic neglect in which Blacks lived.

Estimates from the day suggest that nearly one hundred fifty thousand people joined the march behind the casket.[100] Some of Atlanta's stores were closed out of respect, displaying signs "In Memory of Our Slain Leader Dr. King." Other businesses were closed out of fear, as Rebecca Burns learned from several personal interviews. "Almost all the stores were closed. People were expecting riots, all sorts of stuff. There was a tire place, Goodrich that was closed. It had big glass windows and there were guards with shotguns at the windows."[101] Although the procession was multiracial, the majority of marchers were African Americans. Many Whites stayed home. "A lot of guys just didn't come to work that day. My wife was scared and didn't want me to go downtown."[102]

Once the procession arrived at Morehouse, President Emeritus Benjamin Mays delivered a eulogy. Mays was among the first to claim that King did not belong only to the African American community but to everyone. "He was supra-race, supra-nation, supra-denomination, supra-class and supra-culture. He belonged to the world and to mankind. Now he belongs to posterity."[103] Like other eulogists, he drew comparisons between King and the long tradition of Christian prophets: "Surely this man was called of God to do this work. If Amos and Micah were prophets in the eighth century B.C., Martin Luther was a prophet in the 20th century. . . . If Jesus was called to preach the gospel of the poor, Martin Luther was called to give dignity to the common man."[104]

Near the end of the eulogy, Mays prayed that the assassin would be apprehended, and added, "But, make no mistake, the American people are in part responsible for Martin Luther King's death. The assassin heard enough condemnation of King and of Negroes to feel that he has public support. He knew that millions hated King."[105]

Mays then, rather surprisingly, turned to "Memphis officials" who also "must bear some of the guilt" because the "strike should have been settled several weeks ago. The lowest paid men in our society should not have to strike for a more just wage. A century after Emancipation . . . it should not be necessary for Martin Luther King Jr. to stage marches . . . go to jail 30 times trying to achieve for his people those rights which people of lighter hue get by virtue of their being born white."[106]

He concluded:

> We, too, are guilty of murder. It is time for the American
> people to repent and to make democracy equally applicable to
> all Americans. . . . If we love Martin Luther King, and respect
> him, as this crowd surely testifies, let us see to it that he did not
> die in vain; let us see to it that we do not dishonor his name by
> trying to solve our problems through rioting in the streets. . . .
> But let us see to it also that the conditions that cause riots are
> promptly removed, as the president of the United States is
> trying to get us to do so.[107]

Because of the delays caused by the long march, the planned program
at Morehouse was shortened. Speeches by Mayor Allen, SCLC co-
founder Joseph Lowery, and others were canceled. Eventually, King's
body was taken by hearse to South View cemetery, where he was buried
under a tombstone inscribed, "Free at Last! Free at Last! Thank God
Almighty, I'm Free at Last!"

This was a smaller, more personal ceremony with fewer celebrities.
As one mourner recounted, "I remember how tired the kids were, and
Bernard Lee was carrying Bunny [Bernice King] back to the car and at
that moment I realized that I now knew Martin Luther King was dead.
For five days, we knew he was assassinated, but we knew he was still
with us. At that moment, I knew he was dead."[108]

Crisis Sermons

After King's death, the perceived crisis was existential—"What is happening to this country?"—and material, with 168 cities burning from
riots of various sizes and intensities. As they had after Kennedy's assassination, Americans gathered around their televisions to watch the news
and the funeral. Many Americans went to church, but it was difficult to
assess whether the numbers were unusual in response to events. The two
Sundays after King's assassination were Palm Sunday and Easter Sunday,
a time when most Christian churches experience a temporary spike in
attendance.

Because it is difficult to find the texts of sermons preached in response
to King's death, it is unclear whether ministers prioritized their traditional

Easter sermons over the assassination. If King had died during a less important liturgical time, would more ministers have preached about him? On the other hand, as Coretta Scott King noted, his martyrdom during the Easter season seemed ideally suited for preaching his message. "Even in those first awful moments after the news of King's assassination reached me, it went through my mind that it was somehow appropriate that Martin's supreme sacrifice should come at the Easter season. . . . I thought of how often Martin had drawn analogies in life to Good Friday and Easter. Good Friday, the day of sorrow, the apparent triumph of evil over good. Then Easter Morn and the Resurrection, the coming of Joy, the triumph of life over death."[109]

Several ministers echoed this analogy in the coming weeks. "I have found myself seeing in this man in both his life and his death a Christ figure. His coming to a city that rejected him, his forgiveness of his enemies, his longing for peace, his unwavering faith in the face of possible death, his giving of himself for the sake of the poor and the oppressed. Who could miss the association?"[110] Reverend John Scott Sr. of the Church of Christ entitled his April 14th, 1968, sermon "The Mind of Christ," drawing a long analogy section by section between Martin Luther King and Jesus.[111]

King's death marked the first time I found in the twentieth century that ministers expressed their inability to preach what they truly believed. More than with the prior two crises, they appear theologically disoriented as well as personally stunned. This was particularly true for Black ministers. They were divided into roughly two groups. One group had anticipated that King would suffer a violent and untimely death, and thus primarily preached "what's next" sermons. The other, larger group could not reconcile God's power and love with the slaughter of His most eloquent prophet of that love.

During the previous two crises, ministers confidently expressed the necessity of speaking "God's truth." After King's death, determining what constituted "God's truth" was more challenging. Eventually, over the course of months and sometimes years, ministers found their way. Much has already been written about the consolidation of Dr. King's legacy.[112] But in those first days and weeks after his death, the struggle to make sense of the tragedy was raw as ministers strove to comfort and explain the tragedy to their congregations.

The first challenge was the sense of inferiority many ministers faced when considering their own words against the eloquence of King's. President Johnson, in his address to the nation on April 5, called attention to this loss: "No words of ours—and no words of mine—can fill the void of the eloquent voice that has been stilled."[113] The riots burning across American cities added to the urgency many ministers felt about making their preaching effective, "to preach with power."

Furthermore, there were competing versions of King with which ministers had to come to terms. The mainstream media quickly settled into the March on Washington version of King as a way to frame and understand his leadership. The *New York Times* and the *Washington Post* titled their respective obituaries "Martin Luther King, Jr.: Leader of Millions in Non-Violent Drive for Racial Justice" and "Dr. King, Apostle of Nonviolence, Drew World Acclaim."

In contrast, Coretta Scott King and the SCLC went back to Memphis to support the sanitation strike and to prepare to lead the Poor People's March in Washington, DC, that May. They wanted Martin Luther King to be remembered for his activism, especially for his allegiance to the working poor.

Coretta King also gave a sermon of sorts on May 12 at the Welfare Mother's March in Washington, DC. It was Mother's Day, and she proclaimed, "A future of brotherhood and peace lies in the effective use of 'WOMAN POWER.'" She called for a "campaign of conscience" for all women. She wove nonviolence into a narrative of motherhood: "If any mother wishes to bring life into the world, she becomes obliged to respect and protect the lives of ALL mothers and their children, and to work for a life sustaining peace in the world." She spoke about how nonviolence was a "way of life" expressed in everything one did, from the "greatest actions to the smallest features."[114]

She noted that violence had almost become "fashionable," thus making a life of nonviolence even more difficult. She expanded the conception of violence as well: "I must remind you that starving a child is violence. Suppressing a culture is violence. Neglecting school children is violence. Punishing a mother and her family is violence. Discrimination against a working man is violence. Ghetto housing is violence. Ignoring medical needs is violence. Contempt for poverty is violence. Even the lack of will power to help humanity is a sick and sinister form of violence."[115]

Unlike the ministers who would follow her, she stated, "In spite of the darkness in our times, God has permitted us to see a star of hope." The "star of hope," she proclaimed, was Black mothers. Quoting Langston Hughes's poem "Mother to Son," Coretta reminded her listeners that it had never been easy for Black women, but they had "kept on climbin' . . . although it ain't been no crystal stair." She called out to her listeners, "Do not sit on the landing; your mother has been climbing since before you were born. Get up and carry on."[116]

But many American male Protestant ministers seemed not to heed the call, at least not in the first weeks after King's death. Rather, they were defeated, desperate, and resigned. "In the trauma of grief and mourning, our memories will be short-circuited and we distort the truth about a human life, drawing meanings and morals that are false to the reality."[117] Before King's assassination, ministers had not discussed from the pulpit their own trauma, their own disquiet as a result of a crisis, whether the Pearl Harbor bombing or John F. Kennedy's assassination. They addressed the congregation's doubts—"you might wonder about God's presence"—but that was always quickly followed by a proclamation of God's presence, assurance that the crisis was not of God's making, and insistence that more Christianity, greater church authority, and conscientious dedication to God's plan would resolve the crisis. There was confidence, authority, and resolved certainty.

By April 1968, those elements had begun to decay. The weeks after King's assassination seemed to reveal a crossroads for the United States' clergy, particularly Black ministers. Some turned away from theological principles as the guide for civil rights. They wondered aloud about the role of the church, writ large, in public life. Those ministers who wanted to remain politically active would eventually decide to seek election to political office rather than influence their congregations from the pulpit or from public protest.[118] Others would find refuge in legal processes, and others still would dedicate themselves solely to their own communities, offering spiritual and political solace to their congregations but rarely looking outward. With the death of Martin Luther King, Christian principles seemed to have been routed, crushed by racism and its concomitant violence. Although the Southern Christian Leadership Conference worked tirelessly to assure Christians across the United States that God had not abandoned them and that nonviolence was still viable, doubt cast its foggy haze over many.

In his April 21 sermon, Reverend Samuel Williams began: "For the universe is in the grip of futility. And it is hoping against hope it will be emancipated from the slavery of corruption."[119] There was not much optimism in the sermon; he concluded, "Lord, is there any ground for hope? Creation lies in expectation of being freed from the slavery man has imposed on it. . . . Can we hope and expect man to come right? We can hardly build our hope on man, can we?"[120] Traditionally, this kind of sermon would have turned from what was humanly possible to what was promised by God. Williams's sermon did not make that bend. Instead, it was a Niebuhrian meditation on how human sin had enslaved all of nature. This was particularly poignant because it was preached the Sunday after Easter, when most ministers would have given robust sermons on the viability of resurrection.

As was the case in many of the Kennedy assassination sermons, several ministers claimed that all Americans had killed Dr. King. "King was killed by racial bigotry in his own native land. . . . As a nation we cannot excuse ourselves by saying some sick mind killed King. Our nation did. We did it by the ruse of our continuing evasion of our moral responsibility to a people we made slaves of 400 years ago and have continued some of it ever since."[121] Even more pointedly:

> We [White people] are the reason his people no longer
> followed him. We were the reason the young militant in a
> crowd of blacks could make him look like a "shuffling
> Uncle Tom."[122]

> We failed him and we killed him a little because he bet his
> movement and his method against our consciences that he
> believed would rise up and move the white man out of his
> complacency and apathy about his black brother's plight.[123]

This recognition was an echo of a foundational part of King's own theology: "We are tied together in the single garment of destiny, caught in an inescapable network of mutuality. And whatever affects one directly affects all indirectly. For some strange reason I can never be what I ought to be until you are what you ought to be."[124]

Even Vice President Hubert Humphrey recognized the challenge: "If we do recognize the testament in the life and death of Martin Luther King . . . then truly this tragedy will be remembered, not as the moment when America lost her faith, but as the moment when America found her conscience."[125]

Some White ministers were not persuaded about the United States' collective guilt or the theological analogies for King's demise. "Racism is a two-way street. This ugly reality is not the sole possession of either race. It is a common curse. Let us remember that the man who fired that fatal shot does not represent the white race any more than the colored man in Minneapolis, Minnesota who killed his neighbor represents the Negro race."[126] According to Reverend Ramsey Pollard, there was no collective guilt, just criminal activity.

Another sermon, given by Reverend Francis Sayre at the National Cathedral on April 7, juxtaposed the assassination with the fires burning through the city. He noted that one could hear citizens yelling, "White America killed Martin Luther King." Others vowed, "The Black Man is the Brute." For Sayre, this perspective represented "how hate coagulates itself into the great lumps of generalizations and misunderstandings and rebellions against God!"[127] Sayre considered these as merely two godless opinions that revealed nothing about truth or justice.

It was difficult for ministers writing these kinds of "human depravity" sermons to name racism as the cause of the violence. They were more comfortable with conceptions of human viciousness writ large as the source. Their sermons focused the debate on two elements of King's death. First, they asked whether King's work was moral rather than only political. Second, they explored whether King's assassination had anything to do with theology.

These questions were particularly pertinent to ministers, especially White ministers, who highlighted that King was killed during a workers' strike. He was not actively or obviously engaged in ministerial work, or so they argued, when he was killed. King was not doing "God's work" because it was "obvious that King's purposes are definitely racial (one group only) and that the goal is to stir up more racial tension and anxiety which can only lead to disaster."[128] The only theological feature of King's death from this perspective concerned not King, but God and His willingness to forgive the sinfulness of the shooter.

The statement presented by one hundred Memphis ministers to Mayor Loeb during the April 7 march highlighted the tension. The statement noted that the crisis of King's assassination was caused by a deterioration of human relations and "by a lack of real awareness of the desperate circumstances in which many of our fellow citizens exist and by a lack of climate and public will to put into action the Golden Rule."[129] This was a combination of the secular and the theological, but one quite removed from any articulation of racial justice. Instead, there were eroding human relations, a lack of awareness, and a failure to treat others as one wanted to be treated. None of these were bad recommendations, but they were the beginning of what would become over time the canonization of King into a generic, "content of one's character" kind of leader.

A frequent reference in these early sermons compared King's death in Memphis to Jesus's death in Jerusalem: "And part of our agony over his assassination is not only guilt for the racism we have helped to perpetuate but is an acute embarrassment over what poorly dressed Christians we are."[130] Reverend Elder Hawkins recalled that when Jesus went to Jerusalem, he knew that he was facing his own death: "Behold we are going up to Jerusalem and everything that is written of the Son of Man by the prophets will be accomplished."[131]

Several African American ministers continued this parallel, noting that, like Jesus, King "laid down his life for his friends." This reference to John 15:13 was central to Reverend E. L. Ford's sermon: "He followed the steps of Jesus in his gallant fight to the end. For no greater love can one have, than to lay down his life for his friends."[132]

The multiple sermons that proclaimed King had died for his friends attempted to remove the agency of the White racist. King was not killed; rather, he accepted his death as a way to advance the freedom of his people, his friends. "The highway of the past is littered with the blood and tears of black men and women, who took what they had and made something better."[133]

Some claimed King's death as part of the history of Black suffering. That suffering was identified by God and would be redeemed. In his sermon, Reverend Hawkins continued:

> This ought to be a time of honesty. Let us admit that only a part of the nation recognized the sickness was deep. Fourteen years ago, when the Supreme Court struck down the separate but equal statute, knowing full well that the separate would never be equal. Only a part of the nation saw that the sickness was deep when Medgar Evers was shot. A little larger part, but still only a part saw it when the sickness was writ large as the

little girls of Birmingham were killed. And let's be honest a
little further, many of those who mourn him now, were in the
opposite corner to him before Thursday evening.[134]

Hawkins warned his listeners, comparing the United States to Nazi
Germany, that "the most urgent, the most disgraceful, the most shameful,
and the most tragic problem was silence. The great body of the suburbs
of our cities have been silent. They have not understood, nor identified,
nor believed in Martin Luther King's dream. They've not identified
either, despite what they call themselves, with the dream of him who
went to Jerusalem and died there, that all men might have life and have
it abundantly."[135] It was a powerful sermon linking silence and White
racism with a fundamental failure to follow Jesus. Being a good Christian required speaking up about racial injustices.

There was also the not-so-subtle threat of increased violence to
those secure in their cloistered White suburbs if they did not address
the injustices of the ghetto. White suburbanites might have mistakenly felt secure in their enclaves, but the contagion of "a dream with
its back up against the wall" would spread.[136] In this, Hawkins, like
many others, was referring to Langston Hughes's poem "What Happens to a Dream Deferred?" The last line of the poem asks, "Does it
explode?"[137]

Nonetheless, there were some remnants of ministerial hope in the first
days after King's death. Some ministers declared that all Americans
could now dedicate themselves to the fulfillment of the United States'
"special destiny." This conception, in which Negro liberation was entwined with American destiny, had been foundational to King's project.
In King's "Letter from the Birmingham Jail," he said, "Abused and
scored though we may be, our destiny is tied up with the destiny of
America."[138] In "The Negro and the American Dream," King said, "And
I submit to you that it may well be that the Negro is God's instrument
(*Yeah*) to save the soul of America."[139] But since for many ministers
King had been the manifestation of God's working in history, his
slaughter made it difficult to maintain faith in "American destiny."
The United States had just murdered "God's agent." King's death, the
"ultimate sacrifice," as Reverend Hawkins and Reverend Abernathy
named it, was a debt that must now be paid. The sacrifice had been sense-

less and in vain. Rather than uniting all Americans, it had exposed the country's fissures.

Robert Bellah has argued that gradually in the United States, the nation (rather than the church) emerged as the primary agent of God's meaningful activity in American political history.[140] But with King's death, it felt to many ministers that the reverse was true—that the United States had thwarted, perhaps even destroyed, God's meaningful activity in history. Perhaps this was the difference between a sense of collective response when White Americans realized they had killed one of their own (Kennedy) versus when White Americans realized they had killed the other (King).

A CBS poll taken the week before King's assassination found that 47 percent of White Americans considered Blacks "genetically inferior to whites."[141] Furthermore, a May 1968 survey of three hundred Atlanta Blacks and three hundred Atlanta Whites by the Center for Research in Social Change at Emory University found that 78 percent of Blacks were "shocked and sad" about the death of MLK, whereas only 30 percent of Whites expressed a similar dismay.[142] While only 1 percent of Blacks expressed apathy to the death of King, 14 percent of Whites claimed they were "indifferent" to his loss.[143]

This aspect of mourning King created another feature of King's demise—the spectacle of Black grief for White eyes. As with Kennedy's death, there was considerable attention paid by the media, political leaders, and clerical leaders to how Coretta Scott King grieved. The focus was both racialized and gendered. Harvard president Nathan Marsh Pusey announced this racialized and gendered expectation in his address at the memorial service for Reverend King at Harvard's Memorial Church, April 9, 1968: "One gains a sense of the true quality of the man in observing the totally admirable way in which his wife and children have behaved in these dark days—surely darker and more emotionally debilitating for them than for any of us. It seems to me we can learn from their example, can see what the true character of his influence at its most intimate has been."[144]

Implicit here was that first, "good Negroes" grieved like the King family; they behaved admirably even though they are emotionally devastated; those "bad Negroes" rioting in the street do not have a legitimate claim to grief if the family with the greatest grievance is conducting itself so well. And second, these "good Negroes" were what King was really all about; those "bad Negroes" in the street were not the result of King's influence. Coretta and her family were the exemplars of "good grieving" and of his legacy—"one can see the true character of his influence at its most intimate."

Members of the media who supported King and his work, noted often how much like Jackie Kennedy Coretta was. When Jackie arrived at the funeral, some news sources noted "that both women were wearing black silk suits."[145] And *Jet* magazine described Coretta as "the black Madonna of grief"[146] invoking Catholic images of the Virgin Mary. Even Coretta anticipated the comparison and warned her friend Xernona Clayton that while she wanted her mourning hat to recall Jackie Kennedy's, she didn't want to look like a copycat. They agreed that the veil should be sufficiently transparent that cameras and viewers could see Coretta's facial expressions.[147]

President Pusey's Harvard eulogy was part of the repeated rhetoric that any undesired response by Blacks to King's death was a desecration of his memory. Many White and Black Americans wanted to make the violence about King's memory rather than about White racism. Yet during the years prior to King's assassination, the rhetoric of the Black Power movement had been that "black violence is justified as a response to prior white violence; it is self-defense."[148] King himself had recognized riots as "the language of the unheard."[149] In one of King's final lectures, he had quoted Victor Hugo to explain riots: "If the soul is left in darkness, sins will be committed. The guilty one is not he who commits the sin, but he who causes the darkness."[150]

In the aftermath of King's death, however, Black grief was required to be about King's memory, not the grievances that animated the civil rights movement. As one minister contended: "Why should we press for a civil rights bill as a memory to Martin Luther King? There is no honor in this. The reason should be a humanist one—to free a people, not a memory."[151]

Some Black critics lamented that the funeral had not been an "authentic" Black one:

> Along with millions of others, I watched the funeral on
> television. The proceedings were disgustingly discreet, boringly

low-keyed. . . . When the will is there, Baptists are known to rock a church; soul drips from the ceiling. I wanted there to be wailing and gnashing of teeth. . . . I longed to see the black and white notables flee the pews deeply moved as only black people singing spirituals can move listeners. Instead I watched a "white" funeral in which Mrs. Martin Luther King Jr. was as noble and steadfast as Mrs. John F. Kennedy had been. . . . The soul was gone; the justifiable anger was absent. There should have been anger; Sherman had far less provocation to burn the city than the black people of Atlanta in 1968, where visitors to the funeral were insulted by local whites.[152]

Even Ralph Abernathy said there was something "wrong with the scene. . . . This was Ebenezer Church, yet most of the people jamming the pews were White. So many politicians and celebrities had come for the funeral that there wasn't room for all of Martin's friends and relatives, the people who came to this very church to hear him preach on Sundays."[153]

There was both resentment and pride that so many White leaders came to mourn Dr. King—pride that a Black leader was being acknowledged by the White establishment, and resentment that it had taken King's death to earn it. Many Blacks remembered that when the four girls died at the Birmingham church in 1963, not a single White local, state, or federal official had attended the service. King had eulogized the girls and wired Governor George Wallace with the accusation that "the blood of four little children . . . is on your hands. Your irresponsible and misguided actions have created in Birmingham and Alabama the atmosphere that has induced continued violence and now murder."[154] Some Blacks also recalled that King's name had "inadvertently" been left off the invitation list for President Kennedy's funeral.

Although some scholars have argued that African Americans were "more accustomed to death" and embraced it as "a home going," the unsettled grief of April 1968 suggested otherwise.[155] This was not resignation at the loss of another leader. The mistaken perception that Blacks were more "death accepting" stemmed in part from White America's inability to imagine Black suffering.

Not theologized or eulogized by mainstream America was how the assassination demonstrated the impossibility of the peace for which King had longed. The violent grief of Blacks across the United States was testament to their suffering. But their violent grief after the assassination was dismissed as senseless. In contrast, the violence of White America's grief after 9/11 was elevated to *justice* (manifest in the "just war" on terror and the "justice" killing of Osama bin Laden).

Although many Black ministers tied King's death to Christ's sacrifice, the analogy did not have the same effect as when it was made after JFK's assassination. In 1968, the sacrifice of King could not be redeemed in either the Black or White imaginations. If Black neighborhoods had remained immobilized in private grief, ministers might have been able to use the rhetoric of "how not to die in vain" to redeem King's death. Instead, because of the riots, it was already clear that King had died in vain. His death was completely unnecessary and infuriating.

Jackie Kennedy commented to the press at King's funeral, "When will America learn that if she lives by the sword, she will perish by the sword?"[156] Her words were oddly incongruous. King had not lived by the sword and *still* he died by it. Her comment conflated all the violence—the violence of King's assassination, the violent rioting in the street, the violence that had killed her husband, and (unknown yet) the violence that was about to kill her brother-in-law. Violence was abstracted from its context and imagined as a thing in itself rather than as a symptom. Violence was epiphenomenal, and in this instance a manifestation of the racism that still clung to the United States and its civil rights movement.

As with the death of JFK, many ministers talked about corporate guilt. "Though felled by one demented assassin, all who contributed to American racism and blind prejudice which produced the atmosphere ripe for an act helped to pull the trigger."[157] Some of White America might have assumed responsibility for the assassination, but not the accompanying Black grief. Black grief belonged to Blacks. Even to the Whites who were sympathetic, the violence after King's death was interpreted as a disgrace rather than as symptomatic of racial injustice

With King's assassination, Black grief was unsuccessfully staged in burning cities across the United States. How King was mourned across the racial divide would be recalled again after the beating of Rodney King. The disenfranchised would again occupy the streets in outraged despair while White Americans looked on without recognition that this violence was the public grief of the unheard.

With the death of the prince of peace, many of the United States' Black ministers as well as many White preachers felt defeated. American politics had shown itself unresponsive to Christian principles and even to human goodness. The United States seemed to have confirmed that the country itself was the villain who had killed Kennedy, King, and within weeks, Robert Kennedy. Who knew what others would fall in the future? For the first time, both Black and White ministers wondered aloud whether God could abandon, or perhaps had already abandoned, the United States.

But unlike after Kennedy's assassination, when ministers seemed to double down and reinvest in theological principles, in the years following King's assassination they looked elsewhere for solace, for therapy, and for safety. The alliances they made with a therapeutic model and a redemptive state would become the relationships that would unravel and eventually undo most of the church's autonomy and influence.

The next time Protestant ministers would confront this complex juxtaposition of race and American identity, of violence and public grief, would be during the 1992 Los Angeles uprising and the Oklahoma City bombing. Then ministers would rehearse a well-known playbook—the death of White people is a national tragedy, whereas the death of Black ones is a parochial sadness. A violent White American is an aberration, but Black and Brown violence is always an exemplar of racial identity.

Ministers in the 1990s would not move much beyond the tropes of American social and political life. They no longer proclaimed an alternative from the pulpit. Rather, they confirmed what was, even accepting the status quo in what became the Church of the National Tragedy. American virtue was exemplified not by how citizens shaped the world to their ideals, but how they survived in a world in which those ideals were repeatedly thwarted. By the 1990s, what was believed to unite Americans was their ability to endure through tragedy.

Being an American, not a Christian, became the primary means of recovery. Ministers looked to the state to fill the void left by a world filled with violence and hatred. It was as if they had collectively agreed that God had exempted Himself from American political life and that Christian principles were largely effete relics of a bygone era. All ministers may not have believed that God had abandoned the United States, but the majority certainly no longer thought that He was the clergy's go-to for solving a crisis—therapy and state power were now those primary resources.

CHAPTER FOUR

The Church of the National Tragedy

The Los Angeles Uprisings and the Oklahoma City Bombing

In 1991 Los Angeles, there were two cities. The one where Latasha Harlins was a household name and the other where she was not. Thirteen days after the beating of Rodney King by Los Angeles police officers, fifteen-year-old African American teenager Latasha Harlins walked into a grocery. She grabbed a $1.79 bottle of orange juice, put it into her backpack, and approached the counter with $2 in her hand. The Korean American store owner, Soon Ja Du, suspecting Harlins of shoplifting, grabbed Latasha's sweater. A scuffle between them ensued; Harlins flung the orange juice back at the counter and turned to leave. Du picked up her .38-caliber handgun and shot Harlins in the back of the head, killing her instantly.

A grainy security camera video became the most prominent piece of evidence in the trial six months later. A jury convicted Soon Ja Du of voluntary manslaughter, which held a penalty of up to sixteen years in jail. But a White superior court judge, Joyce Karlin, overruled that judgment and sentenced Du to a ten-year suspended prison term with no jail time, five years of probation, and 400 hours of community service. She also issued a $500 fine. Latasha's aunt, Denise Harlins, recalled: "When I heard the sentence, I screamed, fell to my knees and cried. I just couldn't believe it, I must have died and went to hell."[1]

The death of Harlins was not national news, although her parents and relatives struggled to make her death meaningful to the media. They did not fully succeed, until the White jury in Simi Valley acquitted the police officers of the beating of Rodney King. Then, when South Los Angeles erupted in flames and violence a year later, the name of Latasha Harlins was on the lips of many rioters. "This is for Latasha," claimed a Latinx looter encircled by man-made coronas of torched buildings on the first night of the uprising.[2] The story of Latasha Harlins is a story not only of racial injustice (although it is most certainly that); it is also the story of the ramifications of losses that go unmourned, of displaced grief becoming vengeance, and of racial anguish translated by corporate media into a spectacle of criminality.

In the weeks after the Rodney King verdict and the ensuing violence, American Protestant ministers did not do much to help the nation mourn, to understand the city's grief, or to deconstruct the spectacle of racial violence. At the time, journalist Terry Mattingly was teaching a seminar on "Christian Talk and the Media" at Denver Seminary and he asked his students to find out what pastors had preached about on Sunday (a few days after the riots) and what biblical texts they had used. He also did something very intentional; he asked his White students (about half the class) to go to Black churches in Denver and his Black students (the other half) to go to White churches.[3] The Black students found only one pastor who focused his sermon on the Los Angeles riots, although most did pray for those touched by violence. The White students found that every single Black pastor they called in urban Denver had preached about the riots, "If I remember correctly, every single one of the sermons included references or readings from one or more of the Old Testament prophets."[4]

The primary focus of these sermons was on conceptions of sin—not only the sin of racism but those of fear and hatred: "There is enough sin here to cover us all. Everyone needs to repent and seek justice and reconciliation. Without God, this will be impossible."[5] The ministers, too, were divided among themselves between those who mourned the fifty-three-plus Latasha Harlins who had died in Los Angeles and those who did not recall a single name. Those who did not explicate the racial violence focused on "runaway individualism"[6] and named the Los Angeles violence as part of the nation's spiritual crisis, "which starts with the individual and his relationship with God."[7] Some Black ministers, on the other hand, gave sermons that detailed how racism—the racism of the beating of Rodney King, the racism that prompted the shooting of Latasha Harlins, and the racism that narrated the rage after the Simi Valley verdict as criminality—was the most significant sin.

Within an hour of the not guilty verdict, African American Los Angeles mayor Bill Bradley delivered a message from the pulpit of the First African Methodist Episcopal Church, the oldest Black church in Los Angeles. Over three thousand people had gathered in the sanctuary in anticipation of the reading of the televised verdict. By the time Bradley arrived, there were already angry crowds gathering within blocks of the church. Bradley began: "The jury's verdict will never outlive the images of the savage beating seared forever into our minds and souls. . . . I understand full well that we must give voice to our great frustration. I know that we must express our profound outrage. But we must do so in ways that bring honor to ourselves and our communities."[8] His requests for honorable conduct, of course, went unheeded. In fact, some contemporary commentators thought he had inadvertently fueled the rage by the mere acknowledgment of the "savage beating,"[9] as if the video of the beating had not already confirmed that for most viewers. Minutes after Bradley left the church, the congregants gathered around the church television and watched as Reginald Denny, a White truck driver, and Fidel Lopez, a Hispanic construction worker, were dragged from their vehicles and beaten.

On May 1, 1992, President George H. W. Bush addressed the nation. "What we saw last night and the night before in Los Angeles is not about civil rights. It's not about the great cause of equality that all Americans must uphold. It's not a message of protest. It's been the brutality of a mob, pure and simple. And let me assure you: I will use whatever force is necessary to restore order."[10]

Anger at injustice, Bush maintained, must be managed, processed, properly directed, and sanitized through the legal system. There was a profound irony that Bush demanded that "the civil rights community" must trust the legal process. Had he overlooked the reality that the violence was not primarily because of the police brutality but because the legal process did *not* bring justice? Los Angeles did not go up in flames after the residents watched the videotaped beating of Rodney King. The Los Angeles uprising started after the Simi Valley jury acquitted the police officers of any wrongdoing.

Yet President Bush resolutely continued, "The wanton destruction of life and property is not a legitimate expression of outrage with injustice. It is itself injustice." In this simple rhetorical swipe, Bush conflated the beating of Rodney King, the acquittal of the White officers, and the response of the multiracial community in Los Angeles. He did not offer any possible explanation for why African Americans, Latinxs, or Korean Americans might be legitimately incensed. The president did not acknowledge the reasons for their anger or their right to be angry.

This was a repetition of the occupation of Memphis during the mourning of Dr. King, as well as a preview of the fortification of American cities during protests after the police shootings of numerous unarmed Black men in the summers of 2014 in Ferguson and in 2015 in Baltimore. The rejoinder to Black grief has historically been militarization. The uprising in Los Angeles in 1992 was not a protest, not a rebellion, not a cry for justice from the perspective of White authority. For Whites, it could be nothing other than the destruction of law and order—*a riot.*

The mayhem to which President Bush referred had begun in Los Angeles in response to the acquittal of four White police officers. They had been charged in March 1991 with the beating of an African American man, Rodney King. The traffic stop concluded after a high-speed chase that began on I-210 and ended with King pulled from his vehicle near Lakeview Terrace. An amateur videographer had captured the entire episode on his camcorder from a nearby apartment building. It showed King being struck fifty-six times and kicked an additional six times. Because the chase had spread over nearly eight miles, there were over a dozen Los Angeles police officers by the time King had stopped; these dozen were bystanders who did not intervene.

The official Los Angeles Police Department (LAPD) report described a regular arrest, with the victim suffering only "light" injuries, including a minor abrasion to his face and a split lip. In reality, Rodney King had a broken ankle, a fractured cheekbone, and eleven broken bones at the base of his skull, facial nerve damage, and a severe concussion. The force of the blows had even knocked fillings from his teeth.[11]

Within hours of the acquittal by the predominantly White jury in Simi Valley, an upper-middle-class White suburb about thirty miles northeast of the city, downtown Los Angeles was in upheaval.[12] Southern Los Angeles was engulfed in flames, young men and women smashed storefronts and stole goods, and the LAPD was nowhere to be seen. The police had retreated under command orders because they were "outnumbered and unprepared to handle the situations."[13] Chief of Police Daryl Gates was reportedly at a fundraiser outside the city and later claimed, "It was awful hard to break away."[14] The police force waited, sequestered, for further instructions while the city burned and the violence accelerated.

THE RODNEY KING video was the inauguration of what would become over the next several decades civilian surveillance of the police. It showed what was being done to Black bodies, with the aim of halting that brutality. Unlike the lynching photos of the past that were intended to instill racial terror, these videos were attempts to constrain racist power. The Rodney King video, taken by an Argentinian immigrant, George Holliday, was shared, not as a celebration, but to hold LAPD accountable. George Holliday and his wife had been on their balcony when they saw the police start to beat King. Holliday ran into his apartment to retrieve his new camcorder, and filmed the brutality. Two days later, he called the LAPD to tell them about the video and what he had witnessed. No one at the police station was interested, so he went to television station KTLA. The station aired the video. Within hours, it was a national phenomenon.

The national outrage was like that sparked by the photographs taken of Emmett Till in 1955, with his stoic mother gazing at his ravaged corpse. Mamie Till had insisted on the display of her son's mangled body. "Let the world see what has happened, because there is no way I could describe this. And I needed somebody to help me tell what it was like."[15]

Weeks after the Till funeral, two Black publications, *Jet* and the *Chicago Defender*, published David Jackson's now-iconic photographs. The photos sought to make undeniable what was being done to Black men in the United States. The image of Emmett Till's body was not meant to terrify Black viewers but to urge all Americans to support the developing civil rights movement.[16] Yet the photographs also stirred racial fear with their powerful reminder of what could be done to a Black teenager for the simple accusation of flirting with a White woman.

Nearly forty years later, the security camera footage of Latasha Harlins confirmed how disposable Black children still were in 1991. A mere supposition of guilt was condoned by her murderer as sufficient justification for her execution.[17]

Within weeks of one another, the Rodney King and Latasha Harlins videos exposed that many Americans still perceived Black bodies as necessarily menacing and violent. Even with her back turned, Harlins was envisaged as life-threatening to the armed woman behind the counter. Similarly, the attorney for the prosecution in the Rodney King case, Terry White, noted in his summation: "And according to Sgt. Duke, everything Mr. King did was aggressive. His leg is bent. His foot is not flat. This is aggressive. What could this man do not to be aggressive? Did he have to be unconscious?"[18] It was a rhetorical question. Terry White knew the answer—the only way for a Black man *not* to be perceived as aggressive was for him not to exist. In fact, in Sergeant Stacey Koon's defense, his attorney asserted, "There's only one person who's in charge of this situation and that's Rodney Glen King."[19]

Because of the enduring framing of Black masculinity especially as a toxic combination of bestiality, hypervirility, drug abuse, and superhuman strength, the police officers claimed victimhood. Poet Elizabeth Alexander called this reversal "the myth of white male victimization."[20] Koon's defense attorney, Michael Stone, sought to exonerate his clients this way: "These officers, these defendants do not get paid to lose street fights. They don't get paid to roll around in the dirt with the likes of Rodney Glen King."[21]

With the announcement of the LAPD officers' acquittal, a third video was created by the United States' mainstream media. This was the montage of photojournalist videos taken of the rebellion that roared through South Central Los Angeles for three days and was endlessly aired on televisions across the United States. This was the first modern crisis as spectacle. For days the major television networks, including CNN, showed the riots and fires unfolding in real time. CNN had just established itself as the twenty-four-hour news channel through its coverage of the Gulf War. Journalist John Kiesewetter of the *Cincinnati Enquirer* noted at the time: "Before CNN, events were reported in two cycles, for morning and evening newspapers and newscasts. Now news knows no cycle."[22]

Newscasters interviewed people on the streets and occasionally city leadership. Unlike in other crises before or since, there was no orchestrated management of the response to the verdict—no Jacqueline Kennedy managing the overview, no Coretta Scott King arranging the procession, no first responders bringing people to safety. Instead, there was the endless repetition of recorded violence and the ad hoc gloss of overwhelmed and weary journalists. Media sociologist John T. Caldwell called this production "crisis televisuality."[23] The media apparatus itself was exposed as it struggled to create a coherent narrative while the violence unfurled across the city.

The crisis of the Los Angeles violence, like the crises of Pearl Harbor and the assassinations of President Kennedy and Dr. Martin Luther King Jr., challenged some of the United States' self-understanding while also leaving others unexamined. For example, for many Americans, especially White Americans who trusted that justice would be served by the trial and jury process, the acquittal of the police officers initially shook that confidence. Although 65 percent disapproved of the verdict, the majority of Whites blamed the jury members, not the system.[24] Ninety-six percent of African Americans disagreed with the verdict, but they criticized the judicial system rather than the jurors.[25] The verdict challenged a foundational element of American society for White Americans—the legitimacy and fairness of the judicial system.

But the violence in Los Angeles also confirmed a racist paradigm that had been operative throughout much of American history—the presumption that minorities were always a de facto risk to the peace and stability of any community. It was the presumption that propelled the internment of Japanese Americans after Pearl Harbor, that criminalized the mourning of Dr. Martin Luther King, and that was confirmed for some by the violent desperation manifest in 1992 Los Angeles.

The minority response to the Rodney King injustice (in all its features) challenged another American paradigm—the majority belief that expressions of righteous grievance should adhere to the processes provided by law and order. The Los Angeles rebellion showcased the regular and everyday racial cleavages of which most Americans were blissfully unaware. Dr. Martin Luther King Jr. had reminded Americans in 1966 that riots were a form of political communication; they were the angry articulations of the disenfranchised. A Los Angeles minister, Reverend Cecil Murray, repeated the reminder by paraphrasing a line from a Langston Hughes poem: "What happens to a dream denied? It explodes." But the majority of Americans did not understand the violence in Los Angeles that way. Most reconstructed the crisis—the judgment, the decision—as inexplicable mayhem initiated by the Black community, done by and to itself.

In his book *Screening the Los Angeles Riots,* Darnell Hunt calculated that there were fourteen primary assumptions presented in media coverage of the Los Angeles rebellion. First and most obviously, journalists named the episode a "riot." No definition was given for what that meant or what alternative interpretations might be available.[26] In Hunt's survey of multiple race groups, for example, he discovered that 67.55 percent of Black respondents viewed the events "as mainly protest," whereas the majority of White, Hispanic, and Asian respondents viewed the events "as mainly looting and street crime."[27]

The second and third assumptions made by the mainstream media in Los Angeles was that Black ministers were important representatives, indeed leaders of the Black community (including those protesting), and thus the ministers must be consulted, with the expectation that they would urge peace.[28] A gathering at the AME Church was called a "rally," and newscasters described it this way: "This place, if you recall, was packed. There were three thousand people inside the building. I'm told just as many outside. The main message was, 'stay calm, remain calm. Let's talk out our frustrations at the polling place.'"[29]

Hunt noted that this was a racial stereotype compounded by the third assumption, which focused on congregations' prayers. Prayer was assumed by the mainstream media to be an appropriate strategy for the crisis in the Black community—for that was where the media located the problem. This was a Black problem, not an American one. Just as they did after King's assassination, many reflected on the loss to the Black community rather than to the United States.

During the Los Angeles uprising, Reverend Carl Washington of Peace in the Streets was highlighted multiple times by the media for his recommendation, "Again, ah, there really is nothing left to say, but, ah, it's our job as ministers to go down on our knees in prayer and ask for a higher resource to intervene in this matter." Or again, from multiple local as well as national newscasters, "We want to go back to the AME church where people are raising their voice in protest, in song, and in prayer."[30]

There were two limitations to these assumptions. First, it was not necessarily true that religious leaders had any special authority with the protesters. The belief that they might be able to quell the crowd had no empirical or historical confirmation. In fact, Reverend Washington tried to distance his own congregational community from those protesting: "We are dismayed, but we believe this is from the so-called 'troublemakers' in the community. Those who we have come in contact with have maintained peace."[31] Second, the recommendation for prayer as an approach to the crisis implied that it was not a political crisis but a moral one. The media seemed to suggest that only divine intervention could rectify the turmoil.

By 1992, this had become the mainstream media's anodyne conception of the civil rights movement. The movement was recalled in the White imagination as Black folks arm in arm at leisurely marches, singing "We Shall Overcome." The protests, the sit-ins, and the arrests, as well as the demands made in person to the presidents of the period, were occluded. Reverend Martin Luther King Jr. was canonized while his insights and ideas were overlooked, especially those that might have been germane to the Los Angeles violence: "And I must say tonight that *a riot is the language of the unheard.* And what is it America has failed to hear? . . . It has failed to hear that the promises of freedom and justice have not been met. And it has failed to hear that large segments of white society are more concerned about tranquility and the status quo than about justice and humanity."[32] The mainstream media had rendered invisible not only political history but the very contours of the structural racism and generational poverty that had ignited the rebellion.

Perhaps one of the most disturbing results revealed from Hunt's work interviewing and surveying multiple groups was the way those groups identified with the people they saw on television as "we" or distanced themselves from those represented as "they." White groups tended to identify with the study group, using phrases like "what we just watched." Blacks tended to identify with those they saw: "We cared about Rodney King, man, because that was one of our brothers."[33] In contrast, Black groups tended to identify the media and the police as "they," as the outsiders.[34]

Throughout American crises, who counts as "we" and who is excluded as "they" has determined for whom (or what) Americans mourn. Americans mourned the dead at Pearl Harbor but not those interned afterward. They mourned the death of President Kennedy as a tragedy for all Americans but lamented the assassination of Dr. Martin Luther King as a loss mostly for the Black community. And again, during the Los Angeles rebellion White viewers watched "them" protest but they did not mourn either Latasha Harlins or the fifty-three other people who died over the course of the three days of protest.[35] The protesters in Los Angeles were not "us." They were not Americans with whom the majority of viewers identified or even recognized. The protesters were those "others" who still in 1992 were not "us," and of course, this negation confirmed the necessity and validity of the protest.

When the story of the Los Angeles protest was told as a tale of Black versus White conflict, the Korean American as well as the Latinx community was largely erased. Yet in some ways, they were both at the center of the conflict. A RAND Corporation computer analysis of charges filed in local courts in the peak days of the riots found that 51 percent of the defendants were Latinx and 36 percent were Black.[36] And of those arrests, the majority were reported to Immigration and Naturalization Service (INS) offices and deported, primarily back to Mexico. So Latinxs were both excluded from the hegemonic account of the events despite their place in it and were literally removed (deported) from the story of Los Angeles, despite the origins of the city's very name.[37]

Over three thousand Korean-owned businesses were damaged or destroyed, resulting in over \$350 million of repairs. Elaine Kim, professor of Asian American literature at the time, called the Los Angeles riots "an Asian American legacy of violent baptisms," and said, "The riots are to Korean Americans what internment was for Japanese Americans."[38] Another Korean American called the riots "our rite of passage into American society."[39] Like other immigrant groups, Koreans in Los Angeles were torn between their commitment to their homeland

and their desire to establish more mainstream American lives and identities.

In 1992, Korean Americans traditionally sent significant amounts of money back to Korea for family and friends, partially as a helpful contribution and partially as a confirmation of their American success. Korean American radio and newspapers reported on Korean news as much as, if not more than, California or American news. But by their own account, some Korean Americans enjoyed being "White" in the United States: "We have been living thinking that we come right after whites— clean, gentle and so on—so we've discriminated against other races."[40]

That assumption was shattered during the uprisings. The police did not show up to protect Korean Americans and many felt that media reports on the looting were implicitly urging criminals to come to Koreatown where there was no police presence. "The media showed the looters how easy it was to loot, calling out the looters, it was a real propellant, as if to say—don't worry there are no police here."[41] Some Korean Americans even felt that perhaps Police Chief Daryl Gates had sanctioned the looting to permit the Black community to let off steam.

It was a formidable dilemma. Korean Americans were angry not only that their property and dreams had been destroyed but that they had been misled by their belief that they were included in the American dream. Many described how the riots had led them to realize that the United States really didn't care about minorities and that American citizenship for minorities was worthless.[42]

When Korean Americans sought to protect themselves, they were featured in the media as aggressive and armed foreigners, not as those who had resorted to weapons as a last resort. "They depict us like crazy people holding guns, but they have no ideas of how many Koreans died doing business—people struggling to make it, people who had finally made it, students from Korea about to return, young people, old people."[43] The Korean sense of betrayal was compounded by the looting of Korean businesses by Latinxs. For decades, Koreans and Latinxs had worked together, not only with Latinxs serving in Korean business but in many instances assuming managerial or leadership positions. So it was particularly difficult when Korean business owners saw that nearly half of the looters of their businesses were Latinxs.[44] This complicated matrix had made some wonder if the Los Angeles violence was more a "poor

riot" than a "race riot." Perhaps what the violence represented was not
racial tension but economic despair. Or, perhaps more accurately, what
had kindled the violence was both—a racial tension born out of economic despair and cultural misunderstandings. A juxtaposition between a "model minority" still degraded by White power in opposition
to a Black minority furious that access to upward mobility was forever
deferred.

The way forward was both best described and best enacted by both
the African American and Korean churches in Los Angeles. First, they
did two rather simple things—the African American (and Latinx)
churches urged their congregants to return any known stolen goods.
From the pulpit, ministers encouraged their congregants to "clear their
conscience. . . . We all know it is not right to rob, to be a thief. It is not
possible to act as if nothing has happened. The people who robbed have
an obligation to return these things."[45] Although this recommendation
had limited success, it was more than a simple candlelight vigil. According to some newspaper accounts, both substantial amounts of fur-
niture and clothing were returned. And poignantly, the Los Angeles Times
reported that a child had heeded the request and returned a candy bar.[46]

Many Korean churches distributed lists of losses that Korean businesses had suffered so that members of the congregations could offer
money and manpower to help these businesses get back on their feet.
Structurally, African American churches proposed doing the most. Two
hundred pastors planned to start a venture capital fund across racial and
denominational lines. Other Black churches tried to nurture Black-
owned enterprises. "Suddenly, pastors were talking assets and revenue
and credit limits, sometimes with as much authority as they discuss the
gospel."[47] First AME used money donated by the Walt Disney Company to try to finance "micro loans."[48] Reverend Edgar Boyd, pastor of
the Bethel AME Church on Western Avenue, noted that clergy had
begun to strategize a plan of economic survival before the Rodney King
verdict, but they hadn't expected it to be necessary so quickly. He said:
"We're not just fighting the monster of the immediate needs. We are
fighting a great social and economic monster of racism and injustice that
is unseen."[49] From descriptions and first-hand accounts at the time, there
was an energy and sense of purpose expressed by many church leaders.

Rev. James T. Thompson, associate minister of the Alpha and Omega Baptist Church, exclaimed, "This is what church work is all about. This is what has been missing."[50]

Those initial efforts, however, proved insufficient. A year later, over 70 percent of Korean businesses remained shuttered. Two years later, only half of the federally promised $1.2 billion in relief had been dispensed.[51]

In the autumn of 1992, there were three presidential debates. Neither the Rodney King beating nor its aftermath was mentioned.[52] Within six months, the event had already begun to recede from the United States' public political memory. While there were multiple explanations for this erasure, the one most germane to this chapter is that White Americans blamed the violence on the Simi Valley jury and those jurors' individual racism. Consider this assessment in the *New York Times* on May 4, 1992: "The very lay out of the streets in this well-to-do suburb speaks volumes about how unwelcome strangers are here, about how much safety means to the 100,000 people, most of them white, who have crossed the mountain range and then the Ventura County line to escape the chaos and discomfort of the people."[53] There were no structural or systematic issues that the verdict revealed. Simi Valley might be a racist place, but the United States was not.

Black Americans understood the protests differently and faulted the judiciary system itself:

> This not guilty verdict was sown and harvested in White
> racism, a racism imbibed as holy water by its White creators
> and defenders, an aspergillum used to sprinkle and anoint the
> faithful in holy communion, a racism apotheosized in pulpits,
> glorified in editorial pages, magnified in movies and television,
> sanctified in school textbooks.[54]

From this telling, the problem was not the individual members of that Simi Valley jury. Rather, it was the challenge that all Black men and women faced when attempting to achieve racial justice in a system that defeated them before they had begun. It was a painful reality that would be confronted again two decades later with the killing of Trayvon Martin and the rise of the Black Lives Matter movement.

Theologizing the Violence:
Sin and the Los Angeles Riots

The first Sunday after the verdict was May 3, 1992. That day, Mayor Bradley assured the public that the crisis was mostly over and that he was prepared to lift the curfew.[55] As ministers across the country stepped into their pulpits, many turned to the theology of sin to give a perspective on what they had seen that week in their communities. Using the concept of sin to address political and social problems has long been a rhetorical technique to circumvent political power and to strive to restore the canon of Christianity to the center of American life.

Throughout American history, conceptions of sin have been vital to ministers who were trying to explain various nefarious political developments. Much of the nineteenth-century abolitionist movement centered on conceptions of sin and the stain it placed on American history.[56] The narrative of sin emerged again during the Cold War as part of the fight against "godless communists." It was apparent, too, in parts of the sexual revolution, especially regarding those elements that could be tied to women's equality and the feared destruction of the American family. "The feminist agenda is not about equal rights for women. It is a socialist, antifamily political movement that encourages women to leave their husbands, kill their children, practice witchcraft, destroy capitalism and become lesbians."[57]

During the 1990s, the Moral Majority was losing its footing, but televangelist and Southern Baptist minister Pat Robertson's Christian Coalition was beginning to lead the narrative charge regarding American moral dissolution. By decade's end, *Fortune* magazine would name the Christian Coalition as one of the twenty-five most powerful organizations in American politics.[58] And according to the Christian Coalition, American problems were the result of moral depravity. The use of drugs, the decline of the American family, and the ascendancy of crime were all attributed to the loss of traditional moral values and practices. Patrick Buchanan, an influential conservative politician at the time promoting the United States as a Christian nation, sounded the most apocalyptic: "What we saw in Los Angeles was evil exultant and triumphant."[59]

In distinction to the sinfulness some ministers ascribed to the assassination of President John F. Kennedy in 1963, this 1992 sinfulness was individual, not institutional. It was "a wretchedness of the human heart," not a structural failing of the church. After the assassination of Kennedy, some clergy lamented the negligence of the church to be fully engaged in social and political life. In this view, the church had failed to be fully the church. It was not the depraved human condition that had failed to safeguard the US president; it was the institutional church that had carelessly accepted its sequester into the private sphere.

In contrast, the sermons of 1992 focused on individual culpability. According to these ministers, Christian Americans had failed to live as they should. It was an ugly, brutal world in which Christians struggled to make their way: "There is none righteous, not even one. There is none who understands. There is none who seeks for God. All have turned aside. . . . Their throat is an open grave" (Rom. 3:10–17).[60]

Among the most prominent of these sermons was the one given by Reverend John MacArthur, "The Los Angeles Riots: A Biblical Perspective," on May 3, 1992. MacArthur was the pastor of the Grace Community Church in Sun Valley, California, a community about twenty minutes outside of Los Angeles. MacArthur was also a well-known radio personality on the Christian program *Grace to You,* which according to their website aired over a thousand times daily throughout the English-speaking world.[61]

Reverend MacArthur proclaimed in his lengthy sermon:

> What I want to talk about today is the root of all of these problems and it's a very simple word with three letters called sin. . . . The problem in our city is not lack of jobs. The problem in our city is not lack of opportunity or lack of education. The problem in our city is not too much possessions, materialism. Those are only symptoms of a problem. The problem in our city is the problem of the wretchedness of the human heart. And nobody escapes that. It knows no race. It knows no color. It knows no location. It is pervasive. . . . It pollutes every man and every woman and every part of life.[62]

Like President Bush, the minister named the Los Angeles uprising as being without politics. It was a manifestation of the human condition itself. The anger and violence did not have a particular genesis or even a specific American history; they were expressions of the long course of human disorders. These disorders affected all people, not just Blacks or Koreans, not just city dwellers or the poor. In this way, MacArthur's sermon was inclusive. "And nobody is exempt. Everybody has this polluting stream. It knows no racial bounds."[63] Yet while it ostensibly strove to include "everyone," what it actually did was annul the experience of Blacks, the poor, and the urban. In the sermon, the individual is the analytic category that illuminates reality; thus MacArthur neglects structural categories such as race, gender, class, and their role in contemporary violence. Although Christianity puts the poor, the outcasts, and the pariah at the center of its message, the focus on the individual preached in MacArthur's sermon leaves unexplicated how individuals might become part of those structural castes.

What prompted the crisis was not mentioned in MacArthur's sermon—quite the opposite. When he enumerated his "twelve causes of sin," he asserted, "Anger is a sin. Nobody has a right to be angry. A policeman doesn't have the right to be angry. A criminal doesn't have a right to be angry. Nobody has a right to be angry. The only thing you ever have a right to be angry over is when God is dishonored, holy wrath." There was no possibility in this sermon of righteous anger for justice denied. Justice was not a category in the sermon. When MacArthur turned to the ninth reason for sin, "the loss of respect for authority," he argued that there had been "a concerted effort to destroy the confidence of this population in the people responsible to maintain law and order and now you see the result of it. . . . That is a deadly sin." Unnamed was *the cause* of the loss of confidence. Rodney King was not named. The decision of the Simi Valley jury was not mentioned. Nor was Reginald Denny recalled. In their place, MacArthur told a personal story about the Los Angeles Police Department: "I remember when I was doing a training session for the LAPD one time and had all of their officers and all of their leaders in there and I took them through Romans 13 and I said, 'Do you guys know that you are in authority from God?'" As if that were not sufficient affirmation, MacArthur added, "Therefore he who resists authority has opposed the ordinance of God. These people are not just opposing the police; they're opposing God, almighty holy God."[64]

This was Los Angeles in 1992. And this minister with a national audience was equating police authority with God's authority. The police were alleged to be doing God's work. It is a vast difference from the sermons of 1941, 1963, and even 1968. In 1941, ministers did not believe that any political events, much less crises, were related to God's plan; secular events were exempt from God's interest and highlighted merely the machinations and folly of men.

In 1963, political tragedy was an occasion for ministers to revisit the efficacy of the church. President Kennedy's assassination revealed little about God but much about the failure of the institutional church. The political tragedy was an opportunity for the church to engage more robustly in a kind of public theology.

And in 1968, after the assassination of Dr. King, there was the beginning of a theological reckoning with what God was doing in the world, especially in the United States. Some ministers, Black and White alike, mourned the absence and indeed the potential withdrawal of God from American political life. With King's death, the loss of the prophetic in American politics seemed complete. This was, perhaps, the crescendo of the institutional Christian retreat from politics.

But by 1992, there had been a complex revival in God's (if not the church's) role in American politics. With the rise of evangelicals in political life, especially around social issues, God was imagined to be invested in political issues and their outcomes. God was apparently choosing sides. According to many ministers, God depended on secular processes to fulfill His mandates.

Some ministerial renditions claimed God had empowered the LAPD to enforce His will. It was a tragic decline for the Almighty, though certainly a promotion for the police officers. Even Reverend MacArthur attested to the elevation: "And afterwards there was one old big ole burly crusty sargent [*sic*] with a cigar in his mouth and he came to me and he said, 'Man . . . you said I was appointed by God. . . . Could you tell me that verse again, I've got to use that.' And I said, 'Well you have a right to use that. God is sovereign and God has set these people in authority.'"[65]

In some profound and perhaps uncomfortable ways, MacArthur's sermon illuminated a pivot in the relationship between church and state authority. Civil society was now largely evacuated of the institutional authority and presence of the church.[66] In its place, ministers had ordained as their proxies the servants of the state. In those places where "law and order" were still functional, some of the Protestant ministry attempted to deputize the state (in this instance, law enforcement) with the church's mission. Recognizing that the church could no longer do the work itself, because it no longer had the resources or the credibility to do so, these ministers made an odd and occasionally alarming turn toward appropriating the apparatus of the state for their own purposes. Embedded in this reliance on the state to do God's work was an assumption that the state was responsible for promoting and protecting the common good.

As political theologian William Cavanaugh has argued in "Killing for the Telephone Company," contemporary Christian reliance on the state rests on a series of assumptions: (1) the state is natural and primordial, (2) society gives rise to the state and not vice versa, and (3) the state is one limited part of society.[67] All of these assumptions, according to Cavanaugh, are erroneous in whole or in part, beginning with the fact that the state is not natural; it is a historical construct that the Christian church overlooks at its peril.

The second assumption—that society gives rise to the state rather than vice versa—proceeds as if there were still an autonomous space exempt from the state and its power. The institutional church still operates as if society were self-determining. As French philosopher and social historian Michel Foucault cogently detailed in *The Birth of Biopolitics,* modern power circulates, creates society, and constructs social identities in such a way that there remains no place, no sphere, no element of American culture in which individuals or the church can be fully self-governing, beyond the reach of biopolitics.[68]

The power of the state now generates society, rather than the reverse. From the perspective of the contemporary institutional church, the state and its power reaches everywhere—from military chaplains who wear uniforms to the political economy, invested by the ministry itself with a "prosperity" gospel.[69] What belongs to Caesar has grown exponentially larger than what seemingly belongs to God. When the church relinquished its commitment to "stand against the world" post–World War II, it also largely forfeited its prophetic power. Since the assassination of Dr. King, the prophetic has been mostly mute. Instead, the church has sought to ingratiate itself to the state, to use the mechanisms and processes of the state to augment its own power and authority.

Religious liberalism developed in the place of church authority with a focus on individuals and their singular acts of goodness and sin. The church no longer considered itself (nor was considered, with rare exceptions) as an organization of power or a place coherently committed to the power of organization. To gain power, the church aligned with the state, demanding acknowledgment from institutions it did not control—whether the Supreme Court or the US Congress. The work of the church was reduced to getting out the vote. By the time ministers were preaching about the Newtown tragedy (2012) and Black Lives Matter (2014), the state—in the person of President Barack Obama—would be more adept at mourning and theologizing those deaths than the ministers themselves. It is against this backdrop that the 1992 Los Angeles Protestant clergy must be understood.

When there were news accounts of the role of religious leaders (and these were quite limited), especially as told by the mainstream media, they were edited to fit the narrative that already have become dominant: "good Black religious leaders" prayed, "bad Black people" were those in the streets protesting, and White people who got caught up in the mayhem were innocent victims. One manifestation of this was the video (and follow-up) of Reverend Bennie Newtown rescuing Guatemalan immigrant Fidel Lopez from a beating that nearly took his life. Within minutes of the Reginald Denny beating, rioters pulled Lopez from his delivery truck. They stole $2,000 from him and beat in his forehead with a stereo box. As Lopez lay unconscious, the looters doused him with gasoline and spray-painted his chest, torso, and genitals black.

Reverend Newtown was at home watching television when he saw the live video feed. Recognizing the street, he raced to the scene, Bible in hand, and laid his own body over Lopez, screaming, "If you are going to kill him, you are going to have to kill me, too!" This was sufficient to turn the attackers away. Newtown called for an ambulance, which refused to come to the "dangerous" neighborhood. So Reverend Newtown carried Lopez back to his truck and drove the near-dead victim to the hospital himself, thus saving Lopez's life.[70]

What was revealing was what happened afterward—the episode was mostly forgotten. The story of Reginald Denny became iconic, whereas the Lopez beating and rescue faded from view. The story is not recalled in most scholarship on the Los Angeles uprising. And there was only one article about Fidel Lopez in the *Los Angeles Times,* in which the journalist searched for him a decade after the attack.

Perhaps the reason for the occlusion is obvious. The Lopez story did not "fit" the mainstream media's narrative of the event or the mainstream political version of the Los Angeles "riots." Lopez was Latinx and an immigrant. Reginald Denny was White. Although both men were "rescued" by African American men, the broken body of the White man was perceived as more alarming and heartbreaking than that of the Brown immigrant.

Also, the man who saved Lopez, Reverend Newtown, was himself a former felon. His ministry, Light of Love Outreach, worked with convicts to help them rehabilitate. Newtown had been in and out of prison for dealing drugs, pimping, and armed robbery. He was not the ideal savior for racial reconciliation. What was expedient for the story was a good Black man who rescued a good White man, thus demonstrating that "good Blacks" did not express rage but rescue and that White people were the victims of Black rage, not embedded in its history.

The African Americans who rescued Reginald Denny were glorified by President Bush in his address to the nation, since "they reached across the barriers of color and put their own safety at risk to help others."[71] Like Reverend Newtown, each had been watching television upon deciding that something had to be done. As Lei Yuille left her apartment, one of her neighbors allegedly said to her: "The Rodney King beating was the white man's verdict. That guy in the semi was our verdict."[72] To Yuille, this did not resonate, and she left to try to help. The others, Bobby Green and Curtis Yarborough, said they were simply helping someone in need. According to Green, "Race did not even cross my mind."[73]

Green's attitude confirmed the American fantasy of a color-blind society. Even after the racialized beating and the acquittal of the White perpetrators, as well as the explosive violence of the Black, Latinx, and Korean communities, the majority White community still clung to their trust in a world where "race didn't even cross my mind." As the headlines proclaimed, "Saving One Man's Life Bolsters All Humanity." The rescue of a White body still had that kind of power—it could restore faith in all humanity.

The Reginald Denny rescue also re-created the well-worn taxonomy of "good Blacks" versus "bad Blacks." Those African Americans who rescued White people were "good," whereas those who protested against racism were "bad." Calibrations of virtue for the American Black community have always rested on its acknowledgment by White people, especially when Black people are grieving or expressing their anger at White racism. After the assassination of Dr. King, for example, only those Blacks who demonstrated "respectability" were recognized by White America as fulfilling Dr. King's dream and mourning him appropriately. Black rage and righteous indignation at injustice, on the other hand, had no place in the White master's virtue handbook, whether in 1963 or in 1992.

In 1992, many Americans believed that whatever anger one might have should be aimed at the individual members of the jury who acquitted the four police officers who had beaten Rodney King. They did not understand how the acquittal itself confirmed the structural racism under which Rodney King and many others already suffered. The verdict was not a "one-off mistake" but rather part of an enduring pattern. White America wanted a "law and order" resolution when it was law and order itself—both the police and the jury system—that was at the center of the violence. As one minister noted in his Sunday sermon, the violence did not begin with the riots, "let us see how the seeds of injustice lie within us and the dominant culture from which we benefit."[74] And "the barbarism, destruction and violence we have witnessed here this last week is but a tiny fraction of the barbarism, destruction and violence the United States government has wreaked upon the world."[75]

Not surprisingly, then, the rescue of Reginald Denny became the feel-good story of the calamity. It was the kind of story the mainstream media loved, one that reconciled and evaporated structural, political, and economic disparities. As Rodney King, whose own suffering seemed to be prompting more, asked hours into the protests: "I just want to say—you know—can we all get along? Can we, can we get along? Can we stop making it horrible for the older people and the kids?"[76] It was an aspirational request that much of White America embraced. King was celebrated by the mainstream media. And for King, personally, he marks that moment as the beginning of his own redemption.[77] He moved from being a brutally beaten and humiliated Black man to an agent asking for peace in his community. But for many in the Black community, it was too soon to ask for reconciliation, for "getting along" with its implied amnesia of recent and past injustice. King's request also implied an equivalence between Blacks and Whites in Los Angeles as well as a shared culpability that few accepted.[78] It also made it seem that if the victim had assumed a forgiving posture, the rest of the Black community should do so as well. And forty-eight hours into the protest, most Black Americans were not ready for interracial reunion.

When American violence is Black and collective (i.e., Los Angeles, Ferguson), the sense of a shared sacrifice is lost. But violence against White Americans (i.e., the Oklahoma City bombing; September 11, 2001), in contrast, is often tied to sacrificial ideals. Dead White people are like soldiers in the American military, dying for the common good and for Americans' collective values. Soldiers die as Americans, not as members of a racial category. Dead Black citizens are not afforded this recognition. They are simply dead . . . and Black. Their mortality is not elevated to universal status. Latasha Harlins is a dead Black teenager; she is not elevated to the status of a dead American, representing all of us.

There is no permanent city memorial to the violent deaths in Los Angeles in 1992. There are only videos that rehearse with endless repetition what can still be done to Black bodies. For some viewers, rather than being a vehicle for grief, the videos simply confirm with photographic clarity the close alignment between Black bodies and criminality. Rodney King never became a hero in Americans' collective cultural imagination. He remained a victim whose sacrifice did not redeem the United States. Similarly, there were no calls to ensure that Latasha Harlins did not "die in vain." She was not celebrated as having been sacrificed to recall the United States to racial equity. The image of Rodney King was too embedded in the American narrative of Black bestiality and lawlessness to do that redemptive work. And Latasha was just another victim of incomprehensible tensions between belligerent Black teenagers and struggling, hardworking grocers.

The limits of Black sacrifice would be showcased again with the deaths of Trayvon Martin in 2012 and Michael Brown in 2014. Both Black teenagers were linked too closely with racist conceptions of Black criminality to be recognized as sacrificial heroes or to be acknowledged as part of the jeremiad to reclaim the United States for racial justice. When President Obama identified himself with Trayvon Martin in an early press conference, there was an immediate backlash. The identification made President Obama Black, and as president of the United States, he could not be Black—he had to be beyond color. He had to agree with Bobby Green: "Race didn't even cross my mind."

The Los Angeles African American Clergy and the White Imagination

On the first night of the Los Angeles uprising, Reverend Cecil "Chip" Murray, the leader of the First African Methodist Church in Los Angeles, was praying for peace with members of his congregation. From the church, he could see flames crawling up the sides of a building mere blocks away. He hastily called the fire department, but they refused to come unless they were guaranteed protection. So Reverend Murray and his congregants did just that. Over one hundred of them lined the streets, holding back the tumult while the firemen did their job. Almost instantaneously, Reverend Murray was hailed as a religious exemplar, and his name became a household word across the United States.

Ted Koppel taped *Nightline* in Murray's church, and Murray was interviewed for his reflections. For years afterward, whenever he was asked why African Americans destroyed their own community, Reverend Murray would reply more or less the same way: "Langston Hughes has a poem asking, what happens to a dream deferred? Does it dry up like a raisin in the sun or does it explode? Well, it explodes. That's what happened. The riot was the explosion of a dream deferred."

Part of what distinguished Murray and his church's intervention was that many of their practices moved beyond prayer vigils and temporary memorials. The First African Methodist Church occupied civil society and did the material work that usually was expected of the state. It had been several decades since that had happened. When the Los Angeles fire department refused to fulfill their function because of their fear of Black danger, Murray's church made it possible for the state to do its job. It was a reminder that law and order might still need the church, its members, and its authority. It was a momentary but significant reversal of a decades-long assumption that the church would always beseech the state for what it wanted or needed.

The 1990s were the height of the American culture wars—the struggle over values, beliefs, and practices that centered on questions regarding abortion, homosexuality, pornography, and other morality and so-called lifestyle issues. While some religious groups were enjoying political power, others recognized that the state would never fulfill the church's mission, especially that of the Black church. There was a revelatory story common at the time among some disenfranchised religious groups that had learned this lesson. It went like this: Mixing church and state is like mixing ice cream and manure. It might not make a difference to the manure, but it certainly ruins the ice cream.[79]

Many of the sermons given the first Sunday after the uprisings sought to reverse the premise implicit in the Simi Valley jury's "not guilty" verdict—the assumption that Black men could not be victims; they were always the perpetrators. They were never innocent, never vulnerable. This was a difficult presumption to unravel on May 3, 1992, when videos of the growing violence in Los Angeles had Americans riveted to their televisions. Most of the recorded violence showed Black men setting buildings on fire, looting stores, and beating drivers they had pulled from vehicles. Only later would the full accounting of the violence reveal that more Latinxs had been arrested and charged with looting and other crimes than African Americans. The mainstream media optics of the time had insisted that it was a "Black-led riot."[80]

Los Angeles ministers knew otherwise. On that first Sunday, they tried to tell another version of the story. In her sermon, Reverend Linnea Juanita Pearson explicitly compared Rodney King to a rape victim: "The jury that pronounced that verdict was a jury of the peers of the accused officers. It was not a jury of the peers of Rodney King. And, as so often happens in rape cases—and Rodney King was in a sense raped by those officers of the law—in such a trial the victim becomes the accused, and the verdict of the jury essentially is determined by the attitude that 'he or she asked for it.' This is the way the oppressor class always justifies its oppression."[81] Implicit in this rather awkward analogy was also an attempt to counter the myth of hypervirility and superhuman strength that was often attributed to Black men by a racist culture; Reverend Pearson is challenging the racist assumption that any injury the Black community suffers they either did to themselves or somehow deserve.

There were other approaches taken to establish the history and persistence of the suffering of Black men and women. The first was to describe the moral decay of the dominant culture and how the Black citizens seen looting and vandalizing were merely reenacting what the majority White culture had taught them. "To those who question those poor people who seem to just be taking advantage of the situation, I say, 'They have learned well their lessons from the super-rich. And the barbarism, destruction, and violence we have witnessed here this last week is but a tiny fraction of the barbarism, destruction and violence the United States government has wreaked upon the world in this last decade.'"[82]

The other ministerial response to the violence was to detail how racism itself had initiated, cultivated, and nourished the violence that had exploded in the city. This was a more challenging argument that the United States itself had bred this violence. The actions of the dominant had taught the subordinate how to behave. And American history was littered with examples: "How is it then that these self-appointed media commentators have missed commenting upon the hypocrisy of a government that condemns lawlessness in the streets while condoning and exporting lawlessness abroad: the mining of the harbors in Nicaragua, the torture and death squads in Guatemala, El Salvador and Chile."[83]

These sermons declared that while the actions were criminal, the emotions that prompted the violence were legitimate. "The rage we saw so violently exploding in the streets must be condemned for its viciousness and lawlessness by all decent people. But the feelings of despair, alienation and anger cannot be ignored."[84] And, "let's make sure that the path of judgment goes back many many years, perhaps even centuries, to try to understand behavior, lest we think that rioting or looting is the first kind of violence that occurred instead of seeing that there is a preceding violence that has gone on for years to which some of the rioting is a responsive violence."[85]

This perspective was powerfully repeated by Reverend Jesse Jackson in his sermons across the city. "This is the logical conclusion of twelve years of abandonment from the Reagan and Bush years. There is a connection between neglect, resentment and reaction. . . . What we saw was a kind of spontaneous combustion and you can't have spontaneous combustion without discarded material. And what you find in urban areas is people who have been discarded for a long time. They finally exploded."[86]

The most challenging sermons were those that tried to address the tensions between the Korean American and African American communities. Some ministers simply neglected it altogether. Reverend Jesse Jackson was called out by the *Los Angeles Times* for his silence regarding Korean Americans when he preached six times throughout the city on Sunday, May 3. His only oblique mention, which struck many as contrived, was a frequent reference to Japanese American Olympic gold medalist Kristi Yamaguchi, whose mother had been interned during World War II.[87] Jackson repeatedly noted the unfairness of her internment, but the connection to the Korean grocers who had just lost their businesses at the hands of their Black neighbors remained without explanation.

There were some White ministers who struggled more nobly and forthrightly with the challenge. For example, Reverend Barbara Mudge, minister at an Episcopal Church in Simi Valley itself, preached that first Sunday after the riots: "I have thrown caution to the winds this morning. My prepared sermon based on this Gospel lesson is now scrap paper. I am angry, I am frustrated. We have crucified the Lord . . . again. Nothing excuses the violence of these past few days except the continuing crucifixion of our brothers and sisters in the inner city. We are as much a part of what is happening as if we were setting fires ourselves."[88] This preacher's sermons also struggled with how to make sense of who her congregants were perceived to be ("I was embarrassed by what was being said about the 'ethos' of Simi Valley") and who the congregation *really* was ("It [is] up to us to prove to the folks downtown that we in Simi Valley were just as devastated by the events that had taken place as anyone else").[89] Yet unlike the sermons after Kennedy's assassination, there is no sense in these sermons that the White congregations might also be implicated in the destruction "downtown."

On the other side of the city, the Christian ministers preaching to the Korean American community that had been devastated by the violence counseled forgiveness and understanding. They sought to have their angry and devastated people identified with the suffering of Rodney King, if not directly with the suffering of the African American community. Reverend Linnea Juanita Pearson, whose church was in the center of Koreatown (although she is not a Korean American), began her May 3 sermon with an acknowledgment: "This morning we come together with ashes in our mouths. We come with anger in our hearts. We come with aching in our bodies. We come with bitterness and mourning."[90]

Later in the sermon, she reminded her congregants that "we are all broken" and "we must come together in our brokenness and woundedness, confess our personal and communal sins and ask expiation and forgiveness of one another." She also sought to draw a parallel between Rodney King and Jesus: "And does that face not call to mind that face of another 'criminal' called Jesus of Nazareth who also bore the lashes of the police and the soldiers who were the occupying forces of his land, and who, as armed protectors of the state, like the LAPD, did not allow that any should question their power?"[91]

It was an eloquent sermon both for what it said and for what it did not say. For example, there was no mention of the African American community, with whom her congregants shared Los Angeles, nor of the damage to Korean businesses, which both Latinxs and African Americans had inflicted. There was only one allusion to "poor people who seem to be taking advantage of the situation." But the reverend offered no further assessment of state-sanctioned violence. Rather, she took the well-worn liberal turn of recommending that her congregants practice individual acts of goodness. "We are all sinners, all both victims and victimizers. And, certainly we could all do better." Although she began her sermon with the statement that she would be offering a "societal structural analysis," her recommendations were for individual moral acts, including feeding the hungry, sharing resources, and creating time for "hushed contemplation."[92] There were no recommendations for the development of collective action or for facilitating a "beloved community" with African American or Hispanic neighbors.

At a nearby African American church, Reverend Chester Talton addressed the Korean / African American clash with an assertion that neither of the groups had any power. "We are all struggling, we should not be enemies fighting over fewer and fewer crumbs that fall from the table of the privileged. We could have real power if we could come together and insist on having an equal place at the table."[93] He reminded his listeners that "there is unfinished business in this country; it started before the Koreans or Hispanics became an issue."[94] Although he did not detail what exactly that unfinished business was, the implication was clear from the rest of the sermon that he was referring to the legacy of White racism, segregation, Jim Crow, and chattel slavery. Reverend Chong Ha-Sang in Flushing Queens expressed a similar sentiment to his predominantly Korean American congregation: "Koreans and blacks looked at each other and saw not their brothers and sisters, but their enemies." He suggests that the construction of the other as an enemy is a mistake that is itself the legacy of American racism.[95]

The conflict between the two communities in 1992 was largely because each group had expected more than they had been accorded by White America. Many of the Koreans who lost their businesses were college-educated immigrants who had been thwarted from more professional employment due to regulations and licensing requirements that they could not meet because their education had not been in the United States or because their spoken English was limited.[96] Many Korean immigrants felt considerable resentment that, though they were praised as a "model minority," they were not treated like or as respected as White Americans. The Los Angeles rebellion revealed to Korean Americans their fundamentally degraded status as very little was done to protect them. Initially, their own racism prohibited them from identifying with their African American neighbors, to whom they had long considered themselves superior.

African Americans, as many sermons argued, had been struggling against White oppression much longer than any others. Their ancestors had not chosen to come to the United States. There was a finely calibrated accounting being detailed between the two groups regarding who had suffered more, whose suffering was deserved, and whose was unwarranted. Although there were many community filaments joining the two groups, not the least of which was their shared Christianity, other embedded and largely unacknowledged antagonisms did not require much friction to ignite.

Yet even in the aftermath, there remained some ambiguity about how much or how little the Los Angeles violence had been about Korean/African American conflict. No one in either community suggested that the *cause* of the crisis was this conflict; the suggestion came only from outside interpreters. Although corporate media was obsessed with the utility of this explanatory model at the time, only a few ministers in Los Angeles focused on ethnic conflict as a signature feature of the rebellion.[97] Sadly, one of the early attempts at reconciliation, the Black-Korean Alliance, was disbanded by December 1992 because Korean leaders who joined were roundly mocked or ostracized by their own community.[98]

WHEN PRESIDENT BUSH addressed the nation during the Los Angeles riots, he rebuked what had been seen on televisions across the United States in the preceding forty-eight hours: "None of this is what we wish to think of as American. It's as if we're looking in a mirror that distorted our better selves and turned us ugly. We cannot let that happen. We cannot do that to ourselves."[99] For Bush, the images of the rioting in Los Angeles were uglier than the verdict rendered by the jury in Simi Valley or the beating of Rodney King. It was unclear what this metaphor of Americans being rendered "ugly" was intended to reveal. This was something Bush said Americans should not do to themselves. It was an odd turn of phrase. One cannot help but wonder whether the "ugliness" so long and so often linked to Blackness itself was being invoked.

In the closing minutes of his address, Bush claimed, "I'm one who respects the police." He painted a romantic picture of the first responders who "face danger every day. They help kids. They don't make a lot of money, but they care about their communities and their country."[100] Despite their role in the conflagration in Los Angeles, the police were singled out for commendation. No such acclamation was offered for individuals in the Black community. There was no reminder that the president was "one who respects African Americans. They face danger every day. They help kids. They don't make a lot of money, but they care for their country and their communities."

It would have been so easy and so tellingly accurate to make such an acknowledgment. But that was never said. There are no permanent memorials to the Los Angeles protests because none of what provoked the violence—the police brutality, the not guilty verdict, and the riotous response to it—was ever sufficiently mourned. The city, never mind the nation, could never decide whom or how to mourn. Should all the people who died have been mourned, or just those who could be counted as "innocent victims"?

As President Bush was wont to do at the time, he concluded his address with a story about "the small but significant acts in all this ugliness that give us hope." He mentioned "the people who have spent each night not in the streets but in the churches of Los Angeles, praying that man's gentler instincts be revealed in the hearts of people driven by hate." He told the story of the "savagely beaten" White truck driver, Reginald Denny, who was "alive tonight because of four strangers, four black strangers who came to his aid."[101] It was his only explicit acknowledgment of the racial dimensions of the protests in Los Angeles.

For the president, the twin beatings—of Rodney King and of Reginald Denny—were narrated in such a way as to render both victims invisible. The beatings were collapsed; they canceled one another out and were thus both irrelevant because they were the same. Whites beat Blacks and then Blacks beat Whites. It was a morality tale with a sleight of hand, not political insight. But the name of Rodney King was never uttered.

White America wanted to make Rodney King and Reginald Denny equal in their suffering, while Black America wanted the account to begin long before the beating of Rodney King and to be remembered long into the future. But neither Black nor White Americans knew how to mourn when the suffering was the result of the loss of a business, of personal property, and even something as existential as the fulfillment of the American dream.

Bush had obliquely mentioned the "Korean community" and the concern that Mayor Bradley had for their safety in his address to the nation. "My heart goes out to them and all others who have suffered losses." He did not detail why the Korean community in particular might be at risk. Nor was the safety of Black people mentioned as being of paramount concern. The uprising in Los Angeles was given no context, no history; it was not understood as tethered to a particular place or a particular set of events. Rather, the violence erupted out of nowhere, wreaking a path of destruction that had to be repaired by the state.

Thus, the losses of Korean Americans, as well as those of Latinxs, were largely overlooked because American mourning was about rebuilding, reconciliation, and reuniting; giving an account of racial losses and the discrimination that propelled those losses would have required a more thorough interrogation of the divisive elements of American racial politics.

And like so much of the violence of the last century, this was violence that Americans had done to themselves and thus were in some ways ashamed to recall. It was more expedient to imagine that the violence was what the Black community had done to itself—just as Martin Luther King was somehow responsible for his own assassination, so Black Americans were responsible for their own subordination.

Although President Bush had declared this violence "not American," it was actually quintessentially American as its repetition in Ferguson, Baltimore, and Minneapolis over the coming decades would make irrefutable. This failure to mourn and to memorialize was a harbinger of the rebellion that would again grip American cities in 2015, 2017, and 2020. By failing to mourn, Americans sowed the seeds that would mature grotesquely into more videos of even greater police brutality resulting in the deaths of unarmed African Americans. If the president had named either Latasha Harlins or Rodney King in his address to the nation, would the United States perhaps have begun the intentional process of mourning all of its dead?

Church of the National Tragedy:
The Oklahoma City Bombing, 1995

During the 1960s, influential preacher Harry Emerson Fosdick wrote in his collection *Dear Mr. Brown: Letters to a Person Perplexed about Religion:* "What a strange paradox our life is! We dread tragedy and yet there is nothing on earth that we admire more than a person who handles it triumphantly."[102] And although Fosdick claimed the paradox in the 1960s, the same paradox was revealed and rehearsed in stunning and poignant detail again in the tragic aftermath of the 1995 bombing of the Murrah Federal Building in Oklahoma City, Oklahoma. Unlike the Los Angeles uprising a few years earlier, this violence was understood by most Americans as an opportunity to demonstrate human goodness, to celebrate the homegrown qualities of the American heartland, and to showcase the possibilities of God's enduring presence in Americans' everyday lives.

Of all the events discussed in this book, the tragedy in Oklahoma was grasped and recounted not only by ministers but by the mainstream media as well as by dominant political leaders in the most theological terms. It was a tragedy that the hegemonic narrative evacuated nearly completely of political history or insight. The bomber, Timothy McVeigh, was evil, but all other Americans were rendered good. Sin was reduced to a solitary figure, McVeigh, while the rest of Americans, presumably White, were elevated. Ministers, in particular, made the tragedy cosmic, a battle between good and evil, rather than historical or political: "There is an evil, destructive force in the world. We Disciples (of Christ) don't talk about it too much. But it is there."[103]

The sermons given across the country at the time circled around issues of theodicy. They were focused on Americans' relationship with God. There was a revival feeling to some of the sermons, as if the bombing had provided an opportunity for Christian renewal: "A powerful spiritual presence pervaded the whole incident. People all over the world comment on it. Even agnostics admit something unique happened; those who believe in God are certain what it was. The movement of what Christians call the Holy Spirit. In a word, God is among us."[104]

Ministers as well as others reported sightings of angels and of angel wings in the clouds over the pit of the destroyed building. "I could see the top of the cloud, though. All the angels were facing west. Long wings of incredible dimensions trailed gracefully behind their backs. . . . Angels standing silent vigil over the ruins of the Murrah building."[105] This tragedy was constructed in the media as well as by American ministers as an opportunity to restore faith as well as to demonstrate contemporary Christian American values. In fact, some ministers issued an admonition; Reverend William Simms warned, "The Devil wants you to blame God, he wants us to question God, and he wants you to make God responsible for what has happened."[106] Seeing God's goodness in the ruins was an act of faith.

The ministers focused on theodicy in part because there was no collective historical memory in which they located the violence. The bombing was imagined as a new event; this was the first time such a bombing had happened to Americans. Thus, the survivors too were exceptional. The Oklahoma City bombing was constructed as the first episode of domestic terrorism, as the first attack on the heartland, as well as the first attack on American children.

None of which was true. Two years earlier, in 1993, there had been a terrorist attack on the Twin Towers in New York City, in which six people were killed and over one thousand injured. Before that was the MOVE bombing in Philadelphia in 1985 in which 11 people had been killed, including 5 children, and three years later, the explosion of Pan Am Flight 103 headed toward Detroit, in which 243 passengers and 16 crew members were killed. Among them were not only thirty-five university-age students but young children and their parents. And at Ruby Ridge (1992) and Waco (1993), Americans had been killed, including children who were never sufficiently mourned.

But there was even more recent violence upon which the ministers could have reflected but did not—the attacks on the American Muslim community by their fellow citizens within hours of the Oklahoma City bombing. On April 20, a day after the bombing, Enver Masud, president of the Wisdom Fund, a Washington, DC–area nonprofit organization dedicated to educating Americans about Islam and Muslims, declared: "A society is judged by how well it protects the rights of the least powerful. There are two victims of the Oklahoma tragedy, the innocent dead and the falsely accused."[107] The Wisdom Fund issued a statement naming the Oklahoma blast "a heinous act" as well as condemning as "equally craven, the rush to judgment."[108] The statement compared current Muslim mistreatment in the wake of the Oklahoma bombing "to what was done to Japanese Americans."[109]

The 1995 bombing thus inaugurated the United States' contemporary civil religion, "The Church of the National Tragedy."[110] This term was initially used by Margaret Hirschberg in a concluding paragraph of her essay on Edye Smith Jones, a mother who lost both of her toddler sons in the blast. Hirschberg's essay describes the media's almost obscene focus on Jones's grief and the concurrent sanctification of American motherhood through it. Edye Smith Jones became the emblem of the nation's trauma. Hirschberg notes that even when Jones became a darling of the far-right militia because of her conspiracy theory that the day care workers had been forewarned about the blast, so acute was the American media's desire to find "good from evil" that even this allegiance to militia hate groups was overlooked. She remained the "Madonna of the National Tragedy."[111]

For this chapter, the "Church of the National Tragedy" describes the dominant ministerial response to the bombing as a theology of trauma. Christianity became a place of trauma as well as a therapeutic source of comfort and unity through shared devastation. The catastrophic became the universal human condition with which all, presumably, could identify. Americans were victims and the church was the place where they could dress and heal their wounds. This civil religion would be vibrant again on September 11, 2001, and after the Newtown school shooting.

The Innocent Dead and the Falsely Accused

At 9:02 A.M. on April 19, 1995, a blast ripped through the Murrah Federal Building in downtown Oklahoma City, killing 168 people and injuring more than 200 others. Most of those killed were federal workers specifically targeted by domestic terrorist Timothy McVeigh. McVeigh was a decorated Gulf War veteran who had been radicalized after the Branch Davidian killings at Waco, Texas. The Branch Davidians were a religious sect that was preparing for the second coming at a remote compound. In a fifty-one-day standoff that began with the Bureau of Alcohol, Tobacco, and Firearms (ATF) and concluded with the FBI, seventy-six Branch Davidians, including twenty-five children, were killed when their compound was set on fire April 19, 1993.

McVeigh perceived the Waco siege as a manifestation of government overreach, particularly as it concerned citizens' right to bear arms. He chose the two-year anniversary of the Waco assault for the Oklahoma bombing. It remains unclear to this day whether he knew that his bomb would reach a day care center, although he notoriously insisted that he knew "there had to be blood in order to get the government's attention." When he was arrested within two hours of the bombing, he was wearing a T-shirt inscribed with the words of Thomas Jefferson: "The Tree of Liberty must be watered from time to time with the blood of patriots and tyrants."

Like Lee Harvey Oswald, Timothy McVeigh was feared as "one of us": he was White, had served in the military, and had been born and raised in the heartland of the United States. At some level, his violence was surely revelatory about American conditions. But the mainstream media, as well as the dominant political and ministerial narratives, insisted that he be dismissed as "not like us." In fact, so desperate were many Americans to make the violence "not us" that they first assumed the perpetrators were their Muslim neighbors. For Oklahomans, to maintain their status as a hallowed heartland, McVeigh had to be shunned as an outsider; for politicians and ministers, he was a diabolical individual who was the spawn of Satan, not of the United States itself: "This terrible and senseless tragedy runs against the grain of every standard, every belief, and every custom we hold as a civilized society in the United States."[112]

After the bombing, for the mainstream media Oklahoma City became an agricultural center of preindustrial rhythms, homespun values, barbecues, and church meetings. It was a place of nostalgia. In Oklahoma, goodness was a manifestation of the quotidian. Everyday people doing everyday work. Politicians on the floor of the Senate even used the opportunity to redeem the image of bureaucratic government workers. Senator Feinstein opined:

> So many of those killed or injured were public sector employees, and I believe we should take a moment to consider their sacrifice. All too often, it's easy to abuse those who work in government jobs. They are called bureaucrats and accused of wasting time around water coolers or with their feet up on their desk. But the blast offers another image. . . . They were already hard at work that Wednesday morning when the bomb exploded at 9:04 [*sic*]. They were serving the public.[113]

Aside from the long overdue validation of discarded federal workers, very little of the hegemonic account was accurate. But this was the story Americans told themselves. Never mind that Oklahoma City was a *city*, and a capital city at that. Never mind that Oklahoma City was largely industrial rather than agricultural. And forget that the Murrah building was a federal office building filled with government workers, not church ladies and farmers. Timothy McVeigh was not an anomaly but part of a growing militia of White nationalists who had served in the US military. And of course, overlook that in the first hours after the bombing the good people of Oklahoma were diligent in their anti-Muslim rage.

When McVeigh's identity was confirmed within twenty-four hours of the bombing, although he too was part of the American heartland, his affiliation with militia groups was overlooked and his place in the enduring legacy of American racism discarded. History, facts, and elemental contradictions did not get in the way of the triumphant narrative of good versus evil in the American heartland. So powerful was this narrative regarding Oklahoma that the first item in the "lessons learned" section of the *Oklahoma City Bombing after Action Report* was "the Heartland of America is no longer isolated from the reaction of political action groups of either the extreme left or right."[114] In hindsight, this seems naive. Why did Oklahomans ever believe they were isolated from the very extremists and White nationalist groups that had been cultivated in their own backyards?

Within an hour of the detonation, former congressman Dave McCurdy was on CBS talking about "very clear evidence of fundamentalist Islamic terrorist groups."[115] Supporting his position, McCurdy cited the 1994 propaganda video "Jihad in America." But CBS was not alone. CNN's Wolf Blitzer intoned, "It does appear to have, once again, according to an official, the signature of a Middle East kind of car-bombing."[116] The same day, ABC's John McWethy proclaimed, "The fact that it was such a powerful bomb in Oklahoma City immediately drew investigators to consider deadly parallels that all have roots in the Middle East."[117] Swiftly, terrorism, Islam, and the entire Middle East were buckled together. A crime, terrorism, became a religion, Islam, which was then located in the Middle East.

Even though the "John Doe" sketches released within fewer than twenty-four hours of the bombing revealed a suspect who looked more like a White midwestern boy than a member of the mujahedeen, some journalists persisted. "There is still a possibility that there could have been some sort of connection to Middle East terrorism. One law enforcement source tells me that there's a possibility that they may have been contracted out as freelancers to go out and rent this truck that was used in this bombing and perhaps may not even have known what was involved."[118] There was an acute desire initially for the perpetrators to be "foreigners." If the mayhem had been inaugurated by a fellow American, the challenge to American self-conception would be debilitating.

It was simply too baffling that an American could do this to other Americans.

But there was plenty of available evidence of that very possibility before April 19, 1995. The most readily available was the presidential assassination attempt by Francisco Durant in December 1994. Durant had fired twenty-nine rounds from an SKS automatic rifle at the White House, in the hope of killing President Clinton. Durant hated the government and was a member of the Save America Militia, as well as an avid reader of militia literature. Yet most of the reporting about the assassination attempt focused on whether Durant was mentally ill or merely a disgruntled former GI trying to avenge a drunk driving conviction.[119] Very little of the media assessment focused on the growth of militia groups in the United States.

After the Oklahoma bombing, when militias finally received media attention, their members were still treated as if it were possible that they had "good reasons" for their violence. In a special town hall meeting with a radical militia leader in Michigan, Ted Koppel assured him, "I did promise you would have a chance to say anything you want."[120]

This was but one example of the odd indulgence these figures received over the coming weeks, as if Americans still were in disbelief about right-wing extremism's motives and viciousness. Journalist Jim Naureckas noted at the time: "When the bombing suspects are conservative White men from Middle America—who look like 'us' as 'us' is defined by media decision makers—then there must be a search for understanding. This search at times shaded into a glossing over of the most frightening aspects of the militias."[121]

Surely, the race of the militia men mattered. Can one imagine, as Naureckas hypothesizes, "thousands of black militants acquiring high powered weaponry, openly drilling paramilitary units and announcing for all to hear that sooner or later they would likely have to use their weapons against the U.S. government in order to regain their constitutional rights, and the news media largely ignoring them?"[122] One doesn't have to imagine: recall the mobilization of the National Guard and the military equipment that President Bush had sent into Los Angeles three years earlier because of the largely unarmed outcry by people of color protesting the miscarriage of justice after the mistreatment of Rodney

King at the hands of law enforcement. The media conducted no town hall asking those so-called rioters why they had done what they did or promising them a platform to articulate their grievances.

These biases had a significant impact on Muslim American communities, not only in Oklahoma but across the country.[123] The *Oklahoma Hate and Harassment Report,* compiled by the Project of the Community Peace Coalition, reported that from Wednesday morning until Friday afternoon, when suspect Timothy McVeigh was arrested, Muslims, Arabs, and other communities of color suffered "widespread fear and intimidation, commonplace verbal harassment at school, in public and in the workplace as well as a significant number of physical assaults and hate crimes."[124] There was no concurrent rise of hate crimes against young White militia members. The most serious incident involved a pregnant Iraqi woman, who lost her baby after an April 20 attack on her home in Oklahoma City by people provoked to anger by reports linking Muslims to the bombing.[125] The Council on American Islamic Relations, a Muslim antidefamation organization, recorded 222 attacks against Muslims in the three days after the bombing.[126]

Yet the corporate media colluded in denying this violence and elevating what became known as the "Oklahoma standard." This was the standard of goodness exemplified by Oklahomans in the wake of the tragedy. Search and rescue responders told stories to the media of how their experiences of Oklahoma City were very different from the experiences of those who had worked after the 1993 World Trade Center bombing. In New York, "vendors hiked up the price of bottled water and some rescue workers had to sleep in automobiles. In Oklahoma City, hundreds of volunteers made sure each worker had a cot made fresh each day with a flower and a piece of candy or chocolate on their pillow, as well as clean clothes."[127] Rescue workers also recounted stories of the "Oklahoma dollar": "I left home with only a few dollars, but no one would let me spend a dime. I came home with those same dollar bills in my wallet."[128]

The rescue workers, nurses, and firefighters were all heroes, celebrated in many instances as doing God's work. In his Sunday sermon, Reverend Robert Wise noted: "Today, in that building, with God's infant in his arms, Sam did His will. He [God] needed Sam for a horrible task and Sam came through for him. It's hard to see anything but God's power and purpose, once you realize He was there."[129] First responders were not merely doing their jobs; they were vocational and nearly religious figures.

The Oklahoma bombing was not an occasion to examine the contradiction and challenges of American identity, or of American violence or even the despair of American veterans such as McVeigh who felt abandoned by their government in the American heartland. Instead, the collective response to the violence was framed as a manifestation of American goodness and of everyday American heroism. The inaugural violence was not "about us"—only the heroic American response to the violence revealed American identity. Just as it had been with the violence in Los Angeles, what was measured and characterized was the *response* to grief. What had caused that grief was largely unexamined.

The Protestant clergy followed this same course. Across the nation, they proclaimed that the violence and loss of human life in Oklahoma, particularly the deaths of the children, did not reveal anything about God. They were not interested in the role of religion in the violence or whether the church might have done anything to prevent the tragedy.[130] Rather, God was manifest in the human response—the heroism of the firefighters, the volunteers donating blood, the expertise of the doctors, and the good judgment of the city coordinators who managed the crisis. This was the resonant and active Church of the National Tragedy— Americans' new civil religion.

What Did the Ministers Say?

At the time of the bombing, the state of Oklahoma was more devout than the rest of the United States. Oklahoma City was a deeply Baptist city with nearly fifteen hundred churches. Daily prayers were still published on the front page of the *Daily Oklahoman*, and in 1995 the Association of Statisticians of American Religious Bodies reported that in Oklahoma County, 73 percent of the population belonged to a church or regularly attended religious services, or both, compared with 55 percent in the nation as a whole.

As a result, one of the most difficult elements of the tragedy for ministers was to explain why some people, including children, were killed that day and why others survived. The story of Florence Rogers was a classic example. Florence Rogers, head of the Federal Employees Credit Union, was in her office on the third floor of the Murrah building that morning. Seated around her desk were eight credit union employees, some of whom Rogers had known and worked with for decades. Although they were having a business meeting, spring was in the air, and there was levity in their conversation about the promises of spring.[131]

When the bomb went off at 9:02, Rogers was thrown backward onto the floor, her desk and other office items landing all around her. When she looked up, every one of her colleagues had vanished. "I started hollering, 'Where are you guys? Where are you guys?'" In the next moments, before building and car alarms triggered by the blast began to howl, before fire engine and police sirens wailed, and before cries rang out from the trapped and injured, Rogers experienced an "eerie silence." Alone on a narrow ledge—all that was left of her office floor—below which was a deadly, open pit, she wondered where her colleagues had gone. And later, after being helped to safety, she would wonder at the miracle of her own survival on a day when so many had perished.[132]

Many Christians wanted to claim the survival of Florence Rogers as a miracle, as God's intervention. Rogers, herself, explained her survival, "I soothe myself, I guess you'd say, by saying that God was not ready for me that day."[133] But if God had intervened on behalf of Rogers, why did He not intervene on behalf of other equally good, equally faithful, or equally innocent people? If God was saving some, why didn't He save all? Or at least more . . . like the children in the day care center? At the Community Prayer Service, Bishop Robert Moody gave a reading from Luke 13:1–5 that detailed how the deaths revealed nothing of the goodness of either God or of those killed. He, like other ministers, used the story in which Jesus asked whether His apostles believed that "of those 18 who were killed when the tower of Siloam fell on them—do you think that they were worse offenders than all the others living in Jerusalem? No, I tell you."[134]

The majority of ministers resolved this by insisting that those who survived did not do so because of divine intervention. They had survived by chance, pure and simple. Those who died did so only because of the evil plot of two twisted individuals, Timothy McVeigh and Terry Nichols. As Reverend Bishop preached: "God is a creative God. God does not destroy. God may come across the destruction and enter into it with us, but God is always building, always creating. The ability to make a silk purse out of sow's ear does not imply that the seamstress created the sow's ear."[135]

While this was what many of the ministers preached, the common answer among the congregants remained that those who were saved or spared (i.e., were away from work or arrived late or left early, etc.) did so because of God's intervention. Many of these stories were reported in the Oklahoma newspapers and some were repeated nationwide. One that became nationally popular was the account of Pastor Nick Harris who was spared because he was unexpectedly in his office at First United Methodist Church rather than in the sanctuary where he had held his radio address every week for the last four years.[136]

Another challenge posed for the ministers the Sunday after the Oklahoma City blast was how to discuss the government. Did it matter that the target of the tragedy was a federal building and its federal workers? Was that fact merely incidental or did it have some theological ramifications? After President John F. Kennedy was assassinated in 1963 many ministers felt compelled to think through how an attack on the government reflected on the church. Many decided that the assassination revealed not the failure of the government to protect its president, but the failure of the church to be fully the church. In 1963, the ministers argued that the state needed the church to be the church. The ministers claimed for themselves an important political as well as theological role.

After the Oklahoma City bombing, the majority of ministers took a different perspective. Rather than try to theologize the bombing, that is, rather than try to detail how the bombing reflected or revealed something about the church and its role in the political world, they decided that the bombing was an opportunity for the church to reinvest in the state itself. As noted earlier, this dovetails with the development of the so-called culture wars at the time. In his 1992 speech at the Republican National Convention, Pat Buchanan articulated the perspective and temper of the time: "The agenda [Bill] Clinton and [Hillary] Clinton would impose on America—abortion on demand, a litmus test for the Supreme Court, homosexual rights, discrimination against religious schools, women in combat units—that's change, all right. But it is not the kind of change America wants. It is not the kind of change America needs. And it is not the kind of change we can tolerate in a nation that we still call God's country."[137] And while Buchanan represented a conservative view on these named social issues, there was apparently widespread agreement across the ministerial spectrum that the state was the place to adjudicate theological battles as well as the instrument for implementing God's will. In 1995, the church defended the state, claiming it as itself a manifestation of God's goodness. It was where God's presence was most clearly discerned.

After the Oklahoma City bombing, ministers believed that the state was part of the manifestation of God's goodness. Ministers offered repeated praise for law enforcement, first responders, and government workers.

> We know that in the determination of the rescuers, Christ
> pushes back the stone and rubble.
>   Trusting in your ever vigilant care of us, we pray this night
> for the firefighters and the others who struggle to find the
> victims.[138]

And much of this praise was indeed warranted. What was odd, however, was the ministerial amnesia that neglected to consider why law enforcement, first responders, and government workers had responded so well in Oklahoma when just three years earlier they had responded so negligently in Los Angeles. In 1992, no ministers were claiming law enforcement or first responders as manifestations of God's goodness. And this oversight in the sermons of 1995 rendered race invisible again. No ministers asked whether perhaps first responders were "good" when they had to rescue White people but negligent when they had to protect Black and Brown people. Their goodness was naturalized and the political and racial history of law enforcement ignored.

William T. Cavanaugh, in his essay "Killing for the Telephone Company," notes that for the state to wield power, it must be perceived as representing something more transcendent than, for example, the telephone company. In most instances, that important virtue is "the pursuit of the common good." Indebted to this modern (if mistaken) belief, American ministers sought to provide some kind of transcendence for the Murrah Federal Building and its component Social Security offices, Housing and Urban Development offices, and so forth. In the sermons, the ministers' own predilections required them to somehow show that these offices and their workers excelled beyond their bureaucratic tedium.

This was deeply ironic, since the purpose of the bombing from Timothy McVeigh's perspective was to alert Americans to the dangers, not the promise, of their government. McVeigh intended to punish the government for its role in the deaths of its own citizens at Waco and Ruby Ridge. That the blast served instead to canonize the government and the United States as a whole to many of its citizens marked this episode of domestic terrorism as an epic failure. McVeigh had a profound misunderstanding of the cultural moment.

After the bombing, the church did not offer to provide services—all of that was left to the state; indeed, there was supreme confidence that the state would take care of them. This would also be the pattern after 9/11, after the Newtown school shooting, and after the killing of Trayvon Martin: "the state will take care of it." According to ministers, part of the triumph of Oklahoma City in 1995 was that the state helped the city, volunteers poured in, and victims were not alone in their grief. The entire nation wept with them. One minister prayed for the first responders: "Help them to bring the best of their skill, compassion and energy. . . . *Let them be your hands of care and comfort.* Through them *work your healing* and by everything they do may they demonstrate how much you long to restore us from our brokenness. . . . May the efforts of these friends *be among the greatest of your work.*"[139] In contrast, when Los Angeles was in crisis, the state poured in, but it was the National Guard, not a battalion of volunteers offering bottled water and solace.[140] It's rather obvious, perhaps, but the state as the divine incarnate rescues when the victims are White but punishes when the victims are racialized minorities.

The first responders in Oklahoma City were characterized as instruments of God's will, as minister Tish Malloy preached: "We know that in the determination of the rescuers, Christ pushes back the stones and rubble to give freedom to the bodies and souls of the lost."[141] This canonization of the first responders was a relatively recent phenomenon in post-1960s America; it was an element of the general sanctification of the everyman in American culture. Sociologist and cultural critic Philip Rieff commented in *The Triumph of the Therapeutic* that Americans no longer sought to model themselves on the iconic saint; rather, the model was the ordinary person doing his or her everyday activities.[142]

Traditionally, a saint is someone who is intentionally doing God's work, motivated by a faith tradition or theological commitments. Now, just doing one's job with or without faith or a religious affiliation rendered one a saint. The entrance bar was considerably lowered. One's motivations did not matter; it was the spectacle of one's acts—how they were perceived by others—that anointed you.

Although this might seem like democratization, what it signaled for the church was the loss of authority, the collapse of the holy and the profane, and the mixing of the sacred and the secular into one undifferentiated mass. Traditionally, faith had required obedience to, trust in, and dependence on a transcendent authority; the elevation of the first responders to the sacred heroic suggested that no such delineations were necessary, or perhaps even possible. The church was irrelevant; the camera in the hands of the corporate media now granted sainthood.

This turn to the first responders as sacred actors was not that surprising given that nearly all of the Oklahoma bombing sermons wrestled with why God had allowed this to happen; ministers answered primarily that God was not to be found in the blast but in the recovery. "This was not God's plan! Not my God and I hope not your God."[143] "If you want to talk about the will of God in Oklahoma City, look at the hundreds, thousands of people who have responded to this tragedy. There is the will of God, and don't anyone dare say that that bombing was the will of God!"[144] Yet most minsters, predominantly White, do not pause to ask, "Why is God among the first responders in Oklahoma City but was not among them in Los Angeles? *Is God a racist?*" Implicit here is the assumption that God is responsive to White suffering but indifferent to that of African Americans and others.[145]

If Christians were killed in the bombing, not because they are Christians, but because they were government workers, ministers claimed that the church still had to somehow make these deaths theologically meaningful. The tragedy could not be left beyond their ecclesial reach. So, to achieve this end, the ministers declared that the US government was worth dying for. The state and its workers were rendered sacred in order for these arbitrary deaths not to have been completely in vain. The random political violence of the bombing had to be rescued from its nihilistic crater; the identities of the deceased as federal workers, the work they performed, and the institution for which the dead had toiled were baptized as holy in many of the sermons. The capricious deaths of innocent Americans could not be meaningless; they had to be aligned with something significant, something divine and ultimate—especially because these were primarily dead White Americans.

Ministers recognized that after the Oklahoma City bombing, God was on trial; He, rather than "our fellow Americans,"[146] needed to give an account of Himself—how could He have let this happen? It was the quintessential narcissistic turn. The narcissist is always innocent by his own accounting. It is incomprehensible that he could in any way be liable for his own suffering. There was no interrogation by the ministers as there had been in 1941, 1963, and 1968 about how Christians might have contributed to the elements that produced a racist, violent man such as Timothy McVeigh.

When Dr. Martin Luther King was assassinated, many ministers spent long hours interrogating how it was that the United States had killed its own prince of peace. How had the United States given shelter and sanction to the forces that would be unleashed against Martin Luther King? Ministers in 1995 did not ask this question. They did not wonder aloud about how the United States could have created the hateful contours of Timothy McVeigh and his helpmate, Terry Nichols. How was it possible that the American homeland had cultivated such domestic terrorists?

Instead, McVeigh and Nichols were just exemplars of cosmic sinfulness—evil men. Their crime and its motivations were not imagined to reveal anything significant about the United States. In fact, President Clinton and other national as well as local leaders repeated frequently how these crimes would not intimidate the United States, how the United States would not change or be altered from its course. Immediately, President Clinton proclaimed: "The bombing in Oklahoma City was an attack on innocent children and defenseless citizens. It was an act of cowardice and it was evil. The United States will not tolerate it. And I will not allow the people of this country to be intimidated by evil cowards."[147] Clinton surely knew that there was a politics to the bombing of a federal building on the anniversary of the Waco siege; this was not a cosmic battle between good and evil.

Of course, the bombing was no one's fault but McVeigh's and his assorted accomplices'. But it would have been fruitful if the United States had begun then to sort through the development of hate groups, the rising coordination of militias, and the despair and dissolution in the rural heartland. The ministers did not examine McVeigh in the ways they had examined Oswald. In fact, no single sermon read for this chapter offered any assessment of Timothy McVeigh, although he had been arrested within ninety minutes of the bombing, charged on Friday, April 21, and his name and background given an initial sketch by Saturday, April 22. On that first Sunday, April 23, ministers would have known that the killer had been one of the United States' own homegrown.

So challenging was the question regarding God's goodness in the face of this monstrous slaughter that ministers felt compelled to reveal how God's goodness was literally made manifest in the ruins themselves. In their most cliché forms, these were sermons that reminded congregants of the "silver lining" that follows most misfortunes. Fortunately, most of the sermons resisted this turn. The more poignant ones insisted, like Elie Wiesel,[148] that God suffered with the people of Oklahoma City as well as with all Americans affected by the disaster. As Reverend C. Lawrence Bishop preached, "God's was the first heart to break."[149]

Literally making the site sacred was the chain link fence installed to delineate the bombing site of the Murrah Federal Building. Quickly the fence became a spontaneous memorial festooned with artifacts of comfort and loving attachment. Visitors, rescue workers, and first responders left notes, stuffed animals, candles, and photographs. Even the white helmets from those who had dug through the rubble looking for people and for criminal evidence were hung on the fence. It was a manifestation of spontaneous heartbreak. It was a scene of domestic and quotidian intimacy. In the face of the horrific, the memorial fence sought to reclaim some of the familiarity of everyday life, to restore what had been normal and taken for granted but had been tragically destroyed in the blast.[150]

In the contemporary United States, the spontaneous memorial has come to signal a culture of comfort. As Marita Sturken has detailed in *Tourists of History*, Americans have retreated to a "teddy bear culture" in which they are focused on solace rather than on change, understanding, or even prevention.[151] These temporary memorials are largely exempt from political language or activism. Rather, they are sites of comfort, sometimes of a bizarre infantilization (i.e., a surfeit of stuffed animals) and of reconciliation to what has happened. As Sturken notes, "the teddy bear doesn't promise to make things better; it promises to make us feel better about the way things are."[152]

After the bombing of Pearl Harbor, there were no temporary memorials across the country. The deaths were considered too heroic to be belittled by ephemeral memorabilia. Americans were not seeking solace; they were mobilized for victory. After the assassination of JFK and MLK, Americans did not collect in Dallas and Memphis; although they wrote to the First Lady and to Coretta Scott King, they also continued the civil rights activities as well as marches begun by both the president and Dr. King. After the Los Angeles uprisings, African Americans worked to "rebuild LA"—the motto of the city at that time. But after the Oklahoma bombing and nearly every subsequent American tragedy, Americans created temporary memorials and soothed themselves with their shared sorrow.[153]

These temporary and spontaneous memorials were also a signature feature of the Church of the National Tragedy. The memorials were a ritual practice that joined Americans together in tragic recollection. It was a form of civic participation but an ephemeral one without long-term consequences. The transient memorials were certainly part of public mourning; they occupied public spaces and thus insisted that death and grief be made visible. But this civil practice was revealing in its anodyne lack of prescriptions. It was clearly a terminal feature of the therapeutic— feel better, express emotion, but do nothing substantial—politically or otherwise. The Church of the National Tragedy, like the temporary memorials, was open to everyone: it was a democratic form. One just had to remember where one was, what one was doing when the tragedy occurred, and how one felt when one learned the news. This memory would then join one with other Americans who had their own memories of where they were, how they learned, and what they felt. These stories would then be told and repeated until they created a collective sense of the tragedy, of the shared devastation.

Ministers, too, wanted the Church of the National Tragedy to be full and thus in their sermons constructed an expansive conception of who was a survivor. Ministers embraced nearly all of Oklahoma City residents as survivors. It didn't matter whether they had been in the blast that day, had retired several months earlier, or had just happened to be late to work. All of them were considered survivors and warranted in their anguish.

The tragedies were without a doubt profoundly sad and that desolation was what partially joined Americans together. Yet, although Americans were distraught together in the Church of the National Tragedy, rather quickly the work began of how to find the silver lining, how to make sense of the mayhem, and in that most cliché of phrases, "how to move on." Much of the mourning after the Oklahoma bombing was about being a witness to suffering rather than actually suffering oneself. This was an essential distinction. The anguish in the United States after the Oklahoma bombing had the rather ghoulish misfortune of being a kind of enchantment with being a witness to tragedy and somehow claiming it as one's own. Other scholars have named this fascination with disaster "dark tourism," referring, in part, to the propensity to conflate the trauma victim's loss with one's own sadness while observing the spectacle of devastation. It was a displaced and self-absorbed kind of mourning.

Americans, sometimes led by their ministers, would recall where they were when they heard the news of the bombing, when they saw the first images of the building and the rescue and recovery. They would gather around the altar of their televisions, as they did after the Kennedy assassination, and mourn with the victims and survivors in Oklahoma City. In the Church of the National Tragedy, Americans were joined in unity. Their anguish united them. Invoking this civil religion, Senator Orrin Hatch of Oklahoma declared that the perpetrators were not Americans, "The true Americans are the men, women and children who were killed. . . . Americans are the rescue workers. . . . Americans are *all of us who share the same moral outrage.*"[154] Americans were united in feeling.

A few secular authorities were asking:

> Don't they see the irrationality of praying to this supposedly omniscient and omnipotent deity? If I had known what was about to happen at 9:02 A.M. on April 19, and if I had had the ability to prevent the horror, I would have tried. Wouldn't you? But Billy Graham's all-knowing God (let's pretend he exists) observed the truck being loaded with explosives. He

sat alongside the driver on the trip from Kansas, knowing
what he had in mind. He noticed the laughing children
entering the day-care center. Graham's all-powerful "God of
love" easily could have prevented the detonation. Yet he did
nothing. Graham and Clinton should not be asking their God
for comfort. They should be asking him, "Whose side are you
on?"[155]

But what this 1995 God offered was not the power to prevent heartbreak but rather the necessary therapy to help one recover from it. Ministers recognized a very American and modern God who was at the site
of the Oklahoma bombing. "You, O God, are with us in our pain;/You
grieve with us and for us day by day,/And with us, sharing sorrow, will
remain."[156] This American God did His work through the agents of the
state. His presence was medicinal—not because He performed miracles
but because He was a psychological tonic for traumatic injuries. This
was a God who required very little from humans; rather, He was personified as a reduced version of His previous otherworldly and divine
self. God was present primarily to amplify individual human well-
ness. As Rieff noted in another context, "this hardly means that the
modern individual has abandoned spiritual concerns, but rather that
they (spiritual concerns) have been recast purely as enhancing personal
well-being, instead of serving as a source of love or awe before the
great mysteries."[157]

Immediately after the bombing, President Clinton held a press conference announcing the bombing as evil (as noted above) and concluding
with a recommendation: "Finally, let me say that I ask all Americans
tonight to pray—to pray for the people who have lost their lives, to pray
for the families and the friends of the dead and the wounded, to pray
for the people of Oklahoma City. May God's grace be with them. Meanwhile, we will be about our work."[158] The governmental process of sacralization had begun. God was invoked, His grace summoned, and the
work of the government mobilized.

Later, President Clinton would insist "there is nothing patriotic about
hating your country or pretending that you can love your country but
despise your government."[159] Clinton powerfully tied patriotism with
supporting the state's actions; to do otherwise, he told Michigan State

graduates, was to be linked to the monstrous actions of that government hater, Timothy McVeigh. It was a very fine line Clinton drew between celebrating the freedom to protest and obedience to the rule of law. In that same speech, he addressed members of the militia directly: "If you appropriate our sacred symbols for paranoid purposes and compare yourselves to colonial militias who fought for the democracy you now rail against, you are wrong. How dare you suggest that we in the freest nation on Earth live in tyranny! How dare you call yourselves patriots and heroes!"[160]

The president's rhetoric signaled that he was fighting for something significant. Who counted as a patriot was fundamental to state power and Clinton was reminding the audience who were the *real* patriots: "The real American heroes today are the citizens who get up every morning and have the courage to work hard and play by the rules: the mother who stays up the extra half hour after a long day's work to read her child a story; the rescue worker who digs with his hands in the rubble as the building crumbles about him; the neighbor who lives side-by-side with people different from himself."[161] At the site itself, a chaplain repeated the theme: "Hard hats and heads bowed, we prayed. In the presence of the FBI, DEA, search and rescue teams, and firearms, we prayed. There was no concern about church and state issues, just people in need of God."[162]

After the blast, many ministers encouraged Americans to believe in their government just as they believed in God. Kari Watkins, executive director of the Oklahoma City National Memorial and Museum, put it this way: "Even though people try to bring down the very government we believe in, we will survive, and it will be that same government that will defend the criminals and prosecute the criminals at the same time. And that's a pretty remarkable story."[163] There was an alarming amnesia in many of these "theological" accounts about a foundational claim of Christianity: "Do not be conformed to this world, but be transformed by the renewal of your mind, that by testing you may discern what is the will of God, what is good and acceptable and perfect" (Rom. 12:2). In Christianity, suffering (among other things) was a path to God. In Oklahoma, apparently, the tragedy led most Americans back to the federal government and its goodness rather than to God and His expectations for His people.

While it was certainly not imperative that they do so, many ministers seemed to feel compelled to defend the state. This was different from defending the United States, as they would do in 2001 after September 11. But here they are doing something a bit different: they are defending the institutions of the state and the operation of its power as good. It was without a doubt a political gesture (although not a particularly partisan one), but one that confirmed the validity of the state and sought, perhaps, to align church theology and institutional influence with it. This turn was noteworthy in several respects.

First, there were repeated claims throughout the Oklahoma bombing sermons regarding the loss of American innocence, "we are burying many things—not just people but our innocence."[164] This unpredicted tragedy, they argued, had resulted in American awareness of evil and of unwarranted suffering: "Never in the history of our country have Americans witnessed such senseless barbarism."[165] The assertion required rather willful forgetfulness. The loss of Americans' innocence was lamented after the bombing of Pearl Harbor, after the assassinations of JFK, MLK, and RFK—all in grievous quick succession—as well as after the American losses and humiliations in Vietnam. The loss of American innocence was bemoaned again after the Challenger disaster in 1986 as well as after the explosion of Pan Am Flight 103, which was full of college students returning home just days before Christmas 1988.[166] Apparently, American innocence was something that could be lost and then restored. Like the head of a hydra, it grew back. Or perhaps more accurately, American innocence was the willful forgetting of past adversities. Conceptions of American innocence invoked the indomitable American belief in its own goodness, in the power of its own democratic experiment and its resulting sense of exceptionalism.

American innocence also seemed to represent a naive inoculation from the rest of the world; a kind of fun house mirror in which Americans not only did not see the rest of the world but in which they were blind to the ramifications of their own behavior. American innocence might be renamed "American privilege"—the luxury of not being regularly reminded of episodes of ruin, tragedy, and calamity that were the result of one's own decisions. *American innocence* was the privilege of hegemony. The goodness of American power and its exercise regularly wiped the slate clean. None of this addressed whether the United States was ever innocent.

The sermons after the Oklahoma bombing participated as well in this construction of the American loss of innocence; their explanations also required a kind of intentional amnesia and a sense of exceptionalism. In the White minister's version of American history, the Los Angeles uprising had never happened. The state had always been on the side of right and true and just. This was startling given not only how recent the events in Los Angeles were to the Oklahoma City bombing but also because the first months of the O. J. Simpson trial had made a mockery of law enforcement, as well as of a legal counsel unable to adjudicate the complications of race, gender, and violence in America.[167] It seemed obvious in April 1995 that the United States was quite removed from any conception of innocence. Yet Reverend C. Lawrence Bishop told his congregation: "We are not children anymore. So, for a variety of reasons, we are holding a long, drawn out funeral procession. Because we are burying so many things—not just people but our innocence as well—it's going to last a long, long time."[168]

In the secular age of 1995, Americans might name themselves as Christians, even go to church frequently, but the majority were practicing what Catholic theologian Father Thomas Reeves named at the time as "an innocuous Christianity. It tended to be an easy, upbeat, convenient, and compatible faith. It did not require self-sacrifice, discipline, humility, or an otherworldly outlook. There was very little guilt and no punishment, and the payoff in heaven was virtually certain."[169] Since their congregants were ill equipped to handle the challenges of a demanding, humiliating, and perhaps even a sacrificial faith, ministers had to figure out how to cajole Christian Americans into belief without frightening them away from the church permanently. This was pastoral care as therapy: "God has not rejected us. . . . God's face is toward us. . . . God has heard our cries. God knows our sorrow and grief and pain. But the tears will be wiped away."[170] This was a caretaker God. He required little but gave much. Reeves called this version of Christianity, "consumer Christianity. The 'divine right' of the consumer to choose as he or she pleases has become so common an idea that it operates in millions of Americans like an unconscious tropism. Millions of Americans today feel free to buy as much of the full Christian faith as seems desirable. The cost is low and customer satisfaction seems guaranteed."[171]

So, how did that feature of Christianity work during the crisis of the Oklahoma City bombing? A terrible catastrophe had just occurred. How could Christians be satisfied? First, they could be soothed by ministers who assured them that very little was required of them right now. God was managing everything through his agents of the state, law enforcement, and so forth. Second, God had given them permission to mourn, and to cry; in fact, they were encouraged to mourn for their own long-term psychological benefit. "What do we do with our pain? What do we do with our grief? We need to understand that grief is an emotion, not a disease. . . . We have to understand that everyone will grieve differently. Grief is like snowflakes and fingerprints."[172] Bishop Charles Salatka says it directly: "We pray for ourselves."[173] This tragedy in American history revealed the most acute disintegration of Christianity into therapeutic psychology. So much had Christianity become therapeutic that when clergy arrived at the scene of the Murrah building, they were required to coordinate with psychologists to ensure that they were "qualified" for grief counseling: "We don't want just anyone walking in. This is a site where we must offer both protection and help. Any clergy taking part would have to be highly qualified, and that included earned degrees in the appropriate field."[174]

In her account of how the site was managed, Robin Jones detailed how the "rules" were established and the challenges some of those rules posed for clergy. "Number one priority for any pastoral counselor had to be integrity . . . and an aspect of pastoral integrity was the deliberate abandonment of 'Churchianity.' For a lot of pastors steeped in their denomination, this was very difficult. But the rule was inviolable: No pastor would proselytize for his or her faith or for a specific church."[175]

The man assigned to do the selection and make these determinations was a self-described local businessman who "felt the call of God. There were times when it was really tough, because we turned people away. Turning away incompetence is not tough. Turning away dedicated Christians is. It wasn't that they weren't any good. They certainly were. It was just that they didn't meet the particular requirements we needed in that situation."[176] Clergy only had value when they could lend themselves to the therapeutic. Christianity no longer offered "both protection and help"—only the Church of the National Tragedy could do that.

Therapeutic Christianity also offered multiple kinds of healing services, including the service of the Healing of Memories: "We pray for ourselves. O, God, we are lost, we are broken. We feel anger and frustration. Bless us, O God, that we may bless others along life's way."[177] In other words, God must give the supplicant something before they can do anything for anyone else. This was classic pop psychology from the Norman Vincent Peale era: you have to love yourself before you can love anyone else. It might be good psychology, but it was most certainly a rather narcissistic inversion of the Golden Rule: "In everything, do to others as you would have them do to you" (Matt. 7:12).

The Healing of Memories service was conducted a week after the blast at the Church of the Redeemer. Reverend Robert Wise advised those attending that "a person who makes themselves available to God will receive God's ministry to the fullest extent possible."[178] And what God was providing was *the healing of the horrible memories* that the bombing as well as the rescue and recovery invoked in many people. The service "based on solid scriptural knowledge" asserted that while humankind was locked into time, God was not. God functioned outside of the constraints of time. Therefore, the service helped those traumatized to re-create their memory of the event with God present at every moment, right there in the building.[179]

As Jones recounted, "The participants were asked to picture Jesus Christ right there in the ruined building where He certainly was. After the participants rolled the traumatic aspect of their memories to a conclusion, they released all the destructive experiences, the image and pain, into the arms of the risen Christ."[180] God was the therapist who offered, like the film of the same name, "the eternal sunshine of the spotless mind."[181]

This was Christianity coiled with psychology in a way that reduced Christianity to a form of self-help. Christ becomes a life coach offering solace in grief. Senior minister Michael Anderson of Westminster Presbyterian Church in Oklahoma City even gave a sermon entitled "Transforming Our Trauma," which offered twelve steps for overcoming trauma.[182] This Christianity was not about suffering, the cross, or even the resurrection. This was Christ as a kind of time machine for affliction.

After Pearl Harbor, ministers did not even mention God's role in the tragedy. After JFK's assassination, ministers lamented their own failure and possible culpability. After the death of Dr. Martin Luther King, ministers hesitated in their faith and then theologized themselves away from the political world. In Los Angeles, God was the institutional church providing social services, stepping in as a surrogate for all the ways that the state had failed. And here, in Oklahoma, God was a counselor whose countertransference was so acute that "His heart is the first to break."[183] In fact, to memorialize this grief St. Joseph's Catholic Church, which had been severely damaged in the blast, erected the now well-known statue "And Jesus Wept."[184]

Scholars of religion have coined the term "self-religion" as a way to explain this turn to self-optimization. The goal of religion is to maximize the self, one's potential, to perhaps discover one's true and authentic self. The flourishing of this element of American religion is manifest here in these first sermons after the bombing. It is a rather troubling turn because it is mostly without scriptural or theological support. In the New Testament, Jesus clearly suffers, and he asks his apostles to "take up your cross and follow me." There are no promises of an easy or comfortable life. In fact, Jesus insists that "whoever wants to save his life will lose it" (Matt. 10:39).

Others have noted that this conception of religion as self-maximization is a better fit with late capitalism than with Christianity.[185] The development of the prosperity gospel was only the most obvious expression of that perspective.[186] The foundation of this self-religion, of course, was not the Oklahoma bombing of 1995. The contemporary formulation of self-religion probably began more accurately with the pastoral care theology of Norman Vincent Peale. His best-selling 1952 book, *The Power of Positive Thinking*, deeply influenced the role ministers imagined as appropriate for them to play in their congregants' lives for many decades. Pastoral care had become entwined with psychological therapy. Religious historian Susan Myers-Shirk notes that one of the goals of "pastoral counseling" was to help congregants make connections between the counseling experience and the religious experience.[187] And, unlike during the World War II era when freedom meant primarily the fight against fascism, during the 1960s and beyond, freedom was personalized, linked to "self-realization," and meant making one's own choices and solving one's own problems.[188] And not surprisingly, the constituency for this counseling was predominantly middle class and White. Counseling was one of the privileges of this group.[189]

What the Oklahoma bombing marked was the use of self-help religion during a tragedy. There had been threads of self-help developing for well over forty years before the Oklahoma bombing, but in the aftermath the majority of ministers decided to use the vernacular of the therapeutic with God as a caretaker to console their congregations and to provide answers to their questions of theodicy. It was another element of the Church of the National Tragedy. God was not an agent of political transformation; rather, He was a comforter. He did not help Christians to change the world or even to make sense of it; rather, in this version of Christianity, God merely helped Christians *to feel better* about that world. To echo Marita Sturken in *Tourists of History,* He was a giant teddy bear, soothing Americans with a hug.

There was no prophetic in a therapeutic faith. No demand for excellence to which one was supposed to strive. One merely needed to feel better. This was a version of Christianity without agency—either for its adherents or for its God. Things happened to God's people, as well as apparently to God, and Christianity was about learning how to adjust to these circumstances; one minister proclaimed after the bombing, "In fact God's will was broken with that kind of event."[190] This was not God of the whirlwind who had roared at Job to answer His questions about just punishment.

Instead, the God of the Oklahoma bombing was a diminutive God who accommodated the tragedies of the world, who seemed to have no autonomy from humanity, and who existed primarily to mend the broken hearts of lived experience. This was not a God who demanded a leap of faith, who required sacrifice, who urged particular ways of being. Rather this was a God who existed, who perhaps even came into being, when there was a tragedy. He was, after all, the God of the Church of the National Tragedy. And this anemic God was easily replaced in the days after 9/11 with a state eager to fill the void, one that was ready to become the whirlwind and demand, "Can you hunt the prey for the lion, or satisfy the appetite of the young lions, when they crouch in their dens, or lie in wait in their covert? Who provides for the raven its prey, when its young ones cry to God, and wander about for lack of food?" (Job 38:39–41). Post 9/11, the state would assume the mantle, the agency, and the power once accorded to a now lost or at least willingly subordinated God.

The Oklahoma Bombing: Not the Los Angeles Uprisings

Despite initial appearances to the contrary, there were several important similarities between the Oklahoma bombing of 1995 and the Los Angeles uprisings in 1992. The violence in each was an expression of frustration by alienated and impoverished citizens about the role of their government. In the 1990s, White Americans living in the heartland were sequestered in what historian Osha Gray Davidson named the United States' "rural ghettos."[191] These enclaves were in crisis. There were "pockets of poverty, unemployment, violence and despair that were becoming more and more isolated from the rest of the country. The most American part of America was fast becoming America's Third World."[192] Father Frank Cordero, a Catholic priest in Iowa, called rural homelessness an invisible problem: "We hide poverty much more easily out here than in the cities."[193]

The nostalgic narrative that corporate media promoted after the Oklahoma City bombing did not accurately reflect reality for many Americans living in the heartland. As poverty spiked, the strong tradition of "taking care of one's own" was deeply challenged. It became increasingly difficult just to take care of oneself.[194] Timothy McVeigh and the militia he joined were part of that story. It is now a well-known history—the decimation of small towns by the consolidation of small businesses into a local Walmart, the debt dependence of small farms, and the loss of manufacturing jobs writ large. But in 1995, the rural ghetto was largely invisible to most Americans, just as the frustration of Los Angeles African Americans was largely hidden from the view of the financial center of the city and the wealthy White suburbs that surrounded it.

Tapping into the long tradition of racism and anti-Semitism in the United States, extremist groups became a way for some rural, White, disenfranchised citizens to believe in the possibility of renewed power. It was a chimera, of course, but it was a shiny one, easily accessible and cogently explained, especially after the sieges at Ruby Ridge, Idaho (August 21, 1992), and Waco, Texas (April 19, 1993). After his service in the Gulf War, Timothy McVeigh was disillusioned by American military expenditures abroad. These expenses, he believed, came out of the toil and sweat of everyday Americans and rather than uplifting Americans, the money was squandered on underserving foreigners. He feared that the American government was bloated with taxpayers' money and was willing to sacrifice its own citizens on the altar of imperial ambition. He was also angry, as were many of his fellow militia members, about the government's failure to ensure justice for the Branch Davidians and for Randy Weaver's family at Ruby Ridge.

From the perspective of McVeigh and his militia cohort, the government wielded all the lethal force as was manifest as well to the residents of Los Angeles in the broken ribs and shattered face of Rodney King. Ironically, McVeigh had himself called out the police brutality in Los Angeles; his invective over the deployment of the Seventh Light Infantry into Los Angeles during the protests was not, however, because he feared the harm done to Los Angeles' Black residents, but because he saw the federal use of force as a manifestation of the government's usurpation of local authority.[195] Furthermore, McVeigh believed that the government was not protecting its (White) citizens from unjust execution by its failure to punish those who killed Vicki Weaver and her son at Ruby Ridge and the seventy-five others (including twenty-five children) at Waco, Texas. McVeigh was not concerned about the death or suffering of racialized minorities. McVeigh and his militia cohort were well-established racist bigots whose utopic vision for the United States was White nationalism—what they called the New Era of all-White.[196]

Although the actions of African Americans during those long three days in the spring of 1992 were taken to illuminate race relations in the United States overall, Timothy McVeigh's Whiteness provided no such diagnostic revelation. His race was largely considered irrelevant to his crime. White Americans did not worry about the violent proclivities of White men in the United States after the Oklahoma bombing, but they did worry quite a bit about the Muslims in their midst in the hours before McVeigh's arrest was confirmed. Americans were apprehensive about the militia groups that were forming in the Midwest, but these groups were not given a racial inflection.[197] Even the Southern Poverty Law Center, which compiled the data on the rise of radical Right hate groups, did not interpret the bombing as a racial crime.[198] In contrast, because the participants in the Los Angeles uprising were Black and Korean as well as Latinx, the violence had to be about their race; it must reveal something significant about their racial identity as well as race relations more generally in the United States.

Another distinction between the two events lay in how Americans handled these two violent crises of the 1990s and what they believed the events revealed about American national identity. President Bush was quite clear early in his address to the nation that the Los Angeles uprisings were not American—in fact, they were an "ugly version" of ourselves. The aftermath of the Oklahoma bombing, on the other hand, revealed the United States at its national best. Many of the stories of the Oklahoma bombing centered on the role of mothers in the American heartland. There was an invasive fascination on the grief and suffering of mothers who had lost children in the bombing.[199] As cultural critic Margaret Hirschberg discussed in her provocative essay on Edye Smith Jones, who lost both of her toddler boys in the blast, Jones was followed by the media for well over a year as she struggled to mend herself, mend her marriage, and eventually begin a new family. The grief-stricken Oklahoma mothers were embedded in families, in relationships. Their grief and suffering was our (American) suffering. White grief was universal, while Black grief remained local and particular.

In Los Angeles, the victims of the uprising or police brutality, or both, were themselves interrogated for their own guilt, not mourned for their innocence. They were detailed as solitary figures, not Americans rooted in families and a matrix of relationships. Relationships—mother, father, brother, aunt—did not provide the narrative frame in Los Angeles; rather, there the *suspect* or *offender* was the means of analysis. Several African American commentators noted in newspaper op-eds after the bombing that "white purveyors of hate" were more readily accommodated than their Black counterparts.[200] Others observed, too, that two years later O. J. Simpson was much more despised than Timothy McVeigh: "McVeigh is regarded with far more indifference by the public . . . even though McVeigh was determined to overthrow our government."[201]

In the Oklahoma bombing, race was mostly expunged from the dominant narrative as a category of analysis: "Some of the persons whose stories are told here are black, some white, some Hispanic, some 'other.' We have made no distinction in our text because at that time, in that place, no one made any such distinction whatsoever. Quite simply, no one noticed. Hero and victim bereaved and survivor—all worked and prayed and hugged and mourned together. As the tragedy and the heroism unfolded, race disappeared. In this book we can do no less."[202]

With the erasure, all the victims became White. It was just "easier" (or so the argument went) not to have to address how racial identity might have informed the tragedy and its reverberating aftermath. What became possible, then, was the construction of a united American national identity. The desire after the tragedy was for the universal, for the simplifications that would reunite Americans even after one of their own had turned against his fellow Americans. This point is congruent with Simon Stow's argument in *American Mourning* that historically Americans have preferred a mourning process that propels reconciliation and unity rather than one that interrogates differences and the divisions embedded in American identity.[203]

The visualization of that united American national identity began within hours after the bombing with the iconic photograph of infant Baylee Almon in a firefighter's arms. It was a powerful image taken by an amateur photographer at the scene, Lester Larue. The one-year-old baby was already dead when Captain Chris Fields carried her out of the building; the photograph became the identifying feature of the Oklahoma bombing aftermath. The everyday American hero was trying to save America's children and thus restore national innocence.

Over the ensuing months, the photograph itself would become shrouded in challenges for the unwitting photographer, for Baylee Almon's grieving mother, and for the long-term mental health of the firefighter.[204] But at the time, in the days immediately following the bombing, the image helped to crystallize the narrative of the tragedy. It was an image of both stoic masculinity and cradled domesticity, of heroic rescue and heartbreaking ruin, of the confrontation of the visible American good and the anonymity of the serpentine malicious, and of the possibilities for spiritual redemption and the devastating reality of youthful demise.

The Church of the National Tragedy, as exemplified through this image, was the marker of what united Americans, of what erased tensions and differences. The blast in Oklahoma proclaimed Americans' national innocence: everyone was good and just . . . and White—even the federal workers were canonized as part of the sacred American heartland. Americans triumphed over challenges—bringing hope and justice as well as a helping hand out of the rubble and blood of the building. The Los Angeles uprisings, on the other hand, disclosed the chaotic realities of American identity—the tangled matrix of race and class and law enforcement. In Oklahoma City, the first responders were portrayed as heroes, the angels amidst destruction. In Los Angeles, first responders did not respond, and when they did, Black American citizens suffered bloody faces and broken ribs.

Mourning: Temporary and Forever

If any platitude can explain the Los Angeles uprising and the Oklahoma bombing, it is "We have seen the enemy and it is us." After Los Angeles and Oklahoma, ministers across the political spectrum and racial divide assumed a therapeutic model for mourning—feelings, not actions, were paramount. Most ministers had given up on political actions to manage the crises of modern life. All one could hope to do was survive; hence, the Church of the National Tragedy. Americans became adept at grieving; mourning brought Americans across their political, class, and racial divides together in solemn ceremonial rituals. Tragedy united, if only temporarily.

Thus, in many ways, American ministers were well prepared to preach the Sunday after September 11, 2001. The tragic deaths of Americans living their everyday, freedom-loving lives was something many already knew how to address. And September 11 was even easier to make sense of than either Oklahoma or Los Angeles had been because 9/11 had a built-in foreign enemy who was not one of *us*. Americans were again innocent—there was no American culpability, so ministers could return to a post–World War II narrative of American virtue and valor. First responders were heroes; all Americans were good again and God was clearly on *our* side. With September 11, religion was at the center of the crisis and ministers were called on to think through the magnitude of the theological paradox the violence invoked: how could an all-loving God allow this to happen to an innocent people, a chosen people? And how could another religion, presumably Islam, wish Americans dead?

Unlike after Pearl Harbor, most American ministers after 9/11 were confident that God was communicating through the tragedy; how could He not be—the world's most powerful nation had been humbled by an unknown band of fanatics. This violence had to be about something existential. Something this horrible didn't happen to a country as good as the United States without God's notice. And fortunately for God, the American military stood ready to implement His will and seek His justice. In the tragedy of 9/11, God was communicating and He was prepared for (or dependent on?) the state to implement His will. Protestant ministers may not have made a Faustian pact with the Devil, but in the crisis sermons of September 11, they had certainly made a contract with the state.

CHAPTER FIVE

God's Celestial Army

September 11, 2001

In the first hours after the planes crashed and the buildings burned on September 11, 2001, some ministers had hope for a theological response from American Christians: "The proper response of God's people to this tragedy is not lamenting wicked men or standing paralyzed in the face of so great a loss. . . . This tragedy affords us the opportunity to see ourselves as we have been and now are. It lets us measure ourselves on the scale of something bigger than our comfortable routines and our narrowed perspectives."[1] But within weeks, if not days, some of those very same ministers came to an astute realization: "We may be people who live in two worlds, one foot in the earth, the other in the spiritual realm. But I contend that the foot we have in *this* world bears most of the weight of our priorities and desires and time and attention. The foot we keep in the heavenly realms is light as a feather and atrophied from lack of real use."[2] Reverend William Sloan Coffin more pointedly noted, "Instead of understanding that a lot of people in the world are being unfairly hurt, Americans turned in upon ourselves and became the victim of victimhood."[3] And Reverend Ligon Duncan in a different register but with the same effect: "That was a horrendous occurrence on Tuesday, we've never seen the like of that, and yet in seeing the catastrophe that occurred on Tuesday in New York, and Washington, and just out of Pittsburgh, we only saw a glimpse of what we deserve. We always think that we deserve better, but that's what we deserve, we deserve the judgment of God."[4] But those voices recommending reflection and self-assessment were drowned out and with great alacrity: the dominant ministerial and political narrative of the violence of September 11 became that Americans were victims and that the solution to American grief would be found with that "foot in this world" rather than the one tiptoeing into God's.

The devastation of September 11, 2001, was the first time in a century that Americans put religion directly at the center of a crisis. Indeed, 9/11 was an emergency in which religion was pivotal to understanding the crisis. Within hours, the terrorists were reputed to be Muslim fanatics, and by the next morning the *New York Times* was reporting that Osama bin Laden was "presumed to be the leader" of the group of hijackers.[5] Quickly, the violence was linked to religious beliefs and "the enemy" detailed as a member of a religion little known or understood by most Americans.

American clergy were unexpectedly hurled into the maelstrom. Many were called immediately for pastoral care and counseling at the New York City site and the Pentagon. One pastor, Reverend Kathleen Liles, described her feelings:

> I stopped at St. Luke's Church and used their phone and then at St. Vincent's Hospital to help out there and to talk to the people who were trying to donate blood, and I noted the overwhelming response of people to the clerical collar. They were just so glad that people were clearly involved *as religious people*. I had never before felt that people were so glad to see someone who was identified as a religious person, because usually in New York, they just ignore you. It indicated a real longing for some connection to sacredness in the midst of all that overwhelming horror.[6]

The first official death certificate filed for the terrorist attacks was for Father Mychal Judge, a Franciscan friar and chaplain who was killed by falling debris while giving last rites to a dying firefighter at Ground

Zero.[7] The photograph of his mortally wounded body being carried out of the ruins by five firefighters became an icon of the rescue efforts, an American pietà. The photograph was reminiscent of the image of the firefighter cradling the dead infant, Baylee Almon, after the Oklahoma City bombing.

The 9/11 photo announced the correspondence between the crucified Christ and the wounded American nation. Both were innocent and wrongly punished but resurrected by the Father's love. The loving Father was represented in the photo by the maternal yet masculine first responders. The stage was set for a Christian narrative to explicate the tragedy: White masculinity would rescue the fallen, grief would be invisible and quickly overcome, and the nation would be saved through its atoning suffering. As a Catholic priest told a *New York Times* reporter, "There are no atheists at Ground Zero."[8] Rendered invisible again, as in past tragedies, was the debilitating mourning, particularly the maternal and disempowered grief of the powerless that Michelangelo's sculpture had detailed so profoundly.

Nationwide, most clergy offered consolation with candlelight prayer vigils at crowded churches. The majority of the ministry knew very little about Islam, but they were expected to narrate understanding for ordinary Americans. The crisis was existential, challenging both the theological—*How could God allow so much innocent suffering?*—and the political—*Will America ever be safe again?* There was also some combination of both—*Has America lost its favored status with God?*

The 9/11 attacks were the largest on American soil since Pearl Harbor. Given the media technology available, reporting of the devastation was vivid and traumatic. The coverage became the longest continuously running story in American history, surpassing even the assassination of President John F. Kennedy, which no network had covered for more than seventy consecutive hours. By Saturday morning, September 15, 2001, CBS, NBC, and ABC—the three networks that had also existed at the time of Kennedy's assassination—had been on the air without commercial interruption for ninety hours.[9] Americans watched endlessly repeated video of the planes crashing into the Towers as well as stricken interviews of survivors and desperate grievers.

As with tragedies before, Americans gathered around their television shrines and began the arduous process of making meaning from the absurd. Since there were so few bodies recovered initially, there were limited funerals on which to focus attention in the first several days. There was no theater of a state funeral to secure the community.

Nonetheless, just as the fence around the crumbled Murrah Federal Building in Oklahoma had become a memorial site, so the wrought-iron gate around St. Paul's Chapel at Trinity Church became a canvas where survivors and others could register their grief and their hopes that the lost and missing might still be found alive. Impromptu obituaries emerged from the photos of the missing. Volunteers created a "memorial altar" from the posters and the tokens of remembrance. A national narrative was being birthed.

There were other rituals that became part of the process of mourning and meaning-making. On September 13, rescue workers uncovered a steel beam that had been twisted into a cross; it was dubbed the Ground Zero cross. Its shape and survival became a Christian monument to God's presence and secured the site workers' belief that they were not toiling alone or in vain.

Furthermore, the fact that only one church, St. Nicholas Greek Orthodox Church, had been destroyed was also perceived as significant, especially since St. Paul's Chapel was closer to the destruction and yet had been spared. St. Paul's Chapel was the oldest church building in New York City, the church where George Washington had prayed after his inauguration in 1789. Its endurance and link to the founding of the United States assured Christian Americans that God had not abandoned them. The American project "under God" would continue.

Just as there had been after the Oklahoma City bombing, there were the expected stories of those who were supposed to be at the Twin Towers or on a flight, but who had overslept, had missed their subway stop, or had changed their schedule and thus had lived. Those stories were optimistic, detailed as manifesting God's intervention alongside (despite?) the smoldering carnage manifest in downtown Manhattan, Shanksville, Pennsylvania, and Washington, DC. Reverend Rodney Buchanan repeated such anecdotes:

> As I heard about a person this week who had four friends who were to be at the World Trade Center on Tuesday, September 11. Two of them died. However, one of them slept

through their alarm that morning. . . . The fourth friend fell asleep on the subway ride to work and missed his stop. . . . Why were these two spared and others not? I don't know. They were probably no better or worse than the others. But it does mean that God was at work through this whole thing. How many would be lost if he hadn't been? The death toll could have been in the tens of thousands.[10]

So God saved some ("God was at work"). But largely occluded ("I don't know") was a scriptural justification or theological explanation for why others died for simply being where they were, doing what they were regularly scheduled to do. The theological implications would take months, if not years, to unravel and understand.

Again, as in crises past, the devastation was not only at the sites of the terrorist violence. In the ten days after the attack, the FBI reported more than six hundred incidents of hate against Muslim and Arab men and women. Five hundred furious people mobbed a Chicago-area mosque and refused to leave until they were forced out by police. A Pakistani grocer was murdered in Texas. A man on an anti-Arab rampage in Arizona fatally shot a gas station owner who was an Indian-born Sikh. FBI director Robert Mueller said over and over again that "vigilante attacks and threats against Arab-Americans will not be tolerated," but harassment and violence continued for months.[11]

In a *New York Times* article appearing a week after the horror, a Muslim woman described her dilemma:

> I am so used to thinking about myself as a New Yorker that it took me a few days to begin to see myself as a stranger might: a Muslim woman, an outsider, perhaps an enemy of the city. . . .
> I can only imagine how much more difficult it is for men who look like Mohamed Atta or Osama bin Laden.[12]

Lest this be understood as mere anecdote, a Gallup poll on September 25, 2001, revealed that one-third of Americans favored "such measure as allowing the US government to take legal immigrants from unfriendly countries to internment camps."[13]

This was the fear and violence of the once-secure turning against a perceived threat. This was 1942 America interning its own citizens for fear that they were members of a hidden Japanese fifth column. It was not, however, the rage that burned after the assassination of Rev. Dr. Martin Luther King Jr. or after the not guilty verdict in the beating of Rodney King. Rather, this was the angry realization by ordinary Americans that they were vulnerable, that the unthinking privilege they had enjoyed as unassailable world citizens had been destroyed. This was the fury of those who grasped that they were equal now to others in misery. It was the unmasked wrath of those whose illusions had been exposed.

Slavoj Žižek observed after 9/11 that the collapse of the Twin Towers brought "the real" to the United States. He argued that before September 11, the violence that others suffered elsewhere in the world had been a mere "fantasmatic screen apparition" on the nightly news; after 9/11, that violence became gruesomely present for Americans. In an odd inverse, Žižek notes, American reality was shattered by a spectacle that most watched on their television sets the morning of September 11.[14] A representation had made reality present to an otherwise oblivious America.

It is worth noting that while across the country, Christian Americans flocked to their places of worship in the immediate aftermath of the devastation, the longevity of that seeking for religious solace varied by race, gender, and education. Yet fully 78 percent of all Americans said in the month after the attacks that religion's influence in American life was growing. This was an increase from 37 percent eight months earlier, and the highest mark on this measure in four decades.[15]

At the same time, the American public had a better opinion of Muslim Americans than it did before the attacks. Surprisingly, favorable views of Muslim Americans have continued to rise—from 45 percent in March 2002 to 59 percent (fifteen years and two Middle East wars later) in 2017.

Most African Americans and Hispanics reported that by December 2001, they had returned to their regular religious practices and were neither more nor less religiously active than prior to September 11, 2001. The only group for whom increased religiosity was maintained was White men.[16] They were the ones for whom the violence and violation of the terrorism were the most difficult to process. *How could this happen to us?*

When public intellectual Cornel West used the challenging phrase "the niggerization of America" to describe the United States' experience of September 11, what he was identifying was the suffering and disempowerment that many disenfranchised Americans had been experiencing for centuries. He was not discounting the injury, only aligning it with the experience of many African Americans. "When you're niggerized, you're unsafe, unprotected, subject to random violence, hated for who you are. You become so scared that you defer to the powers that be, and you're willing to consent to your own domination. And that's the history of black people in America."[17]

West was attempting, admittedly in a provocative and perhaps clumsy way, to link 9/11 suffering to previous American suffering. He was offering a cautionary note as well—sometimes when one has been so beaten down, one turns to the powers that be to find redemption. Of course, this was what Americans eventually did. They deferred to the powers that be—primarily the US military—and sought solace and security in ferocious vengeance. They agreed unthinkingly to the sacrifice of some of their own basic freedoms.

Contemporary theorists of cultural trauma have noted that when a society takes some moral responsibility for its own suffering, its citizens are more likely to recognize the suffering of others and thus expand the circle of "we." Those who refuse to assume any liability for their suffering restrict their solidarity with others and thus tend not to assume a moral stance.[18]

In many ways, American Christians did not endorse this scrupulous and dutiful perspective. Ministers neither encouraged their congregants to examine the political origins of terrorist violence nor urged parishioners to identify their suffering with that of others. There were exceptions to this, of course, but the vast majority of the sermons imagined American suffering as without equivalence and of such a magnitude as to have literally reached biblical proportions. American Christians, led by their clergy, thus embraced conceptions of Christian patriotism, innocence, and "sacred evil" that required US military intervention to deliver divine justice. Reverend Marty Baker preached that Satan is actually the force that attacked America: "We do have an enemy. His name is not Osama Bin Laden; nor is it the Taliban. . . . Our enemy is Satan. . . . He has been waging war against God's people since the

Garden of Eden. He specializes in ground troops, air attacks, and covert assaults."[19] In his sermon, Reverend Russell Brownworth concluded that the conditions exist for a "just war." "The American people have the will to respond, there was an evil attack on the unsuspecting and innocent that was clearly evil and the president has said . . . our purpose is to stamp out terrorism, a righteous motive."[20]

The events of the day were traumatic to the nation, in part because the violence disrupted American conceptions of the everyday. Americans were killed merely for being American, and those killed were innocent, good, "us." President Bush named this in the very first line of his address to the nation the night of September 11: "Today our fellow citizens, our way of life, our very freedom came under attack in a series of deliberate and deadly terrorist acts."[21] Reverend Alvin Jackson echoed the claim: "No more can we tell ourselves that we are safe simply because we live in the United States. No more can we cling to the faith that our military and economic might are sufficient to protect us from our enemies. Never again can we derive comfort from our geographic remoteness, located here between these two great moats of the world. Everything changed on 9/11."[22]

Cultural trauma is not natural; it is something constructed by society. For something to be deemed collectively traumatic, society must claim some fundamental injury, the violation of a sacred value, and/or the experience of a horribly destructive social process that demands reparation and reconstruction.[23] The three acts of violence—at the Twin Towers, at the Pentagon, and on Flight 93—were quickly consolidated into one expression encapsulating the date and the emergency number to call for help: 9/11. Many ministers played with the dual meaning, insisting that the attacks were an "emergency call from God."[24] Another very clever preacher built a sermon around Psalm 91:1, "the Lord is my refuge," which she interpreted as "the emergency number to God."[25]

These terrorist acts were particularly traumatic because they challenged fundamental American beliefs: that the United States had no enemies with sufficient power to bring such monstrous destruction to its shores; that the United States was hegemonically secure from acts of terrorism; that the United States was protected by its exceptionalism; and that other nations the world over loved the United States and its people and wished them well, not harm. Each of these beliefs was challenged that Tuesday in 2001. Americans had to seek another version of them-selves, their friends and enemies, and their role in the world.

SIX DAYS AFTER the attacks, President Bush visited the Is-lamic Center in Washington, DC, announcing: "The face of terror is not the true faith of Islam. That's not what Islam is all about. Islam is peace. These terrorists don't represent peace. They represent evil and war."[26] President Bush affirmed the place of Muslims in the United States as "teachers, doctors, members of the military and as moms and dads." He claimed: "It's a great country because we share the same values of re-spect and dignity and human worth. And it is my honor to be meeting with leaders who feel just the same as I do. They're outraged, they're sad. They love America just as much as I do."[27]

So began the civic education of Americans about Islam and Amer-ican Muslims. In a chilling echo of 1941, some clerics called out to their Muslim congregants to prove they were patriotic Americans. Cleric Shedeed told the members of his mosque on Friday, September 14: "Most of the calls we have gotten here have been from people supporting us. But we have to act as Americans. Most of you are American citizens. Fly the flag, donate money to help. If you don't want to act as American citizens, give up your passports."[28]

When FBI agents raided a brownstone in a primarily Arab neigh-borhood in Jersey City, about two hundred Arab men, women, and children cheered the agents on. They broke into chants of "USA!" when the first young man, assumed by the crowd to be a Muslim, was led away in handcuffs. "Burn in hell!" shouted one woman in the crowd. "Get 'em all!" shouted another. As the *New York Times* reported, "Even in this city of 240,000, where 1 in 5 residents is of Arab descent, there are people in the neighborhood [presumably Arabs] who can barely contain their rage toward those who resemble the presumed enemy."[29]

Reverend John A. Huffman Jr. of St. Andrew's Presbyterian Church in Newport Beach, California, told a similar story. On Friday, Sep-tember 14, the head of the local Islamic Center and some of its mem-bers asked to address Huffman's congregation. This unnamed imam, ac-cording to Huffman, "apologized for what had happened and begged us to understand that this was an aberration, not the result of historic Is-lamic teaching."[30] Presumably, the imam thought of this visit as a form of civic education for a congregation that might be tempted to lash out. Yet he apologized—or at least that was what the reverend heard and reported. The apology was part of the economy of the disenfranchised: for what one member of a minority group did, all were held responsible. Did any priests feel compelled to go to synagogues or mosques to apologize for the Christian Timothy McVeigh or the predominantly Christian LAPD?

These efforts by imams across the United States were buried under an avalanche of reporting that insisted Muslims did not sufficiently condemn the terrorists. They did, of course, but those stories were lost in the rapid construction of a new enemy, a religious enemy, a fanatic at war with freedom. Nuance was not possible when one imagined the fight as a metaphysical contest with evil.

Within days, the Honorable Minister Louis Farrakhan was reminding Americans that Muslims were not "foreigners" but an integral part of the African American tradition of the Nation of Islam. He began his address by noting the lineage from Moses and the Torah to Jesus and the Gospel to Muhammad and the Quran.[31] In no uncertain terms, Farrakhan condemned the acts of September 11: "I, on behalf of all the members of the Nation of Islam and on behalf of many millions of Muslims here in America and throughout the world, lift our voices to condemn this vicious and atrocious attack on the United States."[32]

Farrakhan, like President Bush and Christian ministers on the Day of Mourning at the National Cathedral, offered an account of the redemptive power of the tragedy. He detailed how deeply divided the country had been since the election of President Bush and how very ineffective political skill and money had been toward effecting reconciliation. "But tragedy stopped us in our tracks and caused us to reflect on God and tragedy caused the nation to bow down and pray."[33]

Minister Farrakhan made the same argument as conservative Christians when he strove to answer how God could allow this to happen. He referred directly to Reverend Billy Graham's sermon from the day before: "Dr. Graham said that this nation is in need of spiritual renewal and revival, and tragedy has brought us to the beginning of that process. Why does God permit evil? Where was God in this tragedy? In the Qur'an, there is an answer to this."[34] The answer was that Allah knew that "the powerful would not heed a warning coming from an ex-slave or from the weak, so the Qur'an teaches that Allah would seize that nation with distress and affliction, that it might humble itself."[35]

Toward the end of his address, Farrakhan drew a parallel between the 9/11 hijackers and the domestic terrorism of Timothy McVeigh:

> When Timothy McVeigh committed the worst act of terrorism on American soil, the first persons accused of this were members of the Nation of Islam and immigrant Muslims. Many followers of Islam were attacked, and then it was found that the perpetrator of this crime was a White American, a soldier who professed to be a Christian. But no Christian of his denomination was attacked. Even though his crime was the most horrible committed up until that time, nobody said "Christian Timothy McVeigh." They just said, "Timothy McVeigh." Timothy McVeigh's behavior was un-Christian-like, and, those who perpetrated this crime against America, their conduct was absolutely un-Muslim-like.[36]

Muslim scholars and politicians around the world added their voices to the condemnation. "The undersigned, leaders of Islamic movements, are horrified by the events of Tuesday 11 September 2001 in the United States which resulted in massive killing, destruction and attack on innocent lives. We express our deepest sympathies and sorrow. We condemn, in the strongest terms, the incidents, which are against all human and Islamic norms. This is grounded in the Noble Laws of Islam which forbid all forms of attacks on innocents. God Almighty says in the Holy Qur'an: 'No bearer of burdens can bear the burden of another' (Surah al-Israr 17:15)."[37]

Within a week, television stepped into the gap with programs offering a civic education about Islam—everything from the National Geographic documentary *Attack on America: An Islamic Scholar's Perspective* to Oprah Winfrey's hour-long discussion with American Muslim men and women about their faith and perspectives on 9/11.[38] These were framed as promoting the idea that the terrorists did not represent "true" Islam. "True" Islam was about praying to Allah, making a pilgrimage, and memorizing the Qur'an.

The majority of Protestant sermons did not conflate the categories of "Muslims" and "terrorists."

> To lump all Muslims into the category of terrorists is the same thing people do with us as Christians when they claim we're all cruel and bloodthirsty because of what Christians did in the name of Jesus during the crusades of the middle ages.[39]

> The vast majority of Muslims living in the United States are peaceful and law-abiding people. Christians should be the first to recognize this and befriend those who will find themselves shunned by many.[40]

Nonetheless, there were some ministers who traced the antagonism to biblical times.

> Abraham and Sarah were trying to do God's will, but they were doing it in their way. As a result, Sarah's maid, Hagar, gave birth to a son she called Ishmael. The birth of Ishmael caused enormous problems for Abraham and continues to cause problems to this very day. For Ishmael is the father of the Arab nations.[41]

In this way, the conflict was imagined as so old and entrenched as to be without a concise history or the possibility of resolution. This kind of genesis story released Americans from any culpability or recognition of their own participation in the causes of the struggle. In this version, the only person with a tie to American Christianity who "made a mistake" was Abraham of the book of Genesis. Reverend Cooper Abrams put it directly: "The point is that the Muslims have for centuries hated America and what it stands for. . . . This hatred goes back to the birth of Ishmael . . . Muhammad claimed he was a descendent of Ishmael."[42]

Many sermons condemned the anti-Muslim violence that spread across the United States. Sometimes the violence was against Sikhs, whom Americans did not recognize as distinct from Muslims, as well as against anyone who "looked Arab" despite the fact that "looking Arab" was a poorly constructed measure and one that neglected to consider that many Arabs are Christians and not Muslims. One minister adjured: "Be kind to those who would be treated unfairly because of these atrocious acts of hatred. Get rid of prejudice! Did you know that three fourths or more of all Arabs in the USA are Christians? They came to America to escape religious and ethnic persecution. They, like us, are here for freedom. Be kind to Muslims."[43] Another minister worried: "You may be here this morning and the hurt of these past few weeks has begun to manifest itself as hate toward anyone who even looks Islamic. Remember carefully that the One we serve lived His early life in the Middle East. I'm afraid if Jesus walked down one of our streets today, He might be the victim of a hate crime as well."[44]

The discriminatory violence was a painful echo of the hate crimes against Japanese Americans post–Pearl Harbor, when many Americans were unable to distinguish among Chinese, Korean, and Japanese peoples. So acute was that failure that many Chinese and Korean Americans on the West Coast wore pins on their clothing, often incorporating the American flag, confirming, "I am Chinese" or "I am Korean."

In only one of the close to three hundred sermons I read for this chapter did the minister quote at length the response from the American Muslim Council in Washington, DC, to his church's outreach and expressions of support: "We appreciate greatly the meeting with the president of the Unitarian Universalist Association UA and also his letter of support for American Muslims. We are all saddened by the loss of life and we feel compassion for the victims and families. In this time of crisis, it is important for faith communities to come together. We look forward to rebuilding our nation together."[45]

Yet there were competing nonministerial explanations regarding the religious meaning of Islam, one of which was articulated in conservative political commentator Andrew Sullivan's article, "This Is a Religious War," published on October 7, 2001, in the *New York Times Magazine.* Sullivan claimed that the 9/11 terrorists were a manifestation of the violence endemic to religious fundamentalism, whether Christian, Jewish, or Muslim. Over the course of the next months and years, this line of argument would develop into a debate about whether violence was inherent to religious belief and thus whether religion was necessarily counter to modernity and its democratic ambitions.[46]

But while this line of inquiry fascinated academics, it did not become the dominant American narrative. It certainly was not persuasive to the majority of American Christians. Being an "American" was too entwined in the popular imagination with being a Christian for this kind of argument to gain much traction. When President Bush named the terrorists as "attacking civilization," it did not take much to interpret that to mean that (1) the terrorists were not part of civilization, and (2) since religion is foundational to American self-conception, the terrorists were not religious; as Bush named it, they merely had "pretensions to piety."[47] Religion was not the issue—the problem was *which* religion and whether one was an authentic practitioner of it.

American televangelist Reverend Jerry Falwell also stepped into the breach and announced on September 13 that, yes, God was at the center of the crisis and He was punishing the United States because the nation had cast God out of the public sphere: "I really believe the pagans, and the abortionists, and the feminists, and the gays and the lesbians who are actively trying to make that an alternative lifestyle, the ACLU, People for the American Way, all of them who have tried to secularize America. I point the finger in their face and say: You helped this happen."[48]

Reverend Falwell (and fellow televangelist Reverend Pat Robertson) believed with Andrew Sullivan that, yes, this was "a religious war," but the war was being fought by God in order to have His Christian nation rightfully returned to him. The violence of 9/11 was punishment, not to destroy America, but to ignite a Christian revival.

Ironically, Falwell and Robinson were the perfect exemplars of Sullivan's point. Their orthodoxies made them seemingly unfit for the contemporary democratic and pluralistic order. Not unexpectedly, Falwell was swiftly condemned across the political and religious spectrum; he offered an apology that included his "regret that his remarks were taken out of context." He had been having "a theological discussion," he insisted, in a Christian context (his television show, *The 700 Club*). In other words, "real" Christians would understand why he had condemned abortionists, gays, lesbians, and so forth. It was only non-Christians (i.e., those who had been excoriated by Falwell) who presumably misunderstood.[49]

Reverend Falwell was not interested in Islam; he was not trying to understand its principles or forge reconciliation. He was concerned about God acting in American history through the instrument of the jihadists to remind His chosen people that they had neglected their covenant with Him. Unlike the 1960s ministers who after Kennedy's assassination blamed themselves as leaders of the church for overlooking the culture of hate that had facilitated the presidential assassination, these

2001 televangelists scapegoated, blaming not even the jihadists but a specific subset of their fellow Americans; they were convinced that they, themselves, were beyond reproach and were now being called by God to lead the rest of the nation toward its redemption. So certain were they of their own righteousness that they saw confirmation of their worldview everywhere: "Pat, did you notice yesterday? The ACLU, and all the Christ haters, the People for the American Way, NOW, etc. were totally disregarded by the Democrats and the Republicans in both houses of Congress as they went out on the steps and called out to God in prayer and sang, 'God Bless America,' and said, 'Let the ACLU be hanged.'"[50]

Reverend Falwell was referring to the spontaneous singing of "God Bless America" when the Speaker of the House, Representative Dennis Hastert, Republican of Illinois, and the Democratic majority leader, Senator Tom Daschle of South Dakota, addressed the nation immediately before the president's evening address on September 11. "Senators, and House members, Democrats and Republicans, will stand shoulder to shoulder to fight this evil that is perpetrated on this nation," said Hastert. "We will stand together to make sure who perpetrated this evil deed will pay a price."[51]

Daschle called the attacks on the World Trade Center and the Pentagon "an assault on our freedom." He said: "As the representatives of the people, we are here to declare that our resolve has not been weakened by these horrific and cowardly acts. Congress will convene tomorrow." While Daschle used the language of justice, Hastert talked about "fighting evil" and "the evil deed."[52] Rapidly, transcendental purposes were being assigned to the tragedy and the already porous boundary between the state and the church was being negotiated.

President Bush declared Friday, September 14, 2001, as a National Day of Prayer and Remembrance. Note that it was a day of prayer and remembrance, not a national day of mourning, as had been the case for the Oklahoma City bombing in 1995. Americans were not to dwell in grief; rather, they were quickly to construct meaning through memory; mourning was reduced to recollection.

A two-hour-long interfaith, albeit predominantly Protestant, service was held at the Washington National Cathedral in Washington, DC. Other faiths were represented—a Jewish rabbi, a Catholic priest, an Islamic cleric—but each participated in particularly Protestant ways, such as by saying a prayer or reading Scripture. There were no representatives from Eastern religions, such as Buddhism or Hinduism. Perhaps most telling, all the religious leaders processed in and out of the cathedral behind a large metal cross.[53]

The first processional was a military presentation of the colors. A single member of each branch of service carried in a flag representing both the service and the battles in which that service had participated over the course of American history. The US Army Orchestra played "God Bless America." From its first minutes, the service was marked as a state-sanctified space, a militarized zone perhaps, as well as a House of God.

At times it was as if the ministers were hosting a government event. Reverend Holmes Dixon began the service addressing President Bush, "We are grateful that *you have called for this service* and that *you have brought people* to this cathedral church."[54] The implication was that the president had called and gathered the congregation, a role usually reserved for clergy. The service was divided into two segments; the first half emphasized divine grace, love, and calls for peace.[55] It was ostensibly the "religious" part of the event—with Scripture readings, prayers, and even an authoritative sermon from the United States' most recognizable minister, Reverend Billy Graham.

The first hour had all the expected thematic theological elements: the *all for love* ministers such as the Episcopal bishop Reverend Jane Holmes Dixon who officiated the service and proclaimed, "Peoples of all faiths want to say, love is stronger than hate, and that love lived out in justice will prevail."[56] There were the reminders not to respond to evil with evil; Reverend Nathan Baxter, dean of the National Cathedral, urged, "Let us pray for divine wisdom as our leaders consider the necessary actions for national security."[57] And of course there were the bewildering questions about theodicy, addressed most directly by Reverend Billy Graham (who received a standing ovation at the end of his sermon): "God is not the author of evil. Rather evil is part of the mystery of iniquity. . . . From the cross, God declares, I love you. I know the heartaches and the pains that you feel, but I love you."[58] Imam Muzammil Siddiqi of the Islamic Society of North America also spoke about how good and evil are not equal, and that evil must be repelled by good.

Reverend Graham helped to make the transition between the two segments of the memorial as he emphasized what Andrew R. Murphy has called the progressive jeremiad;[59] Reverend Graham encouraged the nation to return to its basic foundations: "but we now have a choice: whether to implode and disintegrate emotionally and spiritually as a people and a nation—or, whether we choose to become stronger through all of this struggle—to rebuild on a solid foundation. . . . That foundation is our trust in God."[60] Graham called the nation back, as Lincoln had, to the better angels of our nature.

Mezzo soprano Denyse Graves followed Reverend Graham by singing the Lord's Prayer. And then, in a rather surprising turn, there was a monetary collection, an opportunity for those at the service, as Pastor Kirby Jon Caldwell (from the United Methodist Church in Houston, Texas) encouraged, to "make an offering this day that will be used for charities that are serving the relief efforts, serving the victims, reclaiming the bodies and ministering to those who are suffering as well as supporting those who are serving and ministering at this time." At the beginning of the service, Reverend Jane Holmes Dixon had previewed that there would be a collection, apparently suggested by President Bush: "And, I am not ashamed to say to you, 'Be generous.'" Perhaps this was an appropriate gesture, although as Peter Jennings remarked on live television, he could not recall another time when there had been a collection during a national memorial.

After the collection, President Bush moved to the altar, speaking from the very same pulpit Reverend Billy Graham had just used. The remainder of the service was a call to action, a reminder of the imperatives of retribution, and an enthusiastic salute to American patriotism. After President Bush spoke, the service concluded with the Navy Sea Chanters leading the congregation in an emotional rendition of "The Battle Hymn of the Republic." The hymn was the perfect culmination of martial ambition—"a fiery gospel writ in burnished rows of steel"—and covenantal theology—"As he died to make men holy, let us die to make men free/While God is marching on." Since the vast majority of those present were Christian politicians, they seemed literally to embody the duality of the service.

Very little about the Christian elements of the National Day of Prayer and Remembrance was unusual—unless one considers, again, that

Rabbi Haberman and Imam Siddiqi were led from the National Cathedral by a prominent Christian cross. The only startling feature was that the president of the United States gave an address. Or was it a sermon? Or did he lead a prayer? Bush quoted President Franklin D. Roosevelt's first inaugural address about "the warm courage of national unity," but President Roosevelt had not led a national prayer service after the bombing of Pearl Harbor.[61] Neither did President Johnson after the assassination of John F. Kennedy. President Clinton did speak, sermonize, and pray at the memorial service for the Oklahoma City bombing, but notably without a pulpit or a cathedral as celestial support. Americans accepted such a role for Clinton in part because they believed he did it so well and in part because it redeemed him as a compassionate and moral man.

So why did President Bush speak at a cathedral service? There was very little discussion at the time about the decision. Americans seemed to expect it. By doing so, President Bush earned a kind of spiritual gravitas. His politics were sacralized. He elevated the United States' political response to the terrorists as a "responsibility to history. To answer these attacks and to rid the world of evil."[62] This was an ambitious obligation for a theologian, never mind an occupant of the executive office. But perhaps the context, the cathedral, made it seem that the task was a legitimate responsibility for a politician.

President Bush was pastoral as well. "Grief and tragedy and hatred are only for a time. Goodness, remembrance, and love have no end. And the Lord of life holds all who die and all who mourn."[63] Bush even made proposals and promises about the afterlife. He was Creon expanding the parameters of what and over whom he ruled. He was a political figure leading the church. The framing power of his address was manifest in the sermons that were preached across the country two days later; many of these echoed the president's judgments, especially about the attack being aimed at American freedom. President Bush had said: "In every generation the world has produced enemies of human freedom. They have attacked America because we are freedom's home and defender. And the commitment of our fathers is now the calling of our time."[64] And two days later, Protestant ministers preached: "Today, the United States shines the light of freedom on the world and is, therefore, the target of evil. . . . Another nation, another day, December 7, 1941, Japan staged a surprise attack on Pearl Harbor. American men and women lost their lives to a godless enemy with wealth and power, but who really won? After a terrible sacrifice, freedom won. . . . Now, given the history of this kind of thing, let me ask you one more time, who will really win? Freedom will win—freedom always wins."[65]

The pageantry was not subtle. The US military wore their dress uniforms and carried their branch of the service's flag. The representatives of the US military were the bookends to the service. Why weren't members of the New York City fire departments or police departments represented? Why weren't survivors given the opportunity to speak or to mourn their loved ones? Why wasn't there even a symbolic representation of the dead? Upon reflection, it remains rather remarkable that the church represented by multiple denominations and faiths gave its altar to the state; the sliver of a boundary between the church and state was shredded. And indeed, as the cameras panned across the congregation gathered in the cathedral, the greatest number of those weeping (sometimes even collapsing into the arms of one another) was during the concluding hymn, "God Bless America."

THUS, BEFORE EVEN the first Sunday sermon was given on September 16, considerable theopolitical work had already been done. So it is not surprising that one of the most striking features of the majority of these sermons is how easily the events of September 11, 2001, were theologized; that is, how readily the events were interpreted by American clergy as indicating something transcendental, as gesturing toward a universal and sacred truth. September 11 was not merely a political disaster; it was an existential crisis.

This was rather different from the interpretation of the bombing of Pearl Harbor, the primary tragedy to which 9/11 was most often initially compared. The Pearl Harbor ministers were primarily interested in addressing how to move from their long-term ministerial and moral opposition to the impending war toward a genuine patriotic but still authentically Christian support of it. They offered their congregations a political interpretation of the violence as well as a patriotic conception of American Christian citizenship. In December 1941, ministers did not theologize the event.

Although any crisis can have both theological and political parameters, with 9/11 ministers gave the profane elements (i.e., the planes, the burning buildings, etc.) theological significance with no political history. The terrorists, the violence, and the massive loss of life were promptly translated into a scriptural narrative of sin, suffering, and redemption. The terrorists became harbingers of both evil and of the human capacity for sin: "We must remember that evil does not wear a turban, a tunic, a yarmulke or a cross. Evil wears the garment of a human heart, a garment woven from the threads of hate and fear."[66] The terrorists were the personification of the fallen condition of humanity. The violence was rendered as an echo of the past suffering of God's people and thus was itself testament to American chosen-ness: "We are not alone. Our forbearers in the faith, God's people Israel had dark dates seared into their souls as well."[67]

Perhaps it is understandable why they did so; it would take many months, if not years, for Americans to understand the history of al Qaeda. Yet so convinced were the majority of ministers of the centrality and exceptionalism of the United States in 2001 that they readily imagined that a cosmic battle was being staged. Ironically, that was what the terrorists believed as well. As Osama bin Laden detailed, "Our religion is under attack. . . . We are a nation whose sacred symbols have been looted.[68]

Ministers recommended that Americans not interpret this violence as the loss of God's patronage but rather as an indication of the United States' place in God's salvation history. "This tragedy is only a picture of the Tribulation this world will face. Jesus will soon come to claim His bride" and "Shallow thoughts explain Tuesday's tragedy as God's judgment on America's collective sin, which ironically mirrors the shallow ideology of the militant wing of Islam."[69]

The deaths of these innocents would be salvaged, they argued, by the United States' future obedience and reconciliation with the Almighty: "God has blessed America, and God desires to continue to bless America . . . through you and me. The challenge is before us."[70] Americans did not die in vain on September 11, 2001; their innocent demise was part of a necessary sacrifice for the redemption of the United States. The tragic deaths were part of the narrative of Christian sacrifice, atonement, and ultimate resurrection: "This wicked, unconscionable evil that was perpetrated on tens of thousands of Americans can be used by God to bring about good."[71]

Repeatedly, one finds in these sermons claims for how the tragedy of 9/11 embraced all humanity, transcended the particularities of history, and was a testament of God's mysterious relationship with His people (i.e., Americans writ large). In these narratives, God's people were not divided by religious affiliation; they were secured and unified under their national identity as Americans. God did not redeem Christians or Jews, or even Muslims; through the tragedy of 9/11, He redeemed Americans. "Today, we grieve together and shudder with fear, yet He is the ultimate answer to whatever questions we may have."[72] What happens to Americans is a template for what happens to everyone.

This claim is not new in American religious history. Since the Puritans and their "errand into the woods," Americans have maintained a sense of their special chosen-ness by God. The first colonies were intended to be a beacon on the hill that would recall lapsed Europeans (particularly British Protestants) back to faithfulness. John Winthrop, aboard the *Arbella* in 1630, encouraged his Puritan passengers, "For we must consider that we shall be as a city upon a hill, the eyes of all people are upon us."[73]

Generations of American presidents would continue the metaphor. President-elect John F. Kennedy said, in an address to the Massachusetts legislature on January 9, 1961:

> Today the eyes of all people are truly upon us—and our governments, in every branch, at every level, national, State, and local, must be as a city upon a hill—constructed and inhabited by men aware of their grave trust and their great responsibilities.[74]

President Ronald Reagan popularized the expression throughout his presidency, frequently noting, "America is a shining city upon a hill whose beacon light guides freedom-loving people everywhere."[75]

President Bush echoed this concept of American exceptionalism when he addressed the nation on the night of September 11, 2001. "America was targeted for attack because we're the brightest beacon for freedom and opportunity in the world. And no one will keep that light from shining."[76] According to Bush, the light itself had attracted the danger; rather than being a source of inspiration, the American beacon had brought violence and death. It was a story that would haunt the narrative of September 11 for years to come. The goodness of the United States—not American power, policy mistakes, or imperial recklessness—had brought violence to its cities. And, as Bush had proclaimed, "No one will keep that light from shining." The threat was already embedded in the analysis.

THE SERMONS PREACHED the first two weeks after September 11 made manifest that the pulpit was a vital public space in the days immediately after the tragedy. Churches were full of a range of believers and American clergy had a unique opportunity to shape the meaning of the catastrophe. As Reverend Harold Dixon preached to his congregation: "People will be drawn to seek God's face because of this overwhelming tragedy. Tragedy of this magnitude leaves people with nowhere else to turn."[77] As part of their preaching that first Sunday, many recounted their struggle to write the sermon: "This was a very hard sermon to write. Let me admit that right up front. I anticipated quite a few people in church this morning, as I suspect is happening all around the country. I knew that I was going to have a very rare opportunity to stand before many more people than I usually do. People searching for answers, for comfort, for hope, for God. I pray to God that I do not disappoint this morning."[78]

Ministers wondered whether to preach the lectionary or to simply address the events of the day. Most decided to use the lectionary. Reverend Mark Henderson told his congregation, "In those times when the noise is the greatest, I have come to rely on the movement and power of our weekly scripture as the grounding for my preaching and for my spirit."[79] In a similar way, Reverend Keith Grogg asserted, "I stayed with the lectionary readings, trying to project a sense that no terrorist could supersede the authority of our established liturgical pattern."[80]

The lectionary for Sunday, September 16, was Jeremiah 4:11–28, Timothy 1:12–17, and Luke 15:1–32; perhaps many ministers chose to remain true to the lectionary because this constellation of readings provided a venue that many perceived as directly related to Tuesday's violence. The Jeremiah reading addressed God's wrath against Jerusalem: "Because you have rebelled against me, declared the Lord, your own conduct and actions have brought this on you" (Jer. 4:18). It was tempting for some ministers to interpret the violence of the flaming jets and crumbling buildings as God's punishment. But most, such as Reverend Jon Gunneman, used the reading with nuance: "Let us not miss the prophetic point of Jeremiah: that in the entanglements of human history and conflict, God's creative spirit will transcend immediate human purposes and perceptions; that almost all human conflict is born out of a history of interactions which on close inspection calls for repentance on all sides."[81]

The Gospel reading from Luke tells the story of the parable of the lost sheep and how a good shepherd searches for even one lost sheep. As first responders dug through Ground Zero rubble, the reading, as many ministers noted, seemed poignantly appropriate; many drew the analogy to God's love: "It is in God's nature to save—because it is in God's nature to love. God seeks the lost, heals the wounded, forgives the offender, and gives hope to those who are in despair. It is what God does."[82]

And finally, the reading from Timothy proclaims that those who have been spared now have "been appointed to God's service." It seemed prophetic that the randomness of who died and who survived would be assigned a sacred task. In his oddly upbeat sermon, "God Is Bigger Than Any Terrorist," Reverend Kenneth Sauer insisted that the evil and violence of September 11 had given Americans a "great commission . . . to preach and proclaim that the grace of our Lord Jesus Christ is bigger than this horrible catastrophe . . . bigger than any terrorists . . . bigger than any hate . . . bigger much bigger than any evil!"[83]

While one would have anticipated that the sermons would address questions of theodicy (which many did), they also made the elements of the day themselves (the burning buildings, the planes, the firefighters) sacramental. For Reverend Jeremiah A. Wright, the destruction of the Twin Towers was comparable to the biblical destruction of Jerusalem. The Twin Towers became a, if not *the*, Holy Temple: "Now get this image clear. Burned. Get it in your mind. He burned the House of the Lord."[84] For Reverend Wright, the Twin Towers were equated with the Jerusalem Temple and the terrorists were the enemies of the Lord, the Edomites. The conflict between the United States and the terrorists easily and literally took on biblical proportions.

Each of the elements of the disaster was made to speak theologically, which is quite different from speaking sacramentally in response to human events. After the assassination of President John F. Kennedy, for example, ministers examined the ways the church had neglected to address violence in American culture. They did not explain the assassination as a communication from God. But with September 11, it was as if ministers now believed that rather than communicating prophetically through dreams as God had once done in the Hebrew Bible or through parables as He did in the Gospels, He now employed the language of the fiery fuselage as a source of divine revelation. Even when the events of the day were given a detailed political history: "Why did they (terrorists) want vengeance? They wanted to avenge the British hegemony over the Arab countries; the death of thousands of Palestinians during the last fifty-three years; the murder of hundreds of Lebanese civilians in the 1980's."[85] They were still justified and understood primarily as theological speech, a divine communication.

In this particular sermon cited above, Reverend Jimenez said that the impetus for the events of 9/11 were named as the same as those that animated Cain's murder of Abel in the Book of Genesis—the loss of honor. Even though Jimenez gave astute political reasons for why the terrorists might have acted, ultimately his explanation was theological—like Cain who felt humiliated when God chose his brother's sacrifice over his own, the terrorists of 9/11 felt humiliated by the United States and sought revenge: "Just as with Cain, a false sense of honor led them to murder."[86] The jihadists were Cain and the American victims were Abel. Like Abel, Americans please God, but like him, they undeservedly suffer the wrath of those "less praised" by the Almighty—implicitly, Muslims in this rendition, although only explicitly in the sermon, the violent jihadists. Unmentioned in this sermon is that Cain is also the first Hebrew penitent who is forgiven by God.[87] The minister does not recommend that Americans take that magnanimous approach to the murderous rage of the terrorists.

Another frequently repeated biblical story, especially by more theologically conservative ministers, was that of the Tower of Siloam. In the biblical account, the tower fell and killed eighteen Galileans while they were praying. Jesus recalled this destruction and reminded His listeners that just because someone died in the tower's wreckage, that did not mean that person was more sinful than those who escaped: "Do you think that these Galileans were worse sinners than all the other Galileans, because they suffered in this way? No, I tell you; but unless you repent, you will all likewise perish. Or those eighteen on whom the tower in Siloam fell and killed them: do you think that they were worse offenders than all the others who lived in Jerusalem? No, I tell you; but unless you repent, you will all likewise perish" (Luke 13:4).

Some ministers used the story in startling ways: "The acts this week are a display of God's mercy and grace that you are still alive. Every human being deserves to be under the rubble dead because we have all sinned against a Holy God. We all fall short of His glory and deserve death."[88] Less bellicose, but still making the same point, Reverend Paul Newell preached:

> Do some suffer more than others in this life because they sin more, because they are worse than others? All we have to do is look around us and see those who seem to get away with evil to answer that question. . . . As tragic and terrorizing as the events of this week have been—let me share with you something even more tragic. Among the thousands who died senselessly this past week—many, many of them not only died needlessly, but they will spend an eternity separated from God in a place He calls hell because they senselessly and needlessly failed to repent of their sins and turn to Jesus Christ for forgiveness and leadership in their lives.[89]

For American Protestant clergy in those early autumn weeks, God was speaking to Americans through the events of 9/11 and the events simultaneously signified both political and divine realities. In those first inchoate days after September 11, the boundaries between religion and politics were not only blurred; they were being renegotiated, destabilized, and reconstituted, as President Bush's address at the National Cathedral highlighted. Rather than simply offering their congregations ways to manage their grief, to comprehend the enormity of the loss, and to begin the first tentative steps toward reconciliation, the majority of these sermons aimed to entwine American politics and Christian theology: "We have a deep faith in God and democracy" and "We are a nation not only under attack but under God."[90]

In this crisis, according to these sermons, the United States itself became a theological category and Christianity a theopolitical resource

for translating and understanding the crisis. Yet although 9/11 was theologized, historically Americans did not theologize other people's conflicts, such as the Balkans War or South African apartheid. Although
Americans might acknowledge that there could be sacred elements
to these conflicts, Americans did not *explain* those political conflicts
theologically. Only American crises were elevated as templates for the
divine.

Although it is one of the regular functions of religion to console its
adherents, in the face of incomprehensible death and destruction the sermons of 9/11 did something more complicated than simply offer their
congregants solace. By claiming the events of September 11 for the sacred, the clergy also participated in the simultaneous depoliticization of
the event *and* the promotion of their own authority. By insisting that
the tragedy was about humanity's relation with God, indeed, specifically
about the United States' relation with God, the majority of the sermons
implicitly made "citizen" a holy category. According to these first sermons, Americans who died that Tuesday were "a people of God"; the
noble first responders such as the firefighters were understood to have
died like Christ, for others. Few of the sermons among these three
hundred read and analyzed charged that September 11 was not about
God; that to ask questions about God in relation to the devastation was
to ask the wrong question: "'Where is God?' seems almost irrelevant. . . .
It [is] the wrong question. . . . The real and interesting question is where
were you before the disaster struck?"[91]

By claiming the elements of the September 11 tragedy, ministers were
implicitly challenging the American convention that there is a wall of
separation between the church and the state. By refusing to read a political event as solely political, or even as *merely* political, the ministers
were trying to regain and expand ecclesial jurisdiction. Implicit was a
critique of liberalism's demand that the church speak in the secular terms
of public reason.[92] The ministers did not contest the division between
church and state in 2001; rather, they detailed a conception of God acting
in the public sphere that necessitated the Christian translation that only
the ministers could provide. God was acting publicly, so the ministers
had no choice but to insert themselves.

Various counterrhetorical strategies can readily be imagined. American clergy could have focused on *how* Christians could/should respond

to the loss and suffering. Theology could have been found not in the events themselves but in the Christian response to them; September 11 could have been understood as an opportunity for Christian witness. There was some of this, of course; some of the ritual practices and spontaneous memorials in the days after September 11 enacted this. The candle lightings across the country, the multiple prayer services, and the newspaper obituaries detailing both the ordinary and extraordinary about each victim were ways of doing this. Yet the words from the pulpit were different.

What many of these 9/11 sermons did, perhaps now obvious with the advantage of hindsight, was make September 11 not merely the fulcrum of political history but of salvation history: "these things are not strange at all. These are things that have been prophesied."[93] In this formulation, then, 9/11 resisted detailed historical and political analysis and the sermons, perhaps inadvertently, laid the groundwork for the narrative support necessary for the wars in Afghanistan and even in Iraq to become not only "patriotic" but also profoundly "Christian."

The majority of the sermons rehearsed a dominant ideology in which America was exempt from politics, or perhaps, more aptly, history. Instead, when "bad things" happen to the United States they must be understood theologically rather than politically. In this paradigm, a tragedy in the United States has universal implications, revealing something about humanity's relationship with the divine, rather than merely historical/political realities.

The crisis of 9/11 was a form of God speaking that required only that Americans and their leaders interpret it correctly. Because theological explanations tend to be without history, an abstracted knowledge of a relationship with the transcendent, American politics was cast, too, as oddly abstracted from history. September 11 was not part of American political history, a tragic outcome to policies in the Middle East, to the legacies of colonialism among Muslim peoples, and so forth. Rather, 9/11 transcended history and became, instead, a sacramental conundrum. Rev. Dr. Daniel P. Matthews, the rector of Trinity Church (New York City), was profound and eloquent on this point: "The dust fell all over the world on 9/11. Not one inch of this earth is without dust. Little villages all over the world, people, nations, religious groups of all traditions, all faiths—everybody is covered with the dust of the World Trade

Center."[94] For Christians, as well as Jews and others, the theological echo "You are dust, and to dust you shall return" (God's curse of Adam, Genesis 3:19) would be clear. Reverend Scott W. Alexander made a similar point, although less eloquently: "There is incredible danger and uncertainty ahead for every human being everywhere on this globe."[95]

Even the consolidation of 9/11 as a time, rather than an event or place, worked well theologically, echoing salvation history with its ready-made pre- and postnomenclature. In her sermon "Alert When He Comes," Reverend Delores Carpenter theologized the answer to the question "Why did we not see this coming?" She did not offer a political or historical account but rather compared American surprise to the Christian failure to be fully expectant about God's imminent return: "We must live our lives in tiptoed expectancy that He is coming any moment."[96] If Americans had been better Christians, awaiting the return of the Messiah, perhaps they would have been ready for the violence that assaulted them on September 11.

In many of the sermons, the clergy asked political questions to which they then gave theological answers. A sermon on "Why didn't we see this coming?" is primarily a political question recast as a theological one. In contrast, asking "Has God abandoned us?" is a theological question that perhaps might find its resolution in politics.

What Is Being Mourned in These Sermons?

Primarily what is mourned in the more than three hundred sermons surveyed here is American innocence: "There is no more innocence for us as a people and a nation."[97] The United States lost its innocence because of the injuries that were done to the country, not because of anything it had done. Some ministers drew parallels between the United States and Job, the righteous, innocent man whom God tested and from whom God took everything: "Without warning, for no reason other than his being blameless and upright, his family and business is wiped out. . . . It was swift. It was unwarranted. It was unthinkable just like what occurred in America on September 11."[98] Again, the United States has no past, no history—only the event of injury. This is what, in another context, political theorist Wendy Brown has called the "fetishization of the wound."[99] It is an identity crafted (and then irreversibly linked) to grievance—a kind of "look what we have lost" stance. The focus on the wound, in the ways Nietzsche provocatively detailed, is also a way to deny any of one's own agency or power. In this instance, the sermons collaborated in a narrative in which American innocence was proclaimed and the country's power erased. The United States was like Job, the innocent victim of forces beyond its control or understanding, or both.

By innocence, most clergy meant that everyday Americans' sense of security—the "taken for grantedness" of their lives—had been annihilated. Americans had been jolted from complacency. Tellingly, almost none of the sermons had details of specific individuals who were lost. Indeed, of the sermons read for this project, only three named specific people. It is worth quoting one of those at length to make manifest the difference the naming makes:

> Five of our extended church family are unaccounted for: our church secretary Charlotte Wallace's husband, Peter who worked on the 100th floor of the North Tower; our church receptionist Keith Blacknall's nephew, David Williams; who was an engineer on the 45th floor of the South Tower; Ginger Ormiston, who was on the 78th floor of Tower Number Two, who was last seen evacuating with a co-worker as she called her husband Jim to let him know she was on her way out; David Rivers, a parent who has been active in our nursery school and who headed the auction last year; and Janet Gustafson, mother of two children, whom most of our own kids in this church have known as a teacher of three and four-year-olds. I name them by name before you because it is important to remember that that is how they, and we, are known by God, unique and special, beloved and desired, treasured and adored.[100]

Another exception to these few is that on the third Sunday after September 11, September 23rd, the story of Todd Beamer was featured in several sermons. Beamer was a passenger on the flight that crashed outside of Pittsburgh who was heard on a telephone line saying to his fellow passengers, "let's roll." This was an expression that Todd Beamer apparently used with his wife and children as they got ready to leave for family outings. The phrase "Let's roll" became a kind of battle cry for several weeks in American media. One minister, Reverend Jack Warford, used the expression seven times in his September 23 sermon as an inspiration for the church, concluding with "this is our mission from Jesus, so *Let's roll!*"[101]

Given that the sermons were given (at the earliest) five days after the tragedy and many two or three weeks later, some names of the dead surely would have been known to various congregations, especially to those in or near the sites of the attacks. Occasionally, the orphaned children were mentioned—the loss of their parents was mourned. But overall, the majority of sermons across the denominational and political spectrum named the loss, the "tragedy" of 9/11, as the damage done to some aspect of national culture: "Our sense of security has been shaken. No longer do our shores and borders seem safe from the hatred and violence in the world. Suddenly, we don't observe from afar the dangers people face in parts of the world torn by terrorism and violent persecution. We now experience the same fear and daily uncertainty as people living in countries of the Middle East, Africa, and other parts of the world. It's not that hatred and violence is new. . . . But it is new to most of us."[102]

And again: "We mourn the loss of loved ones, we mourn the nation gripped in trauma. We mourn the injury to our national pride, this radical shift from overconfidence to uncertainty in the blinking of an eye. We mourn the wreckage of monuments, the Twin Towers symbolizing our money, the Pentagon symbolizing our might.[103]

Others have already noted the ways American mourning practices post-9/11 were more about melancholy than mourning.[104] And this was confirmed by most of these sermons. Rehearsing Freud's classic distinction, American Protestant preachers were more melancholic about the injury done to themselves—"a narcissistic wound"—than they were focused on the ties of relationality that had been lost. They lamented the disruption to their own expectations rather than grieving the loss of individuals. Melancholy maintains the illusion of an autonomous self upon whom pain has been inflicted. It tends to wallow in the unfairness of one's suffering and rehearses the injury to that self rather than recognizing the loss as the absence of another person and of a very specific relationship. Melancholy is an attachment to one's feelings surrounding the loss. When ministers focus on the anger, fear, and insecurity Americans felt after 9/11, they are melancholy. This is a focus on "what has been done to us." Reverend David Washburn's sermon "In the Grips of Crisis" captures the sentiment: "We as individuals, as a community, and as a country, are now victims. . . . We come here this morning, having come face to face with evil. . . . We come angry, numb, grief stricken, horrified and full of pain; and we come into the presence of God and say, 'Make sense of this, oh God. Tell us why.'"[105]

Mourning, in contrast, is an acknowledgment of our dependence on others for our sense of who we are. This is grief which acknowledges, "We are not only constituted by our relations but also dispossessed by them as well."[106] When ministers (those very few) detail the biographies of those who were murdered and the gap left in the community without them, that is mourning. In his sermon "Living by Faith in an Uncertain World," Reverend Ray Pritchard begins: "He must have been in a hurry to get home to see his family. That's the only reason his friends could think of to explain why Thomas Burnett of San Ramon California changed his reservations and took an earlier flight last Tuesday morning. . . . That's why he ended up on United Airlines Flight 93 from Newark to San Francisco."[107]

Americans could no longer take their power for granted, the two oceans they had erroneously believed protected them: "Amid the rubble of steel, glass and human bodies there is *something of our soul* that is lost for the living: *a sense of security* and of justice. There is now vulnerability."[108] Another sermon mourned the loss of national culture: "Lying in the rubble that was the World Trade Center and the damaged section of the Pentagon is *the American sense of well-being*."[109] Security became a theological category, part of the American soul. Indeed, security was detailed as a theological loss, congruent with justice itself. "As hundreds and thousands of rescue workers converge upon the sites of the disaster, as state militias are called to provide order, as the military stands on alert waiting orders to strike back, God's people cannot afford to stand on the sidelines and pretend that life is normal. . . . We face a national crisis and God's people need to respond with a sense of urgency and direction. We are to gather together and seek God's face."[110]

In a testimonial culture, such as contemporary America's, individuals believe that who they are is revealed as much by their self-narratives as by what they do. Americans tend to believe that the stories they tell about themselves produce who they are; the narrative account of self is imagined to make it true, to secure it as real. The proliferation of memoirs, even before the author is close to middle age, as well as the popularity of confessional interviews and television shows all testify to this fascination with self-creation through storytelling.

Particularly germane to identity in this version of American testimonial culture are the sources of injury. Part of the therapeutic legacy of the Freudian "talking cure" is the conviction that if one details the ways one has suffered, one can be released from the debilitating psychological effects of those injuries. Revealing and naming the ways that one has been a victim becomes a path to liberation. Consider the power and popularity of "coming out stories," rape survivor stories, and so forth, especially as proliferated for several decades on talk shows.

By narrating the events of 9/11 as a story of the loss of innocence, these sermons echoed an influential rhetorical element in American culture. By dating the loss of American innocence to Tuesday, September 11, 2001, these sermons occluded most of the American past that the majority of Americans still remembered. Conveniently hidden from view were Watergate, the Vietnam War, and even the Monica Lewinsky scandal—each of which had been decried as an "American loss of innocence." According to the 9/11 sermons, then, American innocence was something that could be lost repeatedly. These sermons, like those after the Oklahoma bombing, were not only inscribing theology into political life; they were also retelling (reconstructing?) political history.

These early sermons created the events of 9/11 as personally connected to each American, not because every American knew or loved people who died in the disaster, but because something intimately connected with their own lives had been destroyed. By naming the loss as cultural or national, the clergy were thus pivotal early on in creating 9/11 as a collective event: it happened to *all of us*. September 11, 2001, was significant not only because of the power of collective memory (i.e., Americans would remember where they were when they heard about the planes crashing into the Towers) but because what was destroyed was now linked theologically to their own lives. One could argue that there is a painful absence in these many sermons because in a bid to include more Americans in the devastation of September 11, many of the clergy left a silent, nearly unmourned gap for those actual individuals who perished that day.

And as one would expect in a narrative focused on the injury to self, rage was the primary emotion many of these early sermons sought to address. Even "God is powerfully mad."[111] While ostensibly seeking to contain their congregants' feelings of anger and to redirect them, most of the sermons also confirmed the validity of the rage. In fact, many of the clergy clearly expressed their own: "I am not immune to emotions of rage and revenge. Whoever perpetrated last week's unjustified violence should be punished."[112] "I am struggling to reconcile my Christian faith with my feelings about the animals who did this."[113] Of course, as expected, the majority of the sermons *also* urged that one not act on that rage: "Pray for those who persecute you. Bless them that revile you."[114]

While anger is an expected element in the stages of grief, it was interesting how quickly American clergy expressed it: "As American citizens, *we are angry*—some of us profoundly and bitterly so. *We are angry* at the terrorists. . . . *We are angry* at any national governments which can be proven to have in any way tolerated, encouraged or supported them. Our anger is, of course, natural and justified."[115]

Many found biblical justification for their anger: "God gives us permission to be angry at a time like this. *'Be angry, and do not sin, do not let the sun go down on your wrath.'* (Ephesians 4:26) Be angry. Anger is a God given emotion."[116] Reverend Davidson Loehr began his sermon: "Where do we begin? For me, it began in anger—in fury. When I heard of the destruction of the World Trade Center Towers and a section of the Pentagon on Tuesday, I wanted loud, bloody revenge. I thought 'Kill the bastards!' I didn't know just who the bastards were, but I wanted them dead."[117]

In clear contrast, the spontaneous memorials that sprang up across the country in those first weeks rarely mentioned anger or rage. Most were focused on sadness, on the loss of individuals, and on feelings of connectedness with the victims. There was poetry and photos and the tracings of hands and feet suggesting the presence of both the mourners and the mourned.[118] Yet the majority of the sermons say little about how to manage *that* kind of grief. For these clergy, sadness is a "safe," manageable, seemingly apolitical emotion, whereas rage demands not only restraint but also a theological response.

As has been detailed throughout this book, who is permitted to be angry and about what is thoroughly racialized. It was acceptable for Americans (presumably primarily White) to be angry about what they had lost in 9/11, but it was not permitted (either theologically or politically) for Black Americans to be angry about the assassination of Rev. Dr. Martin Luther King or the beating of Rodney King. Rather, Black Americans were counseled about befitting, "dignified" ways to respect and mourn the dead. As Reverend Cain Hope Felder asked on September 27, 2001, as American anger flared, "Are African Americans the only ones to be required to turn the other cheek and forgive for righteousness' sake those who persecute them?"[119] As detailed in Chapter 3, after King's assassination there were detailed instructions from White Americans to Black Americans about how they should respond to King's assassination. And anger was decidedly not among the appropriate emotions. There didn't seem to be any appropriate channels for righteous anger in these instances. Japanese Americans, too, were not permitted to be angry about their unjust internment; rather, their stoic accommodation was necessary for marking them as "patriotic."

There was also very little preaching about how Americans should manage their fear. Many ministers actually seemed to cultivate fear: "The American political system is not imperishable. The American military cannot protect us from every destructive force. The financial future is not certain, and you may lose your investment."[120] And as if that were not sufficient, this minister added: "The next phase of terrorism could be an act of chemical warfare that unleashes deadly gas or poisons a city's water supply. . . . It could have been you who died, and it might be you who dies tomorrow. . . . Today the attack could be here. Today it could be a bomb in this very building."[121]

Other ministers, too, seemed to escalate fear by naming all the ways Americans were no longer safe: "Is there any place that's really safe anymore? We used to think that our homes were safe, but we've become more and more aware that our homes are no longer safe. We used to think our workplaces were safe. . . . We used to think our schools were safe, but school-based violence has changed all that."[122]

Most of the ministers who used this tactic did so, as Reverend Piper did, to facilitate their congregants' return to God as their only security: "Perhaps it will take this kind of calamity to help us read the Scriptures for what they are really saying and make us less secure with earthly things so we can be more secure in our Savior and King, Jesus Christ."[123] Nonetheless, there was a very compelling counteranalysis given by the charismatic preacher Rev. Dr. James A. Forbes Jr. at Riverside Church in which he both acknowledged the power of fear but reminded his congregants that God has insisted, "be not afraid."[124]

Repeated frequently in these sermons was the loss of the Twin Towers, which were both mourned and critiqued as symbols of American power and wealth. Although it remained unclear whether Americans perceived the Towers to be symbols of their wealth and power prior to 9/11, after their demolition that is what they became. The Twin Towers were made into "national symbols" of what had been done to "us." *Time* magazine named the Twin Towers "America's Cathedrals." As already detailed, in "The Day of Jerusalem's Fall," Reverend Jeremiah A. Wright Jr. compared the destruction of the Twin Towers to the destruction of Jerusalem.[125] And in his sermon, Reverend Arthur Caliandro asked: "And now the cathedrals are gone. What do we do? Where do we go?"[126] Apparently, the Towers were perceived as having provided some kind of theological, as well as architectural, orientation. As one preacher noted, even heaven trembled at the loss of the Towers: "So in shock was heaven itself, apparently like us . . . I think the clouds themselves were searching all week for those Towers, roaming the sky in sympathy, looking for something prouder and taller than what is left to nuzzle."[127]

The Twin Towers became theopolitical symbols of the myth of the United States itself. For many Americans, new immigrants, and visitors to the United States, the Towers had stood for American exceptionalism and capitalism, for better lives in a new world, for genius and enterprise: "When I saw them burning, for me it was like two people were dying. I feel like I've lost a relative."[128]

The Pentagon, on the other hand, aroused different feelings; that building had been a focal point for protest, symbolizing war, limited access, and secrets and security. It was, as Margaret Yocum notes, "not a spectacular building, low to the ground and folded in on itself . . . it does not loom large on the landscape or in people's imagination."[129] So perhaps it was not surprising that within days the terrorists' attacks were consolidated into *9/11* and the focus was New York rather than the Pentagon or the field in Pennsylvania. Although the consolidation was a date rather than a place, only one or two sermons pointed to the destruction of the Pentagon as "symbolic." The Twin Towers became "us," whereas the Pentagon remained "the government."

It was the sermons that began this odd sanctification of the buildings. The spontaneous memorials that developed at Union Square in New York City, at the Pentagon, and in the field where American Airlines Flight 93 crashed did not declare the buildings "much loved" or the field sacred, nor did they mourn the structural harm done. Part of the reason was that the only thing for certain that was gone were the Towers; the bodies of the victims were still unidentified. Of these three hundred sermons, only Reverend T. D. Jakes preached in gory detail about how the men and women died on September 11, about what might have happened to their bodies: "The media has been very tactful and very tasteful. . . . They've spared us the gory details. They have not given us close-ups of bodies diving out of windows. They've not given us close-ups of body parts. That's all they've been able to find of people. They have not talked about what the heat of jet fuel igniting would do. . . . The heat force was so strong that people chose to dive out of a window from one hundred and four floors up rather than to face the heat."[130] Reverend Jakes recognized that traditionally dead bodies were important to both politics and religion. Dead bodies evoke the awe, uncertainty, and fear associated with cosmic concerns, such as the meaning of life and death. And Jakes's sermon was primarily designed to invoke fear and to foster support for aggression against America's enemies.

Because dead bodies bring us face to face with ultimate questions about what it means to be and to stop being human, about where we have come from and where we are going, all the major faiths have skillfully integrated the practices associated with death into their rituals and burial practices. And politically, corpses have been important, too, because of this perceived link of dead bodies to the sacred. In this way, a religious burial is presumed to sacralize the political order. This is why Creon wanted to claim this power for himself in Sophocles's tragedy,

Antigone. But in the immediate aftermath of September 11, there were no bodies to serve this function.

Yet because corpses are so authoritative both politically and theologically, metaphorical bodies were quickly found. The Twin Towers became the "body of 9/11." The first large-scale memorial to 9/11 was the Towers of Light, an installation of eighty-eight searchlights at the footprints of the World Trade Center (WTC) towers that projected two vertical columns of light into the sky. It is noteworthy that the memorial was quietly renamed Tribute in Light to shift the focus away from the towers; the renaming was an awkward attempt to remind Americans that the towers were a metonym for the human losses, not the loss itself. Nonetheless, the beams of light confirmed the iconic power the buildings had come to assume.

Finally, the last steel column covered with graffiti from the rubble left at the WTC site became a relic of great symbolic value. The column was once a part of Column 1001B—one of forty-seven columns that had supported the South Tower's inner core. Over the course of the work excavating the WTC site, recovery workers placed notes, photos of the missing or the dead, letters, patriotic messages, and identifications from the police or fire department at which some of them served. On May 30, 2002, in a ceremony marking the official end of the recovery effort at Ground Zero, the fifty-eight-ton beam was towed from the scene wrapped in black muslin and an American flag. Two days earlier there had been a private ceremony with the column just for relief and recovery workers. This was a symbolic body if there ever was one, carried out to the sound of "Taps" played by buglers from New York's fire and police departments and "America the Beautiful" played on bagpipes.[131] The column is still preserved and displayed at the National September 11 Memorial and Museum.[132]

How You Die Makes the Death Significant

"To ensure that the dead shall not have died in vain." This aspiration animates many of the 9/11 sermons and is itself part of a long tradition of national mourning in America. What it means for someone "not to die in vain" relies, perhaps ironically, on the living and their behavior; it has relatively little to do with the dead. A person's death is rendered meaningful if the living respond in a noble way, in a way collectively sanctioned to redeem it. President Ronald Reagan, for example, urged Americans in the face of the *Challenger* disaster not to allow the astronauts to have died in vain by continuing to support US space exploration.

So in a parallel vein, on a clear Tuesday morning when nearly three thousand people perished in a matter of minutes, those deaths could be made meaningful and purposeful, in this narrative, if the living dedicated themselves to redemptive behavior: "There is some meaning to be found in the midst of the suffering. . . . There is something redemptive about it, for God's purpose to redeem works through all things, always."[133] Of course, what counted as "redemptive" was what many sermons struggled to detail.

This element of 9/11 mourning was a kind of American progress narrative; something noble, heroic, or valuable must come from death. There must be movement, almost resurrection, from death to life; rather than fully mourn the dead by recounting in detail who had been lost, the relationships destroyed, the skills and contributions thwarted, the American mourning tradition turned quickly to the living to restore value, to find something "productive" about the death.[134] It was as if the victims for whom death should not be in vain were without significance unless the living restored their value to them.

Historian George Mosse notes that during World Wars I and II, the memory of individual suffering was consolidated into the myth of the war experience, a celebration of mass heroism.[135] This was particularly obvious in many of the 9/11 sermons in which much was made of the deaths of firefighters and police officers but considerably less of the average office workers filing papers at their desks. The deaths of the firefighters and police officers were "meaningful" because they died in service to others; indeed, their sacrifice was likened frequently to Christ's. Here is one sermon describing the dust on a dead firefighter's boots: "It was dust that had something holy about it, dust that bore a message of saving love, dust from Calvary."[136] And then more pointedly, "God is like a fireman who runs into a burning building risking his life to save another."[137] Here God is likened to the firefighter, not the other way around.

The focus on the heroic dead was part of the "balm in Gilead" (one of the most repeated phrases in these sermons); it was a way to still see and feel God's hand at work. The sanitized heroic deaths of Tuesday, September 11, also lay the groundwork for the future "heroic military deaths" of American military personnel. Because these sermons had not been able to stay focused long on the horror and loss of individual, ordinary lives, they were not able to impress upon their congregants the brutality and enormity of what had been lost individually. The obituaries in the *New York Times* of each individual who died on 9/11 were an attempt to do this in ways that the sermons, in an attempt to "find God among the rubble," contributed instead to a jingoist rhetoric that found salvation and redemption in heroic death.

The deaths of ordinary people in a fire blast were more difficult to make significant. Jesse Jackson tried to give meaning to these deaths by asserting that people with many differences were "united" in death because they all died in the same way: "There is no ghetto, barrio, suburban hiding places when the hounds of hell bomb. . . . On this past Tuesday the janitors, the maids, the managers, the bosses, those wearing uniforms and those wearing striped suits, lions and lambs, had to lie together when the storms of life did rage."[138] As a result, he said, we the living must remain unified, baptized, and "one in the blood." These deaths will not have been in vain if Americans bring about a new improved humanity. By theologizing the massacre, Jackson tried to write the deaths into a salvation history of redemptive meaning; that is, they died so Americans could recognize their national commonality.

One of the primary challenges the clergy faced in making this bid for no death in vain was that they had to recommend particular behaviors for their congregants to implement to salvage the dead from this void. In his sermon "Our Challenge Now," Reverend David Ball drew a rather unexpected parallel between the dead of 9/11 and those of Abraham Lincoln's "Gettysburg Address." He noted how Lincoln used the field of dead at Gettysburg to motivate Americans to continue the cause of abolition and racial equality: "citizens rededicated themselves to the cause for which the Union soldiers died—the defense of a nation where all are to be treated as equals."[139] Yet the Union soldiers were just that—soldiers committed to Union victory. The 9/11 dead were civilians murdered in an undeclared war. And it remained unclear whether from Ball's perspective the legacy of Jim Crow laws and racial lynching meant that the Union soldiers had, in fact, died in vain. Presumably, all the Confederate soldiers died in vain. For a death not to have been in vain, must the dead's mission have been successful? How does that apply to the average person?

Indeed, Ball was himself at a bit of a loss as to how to give meaning to the carnage of September 11. Yet, like many other clergy, he preached on the necessity of not allowing the victims of 9/11 to have died in vain: "Lincoln took our human impulse to do something, if only to gather to remember the dead, and elevated it to the level of a commitment higher than which I cannot conceive, to ensure that the dead shall not have died in vain."[140] This commitment to the dead was meant as an ethical claim on the living, even if it remained unclear what that commitment entailed.

While there was some preaching about how Americans should live in response to 9/11, most of the recommendations were to send a message to the terrorists. President Bush inaugurated this during his first address to the nation: "These acts of mass murder were intended to frighten our nation into chaos and retreat. But they have failed. Our country is strong."[141] The redemptive behavior was to signal to the terrorists that they had not defeated Americans: "Terrorists want our fear . . . show them they haven't won."[142]

Many of the sermons addressed how the terrorists had not succeeded and how they had radically underestimated the United States and its moral fiber: "What is unexpected here, what was totally unanticipated by the murderers, is the moral fiber of our nation. And that fiber, when it is at its best, is wrapped and bound by the religious bonds of hope and trust in God."[143] Reverend Steve Shepherd, quoting a fellow American, put it more bluntly: "Yesterday, Mr. Bin Laden or whatever your rotten name is, I had an extra value meal, watched my 63" TV, drank the best beer and smoked the finest tobacco money can buy. And, for your information, I'm just the average Joe. So, eat your heart out."[144]

There were precious few recommendations for how Americans should live so as to make sense of the deaths of these ordinary Americans, very little of "a ministry of presence rather than explanations."[145] It was ironic that while most of the sermons insisted that God had been present at the devastation of September 11, the message most ministers suggested the faithful send in return was to the terrorists, *not* to God.

Further confirming the ways "death not in vain" was focused on the living rather than the dead, there was an odd absence in these sermons about the victims' innocence. While theologically, the innocence of Christ would have been an obvious analogy for the victims, when the death of Christ was invoked in these early sermons, the focus was on Christ's suffering and the identification was between "we, the living" who were suffering and Christ, not between the innocent dead and the crucifixion.

Finally, these early sermons perhaps inadvertently created the rhetorical possibilities that would help to justify the wars in both Afghanistan and Iraq—the heroic commitment (and death) of American military men and women who would "give meaning" to the senseless deaths of those who perished on 9/11. And while a full analysis of the rhetoric supporting the invasions of both Afghanistan and Iraq is beyond the scope of this chapter, it is important to recall how the war was supported, in part, by an insistence that it was redemptive work for the dead of September 11.

At the first memorial for 9/11, President Bush said: "These men and women did not die in vain. Their loss has moved a nation to action. What happened to our nation on a September day set in motion the first great struggle in a new century."[146] And ministers would confirm this perspective, sometimes with a rather loose conception of the political theology of just war: "Principle #3 of the JUST WAR theory states, '. . . we must have a reasonable chance to succeed.' Do we? We're America! We are a great superpower! We're #1! Right? Romans 8:12 says, 'If God is for us, who can be against us?' And God is for us! Right? I believe that if God is for us, we will be victorious. But if God is against us, we don't stand a chance."[147]

Furthermore, this rhetoric had additional political ramifications when the US government dissimulated about the deaths of American soldiers who had died from "friendly fire." Recall the story of the death of football star Patrick Tillman, whom the army initially reported was killed when his unit was attacked in an apparent ambush. Within days, the army reportedly knew that Tillman had been killed (shot three times to the head) by confused allied groups; there was no hostile fire involved in the fight. Nonetheless, even the commanding officer, who knew the facts, approved the awarding of the Silver Star, Purple Heart, and a post-humous promotion for Tillman. When the truth was revealed, Tillman's bereft family was incensed.[148] Tillman was supposed to die to redeem the deaths of the victims of 9/11, not rehearse again the meaningless-ness of the initial catastrophe.

The Church / State Divide: What Is Christian Patriotism?

From the perspective of the majority of these sermons, in the aftermath of the bloody violence of 9/11, significant numbers of Americans were no longer worried about the separation of church and state: "Two weeks ago we debated the wisdom and relevance of placing our national motto in school classrooms in Collier County; today, signs all over town read, 'God Bless America.'"[149] Previously *we* as Americans had sidelined God, but now *we* were happy to have God center stage. "Oh, I don't apolo-gize for the following observation. We allow our Supreme Court to make laws that say our students can't pray publicly in the school. Then people want God in the time of need."[150] Often sermons noted that no one pro-tests the day of prayer.

Many of the sermons adopted an almost mocking tone about the so-called church / state divide: "Who was embarrassed to call upon His name? None! Who needed an anchor in this turbulent tragedy? Everyone! What could have taken a generation or two to do was done in one morning. . . . In just one morning, God working within human events to change the world, our nation returned to 'one nation under God' and 'God Bless America.'"[151]

Reverend T. D. Jakes, characteristically, went even further when de-scribing his experience on television: "They (CNN) stopped me and asked, 'Would you just pray?' On CNN. I didn't say TBN, I said CNN. 'Pray for the Nation. . . .' Nobody is arguing about prayer in the schools. Nobody's talking about the separation of church and state. Nobody's saying, 'That prayer offended me.' Nobody's offended now."[152]

There were multiple mentions in sermons of the ways presidential power was seen "bowing to the cross" on the National Day of Mourning: "During Friday's Day of Mourning Services at the National Cathedral, cameras seemed irresistibly drawn to the crucifix . . . and presidential power was seen bowing before the crucified King of creation."[153] For many, this image was a commanding iconography of who and what was *really* in charge.

Nonetheless, while most of the sermons celebrated the influx of Christianity into the public square during the crisis, they were also acutely aware that the violence was itself being attributed to religion, particularly the dangers of these irrational, premodern suicide bombers who believed they were going to paradise as a result of the slaughter of Americans. The US Conference of Catholic Bishops, troubled by those who sought to justify these new forms of terror as a religious act, insisted in their November 14, 2001, statement: "It is wrong to use religion as a cover for political, economic or ideological causes. Whatever the motivation, there can be no religious or moral justification for what happened on September 11. People of all faiths must be united in the conviction that terrorism in the name of religion profanes religion. The most effective counter to terrorist claims of religious justification comes from within the world's rich religious traditions and from the witness of so many people of faith who have been a powerful force for non-violent human liberation around the world."[154]

Yet the clergy were divided as to what the ongoing intervention of the church should be. The traditional Augustinian tension between the "two cities" remained. In one version, Christians were citizens of the "city of God" and should be accountable only to God's kingdom. In these sermons, the political world was condemned as morally bankrupt and 9/11 was, in part, a "sign" of that corruption. These sermons recommended a retreat from the political world and a return to the ways of Christ; Americans were condemned for having made "an idol of our government; too often we place our trust in America, not in God. . . . Only God knows and controls the future. . . . Our power is but an illusion. Therefore, we must turn to Him and to Him alone."[155]

There were both progressive and conservative versions of this retreat. In the conservative account, affairs of state were best left to the government. In these sermons, there was a reluctance to argue for or against retaliation against the terrorists. The "two cities" metaphor enabled the clergy not to have to make any recommendations, although a military response was assumed: "Terrorists are a bad tooth—we must ask our military to extract the terrorists from the planet. . . . We will have to sacrifice with higher gas prices and less freedom at the airport, but this tooth hurts, and it must be extracted."[156] And again: "You and I will not have a say on what will be the military response. But what you and I can be in charge of is the effort to make this world, and the kingdoms of this world, become the kingdoms of our God."[157] Yet even in the bid to focus on God's kingdom, there persisted a plethora of martial metaphors: "The decisive battle has been fought and won in the death and resurrection of Jesus Christ."[158]

For others, in contrast, the crisis was an opportunity for the church to wield more political power, to have greater influence on "the city of man." In these sermons, the catastrophe was read as a failure of the secular state, but the remedy was church intervention. In the progressive version of this narrative, the church's failure to intervene was also a silent accommodation to the impending imperial war: "Churches should refuse to play a bit part in services filled with promises and foreshadowing of war. . . . Christianity requires people for whom being a Christian is not a game. It requires following Jesus and not generals."[159]

Only a small number of these early sermons explicitly asked, "What is a patriotic Christian response to the tragedy?" And among this small number, the answer was that the government had its sphere of responsibility and Christians had theirs. The government would craft its response and Christians must craft theirs.

Surprisingly, there was next to nothing about how Christians might influence the government. Even those who recommended patience ("Be still and know that I am thou God"; Psalm 46:10) did not offer any recommendations for how parishioners should hold government accountable. Rather, most sermons offered an implicit acceptance that there would be a military response and that those in the pews should think more about their relationship with God than about that; "we've been learning from the Psalms that God is our Refuge and our Shelter, that we can't put our faith in bombs or military might, but that we can trust in the power of Almighty God in the midst of our suffering and anxiety about the future."[160]

Some of the most interesting sermons on the question of what would constitute a patriotic Christian response were those given by a small number of African American clergy. As a study on the religious and spiritual responses to 9/11 revealed, White Americans, as the primary creators of the dominant culture, appeared to feel more threatened by the terrorist attacks, as evidenced by their increased emphasis on the importance of religiosity and prayer.[161]

In contrast, African Americans' sermons revealed their ambivalence about the US government: "For many of us, every day catches us in the midst of a love/despair relationship with the United States."[162] There was a bright line between "the government" and "us." While Black congregants were imagined, included, and embraced as "Americans," these African American sermons marked a sharp distinction between themselves as "Americans" and "the government." There was a decided "them" and "us." Of course, there were expressions of a great love for the United States and its people, but there was also decidedly less affection for the US government. "People have been asking about the national government's possible response. . . . What will they do? Well, I say the national government is not them, it's us. It's not their government; it's our government. It's not their decision; it's ours."[163] This was both a telling indictment of Black disenfranchisement and a reminder of Black agency and activism.

While most of the African American ministers made 9/11 a fulcrum of history, they were more likely than their White counterparts to link it to a trajectory of American racism. Nearly half a dozen sermons echoed (without attribution) Malcolm X's infamous response to the assassination of JFK: "America's chickens have come home to roost." Although these sermon writers agreed that 9/11 was a watershed event, they recast it as "in the tradition of American racism."[164] Several referred to Cornel West's expression of the "niggerization of America" and Rev. Dr. Michael Eric Dyson compared the terrorism of 9/11 to the "terrorism in the inner cities and against blacks, including racial profiling and police brutality."[165] Reverend Calvin Butts added: "We know the terror that was called the Christian Knight of the Ku Klux Klan. No, we did not have World Trade Towers. We did not have a multi-trillion-dollar financial district. All we had was our home and our churches. But the terror would ride by night."[166] The Black experience was pivotal to understanding the disaster; Reverend Charles Booth asserted: "Can I tell you why I believe America still lives and why God still has mercy on America? I believe God still has mercy on America because of black people who know how to call on the name of God."[167] Reverend Booth also noted that the answer to the question of why terrorists would want to do this to America was only difficult to answer if one assumed the perspective of the "majority racial group and its narrow self-interest."[168] Influential civil rights preacher Reverend Gardner Taylor echoed the assertion, quoting W. E. B. Du Bois: "Minority people are now peculiarly and I believe providentially endowed by God to speak to the nation and say that pride brings ruin."[169] This was a time for the Black Church to assume a greater prophetic role: "Things that have happened . . . in one context, they are strange, but to those of us who are a part of the Church . . . these things are not strange at all. These are things that have been prophesied."[170] If one understood the tragedy of 9 / 11 as embedded in a violent history, as many African Americans did, then what one remembered when one recalled 9 / 11 would be configured by that American past as well.

BENEDICT ANDERSON ASKS a striking question in *Imagined Communities* (1983): "Why do we not erect monuments to the unknown social democrat or for the unknown liberal as we do for the Unknown Soldier?"[171] His answer, in part, is that social democrats and liberals are not involved in the same business of immorality as the state. For the state, commemoration is a religious project intended to secure some form of immortality. National commemorations make a kind of religious claim to secure the validity of the political realm. Linking death with the apparatus of the state is politically potent.

The unnamed remains of the dead are joined with political authority. The remains (indeed, the very absence of remains in many of these tombs[172]) signal that what is significant is the category *soldier,* not the specific individual who embodied the role. The tombs of the unknown soldiers are meant to unite citizens by memorializing *someone* without a history, without context or particularity except for their service to the state. Which war, in what capacity, with what intention does not matter. Significance resides only in having been a soldier. In many ways, the Tomb of the Unknown Soldier is the creation of what Paul Ricoeur calls in another context "a past that no one remembers."[173] This is a memorial to imagined individuals, known only, as the inscription on the tomb itself details, "to God."[174]

In some striking ways, these first sermons after September 11 were echoes of the project of the Tomb of the Unknown Soldier, crafting a similar kind of patriotism and commemorating a past that never was. For in the first weeks after 9/11, what it meant to be patriotic was to participate in the shared memory being created, to make one's individual memories cohere with the collective memory: "Where were you when you heard? Tuesday's horrors have etched into the calendar of our memories another date that goes down in infamy. We remember where we were when we receive the chilling news of our lives."[175]

Many ministers began their first Sunday sermons recounting as part of the sermon how they heard the news, where they were, how they responded. "Tuesday morning—I was working in my office—preparing the second part of my message on the family . . . AND then Laure called and asked me if I knew what was going on?"[176] And: "Tuesday morning, September 11, 2001, started for me as a day like any other. The usual 6:15 wake of the New York Fast Ferry awoke me."[177]

As with the Tomb of the Unknown Soldier, war and death became the categories by which one's relation to the nation was defined. There were no Tombs to the Unknown Civilians. And the past, which brought the United States to the tragic present, was neglected in favor of a collective memory that rehearsed an endless present. Like the Tomb of the Unknown Soldier, the causes and consequences of the wars fought would be neglected in favor of an eternal vigilance of light and guards protecting the site of imagined community, Ground Zero.

Being patriotic during those first weeks meant that one understood the events of September 11 as a hinge in history and that the elements of the day had more theological than political significance: "The Lord has entrusted us (America) not simply for ourselves but for the sake of all the earth and history. This is a history shaping moment. We are writing the first chapter not of a new millennium, but some would say of a new world."[178] Here, the echoes of Christianity's foundational antagonism with the first-century Roman imperium were loud and clear; in the twenty-first century, however, there was a finely orchestrated nexus of American and Christian imperialism fortuitously melded in these sermons. God has bequeathed the entire world and history to American care. Reverend Craig Barnes ties the theological and the political: "We will unite this great country into a new creation that looks a lot more like the new kingdom Jesus talked about."[179]

Nearly two-thirds of the sermons used some version of "we will never forget where we were when we heard the news of the planes crashing into the Towers." To remember where one was and what one was doing was an ethical demand. To say that one didn't remember where one was or what one was doing that day was understood to be a denial of the near universal implications of the tragedy. To install one's particularities (i.e., I was washing dishes when I heard the news . . .) into the collective memory was to claim the events as personally significant. Even if one did not know anyone who died, the events resonated intimately; the ethics of this memory demanded that one gave an account of oneself in relation to it: "Now we are one people; this tragedy has made us one."[180] Americans could share not only the memory of what had happened but also become participants in it. All other differences were erased; as with the Tomb of the Unknown Soldier, all were unified in the memory of the imaginary one.

While recollections of where one was on Tuesday could echo stories of where one was when President Kennedy was assassinated or where one was when Rev. Dr. Martin Luther King died, the recollections could not name the history that might have made these events possible: the swift renunciation and shunning of anyone who suggested a political history to the events of September 11 was remarkable—whether Peter Jennings because of his critique of President Bush or Pat Robertson for his renunciation of homosexuals and feminists, each was quickly and forcefully rebuked.

This was not a time for partisanship; a collective memory was being authoritatively created and as scholar Avishai Margalit notes, "a shared memory of a historical event goes beyond the experience of anyone alive; it is a memory of a memory that through the division of diachronic labors, ends up as itself an actual event."[181] In other words, the memory of 9/11 would become in the national rhetoric the thing itself. And through this faux participation, an expectation of unity—of patriotism—was created.

In many of the sermons, these recollections of one's whereabouts could be rendered into a "conversion" narrative. "Where were you when you heard the call of the Lord?" Many epiphanies and spiritual renovations were announced in these first sermons: "It was not until Tuesday morning that I actually looked at them closely."[182] Reverend Keller, like many others, told his congregation what to remember: "When we remember the events of this September and we are tempted to become sad . . . we must remember Joseph [Book of Genesis, 37–50]. We must remember the One who will walk with us through the 'Valley of the shadow of death' (Psalm 23:4)."[183] Several preachers noticed theological elements that had eluded them: "Tragedy makes theologians of us all."[184]

Finally, because what it meant to be patriotic in the days after September 11, 2001, had more to do with the creation of a collective memory than with the context and analysis of political beliefs, when clergy did recommend that Christians urge the government to use restraint rather than military force when seeking justice, those propositions had little rhetorical traction. So influential had been the creation of a collective memory of 9/11 as impacting all Americans and uniting everyone in and as "one blood" that calls for peace rang hollow.

By focusing on anger rather than sadness when mourning the dead, by highlighting the loss as national rather than individual, and by claiming the events of September 11 as part of salvation history rather than political realities, American Protestant clergy gave the state the tools it required to begin to wage wars across the Middle East. American clergy helped to inspire the emotions that would validate the state's rhetorical insistence that its military aggression was a fight against evil. Even as there were those clergy who insisted that asking questions about God were the wrong questions in the face of September 11, alternative voices and histories were largely rendered mute in the echo chamber of the pulpit and the state.

For what it meant to be patriotic after 9/11 was to be haunted by the collective memory of 9/11, what Ricoeur named in another context "an incrustation of the past at the heart of the present, the past that does not pass";[185] post-9/11 became a permanent condition.

Perhaps without full realization, many American Protestant clergy promoted the theological reasons for why the events of September 11, 2001, were a watershed event. For them, the primary injury was to national self-esteem and justice. Lost in many of these sermons during the chaotic days of the crisis was the theological mooring "to love your neighbor as you love yourself." Instead, the duty to memory articulated in these sermons was a duty to the past (*no death in vain*) rather than an ethical recollection recognized as an obligation to the future and to one another.

In the crisis sermons of 9/11, the denouement of church power was nearly complete. Ministers preached a nationalist God, who was invested in the United States; a God who used the state to communicate His will, to lead His people, and to point a way forward. Ministers were disoriented by the tragedy, unable to process it theologically; instead, they relied on the state to offer direction as well as solace. President Bush was cited often in these sermons, in ways that President Franklin D. Roosevelt never was.

Presidential power had become priestly. That power would be fully realized in President Obama as he became the "mourner in chief" after the shooting at Newtown and the murders of numerous unarmed Black men. It was a role President Obama willingly embraced and that ministers were grateful for him to assume. Instead of protesting the canned sermon, ministers willingly repeated it. After the Newtown shooting, ministers primarily repeated and/or exegeted President Obama's words.

The elision between the church and the state was achieved. And because of his support among the African American community, President Obama was able to appropriate the prophetic tradition of the Black Church as well. Yet he preached not as a minister in the tradition of Dr. King but as the most powerful man in the world. Even though ministers were grateful to have an ally of such eloquence and erudition in the White House, their need of one revealed the loss of power and autonomy the church had suffered. With that loss, ministers imagined a God, too, who was incomplete without the augmentation of the state. Just as the God of the Oklahoma bombings wept with Americans, this 9/11 God rallied with Americans as they pursued their nationalist interests. This was not a God who countered the status quo; He was a God who facilitated it.

Chapter 6 argues that the Newtown school shooting and the Trayvon Martin sermons were in effect the last crisis sermons because the power of the pulpit had now been nearly completely appropriated by the state. And nothing more eloquently made that point than when President Obama gave the eulogy for Reverend Clementa Pinckney and sang "Amazing Grace" from the pulpit. President Obama, like Creon, presided over the living and the dead, although he at least had the grace to mourn with the ministers the violent assassination of one of their own. President Obama offered the promise that without much amendment church power could be folded into the state, and alarmingly, most ministers seemed to be grateful. From President Bush's bullhorn sermon among the remains of Ground Zero to the faltering voice of President Obama singing from the Charleston altar while ministers applauded, the power of the pulpit had seemingly become just another tool in the arsenal of American power.

CHAPTER SIX

The Enduring American Crisis

Sermons from the Newtown Shooting to Black Lives Matter

In 2015, in response to the multiple violent crises that American ministers were confronting, the self-identified evangelical Christian periodical *Christianity Today* published a pamphlet entitled *Preaching in Moments of Crisis*. The collection was dubbed a "survival guide" and contained previously published essays offering advice on how to manage various homiletical issues that might develop during tragedies, such as "When the News Intrudes," "When a Child Dies," and "The Sacred Conversation That Follows Crisis." While the essays were interesting in their own right, what was perhaps most striking was the addendum printed at the bottom of the table of contents. It read, with capital letters: "PLEASE NOTE: We've worked hard to make sure this information is accurate and legally sound. However, we remind you that this is not a substitute for legal counsel. If you or your church has a legal question, be sure to talk with an attorney."[1] This statement confirmed the trajectory traced in this book and sadly punctuated the denouement of the church's moral, liturgical, and theological authority. Even an expressly theological text for ministers on how to offer solace to their congregations during a crisis was fenced in, presumably by the authors themselves, "the leaders and staff of *Christianity Today*," by a reminder—do not presume that Christian insights are sufficient, do not step beyond the designated and privatized sphere of church authority. Restraint is recommended. Be aware, be circumspect, and if necessary, consult a legal expert and abide.

It is a rather tragic coda to the sermons from the 1940s. The ministers of 2015 seemed to have agreed that religion was private, limited, and perhaps primarily therapeutic; ministers were not expected to challenge the law, to reinterpret it, or even perhaps to violate it. Rather, the church was to align with the law, preferably by consulting an attorney. There was no longer even the faint echo of the 1940s sermons in which ministers refused loudly to do the bidding of the state (recall the protests to the so-called canned sermon proposed by the Civil Defense League) or that insisted that political tragedies were not theological ones. For most ministers in 1941, Pearl Harbor was not a question of theodicy but of political history.

As this book has traced in detail, the arc of church and state authority did not bend toward justice (as Dr. Martin Luther King had hoped); rather, it curved more and more to aggrandized state power at the expense not only of church authority but of civil society itself. The church was merely one of the most obvious losers in this history. As civil society was evacuated of its autonomy, the church, too, merged often nearly invisibly with the government. And this merger occurred not only across denominations but across multiple features of the racial divide as well.

"The most significant transformation in Black life over the last fifty years," African American studies scholar Keeanga-Yamahtta Taylor argues, "has been the emergence of a Black elite, bolstered by the Black political class . . . a layer of Black civil rights entrepreneurs."[2] These Black elites, she argues, have privatized racial inequities and laid much of the burden on their own Black constituents. If the Black church was once the cradle of prophetic resistance to the White majority, by 2015 the Black church had lost much of its authority concurrent ironically with the rise of Black electoral power, manifest perhaps in the election of the first Black president. Yet, like the Black political class, the Black church now also located its own power for change in the government while laying other burdens not on structures and procedures but on the choices and decisions of individual congregants. Perhaps no one has written a more compelling narrative of this transformation than legal scholar James Forman Jr. in his *Locking Up Our Own: Crime and Punishment in Black America,* in which he examines how Black politicians created some of the policies that led to the mass incarceration of their own constituents. And while Black ministers are still among the most fierce advocates for racial justice, as will be exemplified by Hoodie Sunday after Trayvon Martin's killing, they did not deem their ministerial authority sufficient without the supplement of governmentality. This chapter will detail these changes more precisely when it examines the sermons after the killing of Trayvon Martin and the not guilty verdict of George Zimmerman.

In many ways there is no longer a stark church/state divide in America. There is no clear-cut and independent society versus the government. Rather, as William Cavanaugh and Michael Hardt have so persuasively argued, everything everywhere has become merely another articulation of government interest and a further production of its power.[3] The institutions associated with civil society—the schools, the church, prisons, the union, the family—now frequently constitute the locations for the disciplinary deployment of government power.[4] It's not coercive power in a traditional sense but the effects are to evacuate much of civil society of its self-determination. The church can lend its manpower to the government as a way to access some authority, but it does not seem to have an independent way to address violence or even to understand it. The church is no longer a substantial and fully sovereign knowledge-making or service-providing institution. This last chapter on the sermons of the Newtown Sandy Hook school shooting and the killing of Trayvon Martin will explore how this collapse was propelled further by the church's very response to the violence against America's children.

IN FEWER THAN fifteen minutes on Friday, December 14, 2012, twenty children and six adults were killed in what was at the time the deadliest mass school shooting in American history. The tragedy occurred in a small rural town, Newtown, Connecticut, where there had been only one homicide in the decade prior to the morning when the rampage began. The nation was gripped in stunned horror as the names and details of the kindergarten and first-grade victims became known. The otherwise festive and child-centered time of year made the calamity even more difficult for Americans to comprehend. President Obama wiped multiple tears from his eyes as he announced the tragedy a few hours later: "There's not a parent in America who does not feel the overwhelming grief that I do."[5]

Within hours, there were multiple handmade memorials that festooned the road to the school. There were hand-hewn wooden crosses with the name of each child; there were Christmas trees decorated for each victim and there was the now requisite roadside memorial of stuffed animals, balloons, and candles. Prayer vigils were held in town and across the country. The following Friday at 9:30 A.M., church bells across the country rang twenty-six times to honor the victims at the time when the violence had begun. The National Council of Churches also held a moment of silence on that Friday that was observed across the nation, including by President Obama at the White House.

After 9/11, ministers had debated whether to follow the lectionary in their Sunday sermons. They wondered whether the liturgical calendar itself might reveal God's purpose and meaning in the tragic events. It was a genuine question that ministers pursued in the beginning of their sermons—sharing with their congregants the way they had wrestled with the choice and why they decided to preach one way or the other. About half the ministers decided in September 2001 to stay (at least partially or in full) with the lectionary while the rest found consolation in other biblical passages and stories.

A decade later, after the Newtown tragedy in December 2012, whether to preach the lectionary or not was rarely debated. Ministers did not seem to feel tethered to the liturgical calendar. They were confident that current events mandated that they address the tragedy whichever way they could, using whatever they could. Many ministers did not even feel that they were required to refer to the biblical tradition or even to what a "Christian response" to the tragedy might be. Rather, in an era of vast social media and a twenty-four-hour news cycle, many ministers elected to refer to President Obama's eulogy of the Newtown dead on Sunday, December 16, rather than to a biblical story or a theological tradition. His words became the biblical reference—his words were exegeted, expounded, even given history and context. He was truly the "pastor in chief," although he was not telling a biblical story. He did refer to God during the prayer vigil, but it was the speech of a statesman, of a secular authority. President Obama boldly reminded his listeners that they could not safely raise their children without "the help of a nation."[6] As was appropriate, he assured his listeners that the state would solve the problems of family child rearing and safety.

Two days after the tragedy, President Obama attended and spoke at the Newtown Interfaith Memorial Service. The high school auditorium was at capacity with an overflow room holding another thirteen hundred people. The service was televised across the nation. President Obama began his eulogy for the Newtown victims, as any minister would, "Scripture tells us: '. . . do not lose heart. Though outwardly we are wasting away . . . inwardly we are being renewed day by day. For our light and momentary troubles are achieving for us an eternal glory that far outweighs them all.'"[7]

But Reverend Obama did not forget that he was president of the United States: "In the coming weeks, I will use whatever power this office holds to engage my fellow citizens—from law enforcement to mental health professionals to parents and educators—in an effort aimed at preventing more tragedies like this. Because what choice do we have? We can't accept events like this as routine. Are we really prepared to say that we're powerless in the face of such carnage, that the politics are too hard? Are we prepared to say that such violence visited on our children year after year after year is somehow the price of our freedom?"[8] He ended with Scripture and the naming of the dead children: "'Let the little children come to me,' Jesus said, 'and do not hinder them—for to such belongs the kingdom of heaven.'"[9]

During the crisis of the Sandy Hook shooting, the government took the lead, insisting that political will was the divine will. And alarmingly, the church followed this lead. The state, in this case instantiated by President Obama's eulogy at Newtown, provided the foundation for religious reflection. This was near complete appropriation of moral authority by governmental power. Americans were no longer imagined as having a duty to divine God's will as they undertook political goals; rather, those political goals confirmed God's will. The clergy had forfeited their prophetic role; they were not developing new knowledge or challenging the rulers. Instead, they were the state's new priests—the systematizers of the given, wardens of the status quo. So powerful now was the government that it lent its moral authority to the church rather than the reverse.

Long gone were the days when President Roosevelt would seek the validation, perhaps even the permission, of religious leaders for state decisions, including his own momentous decision of taking the nation to war. Roosevelt had written to various religious leaders at the time assuring them that his reason and conduct of the war would dovetail with Christian principles and expectations. He sought religious confirmation of his political aims. No longer. Now the president unabashedly preached, explicitly and without apology, assuming the role and authority of the church.

In response, the church, as exemplified by the Newtown pulpit sermons, drew on the power of the state to confirm its authority. Some of the Newtown ministers gave entire sermons in those first two weeks after the tragedy retelling and elaborating on President Obama's words. "I am profoundly grateful for the ways in which President Obama has led us through these dark, distressing days following the massacre at Sandy Hook Elementary School. He has shown both parental emotion and presidential resolve. Times like these have called upon him not only to speak as president and parent but also to speak from the heart of his faith. He didn't run to become pastor-in-chief, so I sympathize with him for having to find words for the unspeakable at such a traumatized and tender time."[10]

Weeks later, the expression "pastor in chief" would be repeated at President Obama's preinauguration worship service at St. John's Episcopal Church. Atlanta-area pastor Andy Stanley suggested that the president should be called "pastor in chief" for his leadership following the Sandy Hook shootings. Addressing the president in the pews, he said: "Mr. President, I don't know the first thing about being President, but I know a bit about being a pastor. And during the Newtown vigil on December 16th after we heard what you did—I just want to say on behalf of all of us as clergy, thank you. I turned to Sandra [the pastor's wife] that night and said, 'Tonight he's the Pastor in Chief.'"[11]

Although there was a bit of buzz in the religious press about Pastor Stanley's seeming violation of the so-called wall of separation by naming President Obama as "Pastor in Chief" during an inauguration event, most ministers as well as the majority of Americans (as evidenced by online comments and newspaper headlines using the phrase[12]) defended the appellation. This conception of political power and governmental authority as pastoral was revealing beyond the mere nomenclature. Pastoral power, as Michel Foucault has detailed, is power held over a people bound together by faith in their God. It also requires the continual and steady presence of the shepherd. "Pastorship is a kind of constant, individualized and final kindness."[13] And while the shepherd / pastor's efforts are ostensibly focused on the good of the flock, according to Foucault, pastoral power in the hands of the government is ever expanding: "In the Christian conception, the shepherd must render an account—not only of each sheep, but of all of their actions, all the good or evil they are liable to do, all that happens to them."[14] There is no limit to what concerns the pastor, to what the shepherd must be attentive. If the government is mourning the people's dead for them, clearly everything—the practices of the living as well as of the dead—is the terrain of political power. This is a reminder, again, of why Sophocles's *Antigone* continues to have contemporary relevance. As Sophocles detailed, tyranny was on the horizon when the King believed his jurisdiction extended to both the living and the dead, to who can be buried and offered the rites of the sacred and who cannot. Thus, President Obama's assumption of the role of pastor reverberated beyond this single episode. It was, in Foucault's terms, *a technology of power* that produced certain kinds of subjects. Power is not a thing but a relationship and when the government leader is a pastor, he creates a flock—submissive and subordinate.

Two years earlier after the Tucson, Arizona, shooting of Representative Gabby Giffords and the killing of six citizens in a supermarket parking lot, President Obama had been dubbed "mourner in chief." When he had to mourn again a year later in the summer of 2012 for the murder of twelve people in an Aurora, Colorado, movie theater, the phrase resurfaced. Because of the surfeit of violence during President Obama's terms in office, he was frequently before the American people lamenting. In part because of his oratorical gifts, the role of "mourner in chief" seemed naturally to suit him. Nonetheless, why was he the chief eulogist at so many of these vigils?

Of course, the president should attend these events, lend his positional gravitas to the occasion, but should he speak, preach, and set the frame of understanding for these tragic events? What purpose was served? What power was being exercised? What message conveyed? Did his mere presence at the vigils somehow give the deaths meaning? Did the significance of his presence thus imply that the victims had not died in vain, as is so frequently wished? How did the president decide which events to attend? Which to neglect?

President Franklin D. Roosevelt did not eulogize the Pearl Harbor dead. President Lyndon B. Johnson did not eulogize Reverend Martin Luther King Jr., or even President Kennedy for that matter. Johnson did speak of Kennedy's death before Congress, but he did not speak at his funeral or at services held around the country. President Reagan eulogized the seven astronauts killed on the space shuttle *Challenger* in January 1986, but he did that first from the Oval Office and then at a memorial at the Johnson Space Center in Houston where the NASA space program was housed. He did not speak at a church memorial service. President Clinton attended and spoke at the vigil for those killed at the Oklahoma bombings, but that was the first domestic terrorism since Pearl Harbor. And of course, President Bush eulogized the dead after 9/11 at the National Cathedral.

Perhaps not that much politically separates the eulogies among these last three presidents (Clinton, Bush, and Obama), as detailed in each chapter addressing those tragedies, but there was one significant difference. President Obama eulogized so many Americans, traveled so far, and attended so many different events that he became the nation's pastor and that was understood as one of his requisite roles while commander in chief. No one ever called President George Bush pastor in chief. Not only did the American people embrace this role for President Obama but so did the majority of US ministers and other religious leaders. Consequently, national mourning during those eight years was mostly evacuated of theology and replaced by governmentality. The lack of a national vigil for those unarmed Black men killed across the country during the course of 2014 and 2015 made clear that only some lives could be mourned and eulogized by the president of the United States. President Obama did not attend the memorial for Michael Brown in Ferguson, but he did send three White House representatives.[15] No one from the White House attended the journalist James Foley's funeral; he had been beheaded by ISIS ten days after the shooting in Ferguson.[16]

Some lost lives were a national tragedy, calibrated by the government's response or lack thereof, whereas others were merely a source of grief for their loved ones. Some deaths suspended the schedule of a nation and its political leaders. Others did not. And "the prohibition of public mourning doubled the trauma of the loss,"[17] as it had after the assassination of Dr. Martin Luther King, after the beating of Rodney King, and after the deaths of Trayvon Martin and Michael Brown.

Although the conflation of church and state authority seemed almost complete in President Obama's role as pastor, there were some ministers who did challenge Obama's political theology—reprimanding him for not saying what they believed he ought to have said. They did not debate his right to preach; rather, they were chagrined by some of his pseudotheological claims. There was no question regarding his authority (or presumption) to minister, to preach, or to fulfill the role and duties of a pastor. That was not contested. Instead there were only some rather fastidious challenges regarding President Obama's word choice and culminating observations, specifically about the Newtown children. In one sermon (detailed below), for example, the minister's entire sermon was about contesting the final line in President Obama's eulogy. And even though she disagreed with his decision to say that God called the Newtown children home, she was also absolutely confident that President Obama's words were a perfect place to find not only solace and understanding but even God.

Although President Obama was the most common secular referent for many of the Newtown sermons, former Arkansas governor Mike Huckabee was also frequently cited and used to help develop or contest the issues surrounding theodicy. When prompted, Governor Huckabee had responded to questions regarding the Newtown tragedy with, "When we ask why there is violence in our schools, but we've systematically removed God from our schools, should we be so surprised that schools have become a place for carnage because we've made it a place where we don't want to talk about eternity, life, responsibility, accountability?"[18] The backlash to this assertion was swift and widespread; there were nearly as many sermons addressing Governor Huckabee's remarks as there were on President Obama's eulogy. One minister entitled his sermon "An Open Letter to Mike Huckabee" and declared: "I am stunned by the small view of God you have embraced. To speak of kicking God out of our classrooms or prohibiting the presence of God in our school strikes me as blasphemy."[19] The minister continued, "Such an assertion is simplistic at best and only serves to distract us from dealing with *the realistic causes* that comprise the roots of the tragic shootings plaguing our nation: access to the kind of weapons that can kill dozens in an instant . . . a lack of adequate support for mental healthcare and . . . an apathetic attitude toward the plague of bullying in our schools."[20] According to this formulation, God was irrelevant to *"the realistic causes"* of the tragedy. Divine sovereignty had been replaced by the necessity of political intervention. The state could solve this; God could not.

God (and thus, Christianity) also seemed to have nothing to contribute to coping with the tragedy. Christianity offered neither any specific remedy nor apparently even any special understanding of the grief of the community. On the one hand, this reluctance to enmesh Christian principles into a public tragedy might be applauded as a mark of theological sophistication, much like the hesitancy many ministers showed in the 1940s after the bombing of Pearl Harbor. Yet in this instance, the aversion in the Newtown sermons stemmed from a now common acceptance that Christian principles would prove effete in the face of the tragedy. The American experience had demonstrated that it was better to rely on a therapeutic model (à la the Oklahoma bombing) or on the government (à la September 11, 2001). An eviscerated civic sphere, exemplified in this instance by the institution of the church, was no place to turn when the very meaning of life was challenged, or at least so these ministers and most Americans now seemed to believe.

A few ministers tried to defend Huckabee by claiming that by neglecting their relationship with God, Christians had enabled evil to pervade too many elements of their collective civic life, including children's schools. This was reminiscent of the Kennedy sermons in which many ministers blamed the church for being anemic in the face of secularization. But these 2012 sermons were a faint echo of the confidence and insistence those 1963 ministers had that the only way to prevent another assassination and public violence was for the church to be the church and for Christians to renew their faith.

For complicated reasons, many of which have been explicated over the course of the chapters of this book, there is a historical decline of both the moral and institutional authority of the church from the 1940s through to today.[21] In 2012, the church was not as powerful as it was in the 1940s, in the 1960s, and perhaps even as late as the 1990s. What is surprising, however, is that ministers themselves enacted and performed part of this political subordination from the pulpit. This was particularly true of White ministers (who will be contrasted with their Black counterparts after the murder of Trayvon Martin detailed below).

One would have expected that ministers, even in the face of this diminished cultural and institutional influence, would still be using their own biblical and theological traditions from the pulpit to help their congregations mourn the death of the Newtown children and their teachers. One might have reasonably anticipated that they would still be developing Christian understandings of theodicy, of suffering, and so forth. But this was not the case. Instead, the ministers exegeted the words of the state and then offered political appraisals of American gun violence. There was also detailed confession by plenty of ministers of their own relationship with firearms. One minister detailed her recent voting record—indicating that she had regrettably not made ameliorating gun violence a priority when she went to the polls. She named this neglect "a sin" that she said she suspected others in her congregation equally shared.[22]

That ministers expected their congregants "to vote their conscience" was not new. With the rise of evangelicals and fundamentalists in American political life in the 1970s, American Protestants had grown accustomed to thinking through how their religious commitments were made manifest in certain political alignments. Politics was a forum in which theology got done; a place where theology became public and was enacted. What was different was that it was not the religious commitments that were driving the political ones, but rather that there were *only* political commitments.

Political commitments were the theology. Politics was the place where goodness could be made manifest. Again, long gone was the lament of the 1960s ministers after the assassination of Dr. Martin Luther King that politics was the place that "killed the king of peace." Here there was no longer the sentiment that the political sphere was the place where theology got dirty. In 2012 in the midst of tragedy, the only place that the majority of ministers looked for solace was in the public forum and from the presidential pastor in chief. Ministers preached, *He will guide us; tell us how to understand; help us mourn.* President Obama's secular authority was moral authority. And this perception, during the tragedy at least, was not particularly partisan.

Although President Obama spoke at an interfaith vigil, none of the Newtown sermons referred to any of the clergy, including a Methodist minister, a Catholic priest, a rabbi, and a Muslim cleric who had all also spoken. There was no repetition of their words, no reference to what these fellow ministers and religious leaders said or did during the ninety-minute vigil. As a symbolic gesture, for example, all of the clergy at the vigil sat among the mourners rather than gathering together at the front of the auditorium as speakers: "Now there is a reason why all of the clergy are sitting down there and not up here . . . but we wanted to have a symbolic gesture that we ourselves are with you and among you in these coming days."[23]

Also present at the vigil was a Muslim cleric who reminded listeners, "It is in such times of almost unbearable loss that we seek comfort with our Creator and that artificial divisions of faith fall away to reveal a nation of mothers and fathers, brothers and sisters, sons and daughters, all united in a desire to bring healing and renewed hope."[24] His words, too, were never repeated in any of the sermons. Nor were Reverend Jim Solomon's, one of the few ministers who mourned for the children who survived as well as for those who died: "Dear Lord as we leave the children we have lost in your hands, we ask that by your grace, you would empower us to bless and comfort the children who are still here in our hands. Bless them in a special way as they grieve the losses of siblings and friends."[25]

Neglected, too, in favor of repeating the words of governmental authority was the poignant prayer of Methodist minister Jane Sibley. After she had witnessed a state trooper outside her office window crying, she prayed for the first responders, not as cardboard heroes but as injured human beings: "We thank you, Lord, for their gifts and their strength and their courage. So we ask you Lord to walk with them in the days ahead, to surround them with your angels, to give them people who will listen to their story, to listen to what they saw that was not for anyone to ever see, Lord."[26] In contrast to the choices most ministers made after Newtown, these religious leaders adhered more obviously to their theological traditions as they tried to offer solace to the grieving townspeople.

They enacted their belief from their public pulpit rather than turning elsewhere to look for consolation.

The majority of sermons given after Newtown fell into three rather broad categories. About a third of the Newtown sermons wrestled with questions of theodicy, especially regarding why God would allow the innocent to be murdered in this gruesome way. Another third were political creeds either for or against gun control. Here there was some discussion of the American culture of violence that indicted all Americans as partially responsible for the tragedy. And the last third were about how to mourn and still find joy in the coming Christmas holiday.

Overall, the sermons, against the advice given in the pamphlet cited above, exegeted the crisis rather than the Scripture. They tried to explain the violence rather than develop a theological truth. The news itself overshadowed their message and most of the sermons never quite got to Scripture. Many of them focused on gun control and recommendations for legal action. Citizenship replaced discipleship as the church's public key. The liturgy was supposed to do more than simply generate interior motivations to be better citizens. But the church no longer had either the ways or the means to enact its vision in the world. And it mostly no longer even imagined the possibility.

BECAUSE QUESTIONS OF theodicy were, as always, profoundly difficult to address, most of the sermons merely circled around the question without being able to tackle its challenges. Various sermons would ask, *Where was God during the Sandy Hook shooting?* and then give a pat answer, "God weeps" or "No one is more heartbroken than Jesus." Other sermons asked, *Why didn't God intervene?* and again offered little theology, "God has a plan." And finally, among the most common queries, *How are we to reconcile ourselves to a world disrupted by evil?* was frequently answered with "God still loves us" or "This is not what God wants."[27] These were all addendums to the central question of faith posed by the Sandy Hook school shooting, "Why do the innocent suffer?" It was as if ministers themselves were exhausted by the question; they were no longer interested in trying or perhaps were unable to reconcile the rampant violence with their own faith.

Many of the sermons were filled with platitudes: "As dark as the midnight may be, the dawn will come."[28] Over the decades during other crises, ministers have also given sometimes rather contrived answers to questions of theodicy. But these Newtown sermons by and large do not struggle with the issue; they are not meditations on the challenge. They are curt renditions—often in the question and answer form given above—to get to what even the minister seems to acknowledge is not a compelling answer. In a sermon entitled "The Passion of Job," Reverend Christian Wallace asks, "What, why, how did all go so wrong?" A mere dozen words later he preaches, "Even in the Wizard of Oz, Dorothy had to wake up, and so did Job. Problem: Satan; Solution: God."[29]

Well-known minister and best-selling author Reverend Max Locado wrote "A Christmas Prayer" addressed to Jesus: "It's a good thing you were born at night. This world sure seems dark. I have a good eye for silver linings. But they seem dimmer lately."[30] The prayer seeks to reconcile Christmas with the darkness of the Newtown violence: "But you were born in the dark, right? You came at night. The shepherds were nightshift workers. The Wise Men followed a star." The prayer was published in the *Huffington Post* on December 14 and was referred to frequently in sermons, although it did not frame many sermons.

There was at least one, however, that took the darkness at the center of the Christmas story itself quite seriously. Baptist minister Reverend Jim Butcher recounted in his sermon, "The Part of the Christmas Story That Speaks to the Sandy Hook Tragedy," how when Herod learned that he had been deceived by the Magi and that the Savior child had escaped to Egypt with his parents, he ordered that all boys two years old and under be killed. "Then was fulfilled what had been spoken through the prophet Jeremiah: a voice was heard in Ramah, wailing and loud lamentation, Rachel weeping for her children; she refused to be consoled, because they are no more" (Matt. 2:18). Butcher notes that this part of the Christmas story is usually erased because "we try to insulate ourselves from anything unpleasant."[31]

When Butcher poses the theodicy question, he answers with an analysis of how even when Jesus arrived in the world, there was "unspeakable and persistent evil; he came into a world of real sin not to avoid it, but to deal with it." Butcher further elaborates, quoting Solzhenitsyn: "If only there were evil people somewhere insidiously committing evil deeds and it were necessary only to separate them from the rest of us and destroy them. . . . But the line dividing good and evil cuts through the heart of every human being. And who is willing to destroy a piece of his own heart?"[32]

The sermon is noteworthy because of how it contrasts with the majority of Newtown sermons: first, it uses biblical resources rather than politicians or their analysis of political events to explicate a contemporary event; second, it strives for a "theological truth"—the reality of "unspeakable and persistent evil" both in the world and in the human heart—rather than an explication of the crisis itself; and third, it offers Christian resources rather than public policy to address the challenge. It's a remarkably simple formula but one rarely seen in 2012 America.

The Newtown shooting was so profoundly difficult because the "enemy" was not a foreigner; there was no political ideology that propelled the killing. The ministers had to explain evil—where did it come from? Why was it there? When King and Kennedy were assassinated, there were potentially political answers to the murders, although most African American ministers did not find them sufficiently persuasive, particularly after King's death. In Oklahoma and in New York City on September 11, there were clear political enemies, even if one of those enemies, Timothy McVeigh, was himself American.

The Newtown massacre was also disruptive because it was impossible to make the victims into anything other than paragons of innocence—they were children in kindergarten and first grade. Any minister, indeed anyone at all, would struggle to make sense of the mayhem. Yet very few of the sermons addressed doubt about God's goodness or power, which had to be coursing through their congregations. Instead, ministers gave the same answer that might have been given after a fatal car accident or a young person's death after illness. The scale and horror of what had happened did not shake loose the bromides; perhaps because the ministers had already conceded theological defeat, they returned to their comfort zone—ask the government to handle it, give away (or keep) your guns.

One of the most theologically compelling sermons addressing this painful reality was Reverend Emily Heath's "When Joy Feels Impossible: An Advent Sermon for Those Who Mourn for Newtown." She noted that no explanation seemed good enough and concluded, "One of the last things Christ said before he died, in his hour of greatest suffering, was 'My God, my God, why have you forsaken me?' And, really, the shorter version of what he was saying was, 'God, why?' And if Christ himself demanded to know why, what makes us think that we are any different."[33] This "answer" was noteworthy not only for its theological and biblical references but because unlike so many of the other sermons given that weekend in December, it was willing to linger with the inexplicable. It was a clearly Christian response to the tragedy—it was not a political response; it was not a therapeutic response nor a *let's move forward and put this behind us* response. It was one of the very few sermons that addressed doubt and the challenge that the tragedy posed to faith.

It was easier, perhaps, to do what many of the other sermons did instead. They called for gun control. These sermons were reasonably well argued; indeed, some of them were quite persuasive. But none of the gun control sermons were grounded in biblical or theological tradition. A few made a claim similar to those made after the assassination of President John F. Kennedy that because of the culture of violence, all Americans were partially responsible for the tragedy. And television commentator Bill Moyers gave a eulogy reprinted as a "Newtown sermon" in which he echoed the Pearl Harbor motto, "Praise the Lord. Pass the Ammunition." His was primarily a lament for American democracy: "This spilling of innocent blood, this bleeding of democracy's soul. We're losing faith in ourselves, acting as subjects, not citizens, no longer believing that it is in our power to do the right thing."[34]

Most of the gun control sermons had limited or no biblical references; there were no arguments for why gun control was a Christian issue, or how the church itself might be particularly well situated to mobilize for gun control. One might hesitate to call these sermons at all. They were more like political advocacy. In this set of gun control sermons, the Newtown tragedy barely touched Christianity. The shooting was not about God; the death of young children was a political issue, not an opportunity for mourning and deep reflection on purpose or perhaps one's relationship with the transcendent. Many ministers turned their pulpits over quite quickly to the political question of gun control. As noted earlier, one minister offered a long catalogue of her own "sins" regarding gun control: "I haven't spoken up enough about gun violence and when I look back on the entire ballot I cast last month in the elections, not one person I voted for has had the moral or spiritual core inside of them to do what needs to be done on the issue of guns in our country."[35] For Reverend Vince Ocampo, voting incorrectly was a sin. Another sermon demanded simply: "If you have a gun, or guns, in your home, get rid of them. Take them to the police and have them decommissioned. Get rid of them. I don't care if you hunt, or target shoot, or if they are family treasures. Just get rid of them."[36]

Even a prominent rabbi made a similar claim as part of her message regarding the Newtown shooting: "We are at war with guns . . . tragedy and loss is beyond our control, but when we do have the power to exercise some measure of control over how much we must lose and how much we must mourn in life, it is a crime against humanity not to do it."[37]

This approach, inaugurated in the Newtown sermons, would be repeated throughout the remaining tragedies examined in this chapter and culminating in the sermons that addressed Black Lives Matter and the killing of unarmed Black men by law enforcement. Recall that all the sermons examined for this project were given within a week or two of each tragedy. The Sandy Hook shooting was committed on Friday; thus, these Sunday sermons were the first time that many of these ministers would have been addressing their congregations. These sermons were the first words that many believers heard from their minister after the Friday shooting.

Finally, the last set of Newtown sermons were about mourning, or in this case about how quickly one should move away from grief to light and hope. Many ministers were troubled that this tragedy had occurred a mere ten days before Christmas. They seemed to be mourning the loss of the Christmas season as well as the loss of the children and teachers. There was a bit of urgency about shifting beyond the sadness: "I am weeping for the children I don't even know. I am weeping for parents. I am weeping for gifts that were already wrapped. . . . But we can't stay there. Because despair is a stop on the journey, a place where you pull over, look back at what has been lost, and then prepare to journey again."[38] As noted in earlier chapters, there was a cultural reluctance in the United States to linger with grief. One of the ministers astutely noted that the aversion to mourning was in part because Christians thought that belief in God should inoculate them from bad things, "For us, though, God has become anesthetist-in-chief."[39]

Grief was disorienting and revealed American susceptibility to suffering. There was something about grief, which was perceived as unseemly, that was almost un-American. Wasn't it primarily the weak who suffer? The downtrodden who cry out? Most images of wailing women and of those crumpled in sorrow are of unnamed others in remote foreign locations. They were certainly *not us*. Surely, the mighty do not suffer. And yet here were Americans, again, in a post-9/11 world, mourning their own dead children killed by a fellow American. Apparently, Americans still could not recognize the violence as belonging to themselves.

And American clergy, again, tried to resist the implications of the suffering, to block the identification with the lost, downtrodden, and the violated at the center of the Christian theological tradition. It was as if the ministers wanted to go directly from the Good Friday crucifixion to the Sunday resurrection without the long, lonely uncertain day and night of Holy Saturday. The middle day was filled with anxiety and uncertainty; it was a day vacuous with the hollow echo of a tomb.

Christianity has a theology of mourning and it is centered on the crucifixion of Jesus and his resurrection as Christ. As Reverend Gary Hall preached at the Washington National Cathedral the Sunday after the Newtown shooting: "As followers of Jesus, we are led by one who died at the hands of human violence on the cross. We know something about innocent suffering, and we know our job is to heal it and stop it wherever we can."[40]

Traditionally, Christian mourning was intended to be transformative. The process of mourning changed those who mourned. Hence, the Gospel blessing for "those who mourn" (Matt. 5:4). Only one of the Newtown sermons made this point. Reverend James A. Forbes Jr. asked: "We have seen that violence can strike anywhere. Yes, King talked about violence, but he also talked about transformation and healing in the wake of violence. What if history records what happened in Newtown and that leads to a new America?"[41] This was unlike many of the Newtown ministers who sought to expedite the grief, to act as though it was temporary and that the previous order would be quickly restored.

There were several Newtown sermons that addressed whether to light the Advent candle at the Sunday service as required by the liturgical calendar. This last candle was pink and was a symbol of joy. One minister referred to an e-mail she received from someone at "a preaching magazine" advising ministers not to light the pink candle in light of the shooting.[42] But she (and most others) decided to light the candle. Against the recommendation, Reverend Peg Nowling Williams lit the candle because "leaving the candle unlit means darkness wins and my friend, DARKNESS DOES NOT WIN. DARKNESS DOES NOT WIN. But sometimes it seems like it."[43] Father Michael Dolan, a Catholic priest from Avon, Connecticut, insisted that his sermon that Sunday "is going to be a balance . . . how do you respect the present reality . . . when there are joyful things that are happening?"[44] And the minister of First Church of Christ Congregational in West Hartford, Connecticut, asserted, "I will name the pain and acknowledge it . . . but I won't let it become a dominant theme."[45] And because apparently no tragedy was complete without this banality, Pastor Rob Morris at Christ the King Lutheran Church noted, "It is always the darkest nights that have the brightest stars."[46] Evidently, there is always a silver lining even in the slaughter of children.

As explored fully in Chapter 5, the truncated capacity for mourning in the United States marked a narcissistic turn in which mourning became more about the injury to oneself than the loss of the Other. This insight, first advanced by Sigmund Freud in his distinction between mourning and melancholy, helped to explain the American preference for spontaneous and temporary memorials, for expert counseling immediately after the loss of a loved one, and the professionalization of funerals, orchestrated by paid workers rather than family members.

Much has been written about the American capacity for mourning or lack thereof in the wake of 9/11. Since that issue was fully developed in Chapter 5, I merely wish to note that the mourning of the Newtown shooting followed a similar pattern. As one minister revealed: "While it was evident that everyone thought this was a tragedy, the vast majority of people seemed almost to be over it by now [Sunday, December 16]. There was one mom of an elementary aged child who said that she'd had a talk with her child, saying that the child should always pay attention during the drills they have in school. At one point the mom started crying. But she was really the only person who showed any visible emotion about it."[47] The Christian recommendation was to move away quickly from grief; to manage and minimize any extravagant emotions; and, as necessary, to psychologize the grief and to seek the expertise of therapeutic healing.

Although the Newtown tragedy began this chapter's analysis, the shooting did not inaugurate the violence that would come to configure these last dark years in American history. It's difficult to tell when or what initiated this decade of astonishing violence. Was the beginning the assassination attempt on Representative Gabby Giffords and the killing of six others in a Tucson supermarket parking lot in February 2011? Or was it the killing of an unarmed African American teenager, Trayvon Martin, the following February in Sanford, Florida, that established the contemporary culture of violence in the American psyche? Or was violence fully installed in the American way of life with the summertime shooting of twelve people at a movie theater in Aurora, Colorado, and then, again, with the bombing at the Boston Marathon in 2013?

While each of these tragedies punctuated the news cycle and temporarily brought Americans together, again, to assess the tremendous violence that was now a regular part of their experience, it was not until the killing of African American teenager Michael Brown by a White police officer, Darren Wilson, in Ferguson, Missouri, in August 2014 that the entire nation again stopped, held its breath, and tried to understand why. The murder of Michael Brown and the subsequent protests and riots, an echo for many Americans of the slaying of another unarmed African American teenager, Trayvon Martin, the year before, launched the powerful Black Lives Matter movement into the mainstream media. In fact, it was a Facebook post for Trayvon Martin where the phrase "Black lives matter" first appeared.[48]

After the 2014 violence in Ferguson, the Black Lives Matter movement was addressed repeatedly by American ministers—some debated whether to preach about it while others argued about how to preach about it. The killings and the response gripped not only the United States' racial imagination but its religious one as well. After the shooting of Michael Brown, the United States' Black and White Protestant clergy were mobilized in ways not seen since either the assassination of Dr. Martin Luther King in 1968 or the racial unrest in Los Angeles after the Rodney King beating in 1992.

DURING THE SUMMER of 2013, six months after the Newtown shooting, the verdict for the shooting of Trayvon Martin was announced. Trayvon's killer, George Zimmerman, was acquitted by a six-woman jury. A few days after the verdict, President Obama gave one of his most personal assessments of race relations in the United States: "You know, when Trayvon Martin was first shot, I said that this could have been my son. Another way of saying that, is Trayvon Martin could have been me thirty-five years ago. And when you think about why, in the African American community at least, there's a lot of pain around what happened here, I think it's important to recognize that the African American community is looking at this issue through a set of experiences and a history that doesn't go away."[49]

The president went on to detail the ways he had personally experienced racial suspicion simply because he was "being Black." He continued: "There are very few African American men in this country who haven't had the experience of being followed when they were shopping in a department store. That includes me. There are very few African American men who haven't had the experience of walking across the street and hearing the locks click on the doors of cars. That happens to me—at least before I was a senator. There are very few African Americans who haven't had the experience of getting on an elevator and a woman clutching her purse nervously and holding her breath until she had a chance to get off. That happens often."[50]

A year earlier in February 2012, Trayvon Martin had been walking home after buying an iced tea and a bag of Skittles. He was shot and killed by George Zimmerman, a volunteer on "neighborhood watch." The death of the seventeen-year-old unarmed Black boy, who because he was wearing a hoodie was racially profiled by Zimmerman as a threat to the neighborhood, ignited a nationwide conversation on the meaning of race in the United States. But it took nearly a month for the story of the shooting to reach the national press. At first the event was primarily covered only by local Florida outlets. Eventually, ABC News picked up the story on March 10, CNN on March 12, and eventually Fox News on March 19.[51] Analysts credit Trayvon Martin's parents with making their son's death into a national news story.

But the killing was not perceived as a national crisis—it was a tragedy, yes, but it was understood by the majority of White Americans primarily as a tragedy for the Black community. Although White Americans expressed sympathy to Trayvon's parents for their loss, most did not view Martin's death as a reason for all Americans to grieve. Just as Americans sent condolence letters to Coretta King lamenting "her loss," so

White Americans felt compassion for the Martin family. But the death of Trayvon was not lamented as an American loss. The tragedy was partisan, several degrees removed from ordinary White American life. According to a survey done by the Pew Forum at the time, 43 percent of Whites thought that the story was getting too much news coverage.[52]

Perhaps appreciating this racial divide, the president stressed in some impromptu remarks in the Rose Garden a few weeks after the killing: "I think every parent in America should be able to understand why it is absolutely imperative that we investigate every aspect of this. All of us have to do some soul searching to figure out how does something like this happen. When I think about this boy, I think about my own kids. You know, if I had a son, he'd look like Trayvon. I think they [Trayvon's parents] are right to expect that all of us as Americans are going to take this with the seriousness it deserves, and we are going to get to the bottom of exactly what happened."[53]

Two points, slightly in tension with one another, were being made here. First, everyone should care about the death of this boy, and second, the death of this child was particularly poignant to the president because "if I had a son, he'd look like Trayvon." This last comment sparked considerable media attention (and some mockery), but what President Obama was implicitly acknowledging with his recommendations that all Americans *should* care was that Americans did not *already* care. White Americans needed to be prodded and prompted to mourn the loss of this Black American as he, the president, did. He appealed to identity, "as Americans," rather than to conceptions of justice, morality, or of enduring legal or social principles. Implicitly, the president was acknowledging that Americans will only mourn the death of an African American teenager if they can be persuaded that the victim was somehow "one of us." Notably, the president did not invoke civil rights history or in any way draw attention to issues of race.

When President Obama grieved the loss of the Newtown children months later in December of the same year, he issued no reminders to care; it was not necessary to emphasize that all Americans should mourn. The president knew that twenty-six dead predominantly White children and their teachers would be grieved as the national tragedy that it was. And the Newtown deaths were a national tragedy. Just like the condolence letters to Jackie Kennedy mourning the death of her husband as like "the death of my own brother" or "a family member," so Americans mourned the loss of these Newtown children as if they were their own. But Trayvon Martin's death was a national tragedy as well, although not one that was grieved by all. His death focused painful attention on the regular wasting of African American boys' lives by those convinced by the smallest details and the most casual of gestures that these unarmed young Black men were a threat that warranted armed resistance and violent retaliation.

Sadly, this racial gulf that marked the reluctance to mourn for Trayvon was confirmed in the sermons given both immediately after Trayvon's death and in the first days after Zimmerman's acquittal. As one might expect, there was a plethora of sermons about Trayvon's death and the Zimmerman verdict by African American pastors and an alarming paucity of sermons by White clergy.[54] There was commentary at the time in the African American press about this silence and the tardiness with which major church organizations responded to the Zimmerman verdict.[55] In some instances, it took a week for the denomination to release a statement; in other instances, the statement was so bland as to be of no value either culturally or theologically.

Equally noncommittal were those denominations that reminded their congregants that both the Martin family and Zimmerman family were suffering and that their lives had been changed forever. "Some people are upset, angry and frustrated, while others are in full support of the verdict, so where does the church fit in? The church should be there to pray for families, the city of Sanford, and our nation," said Reverend Fred Luter, pastor of Franklin Avenue Baptist Church in New Orleans.[56] Similarly, Bishop Minerva Carcano, president of the United Methodist Commission on Religion and Race, offered this attempt at reconciliation: "I pray that as persons of Christian faith we will help guide the conversation in thoughtful and prayerful ways. The life of a young man has been cut short. His family and closest friends will live with a hole in their hearts. A man has taken a life and will live with that burden the rest of his life. Racism, guns, violence, and the lack of security plague us all."[57]

A bit surprisingly, some African American preachers seemed to take a similar approach by asking their congregants to identify with George

Zimmerman. "I wonder if there are any more George Zimmermans in the house. . . . If there are, let him without sin cast the first stone!"[58] And, more controversially: "You're black before you're anything. You're black before you're Christian, you're black before you're Holy Ghost, you're black before you're anything. Your blackness is greater than your religion. And that's why with you, Zimmerman's guilty."[59]

Only the president of the Southern Baptist Convention, Russell Moore, the first African American leader of that body, added this powerful statement to his denomination's official news service: "Add this [the Zimmerman acquittal] to the larger context of racial profiling and a legal system that does seem to have systemic injustices as it relates to African-Americans with arrests and sentencing, I think that makes for a huge crisis. . . . Most White evangelicals, White Americans, are seeing [the Martin case] microscopically, in terms of this verdict, and most African-Americans are seeing it macroscopically. It's Trayvon Martin, it's Emmett Till, it's Medgar Evers, it's my son, my neighbor's son, my situation that I had. . . . Most white Americans say we don't know what happened that night and they are missing the point."[60]

African American sermons after the Zimmerman verdict identified with the suffering not only of Trayvon but also of his parents and family. "I was not either mentally or emotionally prepared to hear not guilty. Trayvon's parents are in my prayers. Middle Church will mourn with them today as we did when they lost their child to gun violence."[61] A majority of these sermons asserted that what it meant to be a Christian in this tragic situation was to have empathy, to offer solace to those who were suffering: "How should the Christian community respond? . . . Share the sorrow of those being mistreated, for you know what they are going through."[62] Another sermon detailed, "My heart cries out for the mother and the girlfriend, who held up in their heart to sustain and defend, Trayvon Martin's truth."[63] Unlike in the Newtown sermons, these ministers were willing to linger with the pain, to wade through the sorrow. There was no urgency to move past it, to find the silver lining in the tragedy. Rather, this injustice was embedded in a long and tragic history of Black suffering and grief. Many of the sermons retold elements of the civil rights movement; some reached back to slavery and to how Black bodies had long been mistreated and misunderstood. Reverend Tony Lee entitled his Sunday sermon after Martin Luther King's,

"Where Do We Go from Here?" "I wanted Martin speaking on Martin."[64] Reverend Raphael Warnock at Atlanta's Ebenezer Baptist Church preached from his pulpit: "They said his name was Trayvon Martin. But he looked like Emmett Till. At least with Emmett Till someone was arrested. And that was in 1955."[65] These sermons exemplified what scholars of English literature David Eng and David Kazanjian in their essay "Mourning and Loss" have recognized as the "melancholic attachment that enables the past to remain steadfastly alive, bringing its ghosts and specters, its flaring and fleeting images into the present."[66]

The Newtown sermons did not take such a long view of either gun violence or of the killing of innocents. The Newtown ministers did not place the violence in a political context or inside American history. Instead, as is typical in American culture, the White violence at Newtown was categorized as unprecedented and exceptional rather than as part of a long and troubled history of school violence, from the University of Texas at Austin, where a shooter killed fifteen and injured thirty-one in August 1966, and the Columbine High School shooting in 1999, when two gunmen killed thirteen and injured twenty-four, to, most recently, the Virginia Tech High School shooting in 2007, in which thirty-three died and twenty-three were injured. The sermons by White ministers revealed what Toni Morrison has called "racial unconsciousness"; the positioning of oneself as unraced and all others as raced.[67]

Trayvon Martin had already been killed (although the verdict had yet to be given) when the Newtown shooting occurred. Newtown ministers could have referred to the death of Trayvon Martin as another example of the killing of the innocent. Instead, the majority of the Newtown sermons used the tragedy to suggest something uniquely iconic and inexplicable about this particular senseless massacre. Only one of the sermons mentioned the school shooting of five Amish girls in 2005 and none mentioned the shooting in 2006 at Virginia Tech where thirty-five were killed.

With the benefit of hindsight, one cannot help but wonder if interpreting tragedies as exceptionable and unrepeatable events is one of the privileges of American Whiteness. African American ministers interpreted Trayvon's murder as part of the legacy of violence that regularly besieged their community and was part of what it meant to be Black in the United States. Reverend Al Sharpton gave a sermon at the First African Methodist Episcopal Church in Los Angeles on the twentieth anniversary of the Rodney King verdict, several days after the Zimmerman verdict, in which he drew the parallel between the Los Angeles violence of 1992 and Trayvon Martin's death: "Twenty years ago, I came to Los Angeles after the unrest and we protested what had happened with the Rodney King verdict. Flying in this morning from Washington, I thought about what happened 20 years ago and where we are today."[68]

This unwanted inheritance was perhaps most eloquently articulated by Reverend Pamela Lightsey: "So, to put this question to a grieving family, 'Have you lost faith in the justice system?' demonstrates an ignorance of the tragic history of slavery, civil rights, legal racial profiling and now Stand Your Ground laws. *One simply cannot lose what has never been.* The more sensitive question should be: What can we all do to ensure a legal system that ensures justice for all citizens and residents in our country?"[69]

Pastoral solidarity with the grieving was embodied and visibly demonstrated on the one-month anniversary of Trayvon's slaying when Black clergy called for Hoodie Sunday. Black (and some White) clergy across the country adorned their pulpits wearing hoods of various kinds while their members in the pews also donned this symbolic attire.[70] Obviously, the hoodie was not a religious symbol but a political gesture.[71] The sweatshirt hoodie became the symbol of why Trayvon Martin had been perceived as threatening. The hoodie had been interpreted by Zimmerman that night to indicate that the teenager was "a thug." Subsequently, the slain youth was reincarnated with signs and T-shirts proclaiming, "I am Trayvon." The *New York Times* in another context called these "dead man shirts" part of the tradition of African American funerals—a way to honor and to protest the tragic death of members of the community.[72]

Reverend Michael Pfleger asked in his sermon: "Jesus wore a hood. Is he suspicious?"[73] And more pointedly, Reverend Nathaniel Robinson pulled the hood of his sweatshirt over his head and asked his congregants: "Do I look like a criminal? What does a criminal look like? There are some clerics who wear collars and molest little boys. There are political leaders in suits and ties who lie and lead us into wars. Do they look like criminals?"[74]

Hoodie Sunday, as it was called, was a study not only of performative preaching but of the pulpit as a robust place of theopolitics. Sermons by primarily Black ministers helped to propel the civil rights march the following week in Sanford, Florida, where Trayvon had been killed. Ministers as well as activists marched carrying signs: "A Mother's Tears Have No Color" and "Hoodies Don't Kill People, Guns Kill People."[75]

One of the most profound sermons from that Sunday was "A Rizpah Response" by Reverend Howard John Wesley, who retold the story of Saul's concubine, Rizpah, whose two sons David had sacrificed to restore peace with the Gideonites (2 Sam. 21:1–4). Rizpah, like Antigone, insisted that her sons deserved a proper burial and spent five months guarding their corpses until David permitted their burial.

Reverend Wesley, wearing a gray Howard University hoodie, linked the death of Trayvon to the death of the sons of Rizpah; he noted that Rizpah, like the mothers of many dead Black teenagers, was alone for five months with her unburied sons, with no one joining in her sorrow. He enjoined his community: "Wherever you are on the spectrum of life, this [the killing of Trayvon] ought to bother you! . . . Which children are worthy of our outrage? Who qualifies for your outrage? Who is worthy of your marching? Shouldn't you be outraged every time you hear about the taking of a life, regardless of the color of the victim or the perpetrator?"[76] The sermon was a foreshadowing of Claudia Rankin's observation several years later after Ferguson and the Charleston church shooting that Americans live in a country where "dead Blacks are part of normal life."[77] Americans, like the biblical characters, were inured to Black corpses in their public spaces.

Wesley's sermon put mourning at the center of his political theology; he did not exegete the crisis (i.e., the killing of Trayvon Martin) but preached a biblical story that explicated and revealed a way forward. His sermon, through the story of Rizpah, revealed how mourning eventually provoked a political leader, in this case King David, to do the right thing—to acknowledge the unjust killing of Rizpah's sons and to reconcile with her by burying not only her sons but those others who had also been unjustly killed. Similarly, Reverend Wesley called for his congregants to grieve Trayvon Martin as one of their own, not primarily because he was a Black teenager but because he had been killed unjustly.

Wesley was clear that justice as well as racial equity were at stake. His was an invitation to all Americans.

Hoodie Sunday exemplified what Sheldon Wolin has called "fugitive democracy."[78] It was a moment when democracy entwined with loss and created a temporary experience of solidarity and commonality, at least in the Black community. It was a democratic mode of being that was conditioned by bitter experience. Hoodie Sunday was also a profound reminder that whom we mourn, as well as whom we do not, reveals something significant about who we are. And when White America did not mourn the death of Trayvon Martin (and a year later, that of Michael Brown) as robustly as it did the deaths of the Newtown school children, it disclosed something about how White interests were being maintained by that neglect. Paul Gilroy has argued that by decentering race as part of these confrontations, the effect is that the cries of those who suffer sound less than human.[79] That is, by insisting that "race had nothing to do with it," the death of yet another Black child or unarmed Black man becomes another element of "the race-making process," rather than an acknowledgment of systematic injustice. In a crisis, Americans want to proclaim that differences do not matter, that as Americans we rally, unite, and work together. Yet the American history of mourning detailed in this research reveals otherwise.

The chilling repetition here is what happened a year later in pulpits after the Zimmerman verdict in the summer of 2013. Black pulpits were defeated, but not surprised. And White pulpits remained as they had after the killing of Dr. Martin Luther King, full primarily of what was aptly called "white noise."[80] Those sermons mostly offered some commonplace reiterations of the requirements of a "good neighbor." The lectionary reading was the well-known story of the Good Samaritan and it was easy for ministers to address being a good neighbor without thinking too deliberately about the racial context that propelled the slaying of Trayvon Martin.

The verdict that had been delivered late Saturday afternoon did not spark another Hoodie Sunday, although there were a few peaceful marches a few days later. President Obama did not address the nation until a week later, although he released what he called a preliminary statement that seemed intended primarily to calm "rising passions" in the African American community and to forestall any potential violence: "We are a nation of laws, and a jury has spoken. I now ask every American to respect the call for calm reflection from two parents who lost their young son."[81] So there was no pastor in chief to guide the next day's sermons. The nation did not stop and mourn; rather, it continued on. When Obama did address the nation, he gave a powerful speech. He talked about his own experience of being Black and profiled. He continued his use of the more casual "the first president who happened to be African American," rather than the stronger claim, "the first African American president," but his words were artful and insightful.

As noted, the liturgy for the Sunday after the Zimmerman verdict was the story of the Good Samaritan. Many ministers elected to preach the lectionary in part because it dovetailed so well with their moral message regarding the killing of Trayvon Martin. The story of the Good Samaritan is about unexpected kindness by a member of a fiercely despised minority group (the Samaritans). Respectable, so-called good people walk by the man in need, but only the Samaritan stops to offer help. The biblical parable has been used to develop an expansive conception of "neighbor," to recommend kindness to strangers, and more generally as a foundational ethos of Christianity to help those in need.

In the Trayvon sermons, many ministers noted that the story of the Good Samaritan was Jesus's response to a lawyer's inquiry. The lawyer had wanted to know what he should do to inherit eternal life. The implication in the Trayvon sermons is that the lawyer did not know the meaning of the law or that what is important was not the law but the practices entailed by following the law. That analysis resonated with the interpretation of the faulty law and its lawyers that had just released George Zimmerman and ordained him "not guilty."

Some of the sermons also described wished-for hypotheticals in the story of the Good Samaritan. One asked, "What if George Zimmerman had behaved like the Good Samaritan and offered Trayvon Martin a ride home to get him out of the rain that night?"[82] Another minister imagined that in response to the lawyer's question "Who is my neighbor?," Jesus had answered, "A young man who went to the corner store to buy a pack of Skittles and a can of tea."[83]

Some of the sermons struggled with what to do about George Zimmerman's race. Some dubbed him "the light-skinned, neighborhood watch commander."[84] Another designated him as a "Hispanic who passes for white."[85] For some clergy, Zimmerman needed to be rendered "White" for their claims of racial justice to be valid. The National Black Church Initiative made the race of Zimmerman the fulcrum of their anger at "all major Latino Organizations who were silent on the Trayvon Martin Verdict."[86] Their public statement announced: "You will not treat us as second-class citizens in our own country in which you are a visitor and illegal. We are fighting for your dignity, yet when one of your own kills our young you say absolutely nothing."[87] Reverend Al Sharpton helped to quiet this vitriol when he preached: "And the race/ethnicity of Zimmerman or any citizen in this type of scenario doesn't matter, because at the end of the day, it is the race of the victim—Trayvon—that does matter. It is his race and his demographic that is consistently depicted as the threat and negatively portrayed in popular culture."[88]

After the verdict, there were peaceful marches in various cities across the United States and some commentators noted that the nonviolent assemblies defied the expectations that the response to the verdict would be violent.[89] African Americans insisted that the expectation that there would be violence was "racial fear mongering." Newt Gingrich had remarked on CNN that those in the crowds would be "prepared, basically, to be a lynch mob."[90] A former Chicago police officer, Paul Huebl, wrote an op-ed warning: "If you live in a large city be prepared to evacuate or put up a fight to win. You will need firearms, fire suppression equipment along with lots of food and water."[91] His message went viral on social media. As Cobb noted in his *New Yorker* essay on the "non-riots," this language shifted responsibility back onto Trayvon Martin's shoulders and implicitly back on Black people.[92] This language was a disturbing inversion in which the victim now became guiltier than the perpetrator.

WHEN THE CHARACTER of God is given benevolent characteristics—redeemer, lover, creator, friend, healer—there is little or no differences between Black and White Protestants, according to Jason Shelton and Michael Emerson in their work, *Blacks and Whites in Christian America: How Racist Discrimination Shapes Religious Conviction.* However, when the characteristics of God are manifested as either an authority (judge, master, king), familial (father, mother, spouse), or linked to the Black theology of God as liberator, the differences are substantial.[93] For example, slightly fewer than half of White Protestants were extremely likely to view God as a judge, but two-thirds of Black Protestants were extremely likely to do so. Only 21 percent of White Protestants were extremely likely to view God as mother, whereas 57 percent of Black Protestants were extremely likely to view God this way. Fewer than half of White Protestants thought of God as a liberator, whereas two-thirds of Black Protestants were extremely likely to view God as such.[94]

For the purposes of this project, these differences might partially help to explain why White Protestants are historically more willing to abdicate church authority to the state whereas Black Protestants are more reluctant to do so. Black Protestants still believe they have a sovereign authority—God—and since the state has not been just to African Americans, it makes sense that they would depend theologically on God's authority instead. On the other hand, since Whites believe (and have experienced) that the state protects them and since they understand themselves as the state's creator, they are perhaps more willing to abdicate church authority in favor of the state.

This difference was manifest in so many of the sermons after random violence—White Protestants looked for political remedies and Black Protestants looked to God to help them through. This does not mean that Black Protestants were quiescent politically. Rather, it signals that Black Protestants have a conception of God who intervenes more regularly in daily life. This is a God who is more than prepared to fulfill His purposes with or without the state. The God of the White Protestants as detailed in the last chapters seems to be more dependent on the state to fulfill His mission.

A little over a year after George Zimmerman was acquitted on August 9, 2014, eighteen-year-old African American Michael Brown was shot and killed in Ferguson, Missouri, by a White police officer, Darren Wilson. Wilson fired twelve shots in the ninety seconds that began the encounter with Brown, and that ended with the teenager dead on the city street. Although forensic evidence eventually discounted the suspicion that Michael Brown had died with his hands up, the expression "Hands Up, Don't Shoot" became a mantra of the protests and rioting that followed the shooting as well as the decision a few months later not to indict Darren Wilson. The multiple high-profile deaths of unarmed Black men by law enforcement—from Eric Garner (who died as a result of a police chokehold, July 17, 2014) to John Crawford (killed by police in a Walmart store aisle while holding a toy BB gun, August 5, 2014), Akai Gurley (killed by officers in a Brooklyn stairwell, November 20, 2014), and Tamir Rice (a twelve-year-old boy killed within seconds of a police cruiser's arrival at a park in Cleveland, Ohio, November 22, 2014)—provoked the development of the Black Lives Matter movement.

The Black Lives Matter movement (BLM) was founded by African American community activists focused largely on police brutality, racial profiling, and the racial inequities in the US criminal justice system. BLM was catapulted into the national consciousness during the protests in Ferguson after the Michael Brown shooting. BLM is not a religiously inspired or church-involved movement. In fact, many of the BLM activists have sought to distance themselves from the Black Church and what are derisively considered its "respectability politics." The legacy of Booker T. Washington and W. E. B. Du Bois looms over the dismissal of "respectability" and its accommodation of mainstream values and its perceived valorization of the status quo. President Obama has himself been both lauded and accused of "respectability politics." A few days after the unrest in Ferguson, for example, President Obama said: "There are young black men that commit crime. And—and—and we can argue about why that happened—because of the poverty they were born into or the lack of opportunity or the school systems that failed them or what have you. But if they commit a crime, then they need to be prosecuted because every community has an interest in public safety."[95] Several African American leaders took issue with the president's highlighting of Black criminality especially since he seemed to be confirming early in the judicial process the racist suspicion that the Black teenager Michael Brown was somehow responsible for his own death.

BLM was almost immediately burdened with questions about "blue lives" (the lives of police officers), about White lives, about all lives. Didn't all those lives matter, too? And Christian ministers were asking the same questions. For many White Protestants, the Christian response seemed to be, "all lives matter." "Didn't Jesus love everyone?" these sermons rhetorically asked. "You have heard the terms Black lives matter,

White lives matter, police lives matter, Penn Dot road workers lives matter. Until we get to the point that all lives matter, we are playing favorites."[96] Black Lives Matter seemed exclusive, unnecessarily hostile, and without theological foundation. "What had happened to racial reconciliation in America?" some minsters inquired.

A small percentage of ministers simply decided that BLM was too political for the pulpit and said so either by deflecting questions of structural racial injustice into the forensics of the specific case, "we don't know what happened in those final moments of the encounter between Michael Brown and Darren Wilson." Others preached a poignant apolitical identification with the suffering of all, "May I see clearly / That I am the dead in Paris / And I am also their killers / I am the family of the dead in Beirut / And I am the family of their killers / That I am the child of each refugee / And the mother of every despot / I am each ISIL recruit, each American soldier, every exploded hospital and every roadside bomb."[97] This identification with everyone everywhere had the effect, of course, of rendering the empathy rather meaningless. While the initial *Je suis Charlie* was powerful after the Charlie Hebdo massacre, its endless "translation" and repetition after multiple tragedies made it strangely incoherent.[98]

Nonetheless, about half of the United States' Protestant clergy (both Black and White) were engaged by BLM, sensing its possibility for racial justice. A few sermons repeated variations on the following story to their congregants as a way to explain the legitimacy of Black Lives Matter:

> Imagine that you wake up late one night to the sound of your home being burglarized. Through the crack in your bedroom door, you see several figures hauling out your television, computers and nice china to their getaway car parked outside. Thinking quickly, you dial 911 on your iPhone. "911, what's your emergency?" "Help!" you whisper. "My home is being robbed!" "Stay where you are, Miss," the other voice assures you. "We'll look into it." "Thank you," you whisper. "My address is—" "Woah, Ma'am," the voice on the other end says. "Why are you bringing addresses into this?" "What?" you say. "My home is being robbed! Aren't you going to come and stop them?" "Well,

I don't know why you need to make this about your home, ma'am," the operator says. "All houses matter."[99]

Other sermons continued to try to explain how Black Lives Matter was about addressing the current crisis facing young Black men and their deadly encounters with law enforcement. "Brown was cut down at age 18 when bullets shot by a police officer riddled his surrendering body. We have the testimonies of at least two eyewitnesses and a slowly developing story from the police of what happened. But from where I sit, no matter which story one is inclined to believe, Michael Brown has become a symbol, a scapegoat really, of our diseased society, of the U.S. body politick. . . . We are left to ask of God, 'Why are the Michaels of our communities bearing all our iniquities?'"[100]

But even these sermons struggled to find biblical references or a theological component to the unrest. Sermon after sermon given primarily by White ministers either made an ostensibly political argument about the necessity of gun control or more blandly argued for the necessity of "the hard work to affirm the worth and dignity of all people."[101] There were many noble sentiments but very little theology or even biblical references. The closest the sermon cited above came to a religious argument was a reference to Archbishop Desmond Tutu's work in South Africa dismantling apartheid. And this neglect was not limited to one denomination; it was true across denominations. Many White ministers retreated to how "heartbreaking" these stories are and to the confession of their own racism, "It is an emotional issue for all of us—how we feel about police officers and how we feel about Black people."[102] "What we are witnessing in our country today truly breaks my heart. I've said that a lot lately."[103] These were the therapeutic sermons. One's thoughts and feelings were the objects of analysis. Most of the pastoral recommendations were about individual transformation and vague conceptions of "living your faith." Congregants were urged to "get out of your comfort zone," although exactly what that required remained unspecified. There were also frequent sermons by White ministers in which they confessed their racial sins. Being a good Christian meant acknowledging one's sin. Racism was an individual shortcoming that one needed to purge. There was little about why Christianity might demand, require, or expect racial justice. In fact, among the fifty or so sermons read for this section, only one sermon given by a White minister named Black people as also created in the image of God: "The very notion of liberty needs to be distinguished from individual autonomy and license, and the love for the imago dei in our Black brothers and sisters must be united with the creational integrity that God intended them to have."[104]

Among White ministers, it was rather surprisingly conservative evangelicals who often offered the most robust theological defenses of BLM. Pastor Wedgeworth gave the history of the movement, including its founding by queer women activists and worried that the Christian appropriation of the movement without an acceptance of transgender rights might be a violation of the core principles of the movement.[105] He proclaimed: "For the time being, we are willing to work alongside of them [BLM] to achieve important but limited goals. This would be a statement of integrity which communicated appreciation, critique, and limited political solidarity."[106]

Evangelicals' primary disagreement with BLM was that it should be a church-led movement not a secular one. Evangelicals were confident that the church could still do more than the state to achieve racial reconciliation. But BLM was not about racial reconciliation; it was about racial justice. There were many sermons about how the church could accomplish the majority of BLM's aims without violence or animosity— their most frequent critique of BLM. Again, this was a therapeutic approach to the structural issue; racism would be resolved if we all learned, in an echo of Rodney King, "to just get along." Sin in these sermons tended to be individual (i.e., selfishness, greed, laziness) rather than structural or institutional.

There was also a considerable number of both Black and White evangelical preachers who urged evangelicals to distance themselves from the movement. "Here it [BLM] involves using racial guilt to manipulate Christians into supporting a movement that perpetuates a secular social and political narrative that consists of lies and racial paranoia under the guise of fighting racial inequality."[107] Or this: "Support of BLM is a litmus test for racial justice and reconciliation, so the Church must both confirm its agreement with this principle while distancing itself from the movement which has repeatedly made clear that it wants nothing to do with the Christian paradigm. . . . While I wholeheartedly endorse the motivation for wanting to address racial injustice, it seems to me that for Christians, justice must be filtered through the prism of a kingdom paradigm in which Christian ethics dominates."[108]

Evangelical churches across the United States also organized several First Responder Sundays. While some of these days of recognition were attempts to reconcile Black church members with law enforcement, the majority of the First Responder Sundays were meant primarily as a repudiation of Black Lives Matter and its perceived challenge to American conceptions of the heroic.[109]

Not surprisingly, many African American ministers found most of these sermons and activities tiresome. As Reverend Fred D. Robinson noted in his sermon "What God Is Screaming in Ferguson, Missouri": "Most frustrating of all is his [White preacher] solution to the racial powder keg that has produced the Fergusons across the nation: a call for more racially diverse churches. I get tired of that one. His unrelenting insistence reminded me—in the starkest terms—of James Baldwin's prophetic quip, 'Racial progress in America is measured by how fast I become White.'"[110] Another minister in Ferguson noted that in his congregation, White people were saying, "I can't believe this is happening in my city," while the Black members of the congregation were saying, "I can't believe it took this long for this to happen in my city."[111]

The majority of sermons given by Black ministers in these first weeks retold the stories of the American civil rights movement. A few even read sermons from the era. Several reread all or part of Reverend Dr. Vernon Johns's "It's Safe to Murder Negroes," given in May 1949 at the Dexter Avenue Baptist Church in Montgomery, Alabama, after the killing of a Black man by a White police officer near Johns's church.[112] It was chilling that the 1949 sermon was still prophetic in 2014:

> I just want to remind you what the clearest and simplest of these great ten commandments is: Thou shalt not kill. The Birmingham paper says that you have a better chance in 1948 of being murdered in Alabama than anywhere in the U. S. A lot of the people doing the killing are the police officers who should know the law as well as anybody. . . . The officer Orris Thrash killed Amos Star for resisting arrest. Shot him in the back. So, I guess he was resisting while running away. . . . Last week, a White man was fined for shooting a rabbit out of season. But of

course, it's safe to murder Negroes. A rabbit is better off than a Negro because in Alabama niggers are always in season.[113]

By retelling Johns's sermon, ministers reminded congregations of civil rights history while explicitly confirming that the work of that era was not yet finished. Johns's sermon itself ended with a call to action: "And when you stand by and watch your brothers and sisters being lynched it's as if you stood by while Christ was being crucified. . . . Are you afraid that if you speak too loudly, protest too strongly, you will become one of those lynched? Well, you may well be. He who takes not this cross and follows me is not worthy of me. So, there you have the question. Are you worthy of Jesus or are you only worthy of the state of Alabama?"[114]

Reverend Dr. Howard John Wesley, in his sermon "When the Verdict Hurts," began with an echo of Vernon Johns: "How in the world is it that Michael Vick gets two years for killing an animal. But a man kills a black boy and he gets off scot free. I know this is not the button I should be pushing. But what this tells us is that the life of an animal is more protected than our black and brown children."[115] It was a reaffirmation of the "in and out of season rabbits and Negroes" analogy in Vernon Johns's sermon. And Wesley, too, continued with an analogy to the crucifixion of Jesus, who was guilty of nothing but had to carry his own cross to be hanged.[116] This was one of the theological features that many of the sermons by Black ministers highlighted—that the divine is the God of the oppressed.[117] This turn toward liberation theology has deep roots in the African American community. In a recent interview, liberation theologian James Cone noted: "The Jesus of the Biblical and Black tradition is not a theological concept but a liberating presence in the lives of the poor in their fight for dignity and worth. . . . God is indeed on the side of the oppressed."[118]

As Shelton and Emerson showed through their interviews and surveys of Black and White Christians in the United States, Black Christians are more likely to rely on God because they need His help and expect Him to see them through. White Christians are less likely to expect or experience God as a divine liberator because they have other resources for major life problems. Black minister Reverend Washington put it this way: "Blacks don't have the options that Whites have. If a white man has a financial problem, before he leans on God or goes to the church or his pastor, he's got a friend or a relative that's got the economics to help him."[119] Pastor Thomas added that many African Americans think: "If I do my part, then God's going to do His part. So, I have to pray more. I've got to see what the pastor has to say. I've got to see what my prayer partner says about this."[120]

This may also explain why in some of the African American Black Lives Matter sermons there was also more of a discussion of the possibility of miracles. Some were the miracles of history, such as the various achievements of the civil rights movement in the face of alarming odds and the unexpected but grace-filled election of an African American president during their lifetimes. Others were theological miracles. Reverend Kinman preached to a largely African American audience in Ferguson by recalling the story of Peter walking on water: "Jesus tells us to do something impossible. If it isn't someone challenging us to do something that we think is impossible, it's probably not Jesus. . . . If the person said, 'No. Stay in the boat and be comfortable,' Peter would have known, 'Oh, that's not Jesus.' . . . We are born to walk on water . . . we can do impossible things."[121] Although these were sermons focused on miracles, they were not about quiescence; they were calls to action. They were reminders that through Christian activity and divine confirmation, miracles were achievable. These were quite different sermons than those given by White Protestant ministers whose appeals were primarily to the government to legislate, mandate, and respond to the church's demands. In the miracle sermons, African American Christians would ensure by their own civic engagement and Christian activity that God's will would be achieved. Not surprisingly, there were no calls for government intervention.

IT WAS DIFFICULT for many White ministers to understand the rage and violence of Black grief surrounding the deaths of these young unarmed men. When Dr. Martin Luther King Jr. was assassinated and multiple American cities exploded in rage and grief, White America was aghast. How could Black Americans mourn the prince of nonviolence with violence? But the rage was not a commentary on Dr. King's philosophy of nonviolence; it was a response to the violence and the racism that killed him. Similarly, the riots in Ferguson, Baltimore, and Charlotte were markers of the powerlessness and despair of those whose voices were not heard. Although it may be an inadequate and ineffective response to the killing of unarmed Black men, it remains a readily available tool often wielded by the disenfranchised. How the subordinated mourn their dead does not negate the justice of their outrage or diminish the number of their own who are dead.

The challenges continued to develop as ministers (and the country) struggled with the complicated intersections of race and whom and how to mourn. This matrix was highlighted again in November 2014 with the shooting of African American Akai Gurley in a stairwell by a Chinese American rookie police officer, Peter Liang. Liang insisted that his gun had gone off accidentally in the dark and then ricocheted off a wall, striking and accidentally killing Gurley. Liang was subsequently found guilty of manslaughter. At sentencing, the charge was reduced to negligent homicide and he served no jail time. At the time, Liang was the first NYPD officer convicted in a fatal shooting in over a decade. Liang's arrest and conviction mobilized the Chinese American community in New York City, who believed that Liang was being scapegoated because he was himself a racial minority: "The climate is crying out for the indictment of a police officer. . . . [Liang] is being sacrificed for all the injustices that happened."[122] Over ten thousand Chinese Americans marched in protest from Chinatown into the streets of Brooklyn.[123]

There were additional protests in thirty cities across the United States—New York City, Los Angeles, Washington, DC, and Chicago. Many of the Chinese American protesters were waving American flags and declaring, "We are Americans."[124] This citizenship claim was an eerie echo of the declaration many Japanese Americans had made in the days and weeks before their internment in 1942. The protesters said their frustration stemmed from years of persecution. Recalled again was the history of racial conflict between African Americans and Asian Americans which reverberated from the Los Angeles Rodney King beating verdict and the Korean grocer's killing of African American teenager Latasha Harlins.

But some Chinese American activists worried that the protests marked Chinese American chagrin that Liang had not been afforded the "privileges of Whiteness" usually accorded to other officers.[125] Rather than an outcry about justice, some of the protests seemed to validate this worry with their signs and chanting, "White officers shot unarmed black men and got away with it—why can't we?" Black Lives Matter activists responded simply, "An unarmed black man is still dead."

Not unexpectedly, only one of the sermons addressing Black Lives Matter considered this particular Asian/Black matrix of racial complexities. And that one was given by an Asian American minister, Reverend Grace Ji-Sun Kim, who is a Presbyterian minister as well as a professor of theology at the Earlham School of Religion, Earlham College.[126] In her sermon "Crucifixion of Jesus: Scapegoating, Discrimination and the Cross," she drew a parallel between the scapegoating of Jesus to maintain Roman power and the persecution of police officer Peter Liang: "Asian Americans get blamed for the loss of college admission slots for White students, for jobs lost in the United States to Asian immigrants, and for jobs going to China and other Asian countries. All too often, Asian Americans are scapegoated in ways which pit us against other people of color. . . . This form of scapegoating diminishes the long suffering of Asian Americans. These are tools used to reinforce white privilege and white supremacy."[127]

Whom to mourn was again at the center of the funerals for two New York police officers, Raphael Ramos and Weinjian Liu, who were ambushed a month later while sitting in their patrol car in December 2014. The perpetrator claimed on social media that he was planning to kill police officers in response to the killings of Eric Garner and Michael Brown. More than one hundred thousand people attended the funeral for Officer Ramos—the largest police funeral in the city's history. Racial politics were again the central focus when the NYPD police commissioner, William Bratton, began both of his eulogies for the slain officers with, "He represented the blue thread that holds our city together when disorder might pull it apart. . . . These officers were killed for their color—they were killed because they were blue."[128]

Here blue was aligned with black as a category of persecution. It was an intentional rhetorical conflation of racial injustice and the violent death of these police officers. It was also a claim that sought to discard political history and pronounce injustice with an illusion of equivalence: dead police officers were not the same as dead unarmed Black men. The murder of these police officers was criminal, but their deaths were not a manifestation of a structural injustice that had plagued the police community for decades.

President Obama did not attend these police funerals, although Vice President Biden did and he eulogized the officers with an ode to racial pluralism:

> So when an assassin's bullet targeted two officers, it targeted this city and it touched the soul of the entire nation—a city where the son of a Chinese immigrant shared a patrol with a Hispanic minister in training; a city where a single ride on a subway brings you into contact with more people, more lives than many people in this country will encounter in an entire lifetime; a city that educated a young college student with a mother from Kansas, and a father from Kenya who would one day stand before the nation and declare: This is not a black America or a white America or a Latino America or an Asian America; this is the United States of America.[129]

At the end of the funerals for both officers, several hundred New York City police officers turned their backs on Mayor Bill de Blasio in protest for what they perceived as his lack of support for the slain officers. Among other reasons, de Blasio's open endorsement of Reverend Al Sharpton who had strongly criticized police officers in the Eric Garner death, many members of the NYPD blamed de Blasio for the antipolice sentiment that they insisted had fueled the assassination of the two officers, Liu and Ramos.

The deaths after the police shootings necessitated that Americans confront the violence, trauma, and ambivalence of common life.[130] But the confrontation with this ambivalence varied between White and Black Americans. A "spectacular Black death" seemed to be required in order to activate White sympathy.[131] And Black Americans, while understanding the strategic utility of that spectacle, remained as they had for well over a hundred years—angry that a national moral reckoning and outcry for justice still required Black suffering. White death, on the other hand, as manifest in the killing of the officers, was nearly always mourned as an injustice and unwarranted tragedy.

The frequently misunderstood rage manifested by members of the African American community after the shootings of unarmed Black men showcased the costs of collective American lives. It peeled away the veneer and exposed again the wound on which law and order had been built. And, unlike some of the other tragedies of this book, it highlighted that the state was the source of the suffering, not the balm. Perhaps this was why it was so difficult for many in the White Christian community to understand the violence of Black grief in some of the cities that had witnessed the deaths of their Black sons. White Americans expected the state to offer solace. Isn't that what the mourner in chief did? Isn't that what the American creed provided? But how are the disenfranchised, the violated, and the subordinate to express their grief? Their disappointment? Their frustration? Can their mourning be understood, felt, and appreciated when expressed with rage? Or must the subaltern always speak using only the master's ordained vernacular?

PRESIDENT OBAMA DID NOT become mourner in chief again until the domestic terrorism at the African Methodist Episcopal Church in downtown Charleston, South Carolina, on June 17, 2015. President Obama gave the eulogy for the pastor of the AME Church, Reverend Clementa Pinckney. The shooting had occurred during an evening Bible study that the murderer disrupted, killing nine people. The confessed killer asserted that he had intended for the violence to provoke a race war.

In his eulogy, President Obama recalled the history of violence against Black churches "as a means of control, a way to terrorize and oppress . . . an act that he [the killer] presumed would deepen divisions that trace back to our nation's original sin."[132] Yet FBI director James Comey did not think the act qualified as "terrorism" because "based on what I know, I don't see this as a political act."[133] The FBI director was apparently unfamiliar with the political history of White racists killing Black people in churches as a way to coerce behavior and stall the claims to racial equality.

President Obama gave a sermon that was among the most compelling of this dark decade of American violence. For it truly was a sermon, quoting Scripture and reflecting repeatedly on the "power of God's grace." "This whole week, I've been reflecting on this idea of grace. The grace of the families who lost loved ones. The grace that Reverend Pinckney would preach about in his sermons. The grace described in one of my favorite hymnals—the one we all know: Amazing grace, how sweet the sound that saved a wretch like me."[134]

This eulogy for Reverend Clementa Pinckney certainly ranks as among one of the finest speeches about racial justice President Obama gave during his presidency: "For too long, we were blind to the pain that the Confederate flag stirred in too many of our citizens. It's true, a flag didn't cause these murders. But as people from all walks of life, Republicans and Democrats, now acknowledge—including Governor Haley, whose recent eloquence on the subject is worthy of praise—as we all have to acknowledge, the flag has always represented more than just ancestral pride. For many, Black and White, that flag was a reminder of systemic oppression and racial subjugation. We see that now."[135]

And then the eulogy took the quintessentially twenty-first-century theopolitical turn. Political acts became expressions of God's grace. "By taking down that flag [the Confederate flag], we express God's grace. But I don't think God wants us to stop there. . . . Perhaps it [God's grace] softens hearts toward those lost young men, ten and tens of thousands caught up in the criminal justice system and leads us to make sure that system is not infected with bias; that we embrace changes in how we train and equip our police so that the bonds of trust between law enforcement and the communities they serve make us all safer and more secure. . . . We're also guarding against the subtle impulse to call Johnny back for a job interview but not Jamal . . . to do what's necessary to make opportunity real for every American—by doing that, we express God's grace."[136]

The eulogy concluded with a Martin Luther King Jr.–like analysis: "Justice grows out of recognition of ourselves in each other. That my liberty depends on you being free, too."[137] And then President Obama delighted the congregation by beginning to sing the opening stanza of "Amazing Grace."[138]

President Obama was brilliant, eloquent, humble—phenomenally pastoral and still, president of the United States. No one missed an ordained minister, no one needed one. They had Minister Barack. He was the presidential Martin Luther King, but he was not an activist, nor was he prophetic. He was a powerful man of the state who had shown that no one needed church authority and that the vacuum of church authority could be filled by governmentality.

But that glory did not last. Less than a year later when the president was mourning the five police officers executed in Dallas during a peaceful protest, his eulogy was flat and uninspired. Mourning had become too fully politicized for the commander in chief to be perceived as authentic. Even the video of President Obama's funeral oration showed audience members disinterested, sleepy, and sometimes rather annoyed.[139]

President Obama began his eulogy in Dallas as he had all the others, "Scripture tells us . . ." But this eulogy was less theological than the eulogy for Reverend Pinckney but just as political. President Obama called the killing of the police officers "an act not just of demented violence, but of racial hatred."[140] In this eulogy for the police officers, he also recalled the dead unarmed Black men Alton Sterling and Philando Castile, who had been killed by police officers. The protest taking place in Dallas at which these police officers had been ambushed had been in response to the unlawful killing of Black men across the United States. President Obama included them in his eulogy: "I see people who mourn for the five officers we lost, but also weep for the families of Alton Sterling and Philando Castile. In this audience, I see what's possible." He detailed the injuries suffered by Black Americans and asserted: "None of us is entirely innocent. No institution is entirely immune, and that includes our police departments. We know this. . . . We cannot simply turn away and dismiss those in peaceful protests as troublemakers or paranoid."[141]

Although the president countered this assertion with a rather anodyne, "We ask the police to do too much and we ask too little of ourselves," the momentum and energy of the sermon was about White racism. He even referred obliquely to Trayvon Martin with a prayer that all Americans have a "new heart . . . not a heart of stone, but a heart open to the fear and hopes and challenges of our fellow citizens. . . . So that maybe the police officer sees his own son in that teenager with a hoodie, who's kind of goofing off but not dangerous. And the teenager—maybe the teenager will see in the police office the same word, and values and authority of his parents."[142] Obama intended for the juxtaposition to suggest a possibility of mutual recognition but there was no cultural "good cop" equivalent to the hoodie-clad Trayvon Martin. Who would American teenagers conjure as *the good police officer* or even as *the good parent*? The names of the slain police officers were not then (nor are they now) part of the American vocabulary. And Obama did not repeat their names often enough to make them more than "five fellow Americans."[143]

Toward the end of his eulogy, President Obama added, "Insisting we do better to root out racial bias is not an attack on cops, but an effort to live up to our highest ideals."[144] This was a eulogy for police officers killed in the line of duty and Obama was focused on the racial bias of police officers. The trajectory continued: "Protestors can get hurt. They can be frustrated. But even those who dislike the phrase, 'Black lives matter,' surely, we should be able to hear the pain of Alton Sterling's family. We should—when we hear a friend describe him by saying that, whatever he cooked, he cooked enough for everybody, that should sound familiar to us, that maybe he wasn't so different than us. So that we can, yes, insist that his life matters. Just as we should hear the students and co-workers describe their affection for Philando Castile as a gentle soul." Obama then went on to describe how Castile's life also mattered to many different people.

Politically, this was a courageous eulogy. Obama was knitting to-gether the antagonists in the racial drama. But the Dallas eulogy failed, in part because the Charleston one had succeeded so powerfully. In the Charleston eulogy, Pastor Obama had demonstrated that mourning was particular, personal. That Americans did not mourn for all their dead in the same way. And that revelation meant that the mourner in chief was no longer believed—at least by the White majority in Dallas—as caring as much about the slain White police officers as he did about the Black men and women assassinated in a church. In Charleston, Obama sang "Amazing Grace": his grief was intimate; he told the history of the African American struggle in the United States as "we." "Black churches . . . have been, and continue to be community centers where we organize for jobs and justice; places of scholarship and network; places where children are loved and fed and kept out of harm's way, and told that they are beautiful and smart—and taught that they matter. . . . That's what the Black church means. Our beating heart. The place where our dignity as a people is inviolate."[145]

At the Dallas memorial, former president George Bush also spoke about the slain and named the disparity in mourning: "Today, all of us feel a sense of loss, but not equally. I'd like to conclude with a word to the families, the spouses and especially the children of the fallen . . . your loss is unfair. We cannot explain it."[146] Americans do not want to believe that they mourn differently for their fellow Americans. After Newtown, a Connecticut resident insisted: "Mourning is such a personal thing. You don't even have to have children to understand the pain; all you have to have is a heart."[147]

But this is not quite accurate; yes, mourning is personal—it depends on who you are, whom you mourn. Having a heart is not enough to engage all Americans' grief. Rather, there is a history and politics to mourning. After the Oklahoma bombing, President Clinton and First Lady Hillary Clinton held a nationally televised session with a room full of American children to answer their questions about the bombing and to assuage their fears.[148] They were the last presidential family to do so. President Bush and First Lady Laura Bush did not address the nation's children after 9/11; neither did President Obama and First Lady Michelle Obama after the Sandy Hook school shooting or the killing of Trayvon Martin. Surely, young children were rendered similarly afraid and puzzled by the difficult questions such violence undoubtedly raised for them. But the presidential politics of mourning had changed.

In the Charleston eulogy, President Obama had successfully embodied everything the church had once been for both White and Black Americans. It was a beautiful eulogy and a powerful acknowledgment that the church's role in a crisis could be easily embodied by a charismatic state leader. There was nothing wrong with the eulogy; in many ways, it was perfect.

Still, it was Creon giving the eulogy—mourning the dead, with limitless power, while the clergy were sidelined, grateful, perhaps, that Creon was now on the side of justice. By conceding the altar to the presidential minister, the church was complicit in its own disempowerment. It was a profound miscalculation begun, perhaps for understandable reasons, after the assassination of Dr. Martin Luther King, but the consequences continued to accumulate after the bombing in Oklahoma City and the destruction of September 11, when ministers wrestled with the state but ultimately forfeited their power in the hope that they could recoup more by aligning with the state rather than resisting it.

And so in 2015, President Obama stepped onto the stage—eloquent, charismatic, theologically aware—and replaced the prophetic with the therapeutic, installing the pastoral as part of government power, and completing the consolidation of the church and the state. The only remaining resisters, oddly, would be those stragglers left out of the partisan politics who when the party majority changed would again assume their place in the corridors of power where the smell of the white marble replaced the incense of a once transcendent power. Now God had to answer to the secular world, rather than the reverse: "We pray expecting you [God] to work. Prove yourself to them as the God of comfort. Prove yourself to them. . . . Remind them, God that you did not cause this tragedy."[149]

Sermons during this period addressed the crisis, not theological truths. As a White minister said to his congregation after the shooting of Michael Brown, "It is an emotional issue for all of us—how we feel about police officers and how we feel about Black people."[150] How Christians feel is central. Events are personal, individual; justice is not the primary metric. Through all these tragedies, God is distraught, Jesus weeps; their transcendent power is drained by the urgency of human evil. Maybe that's why so many religious leaders urge moving quickly through mourning: "We all feel paralyzed in mourning. That's understandable for today. But for tomorrow, we ask that we sow the seed to prevent it from happening again."[151] Something must be done. And solutions rest with the state rather than in Scripture. As pastor in chief, Barack Obama reminded his flock, "No matter how much you love these kids, you can't do it by yourself. . . . We can only do it together, with the help of friends and neighbors, the help of a community and the help of a nation."[152] Pastor Obama does not invoke God's help; He is no longer necessary in this new theopolitical governmentality.

Postscript: Summer 2020

With the quarantine of COVID-19 and the killing of George Floyd by law enforcement in 2020, Creon and Antigone have returned again as the United States reflects on and struggles to determine for whom to mourn and how. As the elderly, immunocompromised, and Black and Latinx populations succumb disproportionately to the virus, their vulnerability and deaths challenge American conceptions of community. What do we collectively owe them? While their deaths may be particularly poignant to their family members, to what extent are we all collectively responsible for protecting them? What are the restrictions by which Americans should all abide and which can they flaunt in pursuit of that hallowed American value of individual freedom?

As of this writing, there have been over 140,000 American deaths, and President Trump has not assumed the mantle of mourner in chief. It is unclear what kind of crisis would propel him into that role. After the violence in Charlottesville, he chose to thread the needle, "You also had some very fine people on both sides."[153] While he tried to make a moral argument about the racially inflected violence, "racism is evil," he did not lead Americans in mourning then. Trump was also president during the largest mass shooting in American history, the Las Vegas Harvest Festival shooting on October 1, 2017, which killed 58 people and wounded 422. There was no national mourning vigil. President Trump gave no eulogy for the victims. Nor has he done so during the current pandemic, nor in response to the killing of George Floyd; mostly, President Trump has resisted mourning.

And so pastors have been propelled into a virtual pulpit as their congregations, rather than turning away from regular services, demand a word of solace, a place of refuge from the isolation and anxieties of stay-at-home orders. Many churches across the country now are holding creative remote services. Younger ministers are thriving as they showcase their facility with various technologies. One minister posted copies of iPhone photographs of the members of his congregation in the pews so that as he held a virtual service, he could look out and see familiar faces rather than a vacuous void.

Once again, ministers have been pressed to answer existential questions: Why has God allowed this pandemic? How should we understand it? Many ministers have theologized the pandemic as a communication from the divine, not as punishment but as opportunity to assess priorities and values. Christian theologian N. T. Wright has perhaps been the most prominent in this regard: "As the Spirit laments within us, so we become, even in our self-isolation, small shrines where the presence and healing love of God can dwell. And out of that there can emerge new possibilities, new acts of kindness, new scientific understanding, new hope."[154]

But concerns about the pandemic then became displaced by the murder of George Floyd on May 25, 2020. For nearly nine minutes, a

Minneapolis police officer held his knee on George Floyd's neck as the forty-six-year-old Floyd cried that he couldn't breathe and begged for his mother. The video of his death taken by a young teenage girl went viral and Americans responded in ways they had not responded to the deaths of other unarmed Black men, including Trayvon Martin and Michael Brown. BLM protests surrounding Floyd's death—which also included Breonna Taylor and other recently murdered Black Americans—have been ongoing as of this writing.[155] The protests of 2020 have taken place in every state across the country, in towns and rural areas as well as major cities. They appear to include many more White participants than those in Ferguson, although it is not yet clear as of this writing whether these protesters will be involved long term.[156]

Perhaps because so many Americans were sheltered at home, less distracted by their usual routines, they began to advance in their own ethical and existential thinking about what matters most. Amid the confines and losses of the pandemic, the death of George Floyd was grieved by many Americans across the country, including at memorials in Minneapolis, his birth city of Raeford, North Carolina, and his family's home city of Houston, Texas. Floyd's funeral was a national event—the four-hour tribute was televised live and watched by tens of thousands of Americans. The American Stock Exchange held its longest moment of silence in its 228-year history—eight minutes, forty-six seconds—the time it took for Floyd to die under the officer's knee. The silence was coordinated to align with the beginning of Floyd's funeral in Houston on June 9, 2020.[157]

A few days prior to the funeral, on June 4 in Minneapolis, Reverend Al Sharpton gave an address at a memorial service for Floyd. He began with a quotation from Ecclesiastes, "To everything there is a time and a purpose and season under the heaven." And then, Reverend Sharpton turned to a barely veiled criticism of President Trump, who on June 1 had used tear gas to clear protesters outside the White House so he could stand outside St. John's Episcopal Church for a photo shoot holding a Bible: "We cannot use Bibles as a prop and for those that have agendas that are not about justice, this family will not let you use George as a prop."[158] The address was an odd compilation of political criticisms, of celebrity shout-outs, and some self-justification. Sharpton had a social justice thesis and some powerful rhetorical moments, such as when he repeated all the ways that the United States has kept its knee on Black America's necks for 401 years, but overall it was a meandering speech.

At George Floyd's funeral on June 9, however, Reverend Sharpton delivered a powerful sermon. He mourned with intentionality and focus:

> I must also recognize several families that are here that came at great sacrifice, but they wanted to be here to be part of this, because they understand the pain better than anyone, because they've gone through the pain. And I think that we should recognize the mother of Trayvon Martin, will you stand? The mother of Eric Garner, will you stand? The sister of [Botham Jean], will you stand? The family of Pamela Turner, right here in Houston, will you stand? The father of Michael Brown from Ferguson, Missouri, will you stand? The father of Amaud [*sic*] Arbery, will you stand?[159]

Then, exegeting the Pauline letter to the Ephesians, Sharpton preached: "We are not fighting some disconnected incidents. We are fighting an institutional, systemic problem that has been allowed to permeate since we were brought to these shores and we are fighting wickedness in high places." Sharpton also claimed George Floyd as part of God's plan, as part of the biblical tradition and integral to all of God's creation: "God took the rejected stone and made him [George Floyd] the cornerstone of a movement that's going to change the whole wide world. . . . Genesis II said that God formed man. And Jamie, they say he breathed breath, the breath of life to make him a live human being, which means that breath comes from God. Breath is how God gives you life. Breath is not some coincidental kind of thing that happens. Breath is a divine decision that God made. . . . Breath is sanctified, breath is sacred. You don't have the right to take God's breath out of anybody you can't put breath in their body."[160]

The sermon was powerful because it preached justice for George Floyd as part of salvation history; Sharpton claimed Floyd as a carrier of God's breath, a divine gift that no one had the right to extinguish. Sharpton also evocatively used the mantra "I can't breathe" while linking it to the Christian theological tradition. Sharpton also used Christianity to explain justice for George Floyd. Although Sharpton began the sermon demanding a transactional recompense, "because lives like George will not matter until somebody pays the cost for taking their lives," the pace and power of the sermon was his adroit weaving of justice for George Floyd, and of all unjustly killed Black people, into the Gospel tradition. In Reverend Sharpton's account, racial justice was integral to the Christian tradition; the state merely needs to follow its lead.

Similarly, across the country, ministers preached about George Floyd's death. And while it is beyond the scope of this short postscript (and clearly demands comprehensive research and a full explication), a preliminary analysis suggests that many of the parameters detailed in this chapter mourning Trayvon Martin and Michael Brown were exemplified. In his response to fellow White ministers' questions, "Should I Respond to George Floyd's Death on Sunday?," Reverend Michael Lawrence of Hinson Baptist Church in Portland, Oregon, asserted: "My calling is neither as judge nor politician. I'm not responsible to adjudicate what happened in Minneapolis. . . . The principle of moral proximity means I'm most concerned with how my flock are treating each other and treating outsiders, in response to both specific tragic events and the larger context that the event plays into."[161] Reverend Michael Lawrence also added that he would engage in pastoral prayer and "we will probably have a prayer of lament over the brokenness on all sides that led to Mr. Floyd's death."[162]

Notably, Reverend Al Sharpton did not call on anyone to pray. Rather, he asserted that God was acting in the calls for justice for Floyd. Sharpton also did not raise any questions about theodicy. The nationwide response, the protests, the way that Floyd's death had ignited a movement confirmed Sharpton's confidence in God's allegiance, His being "on our side."

But Reverend Lawrence seems to have been misaligned with the sentiments of the American public, as well as with other ministers. In a CBS News survey taken at the time, 57 percent of respondents said police in most communities treat White people better than Black people. Thirty-nine percent said police treat both races equally. Further, 61 percent of Americans said race was a "major factor" in Floyd's death. There was a partisan gap, however, in how respondents answered this question: 87 percent of Democrats said race was a major factor, compared with just 39 percent of Republicans.

More broadly, the public also appeared responsive to the reasons people were protesting. Fifty-seven percent of respondents in one poll felt that, regardless of their actions, protesters' anger was "fully justified," while 21 percent said it was "partially justified," and 18 percent said it was "not at all justified."[163] And 64 percent told Reuters that they were sympathetic to those participating in the protests, while a Morning Consult poll found that 54 percent of adults supported "the protest in general," compared with 22 percent who opposed it.[164] And most important for this research, 47 percent of Christians and 50 percent of non-Christians thought that it was "very important" that religious leaders address racial inequality in the United States.[165] It is striking that even non-Christians (including atheists) thought that religious leaders had a significant role to play in the current crisis.

A preliminary analysis indicates that the majority of ministers returned to common themes. Archbishop Jose H. Gomez, president of the US Conference of Catholic Bishops, made a common assessment: "I am praying for George Floyd and his loved ones, and on behalf of my brother bishops, I share the outrage of the black community and those who stand with them in Minneapolis, Los Angeles, and across the country. The cruelty and violence he suffered does not reflect on the majority of good men and women in law enforcement, who carry out their duties with honor. We know that. And we trust that civil authorities will investigate his killing carefully and make sure those responsible are held accountable."[166] Just as before, there were calls for prayer as well as a condemnation of hatred. It remained difficult for many to name the injustice as racism rather than cruelty, hatred, or sin. Beyond the Christian community, there were a few notable exceptions. Imam Talib 'Abdur Rashid asserted that Muslims must not only "be in the mix" of the fight against racism but "in the vanguard, leading by example, either way."[167] And Rabbi Angela Buchdahl of Central Synagogue in New York City said, "The work of fighting racism cannot be left only to the Black community, just as we know that antisemitism cannot be fought only by Jews."[168]

Again, it is possible that further research will nuance this preliminary analysis, but it suggests that, just as after the killing of Trayvon Martin and Michael Brown, the Black church has taken the lead on linking racial injustice to the Christian tradition. For example, African American clergy led a silent Clergy March in Minneapolis / St. Paul on June 2 and organized medic stations as well as food and supply donation drives. Some of the initiatives, including Reclaim the Block and Black Vision Collective, also called for reallocating resources from the Minneapolis police budget to other community services. The difference this time seems to be that, at least initially, more White ministers are following the Black church's lead than after the killing of either Trayvon Martin or Michael Brown; they are educating themselves and their congregations on racial history and its place in the Gospel stories. One White minister, Reverend Jen Crow, observed while walking in the Clergy March: "Looking around at who I was with, I felt safe because of the other people that were there marching. I did not feel safe because the police and the National Guard were there. That was such a clear moment for me. Here we have literally the police state trying to drown out the voice of the black clergy."[169]

Making an eloquent case for mourning and racial equity in the biblical tradition, African American preacher and activist Reverend William J. Barber II preached at Washington's National Cathedral on June 14, 2020. "So Amos says, God says, we need real lamenting. . . . God says, I need a remnant that will cry in the street and refuse to be comforted. We need from the place of deep love, deep love of humanity. We need public tears and public outcry everywhere. Jesus said, we need love laborers. Amos said, we need real lamentors. I believe that's what we're seeing today in our streets. And it has to keep going—public mourning, mourning rooted in deep love, mourning rooted in the reality that people still believe things don't have to be this way."[170] Here is the provocative optimism of a Black minister calling his national congregants to mourning, to mourning as love, to mourning as the way to change the way things are, and to mourning as a signal to God of the human commitment to justice.

The national mourning of George Floyd has the potential to be transformative because mourning George Floyd is mourning a Black man who is not a celebrity—not a Michael Jackson, not a Whitney Houston, not a Kobe Bryant. This national mourning is significant because neither Floyd's life nor his death were extraordinary. Rather, he lived and died as have many other Black men and women—at the hands of law enforcement. Floyd lived with the so-called ordinary racism that configured his movements and drew the boundaries of his life's possibility. And he died in much the same way. Yet White Americans have largely mourned his death as if his life had been exempt from the regular injustices of structural racism. He was mourned, as he should have been, in his specificity, but primarily for the spectacle of his unjust death. The American infrastructure that reduced his life to those eight minutes and forty-six seconds has been largely hidden from view.

Although Floyd has not been readily translated by the American media as "one of us," he still has been mourned in ways that have the potential to reveal the dominant to themselves, and in ways that may compel the majority of Americans to examine what the features of systemic racism look like. Floyd has been mourned both as an individual and as a member of a family, as so many other African Americans have not been, whether those were African Americans who died during the 1995 Los Angeles protests or even in the Oklahoma City bombing or on September 11, when Americans pretended that *color doesn't matter.* He has also been mourned in ways that look back at the deaths of Dr. Martin Luther King, Latasha Harlins, and Trayvon Martin and recognize a pattern and a legacy. And, finally, Floyd has been mourned in protest of the deaths of other Black men and women that Americans, braced in grim resignation, know are yet to come. These are the mourning practices that Antigone imagined when she defied her powerful uncle, the king, and insisted that everyone's death matters when one is aspiring to create a beloved democratic community.

PART OF THE argument of this book has been that it would be good for American democracy for Protestant ministers to once again claim the autonomy of the Sunday sermon and to use the pulpit as a robust platform for American civic education. The first and most important reason for this is because as this research has shown, a vibrant and erudite pulpit can serve as a limitation on the state; or at least, if not a strict limitation, as a more robust interlocutor for claims that have assumed the moniker of common sense and inevitability. Antigone buried her brother not only to fulfill her obligation to the gods but to proclaim the boundaries of state rule. Antigone fulfilled her religious obligation the first time she buried her brother; there was no need to bury him a second time, unless she was also communicating something to Creon about his political sovereignty.

Yet there are at least two rather obvious concerns with this recommendation for greater sermonic influence. First, there is the potential for this recommendation to risk violating established church/state boundaries. Among democratic advocates, there is a concern that an empowered clergy would impose its theological values on a vulnerable population, exerting undue and undemocratic influence. Furthermore, so the worry goes, Americans would risk continually readjudicating decisions already made, such as same sex marriage, abortion, and so forth. But there is no inevitability or necessary reason to assume that a loud and nuanced pulpit would necessarily reignite a discussion of family values and the culture wars of the 1990s. Nor is there historical evidence to assume that the pulpit would speak with a monolithic voice exerting hegemonic authority. Democracy just needs the pulpit to be independent of the state.

As this book has sought to demonstrate, clergy have sometimes been more predominantly aligned with progressive or liberal values, as they seemingly were during the civil rights movement, and sometimes they have been more compelled by conservative or traditional values, as they were during the 1970s and again during the 1990s. So in 2020, it seems quite possible, for example, that the American pulpit could take a leading role on climate change. The theology for it is already present and while the national discourse is stuck in a standoff about science, the church writ large could make a moral claim for the human obligation to love and protect all creation. Or perhaps sermons could coalesce around the humanitarian crisis at the border, rich with theological possibilities—from Good Samaritan analogies of those abandoned on the side of the road, to the Gospel invocations to heed "the least of my brothers," as well as the sanctuary cities claiming the City of God among the City of Men.

Because, as this book has argued, a sermon is not just about theology; it's also about the rigor of the thinking, about the arguments, the metaphors. It's the performative details. And it is democratic—there is not one pulpit, not one homogeneous, or unified, canned sermon; rather, sermons are part of the long tradition of the American democratic arts used in ensuring a vibrant civil society.

Of course, there is a bit of strategic essentialism in locating the possibility of collective, democratic education and activity in the pulpit. In an influential interview, postcolonialist feminist scholar Gayatri Spivak argued for a kind of strategic essentialism in which minorities, especially racialized minorities, coordinate through debates and activities a shared perspective, without necessarily insisting on the ontology of either their identities or ideological commitments.[171] In other words, "subalterns" can act *as if* they fully embody the category "subaltern" to achieve other ends. This is not hypocrisy; it is what most ministers have done during American political crises. Denominational differences become irrelevant in service to more pressing existential, social, and political ends. Protestant ministers can engage in a kind of strategic essentialism to disrupt the state's framing of both political and social issues.

And now in the summer of 2020 with the quarantine and the protests surrounding the death of George Floyd as well as Breonna Taylor and Ahmaud Arbery, the clergy has another opportunity not only to engage in the debate about police brutality and the killing of unarmed Black men and women but to frame the conversation and political protests as belonging to a robust tradition of Judeo-Christian justice.

The second rather obvious problem with my suggestion that the pulpit would be good for American democracy is to overcome the hurdle that a good sermon cannot be preached to empty pews. As the arc of this book has argued, churches have lost both their authority and, consequently, their membership. Many churches are not full, which means the pulpit must be mobile. And the quarantine of 2020 has provided just such impetus for churches to do so. As mentioned earlier, many ministers used the technologies available to hold regular virtual services and to build a community while congregants were isolated from one another. It was a surprising success and a rather rare update to traditional conceptions of worship and communal gathering. Furthermore, the slower pace of quarantine seems to have propelled renewed interest in the kinds of existential questions with which religious traditions are most adept. Although it is impossible to know whether these commitments will be sustained past the summer of 2020, there is some evidence for optimism.

This optimism rests on the mourning response of many Americans to the death of George Floyd. While the mourning of Floyd has not only been sustained by churches, ministers have played a role in maintaining the link between how and whom we mourn and the claims of racial justice. The pulpit has offered itself not as a place with a single Truth but as a place where seeking the Truth is a lifelong project. The power of the pulpit lies not in taking a specific position but in providing a vocabulary, ways of thinking, and challenges to the governmentality of the contemporary state.

When George Floyd died, American mourning required a different kind of work. This mourning necessitated an examination of the underbelly of American racial politics. To fully mourn Floyd, Americans had to defy the established order, and like Antigone, claim Floyd as worthy of national mourning. American mourning also had to do the work of redeeming the death of Floyd, so that his murder at the hands of law enforcement did not disappear from historical memory, unmarked, irrelevant. For grown men, both Black and White, to cry at the untimely demise of an ordinary, unaccomplished Black man was an act of racial justice. To lift Floyd above his personal biography was to remember the long history of African American suffering and to echo the years of lamentation in the Black community.

Political theorist J. Peter Euben has argued that political theory begins with loss. He tells the story of a woman, Peg Mullen, whose son was killed during the Vietnam War by what was called "friendly fire." Euben notes that as a result of this loss, Mullen begins to theorize; he calls it "when Peg became theoreticized."[172] It is an idea quite akin to Norman Jacobson's conception of a crisis—when the world confronts us with a reality in which our traditional ways of understanding are no longer sufficient to understand it. It's the viral world of COVID-19 and the unjust killing of George Floyd as well as the deaths of named and unnamed others. It's a world of loss. It's a world where the banisters of our thinking no longer seem to support our understanding. And so with ashes in our mouths, we turn to the pulpit with the hope that we will find there the civic education we need not only to comprehend but to transform these losses into justice.

Notes

INTRODUCTION

1.   Correspondents of *Time, Life,* and *Fortune, Dec. 7: The First Thirty Hours* (New York: Knopf, 1942), 109.

2.   Claudia Rankine, "The Condition of Black Life Is One of Mourning," *New York Times,* June 22, 2015, https://www.nytimes.com/2015/06/22/magazine/the -condition-of-black-life-is-one-of-mourning.html.

3.   Walter Maier, "America, Embattled, Turn to Christ!," in *Christ and Country: Radio Messages Broadcast in the Ninth Lutheran Hour* (St. Louis, MO: Concordia, 1942), 106.

4.   Sheldon Wolin, *The Presence of the Past: Essays on the State and the Constitution* (Baltimore, MD: Johns Hopkins University Press, 1990), 13.

5.   Ibram X. Kendi, *Stamped from the Beginning: The Definitive History of Racist Ideas in America* (New York: Nation Books, 2016), 10.

6.   The Oklahoma City bombing was an act of domestic terrorism on April 19, 1995. A truck bombing destroyed the Alfred P. Murrah Federal Building, killing 168 people, including 19 children. Within ninety minutes, Timothy McVeigh was stopped by Oklahoma highway patrolman Charlie Hanger for driving without a license plate and arrested for illegal weapons possession. He was found guilty of eleven counts of murder as well as conspiracy and sentenced to death in 1997. He was executed by lethal injection on June 11, 2001. McVeigh's accomplice, Terry Nichols, was also found guilty and sentenced to 161 consecutive life sentences.

7.   On March 3, 1991, African American Rodney King was beaten by Los Angeles police officers after a high-speed chase during his arrest for drunk driving. A nearby civilian filmed the incident and gave the video to a local television station. The video went viral. Four White officers were eventually tried on charges related to the use of excessive force; three were acquitted, and the jury failed to reach

a verdict on the fourth. Within hours of the verdict in April 1992, Los Angeles erupted in protests and violence, killing 63 people and injuring over 2,000 over the course of six days.

8.   See, for example, Giorgio Agamben, *State of Exception,* trans. Kevin Attell (Chicago: University of Chicago Press, 2005); Leonard Feldman, "Terminal Exceptions: Law and Sovereignty at the Airport Threshold," *Law, Culture and Humanities* 3, no. 2 (2007): 320–344; Carl Schmitt, *The Concept of the Political,* trans. George Schwab (Chicago: University of Chicago Press, 1985; first published in 1932).

9.   Norman Jacobson, *Pride and Solace: The Functions and Limits of Political Theory* (Berkeley: University of California Press, 1978).

10.   J. Peter Euben, "The Politics of Nostalgia and Theories of Loss," in *Platonic Noise* (Princeton, NJ: Princeton University Press, 2003).

11.   See Judith Butler, *Precarious Life: Violence, Mourning and Politics* (New York: Verso Press, 2004).

12.   Louis Althusser, "Ideology and the Ideological State Apparatus," in *On Ideology* (New York: Verso, 2004).

13.   Michel Foucault, *The Birth of Biopolitics: Lectures at the College de France, 1978–1979* (New York: Picador Press, 2008), 157.

14.   Linda Lyons, "Tracking US Religious Preferences over Decades," Gallup, last modified May 24, 2005, https://news.gallup.com/poll/16459/tracking-us-religious -preferences-over-decades.aspx. Note that in the early years, Gallup limited its data on religion to just five categories—Protestant, Catholic, Jewish, "other," and "none." All non-Catholic Christians were coded as Protestants. But beginning in the mid-1970s to the present, Gallup has revised its religion demographic to capture more detail. In 1977, Gallup added "Eastern Orthodox" to the list, and soon after began separating Mormons from the Protestant category in the coding of the question. (Mormon was made an explicit option in 2000.) Significantly, Gallup began coding those who said they were "Christian" but did not specify a denomination as a separate category in 1999, and the number falling into that category has grown since.

15.   Pew Research Center, Religion and Public Life, *The 2014 U.S. Religious Landscape Study,* accessed August 11, 2019, http://www.pewforum.org/religious-landscape -study/.

16.   Pew Research Center, Religion and Public Life, "In US, Decline of Christians Continues at a Rapid Pace," October 17, 2019, https://www.pewforum.org/2019/10 /17/in-u-s-decline-of-christianity-continues-at-rapid-pace/.

17.   It is also noteworthy that although there has been a decrease in what analysts call "religiosity," in 2005 the level of religiosity was about the same as it was in 1945. See Tobin Grant, "Why 1940's America Was Not as Religious as You Think: The

Rise and Fall of Religiosity in the United States," Religion News Service, last modified December 11, 2014, https://religionnews.com/2014/12/11/1940s-america -wasnt-religious-think-rise-fall-american-religion/.

18. See Gary Dorrien, *The Making of American Liberal Theology: Crisis, Irony and Postmodernity, 1950–2005* (Louisville, KY: Westminster John Knox Press, 2006).

19. Paul Moore, *Will the Dust Praise You? Spiritual Responses to 9/11*, ed. R. William Franklin and Mary Donovan (New York: Church, 2003), xiv.

20. P. T. Forsyth, *Positive Preaching and the Modern Mind* (New York: A. C. Armstrong), 3.

21. Ellis Sandoz, *Political Sermons and the American Revolution* (Indianapolis, IN: Liberty Fund, 1998), https://oll.libertyfund.org/pages/political-sermons-and-the -american-revolution.

22. Sandoz, *Political Sermons*.

23. See Sacvan Bercovitch, *The American Jeremiad* (Milwaukee: University of Wisconsin, 1978); and Andrew B. Murphy, *Prodigal Nation: Moral Decline and Divine Punishment from New England to 9/11* (Oxford: Oxford University Press, 2009).

24. See Robert P. Hay, "George Washington: American Moses," *American Quarterly* 21, no. 4 (Winter 1969): 780–791.

25. Harry Stout, *Upon the Altar of the Nation: A Moral History of the Civil War* (New York: Penguin, 2006).

26. Robert M. Reed, *Lincoln's Funeral Train: The Epic Journey from Washington to Springfield* (Atglen, PA: Schiffer, 2014).

27. Michael Burleigh, *Sacred Causes: The Clash of Religion and Politics from the Great War to the War on Terror* (New York: HarperCollins, 2007); David Domke and Kevin Coe, *The God Strategy: How Religion Became a Political Weapon in America* (New York: Oxford University Press, 2010); James L. Guth et al., *The Bully Pulpit: The Politics of Protestant Clergy* (Lawrence: University of Kansas Press, 1997).

28. *Sophocles I: Three Tragedies*, trans. David Grene (Chicago: University of Chicago Press, 1991).

29. See Bonnie Honig, *Antigone Interrupted* (Cambridge: Cambridge University Press, 2013).

30. Judith Butler, *Antigone's Claim: Kinship between Life and Death* (New York: Columbia University Press, 2000), 6.

31. Joseph B. Winter, *Hope Draped in Black: Race, Melancholy and the Agony of Progress* (Durham, NC: Duke University Press, 2016), 7.

32. W. E. B. Du Bois, "On the Passing of the First-Born," chap. 11 in *The Souls of Black Folk* (New York: Norton, 1999; first published in 1903), 132.

33. Du Bois, *The Souls of Black Folk*, 133.

34. Butler, *Antigone's Claim.*

35. Rankine, "The Condition of Black Life Is One of Mourning."

36. Johann Baptist Metz and Elie Wiesel, *Hope against Hope* (New York: Paulist Press, 1999).

37. Martha Hodes, *Mourning Lincoln* (New Haven, CT: Yale University Press, 2016).

38. Langston Hughes, "Justice," https://genius.com/Langston-hughes-justice-annotated.

39. This phrase is from Jon Pahl, *Empire of Sacrifice: Religious Origins of American Violence* (New York: New York University Press, 2010), 6.

40. Hannah Arendt, *Thinking without Banisters: Essays in Understanding, 1953–1975* (New York: Schocken Books, 2018), 328.

41. David Klemm, "Searching for a Heart of Gold: A Ricoeurian Meditation on Moral Striving and the Power of Religious Discourse," in *Paul Ricoeur and Contemporary Moral Thought,* ed. John Wall (New York: Routledge, 2002), 110.

42. M. Craig Barnes, "Response to Crisis: Under Attack, under God," in *First Sunday: Spiritual Responses to the 9–11 Attacks,* ed. Donald R. Elton and Aura A. Elton (Charleston, SC: CreateSpace Independent Publishing Platform, 2011), 61.

43. Susan Berrin uses the expression "unsettles our routines" to describe one of the effects of September 11, 2001, in her introduction to *Living Words IV: A Spiritual Source Book for an Age of Terror* (Newtonville, MA: JFL Books, 2002).

44. Alexis de Tocqueville, *Democracy in America,* trans. James T. Schleifer (Indianapolis, IN: Liberty Fund, 2000; first published, 1835–1840), 1:475.

45. John Huffman, "Response to Crisis: A Biblical Perspective for Our National Tragedy," in *First Sunday,* 116.

46. Huffman, 116.

47. Jacobson, *Pride and Solace,* 10.

48. Richard Rorty, *Philosophy and the Mirror of Nature* (Princeton, NJ: Princeton University Press, 1980).

49. See Rebecca Bynum, "Why Islam Is Not a Religion," *New English Review,* September 2011, https://newenglishreview.org/Rebecca_Bynum/Why_Islam_is_Not_a_Religion/; and Alfred Nock, "The Jewish Problem in America," *Atlantic Magazine,* June 1941, https://www.theatlantic.com/magazine/archive/1941/06/the-jewish-problem-in-america/306268/.

50. Philip Rieff, *Triumph of the Therapeutic: Uses of Faith after Freud* (Chicago: University of Chicago Press, 1966), 43.

51. Sidney Mead, *A Nation with the Soul of a Church* (Macon, GA: Mercer University Press, 1975).

52. James Hennessey, S.J., *American Catholics: A History of the Roman Catholic Community in the United States* (New York: Oxford University Press, 1981), 277–280.

53. Sarah Claerhout, "Review Essay: Religion and the Secular," *Numen* 55 (2008): 601–607, 602.

54. Brandon O'Brien, "Is Patriotism Christian?," *Christian Bible Studies*, June 2011, https://www.christianitytoday.com/biblestudies/articles/spiritualformation /patriotismchristian.html.

CHAPTER 1: "NECESSARY INJUSTICE"

1. Monica Sone, *Nisei Daughter* (Boston: Little Brown, 1953).

2. Correspondents of *Time, Life,* and *Fortune, Dec. 7: The First Thirty Hours* (New York: Knopf, 1942), 45.

3. Roland Herbert Bainton, *Christian Attitudes toward War and Peace: A Historical Survey and Critical Evaluation* (New York: Abingdon Press, 1960), 218.

4. Francis X. Talbot, "Our One Defense," *America* 63 (August 3, 1940): 462.

5. From Reinhold Niebuhr's *Christianity and Power Politics,* quoted in Gerald Sitter, *A Cautious Patriotism: The American Churches and the Second World War* (Chapel Hill: University of North Carolina Press, 1997), 70.

6. "September 11, 1941: Fireside Chat 18: On the Greer Incident," University of Virginia, Miller Center, https://millercenter.org/the-presidency/presidential -speeches/september-11-1941-fireside-chat-18-greer-incident.

7. *Dec. 7,* 111.

8. *Dec. 7,* 26.

9. Recently, the US Department of Defense has offered to exhume and use DNA to identify those buried from the USS *Oklahoma*. Families can then request an individual grave for their loved one. See www.bbc.com/news/world-us-canada -32313713.

10. Emily S. Rosenberg, *A Date Which Will Live: Pearl Harbor in American Memory* (Durham, NC: Duke University Press, 2003), 15; "Pearl Harbor Damage Revealed," *Life,* December 1942, 31–37.

11. Stanley H. Chapman, "The Minister: Professional Man of the Church," *Social Forces* 23 (1944): 202–206.

12. For an image of a Civilian Defense League insignia poster showing the kinds of jobs volunteers did, see http://www.fortmissoulamuseum.org/WWII/detail.php ?id=20.

13. American Public Media, "Eleanor Roosevelt: Civilian Defense," American RadioWorks, http://www.americanradioworks.org/eleanor-roosevelt-civilian-defense/.

14. "'Canned Sermon' of Mayor Scorned," *New York Times,* November 9, 1941, front page, https://timesmachine.nytimes.com/timesmachine/1941/11/09/105406586.pdf. All of the quotations in this paragraph are from this source.

15. "'Canned Sermon' of Mayor Scorned."

16. "Text of Sermon Outline Suggested by Mayor La Guardia to Pastors," *New York Times,* November 9, 1941, https://timesmachine.nytimes.com/timesmachine /1941/11/09/105406723.html?pageNumber=32.

17. "Text of Sermon Outline."

18. "Text of Sermon Outline."

19. "Text of Sermon Outline."

20. "Text of Sermon Outline."

21. "Text of Sermon Outline."

22. "Text of Sermon Outline."

23. "Text of Sermon Outline."

24. "Text of Sermon Outline."

25. "Text of Sermon Outline."

26. Robert Bellah, "Civil Religion in America," *Daedalus* 96 (1967): 1–21.

27. Alexis de Tocqueville, *Democracy in America,* trans. James T. Schleifer (Indianapolis, IN: Liberty Fund Press, 2012), 473.

28. Tocqueville, *Democracy,* 484.

29. See Glenn A. Moots, "The Protestant Roots of American Civil Religion," *Humanitas* 23, nos. 1–2 (2010): 78–106.

30. Minersville School District v. Gobitis 310 US 586 (1940), https://supreme .justia.com/cases/federal/us/310/586/.

31. *Minersville School District,* 310 US.

32. Richard Couto, ed., *Political and Civic Leadership: A Reference Handbook* (Washington, DC: Sage Press, 2010), 509.

33. Theological Declaration of Barmen, http://www.sacred-texts.com/chr/barmen .htm.

34. Theological Declaration of Barmen.

35. Alan Torrance, introduction to *Christ, Justice and Peace: Toward a Theology of the State,* by Eberhard Jungel, trans. D. Bruce Hamill and Alan J. Torrance (Edinburgh: T&T Clark, 1992), xx.

36. Karl Barth, "A Letter to Great Britain from Switzerland," in *The End of Illusions: Religious Leaders Confront Hitler's Gathering Storm,* ed. Joe Loconte (New York: Rowman and Littlefield, 2004), 169.

37. See Melissa Matthes, "American Churches and the Holocaust: The Tragic Struggle between Revelation and Reason in the 1930s," in *The Pilgrimage of Philosophy,* ed. Rene Paddags (South Bend, IN: St. Augustine Press, 2019).

38. E. Brooks Holifield, *God's Ambassadors: A History of the Christian Clergy in America* (Grand Rapids, MI: Eerdmans Press, 2007), 237.

39. See Harry Stout, *New England Soul: Preaching and Religious Culture in Colonial New England* (New York: Oxford University Press, 1986).

40. Roy Abrams, *Preachers Present Arms: The Role of the American Churches and Clergy in World War I and II, with Some Observations on the War in Vietnam* (Scottdale, PA: Herald Press, 1969), 229.

41. Abrams, *Preachers Present Arms,* 229.

42. Abrams, 229.

43. "Editorial," *Christian Century* 35 (November 28, 1918): 3.

44. Rev. Lauritz Larsen, "National Lutheran Council Statement, December 20, 1918," in *Brewing and Liquor Interests and German and Bolshevik Propaganda,* vol. 2, Report and Hearing of the Subcommittee on the Judiciary, United States Senate, S RES 307 & 439: 1806, https://books.google.com/books?id=eNxGAQAAIAAJ.

45. *The Methodist Episcopal Church Fighting America's Fight* (pamphlet), cited in Abrams, *Preachers Present Arms,* 234.

46. *The World Tomorrow* 14, no. 5 (May 1931): 145.

47. Frederick Lynch, *Christian Work* 104, no. 4 (1921).

48. Chicago Federation of Churches, *Unity* 93, no. 14 (June 5, 1924): 219.

49. Abrams, *Preachers Present Arms,* 235.

50. Reinhold Niebuhr, *Leaves from the Notebook of a Tamed Cynic* (Louisville, KY: Westminster John Knox Press, 1929), 43.

51. Harry Emerson Fosdick, "What the War Did to My Mind," *Christian Century* 42, no. 1 (January 5, 1928): 117.

52. Charles Clayton Morrison, "Let the Churches Outlaw War," *Christian Century* 41, no. 5 (January 31, 1924): 134.

53. Albert W. Palmer, "A Road Away from War," June 19, 1940, in *The End of Illusions: Religious Leaders Confront Hitler's Gathering Storm,* ed. Joseph Loconte (New York: Rowman and Littlefield, 2004), 40–41.

54. Rev. Ernest Fremont Tittle, "A Clash of Imperialisms," February 5, 1941, in *The End of Illusions,* 92.

55. Charles Clayton Morrison, "On Saving Civilization," May 8, 1940, in *The End of Illusions*, 54–56.

56. John Haynes Holmes, "The Same Old War," December 11, 1940, in *The End of Illusions*, 75.

57. Already famous in theological circles, Duffy gained wider fame for his involvement as a military chaplain during World War I. Many in his regiment later wrote of Duffy's leadership, and Douglas MacArthur said Duffy was briefly considered for the post of regimental commander. Following the war, Duffy wrote *Father Duffy's Story* (New York: George H. Doran, 1919).

58. Father Francis Duffy, *Unity* 92, no. 14 (December 20, 1923): 214.

59. Sermon from January 1942, quoted in Roland Herbert Bainton, *Christian Attitudes toward War and Peace: A Historical Survey and Critical Evaluation* (New York: Abingdon Press, 1960), 221–222.

60. Homer V. Yinger, "Priorities of the Spirit," *The Pulpit*, February 1942, 31.

61. Jerome Bruner, "OWI and the American Public," *Public Opinion Quarterly* 7 (Spring 1943): 129.

62. Sydney Weinberg, "What to Tell America: The Writers' Quarrel in the Office of War Information," *Journal of American History* 55, no. 1 (June 1968): 73–89.

63. See Barbara Dianne Savage, "'Negro Morale,' the Office of War Information, and the War Department," chap. 3 in *Broadcasting Freedom: Radio, War and the Politics of Race, 1938–1948* (Chapel Hill: University of North Carolina Press, 1999).

64. Wendy Wall, "Our Enemies Within: Nazism, National Unity and America's Wartime Discourse on Tolerance," in *Enemy Images in American History,* ed. Ragnhild Fiebig-von Hase and Ursula Lehmkuhl (Oxford: Berghahn Books, 1997).

65. Wall, "Our Enemies," 214.

66. In the 1990s, the National Conference of Christians and Jews was renamed as the National Conference for Community and Justice. See "Our Story," https://nccj.org/about/our-story.

67. Referring to Black and White Americans, Booker T. Washington said, "In all things purely social, we can be as separate as the fingers, yet one as the hand in all things essential to mutual progress" (Atlanta Exposition Speech, 1895, https://iowaculture.gov/history/education/educator-resources/primary-source-sets/reconstruction-and-its-impact/booker-t).

68. Wendy Wall, "Symbol of Unity, Symbol of Pluralism: 'The Interfaith Idea' in Wartime and Cold War America," in *Making the American Century: Essays in the Political Culture of 20th Century America,* ed. Bruce J. Schulman (New York: Oxford University Press, 2014), 176.

69. Franklin D. Roosevelt, Annual Message to the Congress on the State of the Union, January 1, 1941, https://www.ourdocuments.gov/doc.php?flash=false&doc=70&page=transcript.

70. Yinger, "Priorities of the Spirit," 32.

71. Kenneth Morgan Edwards, "Light of Faith in the Hour of Darkness," *The Pulpit,* February 1942, 35.

72. Edwards, "Light of Faith," 36.

73. Walter Arthur Maier, *For Christ and Country: Radio Messages Broadcast in the Ninth Lutheran Hour* (St. Louis, MO: Concordia, 1942), 33.

74. Charles Clayton Morrison, "A Thought for the Month," *The Pulpit,* January 1942, 23.

75. Federal Council of Churches, Information Service, Department of Research and Education, *Federal Council of the Churches of Christ in America* 21, no. 23 (June 6, 1942).

76. Edwards, "Light of Faith," 38.

77. Paul W. Hoon, "The Words of God in the Mind of Christ," *The Pulpit,* February 1942, 27.

78. Edward Randolph Welles, "Pardon-Power-Peace: An Historic Sermon," *The Living Church* 104, no. 5 (1942): 12. The next four quotations are from this sermon.

79. Norman Schenck, "It Seems to Me," *The Friend* 112, January 1942, 4.

80. Schenck, "It Seems to Me," 4.

81. Peter Marshall, "Why Does God Permit War?," in *The Wartime Sermons of Dr. Peter Marshall* (Dallas: Clarion Call Press, 2005), 69–70.

82. Ferdinand Isserman, "The Wave of the Future," *The Pulpit,* January 1942, 10.

83. Kyle Haselden, "The Burden of the Valley of Vision," *Christian Century Pulpit,* February 1942, 31.

84. While it is beyond the scope of this study, it is worth noting that Quakers, as well as some Roman Catholic nuns, did provide resources and solace to those interned. Their work is a reminder that there were examples at the time of a counternarrative of religious intervention on behalf of Japanese Americans. For a more robust discussion, see Allan W. Austin, *Quaker Brotherhood: Interracial Activism and the American Friends Service Committee, 1917–1950* (Urbana: University of Illinois Press, 2012); and Dorothy Day, "Grave Injustice Done Japanese on West Coast," *Catholic Worker,* June 1942. Day wrote multiple articles and was reprimanded by the Office of Censorship in Washington for disobeying the Code of Wartime Practices of the American Press. The American Friends Service Committee and the British Friends Service Council received the Nobel Peace

Prize in 1947 on behalf of Quakers worldwide for their work with both Japanese Americans and European refugees.

85. Rev. Carl McIntire was the founder and minister of the Bible Presbyterian Church. He also originated the fundamentalist American Council of Christian Churches in 1941, in opposition to the Federal (later National) Council of Churches. He was also a popular religious radio broadcaster, hosting the daily *Twentieth Century Reformation Hour.*

86. Rev. Raphael Harwood Miller, "Training for War or Peace, Which?," *Christian Evangelist* 83 (April 18, 1942): 372.

87. Gerald Sitter, *A Cautious Patriotism: The American Churches and the Second World War* (Chapel Hill: University of North Carolina Press, 1997), 201–203.

88. Sitter, *Cautious Patriotism*, 131.

89. Mulford Sibley and Philip Jacob, *Conscription of Conscience: The American State and the Conscientious Objector, 1940–1947* (Ithaca, NY: Cornell University Press, 1952), 46.

90. This question was particularly controversial and often was mocked and criticized in the religious press.

91. Sibley and Jacob, *Conscription of Conscience*, 61–64.

92. Another important feature of the church-state relationship in the 1940s was the role of military chaplains. During World War I, there were relatively few chaplains and their role was marginal; many served food and did other menial tasks. During World War II, their numbers multiplied dramatically. Almost every military camp built a chapel. Chaplains also served on the front lines with the servicemen. Other than infantrymen, chaplains had the highest percentage of casualties during the conflict. World War II chaplains were charged with the tasks of burial, rituals of mourning, and notification of families. Their liminal position, neither civilian nor military, apparently made them the most appropriate candidates for this heartbreaking but morale-building work.

93. Sibley and Jacob, *Conscription of Conscience*, 157.

94. Roger N. Baldwin, review of *Conscription of Conscience*, in *University of Pennsylvania Law Review* 1010, no. 2 (November 1952): 306–309.

95. Sibley and Jacob, *Conscription of Conscience*, 309.

96. Sibley and Jacob, 317.

97. President Ronald Reagan restored full diplomatic relations with the Holy See in January 1984.

98. John S. Conway, "Myron Taylor's Mission to the Vatican, 1940–1950," *Church History* 44, no. 1 (March 1975): 86.

99. See, for example, Paul L. Blakely, "A Father's Letter That Will Live," *America* 68 (November 22, 1942): 178.

100. Franklin Roosevelt, "Address at Christmas Tree Lighting Ceremony," December 24, 1939, Franklin D. Roosevelt Presidential Library, Master Speech Files, 1898, 1910–1945, File No. 1261, http://www.fdrlibrary.marist.edu/_resources/images/msf/msf01300.

101. Charles Kegley, "Christianity's World Challenge," *The Pulpit*, March 1942, 50.

102. Clergy were not alone in this reprimand. Pearl Harbor commanders Kimmel and Short were charged with dereliction of duty and removed from their commands. The bombing was initially largely perceived as the result of incompetence.

103. Ray Freeman Jenney, "One of Them," in *Best Sermons: 1944 Selection*, ed. G. Paul Butler (Chicago: Ziff Davis, 1944), 41.

104. Ernest Fremont Tittle, "Can Human Beings Be Made Over?," *The Pulpit*, January 1942, 5.

105. There were even well-known caricatures of Mussolini, Tito, and Hitler as the four horsemen; see, for example, https://www.loc.gov/pictures/item/97513117/.

106. Tittle, "Can Human Beings Be Made Over?," 5.

107. Maier was so suspicious of state power that he was a staunch critic of attempts to reinstate Bible reading in public schools. He believed that church-state separation was the best way to protect Christianity.

108. Walter Maier, "America, Embattled, Turn to Christ!," in *For Christ and Country*, 106; Marshall, "Why Does God Permit War?," 70.

109. George Buttrick, "Good and Bad Alike?," *The Pulpit*, January 1942, 8–10.

110. Marshall, "Why Does God Permit War?," 70.

111. Edwin Errett, "The Gates of Hades Shall Not Prevail," *Christian Standard*, September 30, 1939, 935.

112. Harry Emerson Fosdick, *A Great Time to Be Alive: Sermons on Christianity in Wartime* (New York: Harper and Brothers, 1944), 134–144.

113. Cited in Robert Moats Miller, *Harry Emerson Fosdick: Preacher, Pastor, Prophet* (New York: Oxford University Press, 1985), 537.

114. Miller, *Harry Emerson Fosdick*, 533.

115. Howard C. Scharfe, "Now That War Has Come," *Christian Century Pulpit*, February 1942, 37.

116. Scharfe, "Now That War Has Come," 38.

117. Marshall, "Why Does God Permit War?," 73.

118. John Haynes Holmes, "The Causes of the War," in *The End of Illusions*, 80.

119. Paul Scherer, "God's Claims on Man's Mind," *Christian Century Pulpit,* January 1942, 15.

120. Harry Emerson Fosdick, "Keeping Christ above the Strife," January 22, 1941, in *The End of Illusions,* 116.

121. Scharfe, "Now That War Has Come," 39.

122. Clyde Fant Jr. and William Pinson Jr., eds., *Twenty Centuries of Great Preaching,* vol. 11, *Maier to Sangster* (Waco, TX: Word Book, 1971), 3–10.

123. *Dec. 7,* 91.

124. Paul Maier, *A Man Spoke, the World Listened: The Story of Walter A. Maier and the Lutheran Hour* (New York: McGraw-Hill, 1963).

125. Paul Maier, *Walter A. Maier.*

126. Paul Maier, *Walter A. Maier,* 223.

127. Walter Maier, foreword to *For Christ and Country.*

128. Walter Maier, *For Christ and Country,* 86. Note that "under God" was not added to the pledge until 1954 by President Eisenhower, to confirm the United States' distinction from its atheist enemy, the Soviet Union.

129. Walter Maier, *For Christ and Country,* 45, 50.

130. Duncan Ryuken Williams, "From Pearl Harbor to 9/11: Lessons from the Internment of Japanese American Buddhists," in *A Nation of Religions: Politics of Pluralism in Multireligious America,* ed. Stephen Prothero (Chapel Hill: University of North Carolina Press, 2006), 64.

131. Quoted in Ellen Eisenberg, "As Truly American as Your Son: Voicing Opposition to the Internment in Three Western Cities," *Oregon Historical Quarterly* 104, no. 4 (Winter 2003): 542.

132. Emily Roxworthy, *The Spectacle of Japanese American Trauma: Racial Performativity and World War II* (Honolulu: University of Hawaii Press, 2008), 15.

133. Roxworthy, *Japanese American Trauma,* 71.

134. Quoted in Edgar C. McVoy's "Social Processes in the War Relocation Center," *Social Forces* 22, no. 2 (December 1943): 188–190.

135. Duncan Ryuken Williams, "Camp Dharma: Japanese American Buddhist Identity and the Internment Experience of World War II," in *Westward Dharma: Buddhism beyond Asia,* ed. Charles S. Prebish and Martin Baumann (Berkeley: University of California Press, 2002), 193 (emphasis in the original).

136. Public Opinion Poll on Japanese Internment, March 1942, https://exhibitions.ushmm.org/americans-and-the-holocaust/main/us-public-opinion-on-japanese-internment-1942.

137. Cited in Ellen Eisenberg, "As Truly American as Your Son: Voicing Opposition to the Internment in Three Western Cities," *Oregon Historical Quarterly* 104, no. 4 (Winter 2003): 543.

138. Anne Blankenship, *Christianity, Social Justice and the Japanese American Incarceration during World War II* (Chapel Hill: University of North Carolina Press, 2016), 27.

139. Reinhold Niebuhr, "A Blot on Our Record," *Christianity and Crisis: A Bi-Weekly Journal of Christian Opinion,* April 20, 1942, http://providencemag.com/wp-content /uploads/42.8.1.pdf.

140. Blankenship, *Christianity,* 30.

141. Eventually, this organization became known simply as the Committee on National Security and Fair Play.

142. Quoted in Eisenberg, "As Truly American," 551.

143. Eisenberg, 553.

144. Eisenberg, 555.

145. Eisenberg, 555.

146. Brian Niiya, "Manzanar: Photographs by Ansel Adams of Loyal Japanese-American Relocation Center (Exhibition)," Densho Encyclopedia, accessed August 24, 2019, http://encyclopedia.densho.org/Manzanar%3A_Photographs_by_Ansel _Adams_of_Loyal_Japanese-American_Relocation_Center_(exhibition)/.

147. Niiya, "Manzanar."

148. Ansel Adams, *Born Free and Equal: Photographs of the Loyal Japanese-Americans at Manzanar Relocation Center, Inyo County, California, by Ansel Adams* (New York: U.S. Camera, 1944), http://memory.loc.gov/cgi-bin/ampage?collId =gdc3&fileName=scd0001_20020123001bfpage.db&recNum=59.

149. Adams, *Born Free and Equal,* http://memory.loc.gov/cgi-bin/ampage?collId =gdc3&fileName=scd0001_20020123001bfpage.db&recNum=79.

150. "Ansel Adams's Photographs of Japanese-American Internment at Manzanar" (digital collection), Library of Congress, https://www.loc.gov/collections/ansel-adams -manzanar/.

151. Among the many excellent books giving firsthand accounts of the Japanese American internment are John Tateishi, *And Justice for All: An Oral History of the Japanese American Detention Camps* (Seattle: University of Washington Press, 1984); Audrie Girdner and Anne Loftis, *The Great Betrayal: The Evacuation of the Japanese Americans during World War II* (New York: MacMillan, 1969); Dorothy S. Thomas and Richard Nishimoto, *The Spoilage: Japanese American Evacuation and Resettlement during World War II* (Berkeley: University of California

Press, 1946); and Gary Okhihiro and Joan Myers, *Whispered Silence: Japanese Americans and World War II* (Seattle: University of Washington Press, 1996).

152. United States Army, "Final Report: Japanese Evacuation from the West Coast," quoted in Lester Suzuki, *Ministry in the Assembly and Relocation Centers of World War II* (Berkeley: Yardbird, 1979), 32.

153. That there was organized resistance in the camps is an often overlooked piece of history. See Gary Y. Okihiro, "Japanese Resistance in America's Concentration Camps: A Re-evaluation," *Amerasia Journal,* Fall 1973, 20–34; and Norman Jackson, "Collective Protest in Relocation Centers," *American Journal of Sociology* 63, no. 3 (November 1957): 264–272.

154. Morton Grodzins, "Making Un-Americans," *American Journal of Sociology* 60, no. 6 (May 1955): 570–582.

155. Grodzins, "Making Un-Americans," 580.

156. Grodzins.

157. For further development, see Cherstin Lyon, *Prisons and Patriots: Japanese American Wartime Citizenship, Civil Disobedience, and Historical Memory* (Philadelphia: Temple University Press, 2011); Eric Muller, *American Inquisition: The Hunt for Japanese American Disloyalty in World War II* (Chapel Hill: University of North Carolina Press, 2007).

158. NB: Nisei were American citizens (approximately eighty thousand were interned), and the issei—although not eligible for citizenship—were long-term residents of America; many considered America their home and country.

159. Gurney Binford, ed., *The Sunday Before Collection,* http://www.oac.cdlib.org /findaid/ark:/13030/tf867nb2kb/entire_text/.

160. Binford, *Sunday Before,* 2.

161. Binford, 6.

162. Binford, 21.

163. Binford, 30.

164. Binford, 39–40.

165. Binford, 41.

166. Binford, 48.

167. Binford, 31.

168. Binford, 31.

169. Binford, 28.

170. Binford, 26.

171. See Jason Morgan Ward, "No Jap Crow: Japanese Americans Encounter the World War II South," *Journal of Southern History* 73, no. 1 (February 2007).

172. Ward, "No Jap Crow," 35.

173. Ward, 35.

174. Ward, 27–32.

175. Ward, 34–38.

176. Ward, 39–42.

177. Ward, 46.

178. Ward, 36.

179. Ward, 37.

180. Ward, 39.

181. Ward, 39.

182. Ward, 41.

183. Ward, 23.

CHAPTER 2: WE ALL KILLED KENNEDY

1. Quoted in William Findley, "Why God, Why?," in *A Man Named John F. Kennedy: Sermons on His Assassination,* ed. Charles J. Stewart and Bruce Kendall (Glen Rock, NJ: Paulist Press, 1964), 95. After Kennedy's assassination, professor of speech Charles Stewart of Purdue University posted a small advertisement in denominational newspapers and magazines asking ministers to send him copies of the sermons they had given between November 23 and December 2, 1963. He collected 850 sermons, which are now archived at the John F. Kennedy Presidential Library, Boston, MA. These sermons, along with two anthologies, William Fine, ed., *That Day with God: Nov. 24, 1963* (New York: McGraw Hill, 1965), and *A Man Named John F. Kennedy,* are the primary sources I used for this research. Overall, my assessments reflect familiarity with about four hundred sermons.

2. Fine, preface to *That Day with God.*

3. Robert B. Semple, ed., *Four Days in November: The Original Coverage of the John F. Kennedy Assassination* (New York: St. Martin's Press, 2003).

4. Rev. James G. Harris, untitled sermon, University Baptist Church, Fort Worth, TX, November 24, 1963, Charles Stewart Papers, Baptist, Box 4, John F. Kennedy Presidential Library and Museum, Boston.

5. Rev. Norman Meyer, untitled sermon, Faith Lutheran Church, Jefferson City, MO, November 24, 1963, Charles Stewart Papers, Lutheran, Box 3.

6. Rev. Arthur Sherman, "The Death of President Kennedy," Christ Episcopal Church, Warren, OH, November 24, 1963, Charles Stewart Papers, Box 1.

7.   Bradley S. Greenberg and Edwin B. Parker, eds., *The Kennedy Assassination and the American Public: Social Communication in Crisis* (Stanford, CA: Stanford University Press, 1965), 149.

8.   The most violent image of the assassination, Zapruder's film, would not be seen until February 13, 1969, when it was projected at Clay Shaw's trial. Bootleg copies were then circulated. *Life* magazine reproduced thirty frames in black and white in its November 29, 1963, edition, and color frames in its December 6, 1963, issue. A "complete" version of the film was not shown on American television until March 6, 1975, when Geraldo Rivera broadcast it on his talk show, *Good Night America*.

9.   Rev. Billy Graham, "Fleeting Lives," *Hour of Decision*, November 24, 1963, https://www.youtube.com/watch?v=AE97wKQRXuQ.

10.   For the role of television in the tragedy, see Barbie Zelier, *Covering the Body: The Kennedy Assassination, the Media and the Shaping of Collective Memory* (Chicago: University of Chicago Press, 1992).

11.   Greenberg and Parker, *The Kennedy Assassination*, 135–137.

12.   Mohammed A. Bamyeh, *Of Death and Dominion: The Existential Foundation of Governance* (Evanston, IL: Northwestern University Press, 2007), 20.

13.   Ellen Fitzpatrick, *Letters to Jackie: Condolences from a Grieving Nation* (New York: Harper Collins), xvi.

14.   Robert W. Magee, "God Lives! Give Thanks!," St. Charles Christian Church, St. Charles, MO, November 24, 1963, Charles Stewart Papers, Box 3.

15.   Gallup, "In-Depth: Topics A to Z: Religion," https://news.gallup.com/poll /1690/religion.aspx.

16.   Aron Earls, "How Old Are America's Pastors?," Barna Research Study, March 9, 2017, https://factsandtrends.net/2017/03/09/how-old-are-americas -pastors/.

17.   Norman Jacobson, *Pride and Solace: The Functions and Limits of Political Theory* (New York: Routledge, 1986).

18.   Jacobson, *Pride and Solace.*

19.   Jacobson, 10.

20.   Louis H. Valbracht, "One Martyr in the March," in *A Man Named John F. Kennedy,* 172.

21.   Dr. Marvin Hall, "A Man Who Showed Us New Frontiers," First Baptist Church, Hutchinson, KS, November 25, 1963, Charles Stewart Papers, Baptist, Box 1.

22.   Durward McCord, "A Sermon Given at the Westland Methodist Church on Sunday November 24, 1963," Lebanon, TN, Charles Stewart Papers, Box 3.

23. Barry Cater, "Where Is Your Brother?," in *A Man Named John F. Kennedy*, 84.

24. H. B. Roepe, "Sermon Preached at Special Service," First Trinity Lutheran Church, Washington, DC, November 24, 1963, Charles Stewart Papers, Box 3.

25. Thomas Parry Jones, "An American Tragedy," in *A Man Named John F. Kennedy*, 92.

26. See, for example, Rev. Hay, "Father Forgive Them," Lakeville Christian Church, Dallas, TX, November 24, 1963, Charles Stewart Papers, Disciples of Christ, Box 3: "The vast majority of those people who were gathered about the cross of our Master *on that other Friday* so many centuries ago" (emphasis added).

27. Newman Flanagan, "Remarks on the Death of President John F. Kennedy," in *A Man Named John F. Kennedy*, 161.

28. Southern Bell Singers, quoted in Guido Van Rijn, *Kennedy's Blues: African American Blues and Gospel Songs on JFK* (Jackson: University of Mississippi Press, 2007), 127.

29. Van Rijn, *Kennedy's Blues*, 155–158.

30. Van Rijn, 155–158.

31. Rene Girard, *Violence and the Sacred* (Baltimore, MD: Johns Hopkins University Press, 1979).

32. Paul Kahn, *Sacred Violence: Torture, Terror and Sovereignty* (Ann Arbor: University of Michigan Press, 2008), 32.

33. Leroy C. Hodapp, "Reflections on the Death of John F. Kennedy," in *A Man Named Kennedy*, 127.

34. Luke 22:19.

35. Fitzpatrick, *Letters to Jackie*, 79.

36. Fitzpatrick, 160.

37. Theodore H. White, "For President Kennedy: An Epilogue," *Life*, December 6, 1963, https://www.jfklibrary.org/asset-viewer/archives/THWPP/059/THWPP-059-009.

38. White, "For President Kennedy."

39. It is noteworthy that after his death, 97 percent of Blacks, 90 percent of White northern supporters, and 78 percent of White southern supporters considered JFK "an above average president." Before his death, a Gallup poll without racial or regional profiling showed he had a relatively modest approval rating of 59 percent. Twenty-eight percent disapproved, and 13 percent were undecided. Greenberg and Parker, *The Kennedy Assassination*, 167.

40. Robert Reid, "Will There Be Birth?," First Christian Church, Whittier, CA, December 8, 1963, Charles Stewart Papers, Disciples of Christ, Box 1.

41. David J. Jamieson, "The Risks of Freedom," in *A Man Named Kennedy*, 128.

42. Theodore Sorensen, foreword to *Public Papers of the Presidents of the United States: John F. Kennedy, 1963; January 1 to November 22, 1963* (Washington, DC: U.S. Government Printing Office, 1964), vi.

43. Quoted by Roger Wilkins, in Dean R. Owen's *November 22, 1963: Reflections on the Life, Assassination, and Legacy of John F. Kennedy* (New York: Skyhorse, 2013), 81. The quotation comes from a reported conversation that Senator Moynihan (Democrat from New York) had with Mary McGrory (journalist) about whether Americans would laugh again. Moynihan reportedly replied: "Heavens, Mary. We will laugh again. We just won't ever be young again."

44. Dr. Marvin Hall, "The Right to Love and Be Loved," First Baptist Church, Hutchinson, KS, November 24, 1963, Charles Stewart Papers, Baptist, Box 1.

45. Rev. Jo M. Riley, "Our President: In Memory of John Fitzgerald Kennedy," Central Christian Church, Decatur, IL, November 24, 1963, Charles Stewart Papers, Disciples of Christ, Box 1.

46. Clarence E. Parr, "The Light Is Still Shining," First Congregational Church, Albuquerque, NM, November 24, 1963, Charles Stewart Papers, Box 1.

47. Findley, "Why God, Why?"

48. Roepe, "Sermon Preached at Special Service."

49. Errol T. Elliot, "The Death of Our President: A Memorial Sermon," First Friends Church, Indianapolis, IN, November 24, 1963, Charles Stewart Papers, Box 5.

50. Orra G. Compton, untitled sermon, Boston Avenue United Methodist Church, Tulsa, OK, in *That Day with God*, 157.

51. Reid, "Will There Be Birth?"

52. John Donne, "Meditation XVII," https://www.gutenberg.org/files/23772/23772-h /23772-h.htm.

53. Theodore White, cited in *The Camelot Documents*, JFK Laner Productions and Publications, Dallas, TX, http://www.jfklancer.com/pdf/Camelot.pdf.

54. Richard Cardinal Cushing, "Eulogy to John F. Kennedy," in *That Day with God*, 36.

55. Joseph J. Neuville, untitled sermon, St. Mary's Cathedral, Portland, OR, in *That Day with God*, 148.

56. Fine, preface to *That Day with God*.

57. Richard Lyon Morgan, "In the Year President Kennedy Died," in *A Man Named Kennedy*, 106.

58. Francis B. Sayre Jr., "This Man Is Not Worthy of Death," in *A Man Named Kennedy*, 22.

59. John Mark Kinney, "Hate," in *A Man Named Kennedy*, 44.

60. James Reston, "Why America Weeps: Kennedy Victim of Violent Streak He Sought to Curb in the Nation," *New York Times*, November 23, 1963.

61. Arthur M. Sherman, "The Death of President Kennedy," Christ Episcopal Church, Warren, OH, November 24, 1963, Charles Stewart Papers, Box 2.

62. Rev. Stuart P. Benson, "Death of King Uzziah," First Baptist Church, Bellingham, WA, November 24, 1963, Charles Stewart Papers, Box 1.

63. Robert Woodward, untitled sermon, First Baptist Church, Dallas, TX, November 24, 1963, Charles Stewart Papers, Box 1.

64. James Jordon, untitled sermon, Forney Avenue Baptist Church, Dallas, TX, November 24, 1963, Charles Stewart Papers, Box 1.

65. Rev. George Buchanan, "An Ironical Whirlwind of Violence," Shannondale Presbyterian Church, Knoxville, TN, November 24, 1963, Charles Stewart Papers, Box 4.

66. Carl T. Uehling, "And Sorrow and Sighing Shall Flee Away," Trinity Lutheran Church, Akron, OH, November 24, 1963, Charles Stewart Papers, Box 3.

67. This is a paraphrase of George Kateb's definition of patriotism from "Is Patriotism a Mistake?," in *Patriotism and Other Mistakes* (New Haven, CT: Yale University Press, 2006), 8.

68. Kateb, "Is Patriotism a Mistake?," 8–10.

69. Ray Heckendorn, "What Does the Lord Require of Thee?," Boulevard Christian Church, Fort Worth, TX, November 24, 1963, Charles Stewart Papers, Box 1.

70. George Kateb, quoting Ralph Waldo Emerson's *American Scholar*, in *Patriotism and Other Mistakes*, 66.

71. Richard F. Hettlinger, "Our Mechanical, Godless Society," in *A Man Named Kennedy*, 195.

72. Lockett Ballard, "A Certain Responsibility," Trinity Church, Newport, RI, Charles Stewart Papers, Episcopal, Box 2.

73. William A. Myers, untitled sermon, Hamilton, OH (no church name given), Charles Stewart Papers, Baptist, Box 1.

74. William Boehm, "A Great Man Fallen" (no church name or location given), November 24, 1963, Charles Stewart Papers, Box 3.

75. Ray Bristol, "Blessed Are They That Mourn," Midway Hill Christian Church, Dallas, TX, November 24, 1963, Charles Stewart Papers, Box 1.

76. William H. Dickinson, "Living Out Our Faith," in *That Day with God*, 12.

77. William Boehm, "A Great Man Fallen: November 24, 1963" (no church name or location given), Charles Stewart Papers, Lutheran, Box 3.

78. Flanagan, "Remarks on the Death of President John F. Kennedy," 158–160.

79. John C. Wiles, untitled sermon, First Baptist Church, Tucumcari, Mexico, November 24, 1963, Charles Stewart Papers, Baptist, Box 1.

80. Jamieson, "The Risks of Freedom," 132.

81. Rev. Andrew A. Jumper, "The Sins of the Fathers," First Presbyterian Church, Lubbock, TX, November 24, 1963, Charles Stewart Papers, Presbyterian, Box 4. About a dozen sermons incorporated the shooting of Oswald into their text. Others included an addendum when they sent their sermon to Stewart indicating whether they knew Oswald had been shot when they gave the sermon. The majority, however, did not mention the shooting. Those who did mention it, did only that—include it as part of the litany confirming on Sunday whatever position they already had on the Friday of the assassination.

82. Rev. Kenneth H. Gass, "Sermon Preached by the Rector, Dr. Kenneth H. Gass, on the Occasion of the Death of President Kennedy, Sunday, November 24, 1963," St. James Episcopal Church, Birmingham, MI, November 24, 1963, Charles Stewart Papers, Box 2.

83. Rev. T. K. Mullendore, "Expressions of Gratitude, Regret, Remorse and Hope," Bethany Presbyterian Church, Dallas, TX, November 24, 1963, Charles Stewart Papers, Box 4.

84. Rev. William A. Holmes, "One Thing Worse Than This," in *A Man Named Kennedy*, 34–39.

85. Holmes, "One Thing Worse Than This," 35. Also cited in *Christian Century*, January 1, 1964, 30.

86. Earle Cabell, cited in *Christian Century*, January 1, 1964, 29.

87. Cabell, cited in *Christian Century*, January 1, 1964, 29.

88. Frederick Jackson Turner, "The Significance of the Frontier in American History," in *The Frontier in American History* (New York: Henry Holt, 1921); and Perry Miller, *Errand into the Wilderness* (Cambridge, MA: Harvard University Press, 1956).

89. Mullendore, "Expressions of Gratitude, Regret, Remorse and Hope."

90. JFK acceptance speech at the 1960 Democratic National Convention at the Los Angeles Memorial Coliseum, http://www.americanrhetoric.com/speeches/jfk1960dnc.htm.

91. Buchanan, "An Ironical Whirlwind of Violence."

92. Rev. Ewing W. Carroll Jr., "The Great Unfinished Task," Calvary Methodist Church, Largo, FL, November 24, 1963, Charles Stewart Papers, Box 3 (capitalization and emphasis in original).

93. Hall, "A Man Who Showed Us New Frontiers."

94. https://www.bostonglobe.com/news/nation/2013/11/20/iconic-images-jfk-assassination/t4QdO47eiyFlKnkeeGOqlK/story.html?pic=8.

95. Charles Stewart Papers, Box 5, Miscellany.

96. Robert B. Semple Jr., ed., *Four Days in November: The Original Coverage of the John F. Kennedy Assassination by the Staff of the New York Times* (New York: St. Martin's Press, 2003), 84.

97. Booker had established his reputation with his reporting for *Ebony-Jet* on the murder and trial of Emmet Till in Mississippi in 1955–1956. See Simeon Booker, "To Be a 'Negro' Newsman—Reporting on the Emmett Till Murder Trial," https://niemanreports.org/articles/to-be-a-negro-newsman-reporting-on-the-emmett-till-murder-trial/.

98. Simeon Booker, "How John F. Kennedy Surpassed Abraham Lincoln," *Ebony*, February 1964, 25.

99. Rev. Roger Lovette, "Where to Now . . . O, America?," Dawson Baptist Church, Philpot, KY, November 24, 1963, Charles Stewart Papers, Box 1.

100. Thomas Carty, *A Catholic in the White House? Religion, Politics and JFK's Presidential Campaign* (New York: Palgrave MacMillan, 2004), 91.

101. Rev. Martin Luther King Sr. had been a lifelong registered Republican, although he changed his mind after John F. Kennedy called Coretta when his son had been arrested during a peaceful demonstration in Atlanta, Georgia, in October 1960. King had been transported over three hundred miles in the middle of the night and Coretta was worried that he might be killed. Robert Kennedy worked to secure King's release, thus gaining the support of many in the Black community, including King's father. See Susan Bellows, dir. and prod., *American Experience: JFK,* episode 2 (aired in 2013 on PBS).

102. For Julian Bond on JFK's assassination, see Owen's *November 22, 1963,* 69. The Birmingham Movement, or Birmingham Campaign, referred to the civil rights movement organized in early 1963 by the Southern Christian Leadership Conference to dismantle the city's discrimination laws.

103. Greenberg and Parker, *The Kennedy Assassination,* 50–51.

104. Greenberg and Parker, 155.

105. Vivian Jenkins Nelsen, "One Woman's Interracial Journey," in *Ethnic Variations in Dying, Death and Grief: Diversity in Universality*, ed. Donald Irish, Kathleen Lundquist, and Vivian Jenkins Nelsen (Washington, DC: Taylor and Francis, 1993), 22.

106. Jenkins Nelsen, "One Woman's Interracial Journey," 157.

107. William Manchester, *The Death of a President: Nov. 20–Nov. 25, 1963* (New York: Harper and Row, 1967), 48.

108. William R. Grosh, "In the Midst of Life," Calvary Episcopal Church, Kaneohe, HI, December 1, 1963, Charles Stewart Papers, Box 2.

109. Harry Scholefield, "Eulogy to John Fitzgerald Kennedy," First Unitarian Church of San Francisco, November 25, 1963, Charles Stewart Papers, Box 5.

110. Paul E. Kolch, "Sermon-Address," Trinity Lutheran Church, Sacramento, CA, November 24, 1963, Charles Stewart Papers, Box 3.

111. Frederick M. Morris, untitled sermon, St. Thomas Church, New York, November 25, 1963, Charles Stewart Papers, Episcopal, Box 2.

112. Morris, untitled sermon.

113. Editorial, *Wall Street Journal,* November 25, 1963.

114. Daniel Bell, "The Dispossessed," in *The Radical Right* (New Brunswick, NJ: Transaction, 2002), 18.

115. This was included in multiple sermons. See Ray Heckendorn, "What Does the Lord Require of Thee?," Boulevard Christian Church, Fort Worth, TX, November 24, 1963, Charles Stewart Papers, Box 1.

116. Bishop Charles Golden (African American), cited in McCord, "A Sermon Given at the Westland Methodist Church on Sunday, November 24, 1963."

117. Rev. Victor F. Scalise, "Our Great President Is Dead" (radio broadcast with reprinted sermon), Calvary Baptist Church, Lowell, MA, November 24, 1963, Charles Stewart Papers, Box 1.

118. Thomas J. Gibbs Jr., "Personal Reactions to a National Tragedy," Westchester Christian Church, Los Angeles, CA, November 24, 1963, Charles Stewart Papers, Box 1.

119. Curtis McClain, "Our President Is Dead," First Baptist Church, Harrisburg, AR, November 23, 1963, Charles Stewart Papers, Baptist, Box 1.

120. Arthur Slaikeu, "A Profile of Courage," in *A Man Named Kennedy,* 57.

121. James P. Shaw, "Of Common Loss," Trinity Episcopal Church, San Francisco, CA, November 23, 1963, Charles Stewart Papers, Episcopal, Box 2.

122. Charles Mohr, "Johnson Gets Assassination Report," *New York Times,* September 25, 1964, https://timesmachine.nytimes.com/timesmachine/1964/09/25/97420064.html?pageNumber=1.

123. William Archer Wright, "On the Assassination of President Kennedy," Grace Methodist Church, Newport News, VA, November 24, 1963, Charles Stewart Papers, Box 3.

124. William D. Goble, "The Death of President Kennedy," Aynor Baptist Church, Aynor, SC, November 24, 1963, Charles Stewart Papers, Baptist, Box 1.

125. Roger Lovette, "Sermon on the Death of Our President," Dawson Baptist Church, Philpot, KY, November 24, 1963, Charles Stewart Papers, Box 1.

126. Errol Elliott, "The Death of Our President: A Memorial Sermon," First Friends Church, Indianapolis, IN, November 24, 1963, Charles Stewart Papers, Box 5.

127. James G. Harris, untitled sermon, University Baptist Church, Fort Worth, TX, November 24, 1963, Charles Stewart Papers, Baptist, Box 1.

128. Thomas Parry Jones, "American Tragedy," in *A Man Named Kennedy,* 93.

129. Newman Flanagan, "Remarks on the Death of President John F. Kennedy," in *A Man Named Kennedy,* 159.

130. James Jordon, untitled sermon, Forney Avenue Baptist Church, Dallas TX, November 24, 1963, Charles Stewart Papers, Baptist, Box 1.

131. Reinhold Niebuhr, "Tribute to President John F. Kennedy," St. George's Episcopal Church, Stuyvesant Square, NY, November 24, 1963, Charles Stewart Papers, Episcopalian, Box 2.

132. Gordon Hinckley, "Sacrifice Brings Forth Blessings of Heaven," in *A Man Named Kennedy,* 148.

133. O. Carroll Arnold, "It Is Better to Mourn," First Baptist Church, Boulder, CO, November 24, 1963, Charles Stewart Papers, Box 1.

134. Jessica Mitford, *The American Way of Death* (New York: Simon and Schuster, 1963).

135. Paul Osborne, "The Revelation in Assassination," First Unitarian Church, Wichita, KS, November 24, 1963, Charles Stewart Papers, Box 5.

136. Bruce McIver, "Message Following the Assassination of President Kennedy," Wilshire Baptist Church, Dallas, TX, November 24, 1963, Charles Stewart Papers, Baptist, Box 1.

137. Charles Stewart, "The Pulpit in Time of Crisis," *Speech Monographs* 32, no. 4 (November 1965): 428.

138. Emmanuel Levinas, "Time and the Other," in *The Levinas Reader,* ed. and trans. Sean Hand (London: Basil Blackwell, 1989), 40.

139. Julian A. Cave, "On the Death of the President," First Baptist Church, Chester, SC, November 24, 1963, Charles Stewart Papers, Baptist, Box 1.

140. Vincent Bugliosi, *Four Days in November: The Assassination of President John F. Kennedy* (New York: Norton Press, 2007), 88.

141. Carl Uehling, "And Sorrow and Sighing Shall Flee Away," Trinity Lutheran Church, Akron, OH, November 24, 1963, Charles Stewart Papers, Box 3.

142. Scalise, "Our Great President Is Dead."

143. Frederick S. Illick, "Memorial Service," Grace Lutheran Church, Greensboro, NC, November 22, 1963, Charles Stewart Papers, Box 3.

144. Hodapp, "Reflections on the Death of John F. Kennedy," 126.

145. Hodapp, 127.

146. Lyndon B. Johnson, "Address before a Joint Session of Congress," November 27, 1963, https://millercenter.org/the-presidency/presidential-speeches/november-27 -1963-address-joint-session-congress.

147. Cathy Caruth, ed., *Trauma: Explorations in Memory* (Baltimore, MD: Johns Hopkins University Press, 1995), 191n18.

148. Martin Jay, "Against Consolation: Benjamin and the Refusal to Mourn," in *Refractions of Violence* (New York: Routledge, 2003).

149. Louis H. Valbracht, "One Martyr in the March," 22–24.

150. Guy Debord, *The Society of the Spectacle,* Thesis 4 (New York: Zone Books, 1994), 2.

CHAPTER 3: EXISTENTIAL DESPAIR

1.   Arthur M. Schlesinger Jr., *Robert Kennedy and His Times* (New York: Ballantine, 1996).

2.   Robert F. Kennedy (RFK), "Statement on the Assassination of Martin Luther King, Jr.," Indianapolis, IN, April 4, 1968, https://www.jfklibrary.org/learn /about-jfk/the-kennedy-family/robert-f-kennedy/robert-f-kennedy-speeches /statement-on-assassination-of-martin-luther-king-jr-indianapolis-indiana-april -4-1968.

3.   RFK, "Statement."

4.   RFK, "Statement."

5.   RFK, "Statement."

6.   Ellen Fitzpatrick, *Letters to Jackie: Condolences from a Grieving Nation* (New York: Ecco Press, 2010).

7.   Morehouse College Martin Luther King, Jr. Collection, Subseries 1.3, Correspondence: Condolences and Letters Received after Assassination, http://findingaids .auctr.edu/repositories/2/resources/155.

8.   Brady Whitehead, "Preaching Response to the Death of Martin Luther King, Jr." (ThD dissertation, Boston University, 1972). Whitehead was primarily interested in determining the regional differences between how ministers in Atlanta and Memphis responded to King's death. What he discovered was that there was relatively little difference between the two cities regarding whether ministers approved or disapproved of King's work; rather, the primary difference he found was a racial one. The primary determinant of whether a minister supported or disapproved of King's work depended on his race—not his age, education, involvement in community affairs, or whether he lived in Memphis or Atlanta. Ninety-six percent of the questionnaires received from Blacks reported a positive view of

King's work, whereas only 69 percent of those received from Whites did. This confirms, perhaps, with now over forty years of hindsight, what most Americans would expect. Unfortunately, because Whitehead was not as interested in the theology of the sermons, he did not cite specifically from the sermons, so the content is difficult to discern except for the variables that he measured. Whitehead included in footnotes ministers' thoughts expressed to him in notes about what they believed about King and his death even if they suspected their congregations would disagree: "This morning I'm going to stick my neck out further than I ever have before." Another began, "How carefully I have trained my conscience, but in spite of much practice, my efforts of long standing, my ingenuity, there is still a part of my conscience that pains and pricks and irritates. It says to me this day, 'don't play the game, play the man.' This morning regardless of the consequences, I'm permitting this seldom used portion of my heart to ascend the throne."

Yet on the questionnaire, 36 percent of the ministers indicated that they did not feel free to express their honest convictions before their congregations. If only the White ministers are considered, the percentage swells to 49 percent. Ten ministers wrote on their questionnaires comments that indicate they did not feel free to say to their congregations everything they felt needed to be said: "I said . . . as much as I felt I could." "I said what I thought would be heard." "To [sic] much prejudice by my congregation to be rightly understood." One minister reported that he was told he "had better not say one word about Martin Luther King tomorrow."

Whitehead concluded his dissertation with the observation that ten months after King's assassination, thirty-one White ministers had moved from Atlanta and Memphis. Fourteen of these men left no forwarding address. These congregations, he insisted, must ask themselves why this would be true. Was it because these men angered their congregations following King's death? Who decided what the minister would or would not preach?

9. Lyndon B. Johnson, "Address to the Nation," April 5, 1968, http://www.presidency.ucsb.edu/ws/index.php?pid=28783.

10. Lyndon B. Johnson, "Address to Congress," November 27, 1963, http://www.presidency.ucsb.edu/ws/index.php?pid=26198.

11. Lyndon B. Johnson, "Letter to the Speaker of the House," April 5, 1968, https://www.presidency.ucsb.edu/documents/letter-the-speaker-the-house-urging-enactment-the-fair-housing-bill.

12. Lyndon B. Johnson, "Address to the Joint Session of Congress," November 27, 1963, https://cdm15730.contentdm.oclc.org/digital/collection/p15093coll1/id/1118.

13. Johnson, "Letter to the Speaker of the House."

14. Joe Carter, "Five Facts about the Civil Rights Act of 1968," Ethics and Religious Liberty Commission, April 12, 2018, https://erlc.com/resource-library/articles/5-facts-about-the-civil-rights-act-of-1968.

15.   Robert Byrd, quoted in Bruce D'Arcus, "Dissent, Public Space and the Politics of Citizenship: Riots and the Outside Agitator," *Space and Polity* 8, no. 3 (December 2004): 355–370.

16.   The Anti-Riot Act defined any gathering of three or more persons assembled with the intent or perceived threat or even accusation of inciting injury or damage to property as liable for criminal charges. The act was sufficiently broad and vague to be interpreted as necessary to create a legal limit to political protest. The Anti-Riot Act conflated political protest with organized violence.

17.   Milton Rokeach, "Faith, Hope and Bigotry," *Psychology Today*, April 1970, reproduced at https://www.religion-online.org/article/faith-hope-and-bigotry/.

18.   Rokeach, "Faith, Hope and Bigotry."

19.   W. Fields, April 1968, quoted in *Baptist Press*, April 5, 1968, http://media.sbhla
.org.s3.amazonaws.com/2577,05-Apr-1968.PDF.

20.   C. Eric Lincoln, "Key Man of the South: The Negro Minister," *New York Times Magazine*, July 12, 1964, 40, https://timesmachine.nytimes.com/timesmachine
/1964/07/12/119048880.html?pageNumber=221.

21.   James Baldwin, "Letter from a Region in My Mind," *New Yorker*, November 17, 1962, https://www.newyorker.com/magazine/1962/11/17/letter-from-a-region-in
-my-mind.

22.   Elizabeth Hardwick, "The Apotheosis of Martin Luther King," *New York Review of Books*, May 9, 1968, https://www.nybooks.com/articles/1968/05/09/the
-apotheosis-of-martin-luther-king/.

23.   Floyd Bixler McKissick, quoted in William Robert Miller, *Martin Luther King, Jr.: His Life, Martyrdom and Meaning for the World* (New York: Weybright and Talley, 1968), 282.

24.   Simeon Booker, "As DC Burns, President Moves to Head Off Race Confrontation," *Jet*, April 18, 1968, 40.

25.   Thomas Merton, "Thomas Merton on Martin Luther King, Jr.'s Death," in *The Other Side of the Mountain: The End of the Journey*, ed. Patrick Hart (New York: Harper Collins, 1999), 78.

26.   Gardner Taylor, "Is God Dead? Can God Die?," April 14, 1968, Taylor Gardner Collection, Box 20, Folder 18, Robert Woodruff Library, Atlanta University Center.

27.   Robert W. Koons, "The Church That Makes God Sick," Holy Trinity Lutheran Church, Lynchburg, VA, April 7, 1968, Archives Digital Collection, A. R. Wentz Library, Gettysburg Seminary, https://s3.amazonaws.com/arwentz
/docs/Seminary+Archives/Collections/Rev.+Robert+W.+Koons/Koons%2C+Robert
_Box17-Folder5_ChurchThatMakseGodSick_April1968.pdf.

28.   Koons, "The Church That Makes God Sick." Prior to the 1960s, Black obituaries were not published in newspapers. It was only during the process of de-

segregation that the deaths of individual Black men and women were considered appropriate for public notice. See https://digitalcommons.georgiasouthern.edu/willowhillheritage-obituaries/.

29. Herman G. Stuempfle Jr., "Isaiah 53," April 10, 1968, Herman G. Stuempfle Jr. Papers, Box 6, Folder 4, Archives, Boxed Manuscripts, A. R. Wentz Library, Lutheran Theological Seminary at Gettysburg.

30. Martin Luther King Jr., *Stride toward Freedom: The Montgomery Story* (Boston: Beacon Press, 1958), 63.

31. Edler G. Hawkins, "Jerusalem Then—Our Cities Now," Palm Sunday Message, St. Augustine Church, Bronx, NY, Elder G. Hawkins Collection, Box 6, Folder 53, Archives Research Center, Robert Woodruff Library, Atlanta University Center.

32. William Truly, reprinted in Guido Van Rijn, ed., *President Johnson's Blues: African American Blues and Gospel Songs on LBJ, Martin Luther King, Robert Kennedy and Vietnam, 1963–1968* (Netherlands: Agram Blues Books, 2009), 219.

33. Duke K. McCall, Southern Baptist Theological Seminary, Louisville, quoted in "Southern Baptist Leaders Deplore King Assassination," *Baptist Press,* April 5, 1968, 4.

34. "James Baldwin: How to Cool It," *Esquire,* July 1968, http://www.esquire.com/news-politics/a23960/james-baldwin-cool-it/.

35. Kenneth Foote, *Shadowed Ground: America's Landscapes of Violence and Tragedy* (Austin: University of Texas Press, 2003).

36. Simeon Booker, "Ticker Tape USA," *Jet,* April 18, 1968, 13.

37. Rev. Gilbert Schroerlucke, *I Did What I Could: A Memoir* (Louisville, KY: Gilbert Schroerlucke, 2008), 167.

38. Samuel Dubois Cook, "Martin Luther King," *Journal of Negro History* 53, no. 4 (October 1968): 351.

39. Rebecca Burns, "Funeral," *Atlanta,* April 1, 2008, http://www.atlantamagazine.com/great-reads/mlk-funeral-1968/.

40. Rokeach, "Faith, Hope and Bigotry."

41. Rokeach.

42. Rev. William J. Chase, quoted in George Dugan, "Dr. King Is Hailed as 'Peacemaker'; Eulogy of Dr. Read Typifies Palm Sunday Sermons," *New York Times,* April 8, 1968, https://www.nytimes.com/1968/04/08/archives/dr-king-is-hailed-as-peacemaker-eulogy-of-dr-read-typifies-palm.html.

43. Bishop Donegan, quoted in Dugan, "Dr. King Is Hailed."

44. Samuel T. Harris Jr., "The Problem of Civil Disobedience," *Presbyterian Journal* 26 (December 6, 1967): 9.

45. Harris, "The Problem of Civil Disobedience."

46. Church of God leadership, quoted in Julia White Blackwater, "Southern White Fundamentalists and the Civil Rights Movement," *Phylon* 40, no. 4 (1979): 337.

47. L. Calvin Bacon, "Eyewitness at a Funeral," *Pentecostal Evangel,* no. 2827 (July 14, 1968): 20–21.

48. Reuben L. Henry, "Dedicated to the Memory of Martin Luther King, 1968," reprinted in *President Johnson's Blues,* 206–207.

49. Cited in Hardwick, "Apotheosis of Martin Luther King."

50. Hardwick.

51. Taylor Branch, "The Last Wish of Martin Luther King," *New York Times,* Op-Ed, April 6, 2008, http://www.nytimes.com/2008/04/06/opinion/06branch.html.

52. Steve Estes, "'I AM a Man!' Race, Masculinity and the 1968 Memphis Sanitation Strike," *Labor History* 41, no. 2 (2000): 160.

53. Martin Luther King, *All Labor Has Dignity,* ed. Michael Honey (Boston: Beacon Press, 2011), 167.

54. King, *All Labor Has Dignity,* 167.

55. J. Edwin Stanfield, *In Memphis: More Than a Garbage Strike* (Atlanta: Southern Regional Council, 1968).

56. Stanfield, *More Than a Garbage Strike,* 344.

57. Stanfield, 370.

58. Stanfield, 95.

59. Rebecca Burns, *Burial for a King: Martin Luther King Jr.'s Funeral and the Week That Transformed Atlanta and Rocked the Nation* (New York: Simon and Schuster, 2011), 54–55.

60. Burns, *Burial for a King,* 58.

61. J. Edwin Stanfield, *In Memphis: Tragedy Unaverted* (Atlanta: Southern Regional Council, 1968), 6.

62. Hardwick, "The Apotheosis of Martin Luther King."

63. See Karla F. C. Halloway's powerful analysis and retelling in *Passed On: African American Mourning Stories* (Durham, NC: Duke University Press, 2002).

64. Martin Luther King, "Eulogy for the Young Victims of the 16th Street Baptist Church Bombing," September 15, 1963, https://mlkscholars.mit.edu/king-eulogy-1963/.

65. Coretta Scott King, *My Life with Martin Luther King, Jr.* (New York: Holt, Rinehart, and Winston, 1969), 326.

66. Hardwick, "The Apotheosis of Martin Luther King."

67. Conrad Cherry, "Two American Sacred Ceremonies: Their Implications for the Study of Religion in America," *American Quarterly* 21, no. 4 (Winter 1969): 739–754.

68. Anthony Ripley, "Funeral Ignored by Whites but Some Atlanta Stores Close," *New York Times,* April 10, 1968, https://timesmachine.nytimes.com/timesmachine /1968/04/10/issue.html.

69. Henry Louis Gates, ed., "Bobby Hutton," *The African American National Biography* (New York: Oxford University Press, 2008).

70. Richard Lentz, *Symbols, the News Magazines and Martin Luther King* (Baton Rouge: Louisiana State University Press, 1990).

71. Burns, *Burial for a King,* 158.

72. Burns, 158.

73. Max Lerner, "Skyline of Tragic America," *Los Angeles Times,* April 10, 1968, A5.

74. Ben W. Gilbert and the Staff of the Washington Post, *Ten Blocks from the White House: Anatomy of the Washington Riots of 1968* (New York: Praeger Press, 1968), 61.

75. Gilbert, *Ten Blocks,* 63.

76. J. Edwin Stanfield, *In Memphis: Mirror to America? Supplement to Special Report* (Atlanta: Southern Regional Council, 1968), 11.

77. This and the following quotations from the event are taken from a WSB-TV news clip of Coretta Scott King following the assassination of her husband, Dr. Martin Luther King, Jr., speaking at a press conference held at Ebenezer Baptist Church, Atlanta, Georgia, April 6, 1968. Civil Rights Digital Library, http:// crdl.usg.edu/cgi/crdl?format=_video;query=id:ugabma_wsbn_wsbn53564.

78. Ralph Abernathy, "Statement Regarding the Death of Martin Luther King," April 7, 1968, "Funeral" Folder, King Center Archives, Atlanta. This and the following quotations are taken from the original typewritten manuscript.

79. Lauren Hansen, "Keeping the Peace for Martin Luther King, Jr.," *The Week,* accessed in the summer of 2018, http://theweek.com/captured/673288/keeping-peace -martin-luther-king-jr.

80. Rebecca Burns, "The Funeral: An Oral History of the Remarkable Behind the Scenes Effort to Stage Martin Luther King Jr.'s 1968 Funeral," *Atlanta Magazine,* April 1, 2008, http://www.atlantamagazine.com/great-reads/mlk-funeral-1968/.

81. King Papers Project, King's Assassination, April 4, 1968, overview, Martin Luther King Jr. Research and Education Institute, Stanford University.

82. Gary Dorrien, *Breaking White Supremacy: Martin Luther King and the Black Social Gospel* (New Haven, CT: Yale University Press, 2018), 435.

83. Rick Perlstein, *Nixonland: The Rise of a President and the Fracturing of America* (New York: Scribner, 2009), 257.

84. Andrew Manis, "Silence or Shockwaves: Southern Baptists Responses to the Assassination of Martin Luther King, Jr," *Baptist History and Heritage* 15 (October 1980): 23.

85. Typewritten transcript of the service, "Funeral" Folder, King Center Archives, Atlanta.

86. Martin Luther King, "Remaining Awake through a Great Revolution," National Cathedral, Washington, DC, March 31, 1968, Martin Luther King Jr. Research and Education Institute, Stanford University, https://kinginstitute.stanford .edu/king-papers/publications/knock-midnight-inspiration-great-sermons-reverend -martin-luther-king-jr-10.

87. Press conference, Ebenezer Baptist Church, April 6, 1968, http://crdl.usg.edu /cgi/crdl?format=_video;query=id:ugabma_wsbn_wsbn53564.

88. Quoted in UBE Staff, "Remembering Dr. King: Dr. Ron English's Prayer at Dr. King's Funeral," The Union of Black Episcopalians, January 16, 2012, https://www .ube.org/dfc/newsdetail_2/3151112.

89. Martin Luther King had written a book entitled *Where Do We Go from Here? Chaos or Community* (New York: Beacon Press, 1967).

90. English and Abernathy quotes drawn from *Reel America,* "Martin Luther King Jr. Funeral Services," C-SPAN, https://www.c-span.org/video/?443156-1 /martin-luther-king-jr-funeral-coverage-1968.

91. Martin Luther King Jr., "The Drum Major Instinct," Ebenezer Baptist Church, Atlanta, GA, February 4, 1968, https://kinginstitute.stanford.edu/king-papers /documents/drum-major-instinct-sermon-delivered-ebenezer-baptist-church.

92. Rebecca Burns, "Mourning and Message: Martin Luther King Jr.'s 1968 Atlanta Funeral as an Image Event" (master's thesis, Georgia State University, 2008), 12, https://scholarworks.gsu.edu/cgi/viewcontent.cgi?article=1042&context =communication_theses.

93. Alex Haley, "Martin Luther King: The Playboy Interview" (January 1965), *50 Classic Interviews* (Los Angeles: Playboy Enterprises, 2012), Kindle edition.

94. Jonathan Rieder, *The Word of the Lord Is upon Me: The Righteous Performance of Martin Luther King, Jr.* (Cambridge, MA: Belknap Press, 2008), 58.

95. "Martin Luther King: The Great Civil Rights Leader, an Apostle of Non-Violence and Freedom, Dies a Martyr in Memphis," *Life,* April 12, 1968, 74.

96. Martin Luther King Jr., "Eulogy for the Young Victims of the 16th Street Baptist Church Bombing," https://mlkscholars.mit.edu/king-eulogy-1963/.

97. Mika Edmonson, "Family and Cultural Roots," chap. 1 in *The Power of Unearned Suffering: The Roots and Implications of Martin Luther King, Jr.'s Theodicy* (Lanham, MD: Lexington Books, 2017), 3–24.

98. Ralph D. Abernathy, "A Short Letter to My Dearest Friend, Martin Luther King, Jr." (sermon fragment), April 7, 1968, King Center Archives, Atlanta.

99. Abernathy, "Short Letter."

100. Hansen, "Keeping the Peace."

101. Burns, *Burial for a King*, 13.

102. "Dr. Martin Luther King Buried in Atlanta; A Vast Cortege Follows Mule-Drawn Bier," *New York Times*, April 10, 1968, front page.

103. "King Buried in Atlanta."

104. "King Buried in Atlanta."

105. "King Buried in Atlanta."

106. "King Buried in Atlanta."

107. "King Buried in Atlanta."

108. Burns, "Mourning and Message," 16.

109. Scott King, *My Life with Martin Luther King, Jr.*, 320–321.

110. Robert E. Seymour, "Dressed for the Occasion," Binkley Memorial Baptist Church, Chapel Hill, NC, April 14, 1968, Southern Historical Collection, Robert E. Seymour Papers 4554, Louis Round Wilson Special Collections Library, University of North Carolina at Chapel Hill.

111. Reverend John A. Scott Sr., "The Mind of Christ," Church of Christ, White Station, TN, April 14, 1968, http://www.cocws.org/filerequest/2124. The printed announcement of the sermon features a prayerful Dr. King with the sermon title "The Mind of Christ" as caption.

112. See Gary Daynes, *Making Villains, Making Heroes: Joseph R. McCarthy, Martin Luther King Jr. and the Politics of American Memory* (New York: Garland, 1997), 132.

113. Johnson, "Address to the Nation."

114. Coretta Scott King, "Speech for the Welfare Mother's March," Welfare Rights Organization, May 12, 1968, Washington, DC, Emory University Archive.

115. Scott King, "Speech for the Welfare Mother's March."

116. Scott King, "Speech for the Welfare Mother's March"; Langston Hughes, "Mother to Son," https://www.poetryfoundation.org/poems/47559/mother-to-son.

117. Howard Moody, untitled sermon, Judson Memorial Church, New York City, April 7, 1968, Southern Christian Leadership Conference Papers, Robert Woodruff Library, Emory University, Atlanta.

118. Al Sharpton and Jesse Jackson, who have each run for president, are good examples of this reinvented "Black preacher."

119. Samuel W. Williams, "All Created Life Longs for Rescue," April 21, 1968, Samuel W. Williams Collection, Box 19, Folder 47, Robert Woodruff Library, Atlanta University Center.

120. Williams, "All Created Life."

121. Samuel W. Williams, "He Was No Criminal," April 1968, Samuel W. Williams Collection, Box 19, Folder 47, Robert Woodruff Library, Atlanta University Center.

122. Moody, untitled sermon.

123. Moody.

124. King, "Remaining Awake through a Great Revolution."

125. Hubert Humphrey, speech to the National Alliance of Businessmen, April 5, 1968, http://www2.mnhs.org/library/findaids/00442/pdfa/00442-02491.pdf.

126. Ramsey Pollard, untitled sermon, Bellevue Baptist Church, April 8, 1968, reprinted in "King's Death Spurs Memphis Pastors to Action, Sermons," *Baptist Press*, April 8, 1968, http://media.sbhla.org.s3.amazonaws.com/2578,08-Apr-1968.PDF.

127. Francis B. Sayre Jr., untitled sermon, Washington Cathedral, April 7, 1968, https://cathedral.org/wp-content/uploads/2018/01/Dean-Sayre-Sermon-after-MLK-death.pdf.

128. Eleanor K. Harbinson, "Note to the National Cathedral Regarding Why Martin Luther King Should Not Be Permitted to Preach at the Cathedral," February 13, 1968, https://cathedral.org/wp-content/uploads/2018/01/1968-letter-protesting-King-invite.pdf.

129. "King's Death Spurs Memphis Pastors to Action, Sermons."

130. Seymour, "Dressed for the Occasion."

131. Hawkins, "Jerusalem Then—Our Cities Now."

132. E. L. Ford, "The Life and Legacy of Dr. Martin Luther King," in *President Johnson's Blues*, 189.

133. Omie L. Holliday, "King without a Throne," in *President Johnson's Blues*, 171.

134. Hawkins, "Jerusalem Then."

135. Hawkins, "Jerusalem Then."

136. Hawkins, "Jerusalem Then."

137. Langston Hughes, "What Happens to a Dream Deferred?," https://www.poetryfoundation.org/poems/46548/harlem.

138. Martin Luther King Jr., "Letter from the Birmingham Jail," April 16, 1963, https://swap.stanford.edu/20141218230016/http://mlk-kpp01.stanford.edu/kingweb/popular_requests/frequentdocs/birmingham.pdf.

139. Martin Luther King Jr., "The Negro and the American Dream," in *The Papers of Martin Luther King, Jr.,* vol. 7 (Stanford: University of California Press, 2014), 111–122.

140. Robert Bellah, "Civil Religion in America," *Daedalus: Journal of the American Academy of Arts and Sciences* 97 (Winter 1967): 1–21.

141. Michael Honey, *Going Down Jericho Road: The Memphis Strike, Martin Luther King's Last Campaign* (New York: W. W. Norton, 2007), 412.

142. Fred Crawford, Roy Norman, and Leah Dabbs, *A Report of Certain Reactions by the Atlanta Public to the Death of Reverend Doctor Martin Luther King, Jr.,* May 1968, Center for Research in Social Change, Emory University, Atlanta. See also *Racial Attitudes in 15 American Cities,* Institute for Social Research, University of Michigan, June 1968, https://isr.umich.edu/wp-content/uploads/historicPublications/Racialatt itudesinfifteenamericancities_2759_.PDF.

143. Crawford, Norman, and Dabbs, *A Report of Certain Reactions.*

144. Nathan Marsh Pusey, introductory remarks, Memorial Service for Reverend Martin Luther King, Jr., April 9, 1968, Harvard University Archives, UA15.169, Box 416, Ki-Kt, 1967–1968.

145. Cited in Charles Kaiser, *1968 in America* (New York: Grove Press, 1988), 146–148.

146. Simeon Booker, "King's Widow: From Bereavement to Battlefield," *Jet,* April 25, 1968, 6.

147. Burns, *Burial for a King,* 76–77, 116.

148. Robert L. Scott, "Justifying Violence: The Rhetoric of Militant Black Power," *Communication Studies* 19, no. 2 (1969): 97.

149. King, *Where Do We Go from Here?,* 112–113.

150. Martin Luther King Jr., "Impasse in Race Relations," in *Trumpet of Conscience* (Boston: Beacon Press, 1967), 8.

151. Rev. A. E. Bullock, South Fork, CA (denomination and church unknown).

152. John A. Williams, *The King God Didn't Save* (New York: Coward-McCann, 1970), 22–23.

153. Ralph D. Abernathy, *And the Walls Came Tumbling Down: An Autobiography* (New York: Harper and Row, 1989), 461.

154. United Press International, "Six Dead after Church Bombing," *Washington Post,* September 16, 1963, http://www.washingtonpost.com/wp-srv/national /longterm/churches/archives1.htm.

155. See Simon Stow, "Agonistic Homegoing: Frederick Douglass, Joseph Lowery and the Democratic Value of African American Public Mourning," *American Political Science Review,* 104, no. 4 (2010): 681–697.

156. Quoted in Barbara Leaming, *Jacqueline Bouvier Kennedy Onassis: The Untold Story* (New York: St. Martin's Griffin Press, 2015), 237.

157. C. R. Daley, editorial, *The Kentucky Baptist Western Record*, April 5, 1968, 3.

CHAPTER 4: THE CHURCH OF THE NATIONAL TRAGEDY

1.   Julia Wick, "Say Her Name: On the Legacy of Latasha Harlins and the 1992 Riots," in *Arts and Entertainment, LAist*, March 24, 2017, https://laist.com/2017/03/24/latasha_harlins_hammer_museum.php.

2.   Itabari Njeri, chap. 1 in *The Last Plantation: Color, Conflict and Identity: Reflections of a New World Black* (Boston: Houghton Mifflin, 1997), https://archive.nytimes.com/www.nytimes.com/books/first/n/njeri-plantation.html.

3.   Terry Mattingly, "A Broken Nation Hears, According to Elite Press, Vague Sermons on Unity and Reconciliation," July 11, 2016, *GetReligion*, https://www.getreligion.org/getreligion/2016/7/11/a-broken-nation-hears-according-to-elite-press-vague-calls-for-unity-and-reconciliation.

4.   Mattingly, "A Broken Nation."

5.   Mattingly.

6.   Rev. Jonathan B. Coffey, Episcopal, St. James the Less, Scarsdale, NY, quoted in Roberta Hershenson, "In Difficult Times, Church Attempts to Build Spiritual Bridges," *New York Times*, May 24, 1992, https://www.nytimes.com/1992/05/24/nyregion/in-difficult-times-church-attempts-to-build-spiritual-bridges.html.

7.   Rev. Peter Moore, Little Trinity Anglican Church, visiting, St. James the Less, quoted in Hershenson, "In Difficult Times."

8.   Angel Jennings, "He Tried to Cool a City's Anger, Only to Watch Helplessly as It Burned during the 1992 Riots," *Los Angeles Times*, April 28, 2017, https://www.latimes.com/local/lanow/la-me-riots-first-hours-ame-20170426-story.html.

9.   Jennings, "He Tried to Cool a City's Anger."

10.   President George H. W. Bush, "Address to the Nation Regarding the Riots in Los Angeles," May 1, 1992, George H. W. Bush Presidential Library and Museum, https://bush41library.tamu.edu/audiovisual/videos/78. This unintentional echo of Malcom X's "by any means necessary" assumed resonance for many Americans in November 1992 with the release of Spike Lee's biopic of Malcom X.

11.   John Gregory Dunne, "Law and Disorder in Los Angeles," *New York Review of Books*, October 10, 1991, https://www.nybooks.com/articles/1991/10/10/law-disorder-in-los-angeles/.

12.   Although many news accounts described the Simi Valley jury as "all White," among the twelve were a Filipino man and a Hispanic woman. There were no Black jurors.

13. Dunne, "Law and Disorder," 23–29.

14. Quoted in Anna Deavere Smith, *Twilight: Los Angeles, 1992* (New York: Anchor Books, 1994), 180.

15. "How Emmett Till Changed the World," Emmett Till Legacy Foundation, https://emmetttilllegacyfoundation.com/emmetts-story/.

16. *The Body of Emmett Till* (documentary short), *TIME*, http://100photos.time.com/photos/emmett-till-david-jackson.

17. Video of Latasha Harlins at the Korean Empire Liquor Grocery Store, https://www.youtube.com/watch?v=Nm5pp3BBZpA.

18. Terry White, quoted in "Ready . . . Set . . . Burn Part Two," Wagner & Lynch blog, June 13, 2016, https://seoklaw.com/legal-news/ready-set-burn/.

19. Richard Serrano, "2 Views of Rodney King Drawn by Lawyers," *Los Angeles Times,* March 6, 1992, https://www.latimes.com/local/california/la-me-views-rodney-king-lawyers-19920306-story.html.

20. Elizabeth Alexander, "Can You Be Black and Look at This? Reading the Rodney King Video(s)," *Public Culture* 7 (1994): 77–94 (emphasis in original).

21. Michael Stone, quoted in "Ready . . . Set . . . Burn Part Two."

22. Quoted in Kylie Shaw, "News All Day Every Day," *Mass Media Talkback* (blog), October 26, 2014, http://blogs.stlawu.edu/mediaindustries2014/2014/10/26/news-all-day-every-day/.

23. John T. Caldwell, *Televisuality: Style, Crisis, and Authority in American Television* (New Brunswick, NJ: Rutgers University Press, 1995), 302–335.

24. Robert Reinhold, "After Police-Beating Verdict, Another Trial for the Jurors," *New York Times,* May 9, 1992, https://www.nytimes.com/1992/05/09/us/after-the-riots-after-policebeating-verdict-another-trial-for-the-jurors.html.

25. Ronald Jacobs, *Race, Media and the Crisis of Civil Society: From Watts to Rodney King* (Cambridge: Cambridge University Press, 2000), 118.

26. Darnell M. Hunt, *Screening the Los Angeles Riots: Race, Seeing and Resistance* (Cambridge: Cambridge University Press, 1997), 44.

27. Hunt, *Screening*, 128.

28. Hunt, 46–47.

29. Hunt, 48.

30. Phylis Johnson, *KJLH-FM and the LA Riots of 1992: Compton's Neighborhood Station in the Aftermath of the Rodney King Verdict* (Jefferson, NC: McFarland, 2009), 148.

31. Johnson, *KJLH-FM and the LA Riots of 1992*, 148.

32. Martin Luther King Jr., "The Other America," speech at Stanford University, Stanford, CA, April 4, 1967, quoted in Lily Rothman, "What Martin Luther King Jr Really Thought about Riots," *TIME,* April 28, 2015, https://time.com/3838515 /baltimore-riots-language-unheard-quote/. King repeated this sentiment many times throughout his life.

33. Hunt, *Screening,* 131.

34. Hunt, 131–134.

35. Hunt, 130–133.

36. Paul Lieberman, "51% of Riot Arrests Were Latino, Study Says," *Los Angeles Times,* June 18, 1992, https://www.latimes.com/archives/la-xpm-1992-06-18-me-734 -story.html.

37. Eric Bailey, "After the Riots: The Search for Answers," *Los Angeles Times,* May 7, 1992, https://www.latimes.com/archives/la-xpm-1992-05-07-mn-2531-story .html. Los Angeles was named after its Spanish founders in the eighteenth century. And while a full account of the erasure of Latinxs from the narrative of the Los Angeles protests is beyond the scope of this book, their absence is part of how the binary around race (White / Black) was rehearsed in the 1990s.

38. Elaine Kim, "Home Is Where the *Han* Is: A Korean American Perspective on the Los Angeles Upheavals," in Robert Gooding-Williams, *Reading Rodney King, Reading Urban Uprising* (New York: Routledge, 1993), 215–235.

39. Nancy Abelmann and John Lie, *Blue Dreams: Korean Americans and the Los Angeles Riots* (Cambridge, MA: Harvard University Press, 1995), 24.

40. Abelmann and Lie, *Blue Dreams,* 34.

41. Abelmann and Lie, 38.

42. Abelmann and Lie, 40.

43. Abelmann and Lie, 40.

44. Abelmann and Lie, 40.

45. Bettina Boxall and Vicki Torres, "Preachers Urge Worshipers to Improve Society," *Los Angeles Times,* May 4, 1992, 1.

46. Jacobs, *Race, Media,* 121.

47. Nina Easton, "Understanding the Riots: Six Months Later," *Los Angeles Times,* November 18, 1992, 7, https://www.latimes.com/archives/la-xpm-1992-11-19-ss-1080 -story.html.

48. Easton, "Understanding the Riots," 7.

49. Andrea Ford and Lisa R. Omphroy, "A City in Crisis," *Los Angeles Times,* May 3, 1992, 3.

50. Ford and Omphroy, "A City in Crisis," 3.

51. Abelmann and Lie, *Blue Dreams,* 184–191.

52. Jacobs, *Race, Media,* 113.

53. Jane Gross, "In Simi Valley, Defense of a Shared Way of Life," *New York Times,* May 4, 1992, B7.

54. Jacobs, *Race, Media,* 117.

55. Rick Del Vecchio, Suzanne Espinosa, and Carle Nolte, "Bradley Ready to Lift Curfew; He Says L.A. Is 'Under Control,'" *San Francisco Chronicle,* May 4, 1992, A1.

56. See John Morone, *Hellfire Nation: The Politics of Sin in American History* (New Haven, CT: Yale University Press, 2003).

57. Morone, *Hellfire Nation,* 384.

58. Jeffrey H. Birnbaum, "Washington's Power 25," *Fortune,* December 8, 1997, 144–158, http://edition.cnn.com/ALLPOLITICS/1997/11/18/fortune.25/index1.html.

59. Patrick Buchanan, "The War for the Soul of America," *Human Events,* May 23, 1992, quoted in *Blue Dreams,* 5.

60. This section of Romans was referred to or paraphrased in several of the Los Angeles sermons.

61. *Grace to You* radio, https://www.gty.org/radio/.

62. John MacArthur, "The Los Angeles Riots: A Biblical Perspective," Grace Community Church, May 3, 1992, http://www.gty.org/resources/sermons/80-104/the-los-angeles-riots-a-biblical-perspective.

63. MacArthur, "The Los Angeles Riots."

64. MacArthur.

65. MacArthur.

66. While this was initially true primarily for the White church, within a decade, the Black church, too, would have a similar perspective, as will be explored in the next chapter.

67. William Cavanaugh, "Killing for the Telephone Company: Why the Nation-State is Not the Keeper of the Common Good," *Modern Theology* 20, no. 2 (April 2004): 243–274.

68. Michel Foucault, *The Birth of Biopolitics: Lectures at the College de France, 1978–79,* ed. Michel Senellart, trans. Graham Burchell (New York: Picador, 2008).

69. See Kate Bowler, *Blessed: A History of the American Prosperity Gospel* (Oxford: Oxford University Press, 2013).

70. Penelope Miller, "Victim of Mob Assault Meets Man Who Saved His Life," *Baltimore Sun,* May 9, 1992, https://www.baltimoresun.com/news/bs-xpm-1992-05-09-1992130030-story.html.

71. David Bruce, "Terri Barnett, Bobby Green, Titus Murphy and Lei Yuille: African American Heroes of the 1992 Los Angeles Riots," *davidbruce* (blog), July 12, 2012, https://davidbruceblog.wordpress.com/2012/07/03/terri-barnett-bobby-green -titus-murphy-and-lei-yuille-african-american-heroes-of-the-1992-los-angeles -race-riots/.

72. Roger Simon, "Saving One Man's Life Bolsters All Humanity," *Baltimore Sun*, May 8, 1992, https://www.baltimoresun.com/news/bs-xpm-1992-05-08-1992129130 -story.html.

73. Simon, "Saving One Man's Life"; and Bruce, "Terri Barnett."

74. A Christian Confession Conference, Los Angeles Theological Reflection Group, May 15, 1992, in *Dreams on Fire, Embers of Hope: From the Pulpits of Los Angeles after the Riots,* ed. Ignacio Castuera (St. Louis, MO: Chalice Press, 1992), 108.

75. Linnea Juanita Pearson, "Out of the Ashes: A Terrible Beauty Is Born," in *Dreams on Fire,* 32–34.

76. Video of Rodney King's plea during the 1992 Los Angeles Riots, https://www .youtube.com/watch?v=1sONfxPCTUo.

77. Rodney King, *The Riot Within: My Journey from Rebellion to Redemption* (New York: Harper One, 2012).

78. Jerome McCristal Culp Jr., "Notes from California: Rodney King and the Race Questions," *Denver University Law Review* 70, no. 2 (1993): 199–212.

79. Told in Cecil Murray's memoir, *Twice Tested by Fire: A Memoir of Faith and Science* (Los Angeles: Figueroa Press, 2012).

80. Lynn Mie Itagaki, *Civil Racism: The 1992 Los Angeles Rebellion and the Crisis of Racial Burnout* (Minneapolis: University of Minnesota Press, 2016).

81. Pearson, "Out of the Ashes," 31.

82. Pearson, 32–33.

83. Pearson, 33.

84. John Rosove, "Remarks in the Wake of the LA Riots," in *Dreams on Fire,* 26.

85. Rev. Dr. Ignacio Castuera, "Breath from the Four Winds," Hollywood United Methodist Church, in *Dreams on Fire,* 77.

86. Miles Corwin, "Riot Aftermath: Man with a Mission: Jesse Jackson Follows Cries around the Globe," *Los Angeles Times,* May 6, 1992, 5, https://www.latimes .com/archives/la-xpm-1992-05-06-mn-1260-story.html.

87. Corwin, "Riot Aftermath," 5.

88. Barbara Mudge, "We Are an Easter People," in *Dreams on Fire,* 57–58.

89. Mudge, 58.

90. Pearson, "Out of the Ashes," 29.

91. Pearson, 36.

92. Pearson, 35–37.

93. Chester Talton, "How Have You Helped Me?," in *Dreams on Fire*, 41.

94. Talton, 42.

95. Robert D. McFadden, "Riots in Los Angeles: Pleas for Peace and Justice from Pulpits in Dozen [*sic*] Cities," *New York Times*, May 4, 1992, https://timesmachine .nytimes.com/timesmachine/1992/05/04/360092.html?pageNumber=26.

96. Abelmann and Lie, *Blue Dreams*, 101.

97. See Abelmann and Lie, 148–180.

98. Associated Press, "Group to Improve Black-Korean Relations Disbands in Los Angeles," *New York Times*, December 26, 1992, https://www.nytimes.com/1992/12 /26/us/group-to-improve-black-korean-relations-disbands-in-los-angeles.html; and Jack Doherty, "Black-Korean Alliance Says Talk Not Enough, Disbands," *Los Angeles Times*, December 24, 1992, https://www.latimes.com/archives/la-xpm-1992 -12-24-mn-3564-story.html.

99. President George H. W. Bush, Oval Office Speech to the Nation, May 1, 1992, C-SPAN transcript, https://www.c-span.org/video/?c4536094/bush-la-riots.

100. Bush, Oval Office Speech to the Nation.

101. Bush.

102. Harry Emerson Fosdick, "How to Handle Tragedy," chap. 18 in *Dear Mr. Brown: Letters to a Person Perplexed about Religion* (New York: Harper and Brother, 1961), 121.

103. Rev. C. Lawrence Bishop, "Resurrection in the Midst of Tragedy," Edmond Trinity Christian Church, April 23, 1995, in *And the Angels Wept: From the Pulpits of Oklahoma City after the Bombing*, ed. Marsha Brock Bishop and David P. Polk (St. Louis, MO: Chalice Press, 1995), 77.

104. Robin Jones, *Where Was God at 9:02? Miraculous Stories of Faith and Love from Oklahoma City* (Nashville, TN: Thomas Nelson, 1995), 33–34.

105. Jones, *Where Was God?*, 65–72.

106. Rev. William Simms, "Reflections on a Nightmare," Wildewood Christian Church, April 23, 1995, in *And the Angels Wept*, 87.

107. Quoted in the Wisdom Fund, "Oklahoma City Bombing: Innocent Dead, Falsely Accused," April 20, 1995, http://www.twf.org/News/Y1997/Victims.html.

108. Wisdom Fund, "Oklahoma City Bombing."

109. Wisdom Fund.

110. Margaret Hirschberg, "The Real of Edye-Icon: Edye Smith, the Oklahoma Bombing, and the Mobilization of Ideologies," *Genders* 29 (June 1, 1999), https://www.colorado.edu/gendersarchive1998-2013/1999/06/01/real-edye-icon -edye-smith-oklahoma-city-bombing-and-mobilization-ideologies.

111. Hirschberg, "The Real of Edye-Icon."

112. Rev. Billy Graham, Oklahoma Bombing Memorial Prayer Service Address, April 23, 1995, https://www.americanrhetoric.com/speeches/billygrahamoklahom abombingspeech.htm.

113. Barbara Feinstein, "Tribute to the Victims of Oklahoma City Bombing," Congressional Record 141 (69), Senate, April 27, 1995: S5749–S5751, https://www .govinfo.gov/content/pkg/CREC-1995-04-27/pdf/CREC-1995-04-27-senate.pdf.

114. Oklahoma Department of Civil Emergency Management, *Oklahoma City Bombing after Action Report,* April 19, 1995, https://www.ok.gov/OEM/documents /Bombing%20After%20Action%20Report.pdf.

115. Dave McCurdy, quoted in Jim Naureckas, "The Oklahoma City Bombing: The Jihad That Wasn't," *FAIR,* July 1, 1995, http://fair.org/extra/the-oklahoma-city -bombing/.

116. Naureckas, "The Jihad That Wasn't."

117. Naureckas.

118. Naureckas.

119. Naureckas.

120. ABC Special, "Nightline Town Meeting: Trouble in the Heartland," April 25, 1995, https://www.youtube.com/watch?v=BQHieAlExJo.

121. Naureckas, "The Jihad That Wasn't."

122. Naureckas.

123. See Larry Stammer and Carla Hall, "Terror in Oklahoma City: American Muslims Feel Sting of Accusations in Bombing's Wake," *Los Angeles Times,* April 22, 1995, https://www.latimes.com/archives/la-xpm-1995-04-22-mn-57460 -story.html.

124. Project of the Community Peace Coalition, *Oklahoma Hate and Harassment Report,* Spring 1995, http://www.themodernreligion.com/assault/okla-report.html.

125. Melinda Henneberger, "Terror in Oklahoma: Bias Attacks," *New York Times,* April 24, 1995, B10.

126. James Brooke, "Attacks on Muslims Surge Even as Their Faith Takes Hold," *New York Times,* August 28, 1995, http://www.nytimes.com/1995/08/28/us/attacks -on-us-muslims-surge-even-as-their-faith-takes-hold.html.

127. Edward T. Linenthal, *The Unfinished Bombing: Oklahoma City in American Memory* (Oxford: Oxford University Press, 2001), 48.

128. Quoted in Linenthal, *The Unfinished Bombing*, 48.

129. Robert Wise, sermon, quoted in Jones, *Where Was God?*, 174.

130. Although American clergy would not have immediately known this, McVeigh was later found to be sympathetic to a Far Right political organization, the Covenant, the Sword and the Arm of the Lord (CSA), which had been dedicated to Christian identity and survivalism. The group had been active in the United States since the 1970s and was considered by the FBI to have been one of the most dangerous domestic terrorist organizations throughout the 1980s. CSA was eventually disbanded, but its influence reverberated for many years.

131. Florence Rogers, Oklahoma City survivor, FBI video, https://www.fbi.gov /video-repository/newss-florence-rogers-survivor-of-oklahoma-city-bombing /view.

132. Rogers, FBI video.

133. Rogers.

134. Bishop Robert M. Moody, Episcopal Diocese of Oklahoma, Community Prayer Service, First Christian Church, April 20, 1995, in *And the Angels Wept*, 42.

135. Bishop, "Resurrection in the Midst of Tragedy," 77.

136. Emily M. Bernstein, "Terror in Oklahoma: The Displaced; Its Building Shattered, but Church Survives," *New York Times*, April 24, 1995, https://www .nytimes.com/1995/04/24/us/terror-in-oklahoma-the-displaced-its-building-is -shattered-but-church-survives.html.

137. Pat Buchanan, "1992 Republican National Convention Speech," Patrick J. Buchanan—Official Website, August 17, 1992, https://buchanan.org/blog/1992 -republican-national-convention-speech-148.

138. Gene Garrison, untitled sermon, First Baptist Church, Oklahoma City, OK, in *And the Angels Wept*, 41.

139. Joseph Solomon, untitled sermon, Oklahoma United Methodist Conference, First Christian Church, April 20, 1995, in *And the Angels Wept*, 42 (emphasis added).

140. And with the acknowledged benefit of hindsight, one wonders how events might have played out differently if volunteers of comfort rather than armed guards had flooded Memphis and Washington, DC, after King's assassination, after the not guilty verdict in Simi Valley, after the killing of Trayvon Martin or Michael Brown, or even today, after the killing of George Floyd.

141. Tish Malloy, "We Have Seen the Lord," Village United Methodist Church, Oklahoma City, OK, April 23, 1995, in *And the Angels Wept*, 71.

142. Philip Rieff, *The Triumph of the Therapeutic: Uses of Faith after Freud* (Chicago: University of Chicago Press, 1966), 8–10.

143. Bishop, "Resurrection in the Midst of Tragedy," 77.

144. Thomas R. Jewell, "Why?," Disciples of Christ Church, Oklahoma City, OK, April 23, 1995, in *And the Angels Wept*, 62.

145. There is a well-known book published in the 1970s, *Is God a White Racist?: A Preamble to Black Theology* (Boston: Beacon Press, 1973), by William R. Jones, that asks this question as a way to try to think through both Black and White ministers' willingness to accept African American suffering to preserve conceptions of a benevolent God. The book offers a radical and sometimes sardonic look at the assumptions sometimes made by a "color-blind" ministry.

146. This was President Clinton's signature phrase in his address to the nation at the memorial service for the Oklahoma City bombing on April 23, 1995.

147. President William J. Clinton, Remarks from the Briefing Room on the Bombing of the Alfred Murrah Federal Building, April 19, 1993, https://www.govinfo.gov/content/pkg/PPP-1995-book1/html/PPP-1995-book1-doc-pg552.htm.

148. Holocaust survivor Elie Wiesel was perhaps the most well-known person to write and speak about a suffering God in a world of despair and alienation. See his *Night* (New York: Hill and Wang, [1972] 2006), *The Trial of God* (New York: Random House, 1979), and *A Beggar in Jerusalem: A Novel* (New York: Random House, 1970).

149. Bishop, "Resurrection in the Midst of Tragedy," 78.

150. Edward T. Linenthal, "The Predicament of the Aftermath: Oklahoma City and September 11," in *Resilient City: How Modern Cities Recover from Disaster*, ed. Lawrence J. Vale and Thomas J. Campenella (Oxford: Oxford University Press, 2005), 65.

151. Marita Sturken, *Tourists of History: Memory, Kitsch, and Consumerism from Oklahoma City to Ground Zero* (Durham, NC: Duke University Press, 2007).

152. Sturken, *Tourists of History*, 7 (emphasis added).

153. There is no permanent memorial to the Los Angeles dead, although there are permanent memorials for most of the other tragedies addressed in this book. There is the Arizona Memorial at Pearl Harbor with its eerie, watery grave of the dead, and the morbid Sixth Floor Museum at Dealey Plaza positioned on the very spot from which Lee Harvey Oswald shot and killed the president. There's the memorial at the Lorraine Motel in Memphis, complete with period cars parked in the lot beneath the terrible balcony on which King was assassinated as well as the Oklahoma City Memorial and National Museum with its field of 168 empty chairs. And, finally, there is the recently completed 9/11 National Memorial and Museum at what was for many years known in the United States as Ground Zero. While part of the symbolic continuum, these permanent memorials serve a different cultural and political purpose than those that were spontaneously created immediately after a tragedy. There are several fascinating books on this contemporary turn to "dark tourism." See Brigitte Sion, *Death Tourism: Disaster Sites as Recreational*

Landscape (Chicago: Seagull Books, 2014); and Malcolm Foley and John Lennon, *Dark Tourism: The Attraction of Death and Disasters* (London: Thomson Learning, 2000). For more on temporary memorials, see, for example, Erika Doss, *Memorial Mania: Public Feeling in America* (Chicago: University of Chicago Press, 2010); and Kirk Savage, *Monument Wars: Washington DC, the National Mall and the Transformation of the Memorial Landscape* (Berkeley: University of California Press, 2011).

154. Orrin Hatch as quoted in Linenthal, *The Unfinished Bombing*, 20.

155. Dan Baker, "Christian Terrorism in Oklahoma City," Freedom from Religion Foundation, May 1995, https://ffrf.org/component/k2/item/18402-christian -terrorism-in-oklahoma-city.

156. Rev. Joy Patterson, "When Senseless Violence Takes Those We Love," adapted from Chalice Hymnal #512 Candlelight Vigil, Oklahoma City, April 21, 1995, in *And the Angels Wept*, 46.

157. Rieff, introduction to *The Triumph of the Therapeutic: Uses of Faith after Freud* (Chicago: University of Chicago Press, 1966), v, viii.

158. President William J. Clinton, press conference, April 19, 1995, https://www.c -span.org/video/?c4588892/president-clinton-oklahoma-city-bombing.

159. Peter Keating, "Remembering Oklahoma City and How Bill Clinton Saved His Presidency," *New York Magazine*, April 19, 2010, http://nymag.com/daily /intelligencer/2010/04/remembering_oklahoma_city_and.html.

160. President William J. Clinton, "Remarks at the Michigan State University Commencement Ceremony in East Lansing, Michigan, May 5, 1995," American Presidency Project, https://www.presidency.ucsb.edu/documents/remarks-the -michigan-state-university-commencement-ceremony-east-lansing-michigan.

161. Clinton, "Remarks at the Michigan State University Commencement Ceremony."

162. Jones, *Where Was God?*, 61.

163. Federal Bureau of Investigation, "The Oklahoma City Bombing: 20 Years Later," https://stories.fbi.gov/oklahoma-bombing/.

164. Bishop, "Resurrection in the Midst of Tragedy," 74.

165. Governor Frank Keating, "A Time for Healing," Oklahoma State Fair Arena, April 23, 1995, in *And the Angels Wept*, 48.

166. Consider just this small sample of books (and articles) about the loss of American innocence: Eliot Asinof, *1919: America's Loss of Innocence* (New York: Donald I. Fine Press, 1990); Stephen Cone, *Loss of Innocence: A History of Hotel Company, 2nd Battalion, 7th Marines in Vietnam* (Victoria, BC: Friesen Press, 2012); Richard North Patterson, *Loss of Innocence* (New York: Quercus, 2014); and Jon Margolis, *The Last Innocent Year: America in 1964* (New York: Harper Perennial, 2000).

167. Opening statements in the O. J. Simpson trial were given January 24, 1995.

168. Bishop, "Resurrection in the Midst of Tragedy," 74.

169. Thomas Reeves, "Not So Christian America," *First Things*, October 1996, https://www.firstthings.com/article/1996/10/001-not-so-christian-america.

170. Lura Cayton, "God's Face Is Toward Us," Capitol Hill Christian Church, OK, in *And the Angels Wept*, 26.

171. Reeves, "Not So Christian America."

172. Earl A. Grollman, "What Do We Do with Our Pain?," First Christian Church, April 23, 1995, in *And the Angels Wept*, 29.

173. Bishop Charles Salatka, Community Prayer Service, First Christian Church, April 20, 1995, in *And the Angels Wept*, 45.

174. Jones, *Where Was God?*, 124.

175. Jones, 124.

176. Jones, 127.

177. Charles Salatka, Roman Catholic Archdiocese of Oklahoma City, Community Prayer Service, April 20, 1995, in *And the Angels Wept*, 45.

178. Jones, *Where Was God?*, 168.

179. Jones, 170.

180. Jones, 173–174.

181. Director Michel Gondry's 2004 film starring Kate Winslet and Jim Carrey, *The Eternal Sunshine of the Spotless Mind*, https://www.imdb.com/title/tt0338013/.

182. *Transforming Our Trauma*, episode 13, "We Will Always Remember: The Oklahoma City Bombing," sermon by Rev. Michael D. Anderson, April 23, 1995, http://realmysteries.us/we-will-always-remember-the-oklahoma-city-bombing-episode-13/.

183. Bishop, "Resurrection in the Midst of Tragedy," 78.

184. "And Jesus Wept—Oklahoma City, Oklahoma—Statues of Religious Figures," Waymarking, http://www.waymarking.com/waymarks/WMB4R3_And_Jesus_Wept_Oklahoma_City_OK.

185. Kate Bowler, *Blessed: A History of the American Prosperity Gospel* (Oxford: Oxford University Press, 2013).

186. See Joel Osteen, *Your Best Life Now: 7 Steps to Living at Your Full Potential* (New York: Faith Words, 2004); and Rev. T. D. Jakes, *Loved by God: The Spiritual Wealth of the Believer* (Bloomington, MN: Bethany House, 2003).

187. Susan Myers-Shirk, *Helping the Good Shepherd: Pastoral Counselors in a Psychotherapeutic Culture, 1925–1975* (Baltimore, MD: Johns Hopkins University Press, 2009), 195.

188. Myers-Shirk, *Helping the Good Shepherd,* 114–118.

189. Myers-Shirk, 119.

190. Pastor Don Alexander, Community Prayer Service, First Christian Church, April 20, 1995, in *When the Angels Wept,* 35.

191. Osha Gray Davidson, *Broken Heartland: The Rise of America's Rural Ghetto* (Iowa City: University of Iowa Press, 1996).

192. According to Davidson, the poverty rate in rural ghettos was almost equal to that found in inner-city areas in the late 1980s and the 1990s. See Davidson, *Broken Heartland,* 8, 143.

193. Davidson, 81.

194. Davidson, 82.

195. Davidson, 82.

196. John Kifner, "The Gun Network: McVeigh's World—A Special Report," *New York Times,* July 5, 1995, https://timesmachine.nytimes.com/timesmachine/1995/07/05/709095.html?pageNumber=2.

For a comprehensive analysis of White nationalism and McVeigh's violence, see Kathleen Belew, *Bring the War Home: The White Power Movement and Paramilitary America* (Cambridge, MA: Harvard University Press, 2018), especially chap. 9, which specifically addresses the Oklahoma City bombing.

197. In fact, after the Oklahoma bombing, membership in the militia groups across the Midwest dropped precipitously. See Randy E. Barnett, "Guns, Militias and Oklahoma City," Georgetown Law Faculty Publications and Other Works, 1995, https://scholarship.law.georgetown.edu/facpub/1541.

198. Southern Poverty Law Center, *Terror from the Right: Plots, Conspiracies and Racist Rampages since Oklahoma City* (2012), https://www.splcenter.org/sites/default/files/d6_legacy_files/downloads/publication/terror_from_the_right_2012_web_0.pdf.

199. Hirschberg, "The Real of Edye-Icon."

200. See Nell Painter, "Hate Speech in Black and White," *Baltimore Sun,* May 8, 1995, http://articles.baltimoresun.com/1995-05-08/news/1995128168_1_muhammad-farrakhan-city-bombing.

201. Wilbert Tatum, "Claude Lewis Looking at America," *New York Amsterdam News,* May 31, 1997.

202. Author's note, in Jones, *Where Was God?,* xi.

203. Simon Stow, *American Mourning: Tragedy, Democracy and Resilience* (Cambridge: Cambridge University Press, 2017).

204. See Melanie Eversley, "Iconic Oklahoma City Photo Caused Twists and Turns," *USA Today,* April 18, 2015, https://www.usatoday.com/story/news/2015/04/18/oklahoma-city-photo/25957831/.

CHAPTER 5: GOD'S CELESTIAL ARMY

1.   Rev. Tim Woodroof, "Looking for a Christ-like Response," Otter Creek Church, Nashville, TN, September 16, 2001, http://timwoodroof.com/information/sermon-resources/we-can-be-heroes-sermons-preached-in-the-aftermath-of-911/looking-for-a-christ-like-response/.

2.   Rev. Tim Woodroof, "The Failure," Otter Creek Church, Nashville, TN, September 23, 2001, http://timwoodroof.com/information/sermon-resources/we-can-be-heroes-sermons-preached-in-the-aftermath-of-911/the-failure/.

3.   Rev. William Sloan Coffin, "A Lover's Quarrel with America," Old Dog Documentaries (released 2004), https://www.olddogdocumentaries.org/product/william-sloane-coffin-a-lovers-quarrel-with-america/.

4.   Rev. J. Ligon Duncan, "God's Purpose to Display His Mercy," First Presbyterian Church, Jackson, MS, September 23, 2001, https://www.fpcjackson.org/resource-library/sermons/god-s-purpose-to-display-his-mercy-against-the-backdrop-of-evil.

5.   "US ATTACKED: Hijacked Jets Destroy Twin Towers," *New York Times,* September 12, 2001, front page and A21.

6.   R. William Franklin and Mary Sudman Donovan, eds., *Will the Dust Praise You?: Spiritual Responses to 9/11* (New York: Church, 2003), 31–32.

7.   NPR special series, *Reflecting on Sept. 11, 2001,* "Slain Priest: Bury His Heart, but Not His Love," September 9, 2011, https://www.npr.org/2011/09/09/140293993/slain-priest-bury-his-heart-but-not-his-love.

8.   Serge Schemann, "President Vows to Exact Punishment for 'Evil,'" *New York Times,* September 12, 2002, https://www.nytimes.com/2001/09/12/us/us-attacked-president-vows-to-exact-punishment-for-evil.html.

9.   Bill Carter and Jim Rutenberg, "After the Attacks: Television," *New York Times,* September 15, 2001, https://www.nytimes.com/2001/09/15/us/after-the-attacks-television-viewers-again-return-to-traditional-networks.html.

10.   Rodney Buchanan, "Trusting in the Goodness of God," United Methodist Church, Howard, OH, September 23, 2001, https://www.sermoncentral.com/sermons/trusting-in-the-goodness-of-god-rodney-buchanan-sermon-on-god-s-provision-39550.

11.   Susan Baer and David L. Greene, "'Face of Terror Not True Faith of Islam,' Bush Declares," *Baltimore Sun,* September 18, 2001, https://www.baltimoresun.com/bal-te.bush18sep18-story.html.

12.   Anika Rahman, "Fear in the Open City," *New York Times,* September 19, 2001, https://www.nytimes.com/2001/09/19/opinion/fear-in-the-open-city.html.

13.   Jeffrey M. Jones, "The Impact of the Attacks on America," Gallup, September 25, 2001, https://news.gallup.com/poll/4894/impact-attacks-america.aspx.

14. Slavoj Žižek, *Welcome to the Desert of the Real! Five Essays on September 11 and Related Dates* (London: Verso Books, 2002), 16.

15. "Post 9/11 Attitudes," Pew Research Center: US Politics and Policy, December 6, 2001, https://www.pewresearch.org/politics/2001/12/06/post-september -11-attitudes/.

16. Jeremy E. Uecker, "Religious and Spiritual Responses to 9/11: Evidence from the Add Health Study," *Society and Spectator* 28 (5): 477–509.

17. Cornel West, "On the Niggerization of America," accessed in the summer of 2019, https://ce399resist.wordpress.com/2011/09/13/america-been-niggerized-since -911-cornell-west/.

18. Jeffrey Alexander, "Toward a Theory of Cultural Trauma," in *Cultural Trauma and Collective Identity*, ed. Jeffrey Alexander et al. (Berkeley: University of California Press, 2004), 1.

19. Rev. Marty Baker, "Understanding the Enemy," Stevens Creek Community Church, Augusta, GA, September 23, 2001, https://www.sermoncentral.com /sermons/understanding-the-enemy-marty-baker-sermon-on-satan-39597.

20. Rev. Russell Brownworth, "Just War or Another Act of Madness?," Cedar Lodge Baptist Church, Thomasville, NC, September 23, 2001, https://www .sermoncentral.com/sermons/just-war-or-just-another-act-of-madness-russell -brownworth-sermon-on-peace-39574.

21. President George W. Bush, "Address to the Nation on the Terrorist Attacks," September 11, 2001, American Presidency Project, http://www.presidency .ucsb.edu/ws/index.php?pid=58057.

22. Alvin Jackson, "How Can Everything Be All Right?," National City Christian Church, Washington, DC, September 16, 2001, in *Shaken Foundations: Sermons from America's Pulpits after the Terrorist Attacks*, ed. David Polk (St. Louis, MO: Chalice Press, 2001), 38.

23. Alexander, "Toward a Theory," 11.

24. Rev. Jack Warford, "911," Aletheia Christian Fellowship, Lake Elsinore, CA, September 16, 2001, https://www.sermoncentral.com/sermons/911-jack-warford -sermon-on-forgiveness-for-others-39189?ref=SermonSerps.

25. Leslie Trombly, "Day of Infamy," Angels of God, Bellevue, NE, September 16, 2001, https://www.sermoncentral.com/sermons/day-of-infamy-leslie-trombly-sermon -on-disappointment-39449?ref=SermonSerps.

26. President George W. Bush, "Islam Is Peace," Islamic Center, Washington, DC, September 17, 2001, https://georgewbush-whitehouse.archives.gov/news/releases /2001/09/20010917-11.html.

27. Bush, "Islam Is Peace."

28. Quoted in Gustav Niebuhr, "After the Attacks: A Day of Worship; Excerpts from Sermons across the Nation," *New York Times*, September 17, 2001, https://www .nytimes.com/2001/09/17/us/after-the-attacks-a-day-of-worship-excerpts-from -sermons-across-the-nation.html.

29. Hector Tobar, "FBI Draws Cheers with NJ Sweep," *Los Angeles Times*, September 16, 2001, http://articles.latimes.com/2001/sep/16/news/mn-46443.

30. John A. Huffman Jr., "Response to Crisis: A Biblical Perspective for Our National Tragedy," in *First Sunday: Spiritual Responses to the 9–11 Attacks,* ed. Donald Robert Elton and Aura Agudo Elton (self-published by Elton and Elton, 2011), 109–110.

31. Louis Farrakhan, "The Nation of Islam Responds to Attacks on America," press conference transcript, Mosque Maryam, Chicago, IL, September 16, 2001, https://www.noi.org/nation-of-islam-responds-911-attacks-on-america/.

32. Farrakhan, "The Nation of Islam Responds."

33. Farrakhan.

34. Farrakhan.

35. Farrakhan.

36. Farrakhan.

37. Charles Kurzman, "Islamic Statements against Terrorism," University of North Carolina, http://kurzman.unc.edu/islamic-statements-against-terrorism/.

38. See http://news.nationalgeographic.com/news/2001/09/0927_imampart1.html (page no longer available; aired on the National Geographic Channel on September 28, 2001) and https://www.youtube.com/watch?v=CkCvEgukWB0.

39. Rev. Timothy Peck, "Praying about Our National Crisis," Life Bible Fellowship Church, Upland, CA, September 16, 2001, https://www.sermoncentral.com/sermons /praying-about-our-national-crisis-timothy-peck-sermon-on-lord-s-prayer-39257.

40. Rev. Steven Shepherd, "Existing Evil, Exhausting Evil," First Christian Church, Jonesboro, AR, September 16, 2001, https://www.sermoncentral.com /sermons/existing-evil-exhausting-evil-steve-shepherd-sermon-on-war-61879.

41. Rev. Marty Baker, "Understanding the Enemy," Stevens Creek Community Church, Augusta, GA, September 23, 2001, https://www.sermoncentral.com /sermons/print?sermonId=39597.

42. Rev. Cooper Abrams III, "To Whom Are They Terrorists?," Calvary Baptist Church, Tremonton, UT, September 16, 2001, https://www.sermoncentral.com /sermons/to-whom-are-they-terrorists-cooper-abrams-iii-sermon-on-hardship-of -life-39393.

43. Rev. Ronald Keller, "Hope in Times of Disaster," Church of the Nazarene, Coraopolis, PA, September 16, 2001, https://www.sermoncentral.com/sermons/hope -in-times-of-disaster-ronald-keller-sermon-on-bible-truth-39575?ref=SermonSerps.

44. Rev. Paul Newell, "What Jesus Would Say to a Muslim," Church for Family (Baptist), Beaumont, CA, September 22, 2001, https://www.sermoncentral.com /sermons/what-jesus-would-say-to-a-muslim-paul-newell-sermon-on-evangelism -the-lost-39547.

45. Newell, "What Jesus Would Say to a Muslim."

46. Andrew Sullivan, "This Is a Religious War," *New York Times Magazine,* October 7, 2001, https://www.nytimes.com/2001/10/07/magazine/this-is-a-religious -war.html.

47. President George Bush, "Address to a Joint Session of Congress and the American People," United States Capitol, Washington, DC, September 20, 2001, https:// georgewbush-whitehouse.archives.gov/news/releases/2001/09/20010920-8.html.

48. Jerry Falwell, quoted in partial transcript from episode "You Helped This Happen," *700 Club,* September 13, 2001, http://www.beliefnet.com/faiths/christianity /2001/09/you-helped-this-happen.aspx.

49. Falwell, "You Helped This Happen."

50. Falwell.

51. Alison Mitchell and Katharine Q. Seelye, "A Day of Terror: Congress; Horror Knows No Party as Lawmakers Huddle," *New York Times,* September 12, 2001, https://www.nytimes.com/2001/09/12/us/a-day-of-terror-congress-horror-knows -no-party-as-lawmakers-huddle.html.

52. Mitchell and Seelye, "A Day of Terror."

53. See ABC News, special report, with Peter Jennings, minutes 3:15:57–3:16:23, https://www.youtube.com/watch?v=rIrvgnX753Y.

54. National Prayer Service, September 14, 2001, C-Span video, https://www.c -span.org/video/?166031-1/national-prayer-service (emphasis added).

55. Mary Sanders, "A Mighty Fortress Is Our Battle Hymn of the Republic: Episcopal Liturgy and American Civil Religion in the National Prayer Service on 14 September 2001," *Anglican and Episcopal History* 85, no. 1 (2016): 68.

56. National Prayer Service, https://www.c-span.org/video/?166031-1/national -prayer-service.

57. National Prayer Service.

58. National Prayer Service.

59. Andrew R. Murphy, *Prodigal Nation: Moral Decline and Divine Punishment from New England to 9/11* (New York: Oxford University Press, 2009).

60. National Prayer Service, https://www.c-span.org/video/?166031-1/national -prayer-service.

61. Franklin D. Roosevelt, First Inaugural Address, March 4, 1933, https://www .americanrhetoric.com/speeches/fdrfirstinaugural.html.

62. President George W. Bush, National Day of Prayer and Remembrance, September 13, 2001, https://www.presidency.ucsb.edu/documents/remarks-the-national-day-prayer-and-remembrance-service-0.

63. Bush, https://www.presidency.ucsb.edu/documents/remarks-the-national-day-prayer-and-remembrance-service-0.

64. President George W. Bush, National Day of Prayer and Remembrance, September 13, 2001, Washington National Cathedral, Washington, DC, https://www.c-span.org/video/?166031-1/national-prayer-service.

65. Rev. Jack Allen, "Sometimes the Roof Falls In," Cottonwood Church, Albuquerque, NM, September 16, 2001, https://www.sermoncentral.com/sermons/sometimes-the-roof-falls-in-jack-allen-sermon-on-death-39369?page=2&wc=800.

66. Nathan Baxter, "Finding What Is Lost," Washington National Cathedral, Washington, DC, September 16, 2001, in *Shaken Foundations*, 18.

67. David A. Shirey, "Looking through the Glass," Southport Christian Church, Indianapolis, IN, September 16, 2001, in *Shaken Foundations*, 96.

68. Interview with Osama bin Laden, *Frontline* (1998), in *September 11: Religious Perspectives on the Causes and Consequences*, ed. Ian Markham and Ibrahim Abu-Rabi (Oxford: One World, 2002), 149. For a full analysis of the conception of a cosmic battle and total war in both Islam and Christianity related to September 11, 2001, see Mark Juergensmeyer, *Terror in the Mind of God: The Global Rise of Religious Violence* (Berkeley: University of California Press, 2000); and Bruce Lincoln, *Holy Terrors: Thinking about Religion after 9/11* (Chicago: University of Chicago Press, 2002).

69. Rev. Scottie Pitts, "A Strong Reminder," Philadelphia United Methodist Church, Philadelphia, PA, September 14, 2001, https://www.sermoncentral.com/sermons/a-strong-reminder-scottie-pitts-sermon-on-god-the-father-39305; Allen, "Sometimes the Roof Falls In."

70. Luther Alexander Jr., "Been There; Done That," in *The Sunday after Tuesday: College Pulpits Respond to 9/11*, ed. William Willimon (Nashville: Abingdon Press, 2002), 28.

71. David Swensen, "Reflections on America's Tragedy," Winthrop Street Baptist Church, Taunton, MA, September 16, 2001, https://www.sermoncentral.com/sermons/reflections-on-america-s-tragedy-david-swensen-sermon-on-god-in-the-hardships-39391?ref=SermonSerps.

72. David Sylvester, "When Tragedy Hits Home," Today's Pulpit, Amarillo, TX, September 14, 2001, https://www.sermoncentral.com/contributors/david-sylvester-profile-6547?ref=SermonDetails.

73. Governor John Winthrop, "A Model of Christian Charity," 1630, https://www
.winthropsociety.com/doc_charity.php.

74. Congressional Record, January 10, 1961, vol. 107, Appendix, p. A169, quoted
in *Respectfully Quoted: Dictionary of Quotations*, https://www.bartleby.com/73
/1611.html. For full exploration of this metaphor and concept, see Daniel Rod-
gers, *As a City on a Hill: The Story of America's Most Famous Lay Sermon* (Princeton,
NJ: Princeton University Press, 2018); and Abram van Engen, *City on a Hill: A History of American Exceptionalism* (New Haven, CT: Yale University Press, 2020).

75. Quoted in Kimberly Winston, "From Theological Tenet to Political Password,"
BeliefNet, February 2002, https://www.beliefnet.com/news/politics/2004/02/from
-theological-tenet-to-political-password.aspx.

76. President George W. Bush, "Address to the Nation," September 11, 2001,
http://archive.boston.com/news/packages/underattack/globe_stories/0912/_Today
_our_very_freedom_came_under_attack_+.shtml.

77. Rev. Harold Dixon, "America under Attack—A Christian Response," Calvary
Baptist Church, Waldorf, MD, September 12, 2001, https://www.sermoncentral
.com/sermons/america-under-attack-a-christian-response-harold-dixon-sermon
-on-forgiveness-general-39238?ref=SermonSerps.

78. Rev. Ed Blonski, "America under Attack: Our Response," Lutheran, Beaver
Dam, WI (no church given), https://www.sermoncentral.com/sermons/america
-under-attack-our-reponse-ed-blonski-sermon-on-endurance-39629.

79. Rev. Mark Henderson, "For the Living of These Days," Federated Church of
Sandwich, Center Sandwich, NH, September 16, 2001, http://www.textweek.com
/response/for_the_living_of_these_days.htm.

80. Rev. Keith Grogg, "Hope amid the Ruins," Carolina Beach Presbyterian
Church, Carolina Beach, NC, September 16, 2001, in *First Sunday,* 90.

81. Rev. Jon Gunneman, "Naming the Terror: The Human Heart and the Spirit of
God," *Christian Century,* September 26, 2001, 4–5.

82. Rev. Andrew Chan, "A Response to the Carnage and Human Suffering," Richmond Chinese Evangelical Free Church, Richmond, VA, September 16, 2001,
https://www.sermoncentral.com/sermons/a-response-to-the-carnage-and-human
-suffering-andrew-chan-sermon-on-forgiveness-general-39191?ref=SermonSerps.

83. Rev. Kenneth Sauer, "God Is Bigger Than Any Terrorist," Parkview United
Methodist Church, Newport News, VA, September 16, 2001, https://www
.sermoncentral.com/sermons/god-is-bigger-than-any-terrorist-kenneth-sauer
-sermon-on-jesus-teachings-39244?ref=SermonSerps.

84. Rev. Jeremiah A. Wright Jr., "The Day of Jerusalem's Fall," Trinity United
Church of Christ, Chicago, IL, September 16, 2001, in *09.11.01: African American*

Leaders Respond to an American Tragedy, ed. Martha Simmons and Frank A. Thomas (Valley Forge, PA: Judson Press, 2001), 83.

85. Pablo A. Jimenez, "Elusive Honor," La Hermosa Christian Church, New York, NY, October 14, 2001, in *Shaken Foundations,* 108.

86. Jimenez, "Elusive Honor."

87. While a full biblical exegesis is beyond the scope of this chapter, it is noteworthy that even though God forgives Cain, He also marks him. There is something quite profound being enacted in this story about the relation between forgiveness and memory. Although God forgives Cain, the mark ensures that neither God nor Cain will forget what Cain had done.

88. Rev. Jason Lancaster, "Spiritual View of the 911 Attacking of America," Christian and Missionary Alliance Church, Santa Monica, CA, September 16, 2001, https://www.sermoncentral.com/sermons/spiritual-view-of-the-911-attacking -of-america-jason-lancaster-sermon-on-god-in-the-hardships-39192?page=3&wc =800.

89. Rev. Paul Newell, "When Tragedy Strikes—God Answers," Church for Family, Beaumont, CA, September 23, 2001, https://www.sermoncentral.com /sermons/when-tragedy-strikes-god-answers-paul-newell-sermon-on-what-is -evangelism-39523.

90. Baxter, "Finding What Is Lost"; Rev. Tim Dearborn, "Will Life Ever Be the Same Again? Reflections on John 2," Seattle Pacific University, in *The Sunday after Tuesday,* 67.

91. Peter J. Gomes, "Outer Turmoil, Inner Strength," Memorial Church, Harvard University, in *The Sunday after Tuesday,* 95. It is noteworthy that a year later, many religious leaders argued that September 11, 2001, was not about God. See *Frontline,* "Faith and Doubt at Ground Zero," September 3, 2002, https://www.pbs.org/wgbh /pages/frontline/shows/faith/.

92. See John Rawls, *Political Liberalism* (New York: Columbia University Press, 1993).

93. Charles Booth, "What's Going On?," Mount Olivet Baptist Church, Columbus, OH, September 16, 2001, in *African American Leaders Respond,* 48.

94. Rev. Dr. Daniel P. Matthews, Sunday Sermon, September 16, 2001, in *Will the Dust Praise You?,* xv.

95. Rev. Scott W. Alexander, "What Is on Our Hearts Today," River Road Unitarian Church, Bethesda, MD, September 16, 2001, in *Will the Dust Praise You?,* 29.

96. Rev. Delores Carpenter, "Alert When He Comes," Michigan Park Christian Church, Washington, DC, September 16, 2001, in *African American Leaders Respond,* 58–66.

97. Barbara Carlson, "Deliver Us from Evil," Unitarian Universalist Church, Bloomington, IN, in *The Sunday after Tuesday,* 62.

98. Rev. Andrew Chan, "Questions We Have for God in the Attack on America," Richmond Chinese Evangelical Free Church, Richmond, VA, September 14, 2001, https://www.sermoncentral.com/sermons/questions-we-have-for-god-in-the -attack-on-america-andrew-chan-sermon-on-god-in-the-hardships-39307?ref =SermonSerps.

99. Wendy Brown, *States of Injury: Power and Freedom in Late Modernity* (Princeton, NJ: Princeton University Press, 1995).

100. Rev. Jon M. Walton, "How in God's Name?," First Presbyterian Church, New York, NY, September 16, 2001, in *Shaken Foundations,* 90. Each of the people named in this sermon was eventually confirmed dead. See also Rev. Rick Gillespie-Mobley, "And Where Was God," Greenville New Life Community Church, Cleveland, OH, September 16, 2001, https://www.sermoncentral.com/sermons /and-where-was-god-rick-gillespie-mobley-sermon-on-god-in-the-hardships -39302?ref=SermonSerps.

101. Rev. Jack Warford, "Easing Back into Business as Usual," Aletheia Christian Fellowship, Lake Elsinore, CA, September 23, 2001, https://www.sermoncentral .com/contributors/jack-warford-profile-63107?ref=SermonDetails.

102. Rev. Joel Curry, "Christ Jesus Our Hope as We Face National Tragedy," Oak Park Evangelical Free Church, Warsaw, IN, September 16, 2001, https://www .sermoncentral.com/sermons/christ-jesus-our-hope-as-we-face-national-tragedy -joel-curry-sermon-on-god-brings-hope-39377?ref=SermonSerps.

103. Jesse Louis Jackson Sr., "No Test, No Testimony," September 16, 2001, in *African American Leaders Respond,* 107.

104. For one example, see David L. Eng and David Kazanjian, eds., *Loss: The Politics of Mourning* (Berkeley: University of California Press, 2002).

105. Rev. David Washburn, "In the Grips of Crisis," Chestnut Grove Baptist Church, Earlysville, VA, September 16, 2001, https://www.sermoncentral.com /sermons/in-the-grips-of-crisis-david-washburn-sermon-on-death-39402.

106. Judith Butler, *Precarious Life: The Powers of Mourning and Violence* (New York: Verso Books, 2004), 24.

107. Rev. Dr. Ray Pritchard, "Living by Faith in an Uncertain World," Calvary Memorial Church, Oak Park, IL, September 16, 2001, https://www.keepbelieving .com/sermon/2001-09-16-Living-by-Faith-in-an-Uncertain-World.

108. Baxter, "Finding What Is Lost," 15 (emphasis added).

109. Jackson, "How Can Everything Be All Right?," 38 (emphasis added).

110. Rev. Mike Maggard, "Dealing with Disaster," Crossroads Community Church, Naples, FL, September 16, 2001, https://www.sermoncentral.com/sermons /dealing-with-disaster-mike-maggard-sermon-on-disappointment-39269.

111. Bonnie Rosborough, "What Is Broken, Matters," Broadway United Church of Christ, New York, NY, September 16, 2001, in *Shaken Foundations,* 76.

112. William McDonald, "As It Was in the Beginning," Tennessee Wesleyan College, Athens, TN, in *The Sunday after Tuesday,* 136.

113. Rev. Timothy Carson, "The Shaking of the Foundations," Webster Groves Christian Church, St. Louis, MO, September 16, 2001, in *Shaken Foundations,* 85.

114. McDonald, "As It Was in the Beginning," 136.

115. Rev. George Antonakos, "God, Don't You Care?," Central Presbyterian Church, Baltimore, MD, September 16, 2001, in *First Sunday,* 33.

116. Community Prayer Service at Lakeville High School, Cortland Trinity Baptist Church, Cortland, OH, September 12, 2001, https://www.sermoncentral.com /sermons/america-s-response-to-terrorism-daniel-barker-sermon-on-anger-42051 (emphasis added).

117. Rev. Davidson Loehr, "Responding to the Violence of 9/11," First Unitarian Universalist Church, Austin, TX, September 16, 2001, https://www.uua.org /worship/words/sermon/responding-violence-september-11th.

118. See Jack Santino, ed., *Spontaneous Shrines and the Public Memorialization of Death* (New York: Palgrave Press, 2006).

119. Rev. Cain Hope Felder, "An African American Pastoral on Recent Acts of Terrorism in America" (no location given), September 27, 2001, in *African American Leaders Respond,* 18.

120. Rev. John Piper, "A Service of Sorrow, Self-Humbling and the Steady Hope in our Savior and King, Jesus Christ," Bethlehem Baptist Church, Minneapolis, MN, September 16, 2001, https://www.desiringgod.org/messages/a-service-of -sorrow-self-humbling-and-steady-hope-in-our-savior-and-king-jesus-christ.

121. Rev. Darrell Brazell, "In This Time of Crisis," Wheatland Church of Christ, Lawrence, KS, September 16, 2001, in *The Sunday after Tuesday,* 43.

122. Rev. Jimmy Davis, "Amid Uncertainty, God Is Our Strength," Bayview Baptist Church, Columbia, SC, September 16, 2001, https://www.sermoncentral.com /sermons/amid-uncertainty-god-is-our-strength-jimmy-davis-sermon-on -endurance-39149?ref=AllSermonPrep.

123. Piper, "A Service of Sorrow."

124. Rev. Dr. James A. Forbes Jr., "A Sermon from 9/16/01: Is There Any Word from the Lord?," Riverside Church, New York, NY, September 16, 2001, https://www

.huffingtonpost.com/rev-dr-james-a-forbes-jr/sermon-911-is-there-any-word
-from-the-lord_b_956107.html.

125. Yet Rev. Wright finally shows how in the last line of this same psalm in which babies are dashed against rocks there is a referendum against violence and the way hatred begets hatred.

126. Arthur Caliandro, "To Mourn, Reflect and Hope," Marble Collegiate Church, New York, NY, September 16, 2001, in *Shaken Foundations*, 45.

127. Walton, "How in God's Name?," 91.

128. Iranian immigrant quoted in Margaret Yocum's "'We'll Watch Out for Liza and the Kids': Spontaneous Memorials and Personal Response at the Pentagon, 2001," in *Spontaneous Shrines*, 78.

129. Yocum, "'We'll Watch Out for Liza and the Kids,'" 77–78.

130. Rev. T. D. Jakes, "The Gathering of America," Potter's House, Dallas, TX, September 16, 2001, in *African American Leaders Respond*, 22.

131. Harriet Senie, "Mourning in Protest: Spontaneous Memorials and the Sacralization of Public Space," in *Spontaneous Shrines*, 50.

132. "Interpreting the Last Column Stories: The Stories behind the Markings," 9/11 Memorial and Museum blog, May 17, 2017, https://www.911memorial.org/blog/interpreting-last-column-stories-behind-markings.

133. Rosborough, "What Is Broken, Matters."

134. It is noteworthy that Americans seem to demand that "death not be in vain" primarily when the loss is significant or emotionally powerful in some way, or both. Americans demand that the death not be in vain when the young die, particularly in accidents or illness, or when there are a large number of deaths from a random cause. Americans do not traditionally demand, in contrast, that the death of the elderly not be in vain.

135. George Mosse, *Fallen Soldiers: Reshaping the Memory of the World Wars* (Oxford: Oxford University Press, 1991).

136. Heidi Neumark, "Beautiful Feet," University of Chicago, Rockefeller Chapel, October 6, 2001, in *Shaken Foundations*, 34.

137. Thomas J. Reese, SJ, "The Mystery of Grace," St. Ignatius Loyola Church, New York, NY, September 16, 2001, in *Shaken Foundations*, 112.

138. Jesse Jackson Sr., "No Test, No Testimony," September 16, 2001, in *African American Leaders Respond*, 105.

139. Dave Ball, "Our Challenge Now," Denison University, Granville, OH, in *The Sunday after Tuesday*, 30.

140. Ball, "Our Challenge Now," 31.

141. Bush, "Address to the Nation on the Terrorist Attacks."

142. Calvin Butts, "Manage Your Fear," September 16, 2001, Abyssinian Baptist Church, Harlem, NY, in *African American Leaders Respond,* 99.

143. Carson, "The Shaking of the Foundations," 83.

144. Shepherd, "Existing Evil, Exhausting Evil."

145. A powerful counter was Barbara K. Lundblad's "Fragments," Union Theological Seminary, New York, NY, September 13, 2001, in *Shaken Foundations,* 22.

146. President George W. Bush, "President Bush's Remarks on September 11, 2002," https://www.cnn.com/2002/US/09/11/ar911.bush.speech.transcript/index.html.

147. Rev. Peter Baumgartle, "Just War," First Capital Christian Church, Corydon, IN, September 16, 2001, https://www.sermoncentral.com/sermons/just-war-peter -baumgartle-sermon-on-hardship-of-life-39474.

148. Wikipedia, s.v. "Pat Tillman," accessed in the summer of 2019, http://en .wikipedia.org/wiki/Pat_Tillman.

149. Rev. Mike Maggard, "Dealing with Disaster," Crossroads Community Church, Naples, FL, September 16, 2001, https://www.sermoncentral.com/sermons /dealing-with-disaster-mike-maggard-sermon-on-disappointment-39269?ref =SermonSerps.

150. Rev. Harry Wood, "What Shall America Do?," Lamb Worship Assembly, Germanton, NC, September 16, 2001, https://www.sermoncentral.com/sermons /what-shall-america-do-harry-wood-sermon-on-truth-43660?ref=SermonSerps.

151. Rev. Vashit Murphy McKenzie, "It's Time to Move Forward" (no location given), September 16, 2001, in *African American Leaders Respond,* 127–128.

152. Jakes, "The Gathering of America," 26.

153. Dearborn, "Will Life Ever Be the Same Again?," 69.

154. "A Pastoral Message: Living with Faith and Hope after September 11," US Conference of Catholic Bishops, November 14, 2001, http://www.usccb.org /issues-and-action/human-life-and-dignity/september-11/a-pastoral-message -living-with-faith-and-hope-after-september-11.cfm.

155. Rev. Darrell Brazell, "Why Did This Happen?," Wheatland Church of Christ, Lawrence, KS, in *The Sunday after Tuesday,* 40.

156. Allen, "Sometimes the Roof Falls In."

157. Walter Thomas, "That's Enough," New Psalmist Baptist Church, Baltimore, MD, September 16, 2001, in *African American Leaders Respond,* 45.

158. Tony Campolo, "The Best of Times, the Worst of Times," Eastern University Chapel, St. Davids, PA, in *The Sunday after Tuesday,* 59.

159. Michael Budde, "Putting Away Childish Things," sermon given as DePaul University chaplain, Chicago, IL, in *The Sunday after Tuesday*, 49.

160. Rev. Mike Hays, "The Source of My Hope," Britton Christian Church, Oklahoma City, OK, September 26, 2001, https://www.sermoncentral.com/sermons/the-source-of-my-hope-mike-hays-sermon-on-god-s-sovereign-will-39711?ref=SermonSerps.

161. Uecker, "Religious and Spiritual Responses to 9/11."

162. Rev. Gail E. Bowman, "After the Cistern," Dillard University, New Orleans, LA, September 14, 2001, in *African American Leaders Respond*, 6.

163. Bowman, "After the Cistern," 10.

164. Wright, "The Day of Jerusalem's Fall," 87.

165. Rev. Dr. Michael Eric Dyson, "What Have I Left?," September 16, 2001, in *African American Leaders Respond*, 73.

166. Butts, "Manage Your Fear," 100.

167. Booth, "What's Going On?," 57.

168. Felder, "An African American Pastoral," 17.

169. Rev. Gardner C. Taylor, "Reconciliation: Beyond Retaliation," Concord Baptist Church, Brooklyn, NY, September 18, 2001, in *African American Leaders Respond*, 36.

170. Booth, "What's Going On?," 49.

171. Benedict Anderson, quoted in Avishai Margalit's *Ethics of Memory* (Cambridge, MA: Harvard University Press, 2002), 25.

172. In 1999, the Pentagon announced that because of the scientific advances of DNA screening, henceforth no new remains would be added to the Tomb. This was in part the result of an embarrassing episode in which the identity of a soldier of the Vietnam War was discovered and his remains had to be removed from the Tomb.

173. Paul Ricoeur, *Memory, History, Forgetting*, trans. Kathleen Blamey and David Pellauer (Chicago: University of Chicago Press, 2004).

174. With the development of DNA forensics, it is increasingly unlikely that any remains are forever unknown. In fact, there are no remains in the Tomb of the Unknown Soldier for the Vietnam War. The last remains were identified and returned to the family in the late 1990s. Some of the survivors of 9/11 have complained that there is no equivalent Tomb of the Unknowns for Ground Zero. As of 2018, eleven hundred remains from the site are still unidentified. Those remains are in a repository alongside the 9/11 museum. Yet, as one mother noted, "Keeping remains at the repository is painful and insulting. . . . The room has no sanctity, no religiosity, no atmosphere or respect like an interfaith chapel would." Jon Schuppe, "Still

Missing: Unidentified Remains Leave a Lingering Void for 9/11 Families," NBC News, September 5, 2016, https://www.nbcnews.com/storyline/9-11-anniversary /still-missing-unidentified-remains-leave-lingering-void-9-11-families-n642076.

175. Shirey, "Looking through the Glass," 96.

176. Rev. Steve Malone, "In God We Trust," Southeast Christian Church, Orlando, FL, September 16, 2001, https://www.sermoncentral.com/sermons/in-god-we-trust -steve-malone-sermon-on-god-in-the-hardships-39422?ref=SermonSerps.

177. Rev. Christopher J. McMahon, "A Day That Changed the World," United States Merchant Marine Academy, Unitarian Universalist Congregation, South Fork, NY, September 16, 2001, https://www.uua.org/sites/live-new.uua.org/files /documents/mcmahonchristopher/changed_world.pdf.

178. Dearborn, "Will Life Ever Be the Same Again?," 69.

179. Rev. M. Craig Barnes, "Response to Crisis: Under Attack; Under God," National Presbyterian Church, Washington, DC, September 16, 2001, in *First Sunday*, 64.

180. Nancy A. De Vries, "Your Glory, O Israel, Lies Slain on the High Places," Colgate University Church, Hamilton, NY, in *The Sunday after Tuesday*, 72.

181. Margalit, *Ethics of Memory*, 51.

182. Shirey, "Looking through the Glass," 99.

183. Rev. Ronald Keller, "When Hearts and Faces Are Sad," Church of the Nazarene, Moon Township, PA, September 23, 2001, https://www.sermoncentral.com /sermons/when-hearts-and-faces-are-sad-ronald-keller-sermon-on-human-body -39718?ref=SermonSerps.

184. William Willimon, introduction to *The Sunday after Tuesday*, 14.

185. Ricoeur, *Memory, History, Forgetting*, 54.

CHAPTER 6: THE ENDURING AMERICAN CRISIS

1. Leaders and staff of Christianity Today, *Preaching in Moments of Crisis* (n.p.: Christianity Today, 2015), https://www.bclstore.com/products/preaching -in-moments-crisis.

2. Keeanga-Yamahtta Taylor, *From #BlackLivesMatter to Black Liberation* (Chicago: Haymarket Press, 2016), 15.

3. William T. Cavanaugh, *Theopolitical Imagination: Discovering the Liturgy as a Political Act in an Age of Global Consumerism* (London: Bloomsbury Press, 2002); Michael Hardt, "The Withering of Civil Society," *Social Text* 45 (Winter 1995): 27–44.

4. Wendy Brown, *Undoing the Demos: Neoliberalism's Stealth Revolution* (New York: Zone Books, 2015); and Michael Hardt, "The Withering of Civil Society," *Social Text* 45 (Winter 1995): 27–44.

5. President Obama Speaks on the Shooting in Connecticut, December 14, 2012, https://obamawhitehouse.archives.gov/blog/2012/12/14/president-obama-speaks -shooting-connecticut.

6. President Obama at Sandy Hook Prayer Vigil, December 16, 2012, NPR transcript, https://www.npr.org/2012/12/16/167412995/transcript-president-obama-at -sandy-hook-prayer-vigil.

7. President Obama at Sandy Hook Prayer Vigil

8. President Obama at Sandy Hook Prayer Vigil.

9. President Obama at Sandy Hook Prayer Vigil.

10. Rev. Shannon Daley Harris, "God's Call to Seek Change, Not Comfort, to Keep Our Children Safe," *Huffington Post,* December 21, 2012 (updated February 20, 2013), http://www.huffingtonpost.com/rev-shannon-daleyharris/gods-call -is-to-seek-change-not-comfort-to-keep-our-children-safe_b_2347333.html (emphasis added).

11. Andy Stanley, "Did Andy Stanley Really Mean Obama Is Pastor in Chief?," interview by Mark Galli, *Christianity Today,* January 25, 2013, https://www .christianitytoday.com/ct/2013/january-web-only/andy-stanley-obama-inauguration -pastor-in-chief.html.

12. See, for example, George Condon, "President Obama: Mourner in Chief," *The Atlantic,* May 22, 2013, https://www.theatlantic.com/politics/archive/2013/05 /president-obama-mourner-in-chief/443001/; Tom Ehrich, "President Obama: Mourner in Chief," *Washington Post,* April 30, 2013, https://www.washingtonpost .com/national/on-faith/president-obama-mourner-in-chief/2013/04/30/3f89e656 -b1a5-11e2-9fb1-62de9581c946_story.html; Mark Mardell, "America's Mourner in Chief," BBC News, April 13, 2013, https://www.bbc.com/news/world-us-canada -22210030.

13. Michel Foucault, "Omnes et Singulatim: Towards a Criticism of 'Political Reason'" (The Tanner Lectures on Human Values, delivered at Stanford University, October 10 and 16, 1979), 229, https://tannerlectures.utah.edu/_documents/a -to-z/f/foucault81.pdf.

14. Foucault, "Omnes et Singulatim," 236.

15. L. Carol Ritchie, "Three White House Aides to Attend Michael Brown's Funeral Service," NPR, August 24, 2014, https://www.npr.org/sections/thetwo-way /2014/08/24/342868844/3-white-house-aides-to-attend-michael-browns-funeral -service.

16. David Martosko, "White House Sent Three Officials to Michael Brown Funeral but ZERO to James Foley Memorial Service," Dailymail.com, August 26, 2014, https://www.dailymail.co.uk/news/article-2734029/White-House-sends-three -officials-Michael-Brown-funeral-ZERO-James-Foley-memorial-service.html.

17. David McIvor, "Bringing Ourselves to Grief: Judith Butler and the Politics of Mourning," *Political Theory* 40, no. 4 (2012): 409–436.

18. Governor Mike Huckabee, Fox News, December 14, 2012, https://www .youtube.com/watch?v=PtRM1LCCbTk.

19. Rev. Dr. C. Welton Gaddy, president, Interfaith Alliance, Northminster Baptist Church, Monroe, LA, "An Open Letter to Mike Huckabee," *Huffington Post*, December 18, 2012 (updated February 17, 2013), http://www.huffingtonpost.com/rev -dr-c-welton-gaddy/an-open-letter-to-mike-huckabee_b_2323040.html (emphasis in original).

20. Gaddy, "An Open Letter to Mike Huckabee."

21. See also Martin E. Marty's multivolume history, *Modern American Religion* (Chicago: University of Chicago Press, 1987); and Gary Dorrien's multivolume history, *The Making of American Liberal Theology* (Louisville, KY: Westminster John Knox Press, 2006).

22. Rev. Shannan R. Vince Ocampo, "Advent 3: A Newtown Shooting Sermon," Watchung Avenue Presbyterian Church, North Plainfield, NJ, in *A Good Word: Sermons, Prayers and Liturgies in Response to the Shooting at Sandy Hook Elementary, Newtown, CT on December 12, 2012*, 233, https://fpcma.files.wordpress.com/2012/12 /a-good-word.pdf.

23. Rev. Matthew Crebbin, Newtown High School Vigil, December 16, 2016, https://www.c-span.org/video/?309977-1/president-obama-newtown-connecticut -prayer-vigil.

24. Jason Graves, director of Youth Affairs and Muadh Bhavnagarwala, Student Al Hedaya Islamic Center, "December 16th 2012 Statement at Newtown High School Vigil with President Obama," press release, http://www.hedayacenter.org /press-release-4.

25. Rev. Jim Solomon, Newtown High School Vigil, December 16, 2016, https://www.c-span.org/video/?309977-1/president-obama-newtown-connecticut -prayer-vigil.

26. Rev. Jane Sibley, Newtown High School Vigil, December 16, 2016, https://www .c-span.org/video/?309977-1/president-obama-newtown-connecticut-prayer-vigil.

27. Father Seth Brooker, St. Luke's Anglican Church, East Aurora, NY, December 16, 2012, https://www.facebook.com/notes/east-aurora-advertiser/sermon -on-newtown-conn-shooting/501763243177741.

28. Rev. Dr. Jim Nelson, "Will the Sun Ever Rise Again?," Neighborhood Unitarian Universalist Church, Pasadena, CA, December 17, 2012, http://www.ocregister.com/articles/shooting-380872-world-school.html.

29. Rev. Christian Wallace, "The Passion of Job," The People's Ministry, Baptist, Memphis, TN, December 17, 2012, https://www.sermoncentral.com/sermons/the-passion-of-job-christian-wallace-sermon-on-justice-172044.

30. Rev. Max Locado, "A Christmas Prayer," *Huffington Post,* December 14, 2012, https://www.huffpost.com/entry/a-christmas-prayer_2_b_2302548.

31. Rev. Jim Butcher, "The Part of the Christmas Story That Speaks to the Sandy Hook Tragedy," Madison Baptist Church, Madison, WV, December 18, 2012, https://www.sermoncentral.com/sermons/the-part-of-the-christmas-story-that-speaks-to-sandy-hook-tragedy-jim-butcher-sermon-on-christmas-172058.

32. Butcher, "The Part of the Christmas Story."

33. Rev. Emily Heath, "When Joy Feels Impossible: An Advent Sermon for Those Who Mourn for Newtown," United Church of Christ, Congregational Church, Exeter, NH, December 16, 2012, https://emilycheath.com/2012/12/16/when-joy-feels-impossible-an-advent-sermon-for-those-who-mourn-for-newtown/.

34. Bill Moyers, "Remember the Victims, Reject the Violence," *Huffington Post,* December 21, 2012, https://www.huffpost.com/entry/watch-remember-the-victim_b_2341949.

35. Vince Ocampo, "Advent 3," 233.

36. Nelson, "Will the Sun Ever Rise Again?"

37. Rabbi Jennifer Krause, "Brothers in Arms; Isaac, Ishmael, and Sandy Hook," 92nd Street Y, Manhattan, NY, *Huffington Post,* December 20, 2012 (updated February 19, 2012), http://www.huffingtonpost.com/rabbi-jennifer-krause/brothers-in-arms-isaac-ishmael-and-sandy-hook_b_2333587.html.

38. Rev. Marci Glass, "Joy to the World," Southminster Presbyterian Church, Boise, ID, December 16, 2012, https://marciglass.com/2012/12/16/joy-to-the-world/.

39. Pastor Rob Brendie, Denver United Church, Evangelical, Denver, CO, quoted in Dan Gilgoff and Eric Marrapodi, "Massacre of Children Leaves Many Asking, 'Where's God?,'" *CNN Belief Blog,* December 14, 2012, http://religion.blogs.cnn.com/2012/12/14/massacre-of-children-leaves-many-asking-wheres-god/.

40. Rev. Gary Hall, dean of Washington National Cathedral, "Enough Is Enough," December 16, 2012, http://www.livingchurch.org/enough-is-enough.

41. Rev. James A. Forbes Jr. (retired), "For the Healing of Newtown," Riverside Church, New York, NY, January 20, 2013, extracted in "Minister: Newtown Needs MLK's Words of Hope," CBS News, January 21, 2013, http://www.cbsnews.com/news/minister-newtown-needs-mlks-words-of-hope/.

42. Rev. Peg Nowling Williams, Intentional Interim Minister, Community United Church of Christ, Baptist, Raleigh, NC, "Darkness Doesn't Win," *Huffington Post*, December 20, 2012 (updated February 20, 2013), http://www.huffingtonpost .com/rev-peg-nowling-williams/darkness-doesnt-win_b_2346519.html.

43. Nowling Williams, "Darkness Doesn't Win" (emphasis in original).

44. Father Michael Dolan, Church of Saint Ann, Avon, CT, interview by Kenneth Gosselin in "Sermons: Out of Darkness," *Hartford Courant*, December 23, 2012, https://www.courant.com/news/connecticut/newtown-sandy-hook-school-shooting /hc-christmas-message-newtown-shootings-20121223-story.html.

45. Rev. Geordie Campbell, First Church of Christ Congregational, West Hartford, CT, interview by Kenneth Gosselin in "Sermons: Out of Darkness."

46. Pastor Rob Morris, Christ the King Lutheran Church, Newtown, CT, interview by Kenneth Gosselin in "Sermons: Out of Darkness."

47. Pastor Pete Vecchi, "Follow Up: The Sermons after the Connecticut Shootings," NazNet, http://www.naznet.com/community/showthread.php/10561-Follow -up-The-Sermons-After-the-Connecticut-Shootings?s=0f24cd87f8aa520a0e5c01e 001fc170e (webpage no longer available).

48. Jessica Guynn, "Meet the Woman Who Coined #BlackLivesMatter," *USA Today*, March 4, 2015, http://www.usatoday.com/story/tech/2015/03/04/alicia-garza -black-lives-matter/24341593/.

49. President Barack Obama, "Remarks by the President on Trayvon Martin," July 19, 2013, White House, Office of the Press Secretary, https://www.whitehouse .gov/the-press-office/2013/07/19/remarks-president-trayvon-martin.

50. Obama, "Remarks by the President on Trayvon Martin."

51. Nick Summers, "Fox News Coverage of the Trayvon Martin Case Criticized," *Daily Beast*, March 21, 2012, http://www.thedailybeast.com/articles/2012/03/20/fox -news-coverage-of-the-trayvon-martin-case-criticized.html.

52. "Wide Racial, Partisan Gaps in Reactions to Trayvon Martin Coverage," Pew Research Center: US Politics and Policy, April 3, 2012, https://www.people -press.org/2012/04/03/wide-racial-partisan-gaps-in-reactions-to-trayvon-martin -coverage/#too-much-coverage.

53. President Obama in the Rose Garden, March 23, 2012, https://obamawhitehouse .archives.gov/blog/2013/07/19/president-obama-trayvon-martin-could-have -been-me.

54. Jeffrey Weiss, "White Churches Uncommonly Quiet after Zimmerman Verdict," *CNN Belief Blog*, July 20, 2013, http://religion.blogs.cnn.com/2013/07/20/on -zimmerman-verdict-a-loud-silence-from-white-churches/; Troy Jackson, "Silence Is Golden: The White Church and Race in America," *Sojourners*, July 22, 2013,

https://sojo.net/articles/remembering-trayvon/silence-golden-white-church-and
-race-america.

55. See Rev. Jose Humphreys, "An Invitation to Disruption: Call to White
Churches," *Patheos*, August 19, 2014, http://www.patheos.com/blogs/rhetoricraceand
religion/2014/08/an-invitation-to-disruption-a-call-to-white-churches.html.

56. Rev. Fred Luter, Franklin Avenue Baptist Church, New Orleans, LA, quoted
in Weiss, "White Churches Uncommonly Quiet."

57. Kathy Gilbert, "Reflections on What the Trayvon Martin Case Means for
Christians," Pacific Northwest Conference, July 15, 2013, https://www.pnwumc.org
/news/reflections-on-what-trayvon-martin-case-means-for-christians/.

58. Rev. Steven G. Thompson, "I'm George Zimmerman," Leonard Baptist Church,
St. Louis, MO (preaching date not given), posted August 3, 2013, https://www
.sermoncentral.com/sermons/i-m-george-zimmerman-steven-g-thompson
-sermon-on-judging-others-177977.

59. Rev. Dr. James David Manning, ATLAH World Missionary Church, New
York, NY, quoted in Jason Howerton, "Lightning Rod NYC Pastor's Stunningly
Confrontational Sermon on Trayvon Martin: 'You See the World through Your
Black Eyes,'" *TheBlaze*, July 17, 2013, https://www.theblaze.com/news/2013/07/18
/lightning-rod-nyc-pastors-stunningly-confrontational-sermon-on-trayvon
-martin-you-see-the-world-through-your-black-eyes.

60. Russell Moore, quoted in Michelle Boorstein, "Zimmerman Was 'Wrong,'
Says Southern Baptist Convention Official," *Washington Post*, July 16, 2013,
https://www.washingtonpost.com/national/on-faith/zimmerman-was-wrong
-says-southern-baptist-convention-official/2013/07/16/2002f144-ee39-11e2-bed3
-b9b6fe264871_story.html.

61. Rev. Jacqueline Lewis, untitled sermon, Middle Collegiate Church, New
York, NY, quoted in Rev. Paul Brandeis Raushenbush, "Trayvon Martin 'Not
Guilty' Verdict Sparks Hoodie Sunday at Black Churches," *Huffington Post*,
July 14, 2013, https://www.huffpost.com/entry/trayvon-martin-hoodie-sunday
_n_3594302.

62. Rev. Roosevelt Wright, "Iced Tea and Skittles," New Tabernacle Baptist
Church, Monroe, LA, March 2012, http://www.sermoncentral.com/sermons/ice
-tea-and-skittles-roosevelt-wright-sermon-on-justice-165610.asp.

63. Rev. Dr. Gale Ragan-Reid, "Trying Times: When We Started," True Fellowship Church, Camilla, GA, July 2013, http://www.sermoncentral.com/sermon-series
/trying-times-sermon-series-by-dr-gale-a-ragan-reid-95620-540.asp.

64. Rev. Tony Lee, "Where Do We Go from Here?," Community of Hope, AME
Church, Temple Hills, MD, July 13, 2013, quoted in Raushenbush, "Trayvon
Martin 'Not Guilty' Verdict Sparks Hoodie Sunday."

65. Rev. Raphael Warnock, untitled sermon, Ebenezer Baptist Church, Atlanta, GA, March 25, 2012, excerpted in Associated Press, "Churches Express Pain, Ask for Justice in Trayvon Martin Case," *Deseret News,* March 25, 2012, https://www .deseret.com/2012/3/25/20402589/churches-express-pain-ask-for-justice-in -trayvon-martin-case. NB: George Zimmerman was not arrested until six weeks after the shooting.

66. David L. Eng and David Kazanjian, "Mourning and Loss," in *Loss: The Politics of Mourning* (Berkeley: University of California Press, 2002), 4.

67. Toni Morrison, preface to *Playing in the Dark: Whiteness and the Literary Imagination* (Cambridge, MA: Harvard University Press, 1992), xii.

68. Irene Byon, "L.A. Riots: Rev. Al Sharpton Encourages Further Change," *Neon Tommy,* Annenberg Media Center, University of Southern California, April 29, 2012, http://www.neontommy.com/news/2012/04/la-riots-video-rev-al-sharpton -encourages-further-change.

69. Gilbert, "What the Trayvon Martin Case Means" (emphasis in the original).

70. This Hoodie Sunday was an echo of the Million Hoodie March that had been held in New York City in March after the shooting.

71. Laura Nelson, "Sanford Removes Trayvon Martin Memorial, Outraging Some Activists," *LA Times,* July 10, 2012, http://articles.latimes.com/2012/jul/10/nation /la-na-nn-memorial-trayvon-martin-20120710. There was a similar discussion, although without any controversy, about when to remove the memorials, including sixty-five thousand teddy bears, in Newtown, CT. See Ray Rivera, "Asking What to Do with Symbols of Grief as Memorials Pile Up," *New York Times,* January 5, 2013, http://www.nytimes.com/2013/01/06/nyregion/as-memorials-pile-up-newtown -struggles-to-move-on.html.

72. Emily Yellin, "New Orleans Epitaph: Dead Man Shirts," *New York Times,* April 17, 2000, A15.

73. Rev. Michael Pfleger, untitled sermon, St. Sabina Catholic Church, Chicago, IL, March 25, 2012, excerpted in Jim Jaworski, "Pfleger on Trayvon Martin Shooting: 'Protect Our Children,'" *Chicago Tribune,* March 25, 2012, https://www .chicagotribune.com/news/breaking/chi-michael-pfleger-trayvon-martin-st. -sabina-story.html.

74. Rev. Nathaniel Robinson, untitled sermon, March 25, 2012, Greater St. Paul AME Church, Coconut Grove, FL, excerpted in James D. Davis and Mike Clary, "Sermons Carry Message of Solidarity for Trayvon Martin," *Sun Sentinel,* March 26, 2012, https://www.sun-sentinel.com/fl-trayvon-martin-church-20120325 -story.html.

75. Associated Press, "Trayvon Martin Death: Thousands March in Town Where Teenager Was Shot," *The Guardian,* March 31, 2012, https://www.theguardian.com

/world/2012/mar/31/trayvon-martin-protest-march-sanford. NB: "Hoodies Don't Kill" was a response to journalist Geraldo Rivera's assertion that Martin's hoodie was as responsible for Trayvon Martin's death as George Zimmerman. See https://video.foxnews.com/v/1525652570001#sp=show-clips.

76. Rev. Dr. Howard John Wesley, "A Rizpah Response," Alfred Street Baptist Church, Alexandria, VA, March 25, 2012, https://www.youtube.com/watch?v=vkg2_pVfjMU.

77. Claudia Rankin, "The Condition of Black Life Is One of Mourning," *New York Times,* June 22, 2015, https://www.nytimes.com/2015/06/22/magazine/the-condition-of-black-life-is-one-of-mourning.html.

78. Sheldon Wolin, *Fugitive Democracy: And Other Essays* (Princeton, NJ: Princeton University Press, 2016).

79. Paul Gilroy, *Postcolonial Melancholia* (New York: Columbia University Press, 2006), 41–57.

80. Elizabeth Drescher, "White Noise: Christian Whispers and Shouts on the Trayvon Martin Case," July 15, 2013, https://elizabethdrescherdotcom.wordpress.com/2013/07/15/white-noise-christian-whispers-and-shouts-on-the-trayvon-martin-case/.

81. President Barack Obama, "Statement by the President," July 14, 2013, https://obamawhitehouse.archives.gov/the-press-office/2013/07/14/statement-president.

82. Episcopal bishop Greg Brewer, Central Florida, "The Issue Is Justice, Not Merely Race," *Christianity Today,* July 13, 2013, https://www.christianitytoday.com/edstetzer/2013/july/issue-is-justice-not-race.html.

83. Rev. Beverly A. Bartlett, "Go and Do Likewise," Madison Avenue Presbyterian Church, July 21, 2013.

84. Rev. Greg Gregory, "Christians Are Abnormal in How They Relate to Enemies and Abuse," River of Life Church, Baptist, Enterprise, FL, April 2012, http://www.sermoncentral.com/sermons/christians-are-abnormal-in-how-they-related-to-enemies-and-abuse-gene-gregory-sermon-on-forgiveness-for-others-169044.asp?Page=2.

85. Wright, "Iced Tea and Skittles."

86. The National Black Church Initiative (NBCI) is a coalition of thirty-four thousand African American and Latinx churches working to eradicate racial disparities in health care, technology, education, housing, and the environment. See http://www.naltblackchurch.com.

87. Rev. Anthony Evans, president of the National Black Church Initiative, "NBCI Condemns All Major Latino Organizations Who Were Silent on Trayvon Martin Verdict," press release, October 28, 2013, https://www.naltblackchurch.com/pdf/latino-silence.pdf.

88. Rev. Al Sharpton, "Why Race Matters in the Trayvon Martin Tragedy," TheGrio, March 19, 2012, http://thegrio.com/2012/03/19/rev-al-sharpton-why-race -matters-in-the-trayvon-martin-tragedy/.

89. Jelani Cobb, "After the Verdict: The Zimmerman Non-Riots," *New Yorker,* July 15, 2013, http://www.newyorker.com/news/news-desk/after-the-verdict-the -zimmerman-non-riots.

90. Cobb, "After the Verdict."

91. Cobb.

92. Cobb.

93. Jason Shelton and Michael Emerson, *Blacks and Whites in Christian America: How Racist Discrimination Shapes Religious Conviction* (New York: NYU Press, 2012).

94. Shelton and Emerson, *Blacks and Whites in Christian America,* 122.

95. President Barack Obama, "Statement by the President," August 18, 2014, https://obamawhitehouse.archives.gov/the-press-office/2014/08/18/statement -president.

96. Rev. Anthony Zibolshi, "The Heart Matters," Rosedale Church of the Nazarene, Middletown, PA, July 2016, http://www.sermoncentral.com/sermons/the -heart-matters-anthony-zibolski-sermon-on-heart-202604.asp.

97. Rev. Lena Gardner, "Black Lives Matter Sermon," Michael Servetus Unitarian Society, Fridley, MN, November 15, 2015, https://www.questformeaning.org /spiritual-themes/challenge-and-transformation/black-lives-matter-sermon.

98. "Je suis Charlie" (French for "I am Charlie") is a slogan and a logo created by French art director Joachim Roncin and adopted by supporters of freedom of speech and freedom of the press after the January 7, 2015, shooting in which twelve people were killed at the offices of the French satirical weekly newspaper *Charlie Hebdo.*

99. *Relevant* staff, "The Problem with Saying 'All Lives Matter,'" *Relevant,* June 5, 2020, https://www.relevantmagazine.com/current/the-problem-with-saying-all -lives-matter/.

100. Rev. Valerie Bridgeman, visiting associate professor of homiletics and the Hebrew Bible, Methodist Theological School in Ohio, "Wounded for Us," *Huffington Post,* August 15, 2014 (updated December 6, 2017), http://www.huffingtonpost.com /rev-dr-eric-d-barreto/preaching-reflections-on-michael-brown_b_5682974.html.

101. Gardner, "Black Lives Matter Sermon."

102. Rev. Michael Hodges, "After Ferguson," Christ Church, Andover, MA, December 7, 2014, http://www.christchurchandover.org/sermons/article404616c8529826 .htm.

103. Rev. Barry Johnson, "Do We Trust God?," Grace Christian Center, Dayton, OH, August 2016, http://www.sermoncentral.com/sermons/do-we-trust-god-barry -johnson-sermon-on-police-officers-203510.asp.

104. Rev. George Yancey, "We Need a Christian Version of Black Lives Matter," *The Stream*, January 17, 2016, https://stream.org/need-christian-version-black-lives -matter/.

105. Pastor Steven Wedgeworth, "Should Evangelicals Hijack Black Lives Matter?," *Mere Orthodoxy*, January 11, 2016, https://mereorthodoxy.com/should-evangelicals -hijack-black-lives-matter/.

106. Wedgeworth, "Should Evangelicals Hijack Black Lives Matter?"

107. Derryck Green, "InterVarsity Seduced by Compartmentalized Justice," *Juicy Ecumenism*, Institute on Religion and Democracy blog, December 31, 2015, https://juicyecumenism.com/2015/12/31/35285/.

108. Lisa Robinson, "Some Honest Thoughts on #BlackLivesMatter, the Church, and Real Reconciliation," *Theothoughts* (blog), May 13, 2016, https://theothoughts .com/2016/05/13/some-honest-thoughts-on-blacklivesmatter-the-church-and-real -reconciliation/.

109. Jason Vallee, "Blessing of the First Responders Set for Sunday," *Westerly Sun*, September 28, 2016, https://www.dailydispatch.com/StateNews/RI/2016/September /28/Westerly.Blessing.of.the.First.Responders.set.for.Sunday.aspx. See Chapter 4 for another version of the story of first responders as America's heroes.

110. Rev. Fred D. Robinson, "What God Is Screaming in Ferguson, Missouri," Baptist, Charlotte, NC, *CNN Belief Blog*, August 23, 2014, https://religion.blogs.cnn .com/2014/08/23/what-god-is-screaming-in-ferguson-missouri/.

111. Rev. Mike Kinman, dean of Christ Church Cathedral, St. Louis, MO, quoted in Leah Gunnings Francis, *Ferguson and Faith: Sparking Leadership and Awakening Community* (St. Louis, MO: Chalice Press, 2016), 48.

112. Rev. Vernon Johns, "It's Safe to Murder Negroes," Dexter Avenue Baptist Church, Montgomery, AL, May 1949, http://www.thehundred-seven.org /vernonjohns_sermon.pdf. See also "Early Years in Montgomery, 1948–1950," chap. 23 in *The Life and Times of the Prophet Vernon Johns: Father of the Civil Rights Movement*, by Patrick Louis Cooney (n.p.: 1998), http://www.vernonjohns.org/tcal001 /vjvjmnterl.html (webpage no longer available).

113. Rev. Wayne Croft Sr., St. Paul's Baptist Church, West Chester, PA, July 10, 2016, http://abhms.org/about-us/mission-stories/safe-murder-negroes-america/.

114. Croft.

115. Rev. Dr. Howard John Wesley, "When the Verdict Hurts," Alfred Street Baptist Church, Alexandria, VA, July 18, 2013, https://www.youtube.com/watch?v =hqhOe85_vA8.

116. Wesley, "When the Verdict Hurts."

117. Gunnings Francis, *Ferguson and Faith*, 22.

118. James Cone, quoted in an interview in Shelton and Emerson's *Blacks and Whites in Christian America*, 44.

119. See Jason Shelton and Michael Emerson, "Shaded Morality: Not So Black and White," chap. 6 in *Blacks and Whites in Christian America*, 129.

120. Shelton and Emerson, "Shaded Morality," 126.

121. Gunnings Francis, *Ferguson and Faith*, 46.

122. Vivian Yee, "Indictment of New York Officer Divides Chinese-Americans," *New York Times*, February 22, 2015, https://www.nytimes.com/2015/02/23/nyregion /in-new-york-indictment-of-officer-peter-liang-divides-chinese-americans.html.

123. Frank Shyong, "Why This Cop's Conviction Brought Thousands of Asian Americans into New York's Streets," *Los Angeles Times*, April 13, 2016, http://www .latimes.com/nation/la-na-liang-brooklyn-shooting-20160413-story.html.

124. Timmy Lu, "There Is No Chinese Side of Justice," *Reappropriate* (blog), February 27, 2016, http://reappropriate.co/2016/02/there-is-no-chinese-side-of-justice/.

125. Jay Caspian Kang, "How Should Asian Americans Feel about the Peter Liang Protests," *New York Times Magazine*, February 23, 2016, http://www.nytimes.com /2016/02/23/magazine/how-should-asian-americans-feel-about-the-peter-liang -protests.html.

126. Rev. Grace Ji-Sun Kim, "Crucifixion of Jesus: Scapegoating, Discrimination and the Cross," *Huffington Post*, March 25, 2016, http://www.huffingtonpost.com /grace-jisun-kim/crucifixion-of-jesus-scap_b_9512372.html.

127. Ji-Sun Kim, "Crucifixion of Jesus."

128. See William Bratton, "Eulogy for Police Officer Rafael Ramos," accessed in the spring of 2019, https://assets.documentcloud.org/documents/1386203/bratton -eulogy-for-officer-ramos.pdf.

129. Vice President Joseph Biden, "Remarks by Vice President Biden at a Service for NYPD Officer Rafael Ramos," Christ Church, Glendale, NY, December 27, 2014, White House, Office of the Vice President, https://obamawhitehouse .archives.gov/the-press-office/2014/12/27/remarks-vice-president-biden-service -nypd-officer-rafael-ramos.

130. Judith Butler, *Precarious Life: The Power of Mourning and Violence* (London: Verso, 2004).

131. Shatema Threadcraft, "Spectacular Black Death," Institute for Advanced Study, 2018, https://www.ias.edu/ideas/threadcraft-black-death.

132. President Barack Obama, "Remarks by the President in Eulogy for the Honorable Reverend Clementa Pinckney," College of Charleston, Charleston, SC,

June 26, 2015, https://obamawhitehouse.archives.gov/the-press-office/2015/06/26/remarks-president-eulogy-honorable-reverend-clementa-pinckney.

133. James Comey, quoted in "FBI Director: Charleston Shooting, Not Terrorism," WHAM-TV, June 20, 2015, https://web.archive.org/web/20150628135934/ http://13wham.com/news/features/nation-news/stories/fbi-director-charleston-shooting-not-terrorism-3408.shtml.

134. Obama, "Eulogy for the Honorable Reverend Clementa Pinckney."

135. Obama, "Eulogy for the Honorable Reverend Clementa Pinckney."

136. Obama, "Eulogy for the Honorable Reverend Clementa Pinckney."

137. Obama, "Eulogy for the Honorable Reverend Clementa Pinckney."

138. President Obama singing "Amazing Grace" at the memorial service for Honorable Reverend Clementa Pinckney, College of Charleston, Charleston, SC, June 26, 2015, https://youtu.be/INo5jVNBs64.

139. President Obama's Dallas Police Memorial Speech, July 12, 2016, http://www.cnn.com/videos/us/2016/07/12/barack-obama-dallas-police-memorial-entire-speech-sot.cnn.

140. President Barack Obama, Eulogy at the Dallas Police Officers Memorial Service, Morton H. Meyerson Symphony Center, Dallas, TX, July 12, 2016, *TIME* transcript, http://time.com/4403543/president-obama-dallas-shooting-memorial-service-speech-transcript/.

141. Obama, Eulogy at the Dallas Police Officers Memorial Service.

142. Obama, Eulogy at the Dallas Police Officers Memorial Service.

143. Obama, Eulogy at the Dallas Police Officers Memorial Service.

144. Obama, Eulogy at the Dallas Police Officers Memorial Service.

145. Obama, "Eulogy for the Honorable Reverend Clementa Pinckney."

146. President George W. Bush, Dallas Police Officers Memorial Service, Morton H. Meyerson Symphony Center, Dallas, TX, July 12, 2016, *TIME* transcript, http://time.com/4403510/george-w-bush-speech-dallas-shooting-memorial-service/.

147. Ray Rivera, "Asking What to Do with Symbols of Grief, as Memorials Pile Up," *New York Times,* January 5, 2015, https://www.nytimes.com/2013/01/06/nyregion/as-memorials-pile-up-newtown-struggles-to-move-on.html.

148. President Clinton and First Lady Hillary Clinton address children about Oklahoma bombing during weekly presidential radio address, April 22, 1995, https://www.youtube.com/watch?v=nl59FA3STGc.

149. Rev. Nathan Albert, "A Prayer: God of All Comfort and Grace," in *A Good Word,* 6.

150. Hodges, "After Ferguson."

151. Rabbi Arnold Rachlis, University Synagogue, Irvine, CA, quoted in Roxana Kopetman and Doug Irving, "Local Sermons Call on Faith, Action in Response to School Shootings," *Orange County Register,* December 17, 2012, http://www.ocregister.com/articles/shooting-380872-world-school.html.

152. President Obama at Sandy Hook Prayer Vigil.

153. President Donald J. Trump, quoted in Rosie Gray, "Trump Defends White-Nationalist Protesters: 'Some Very Fine People,'" *The Atlantic,* August 15, 2017, https://www.theatlantic.com/politics/archive/2017/08/trump-defends-white-nationalist-protesters-some-very-fine-people-on-both-sides/537012/.

154. N. T. Wright, "Christianity Offers No Answers about the Coronavirus. It's Not Supposed To," *TIME,* March 29, 2020, https://time.com/5808495/coronavirus-christianity/.

155. See "Police in the U.S. Killed 164 Black People in the First 8 Months of 2020. These Are Their Names. (Part II: May-August)," CBS News, accessed October 19, 2020, https://www.cbsnews.com/pictures/black-people-killed-by-police-in-the-us-in-2020-part-2/80/.

156. Willie Brown, "Young Whites Awaken to 400 Years of American Racism," *San Francisco Chronicle,* June 6, 2020, https://www.sfchronicle.com/bayarea/williesworld/article/Young-whites-awaken-to-400-years-of-American-15321313.php.

157. John McCrank, "NYSE Holds Nearly Nine-Minute Silence in Honor of George Floyd," Reuters, June 9, 2020, https://www.reuters.com/article/instant-article/idUSKBN23G2IM.

158. Katie Rogers, "Protesters Dispersed With Tear Gas So Trump Could Pose at Church," *New York Times,* June 1, 2020 (updated September 17, 2020), https://www.nytimes.com/2020/06/01/us/politics/trump-st-johns-church-bible.html; George Floyd Memorial in Minneapolis, transcript, accessed in the summer of 2020, https://www.rev.com/transcript-editor/shared/fk8VThpYSdwzNOmZ-uLgMdBCkiNoTwi7R29TGK64fGOf43DCdcpm3Av9oDFP2DUD-i5R-oFHzeSSf6GOC1ZyIAJGs_g.

159. Rev. Al Sharpton, George Floyd Funeral Eulogy, June 9, 2020, transcript, https://www.rev.com/blog/transcripts/reverend-al-sharpton-george-floyd-funeral-eulogy-transcript-june-9.

160. Sharpton, George Floyd Funeral Eulogy.

161. Rev. Michael Lawrence, "Should I Respond to George Floyd's Death on Sunday?," Hinson Baptist Church, Portland, OR, May 30, 2020, https://www.9marks.org/article/should-i-respond-to-george-floyds-death-this-sunday/.

162. Lawrence, "Should I Respond to George Floyd's Death?"

163. Geoffrey Skelley, "How Americans Feel about George Floyd's Death and the Protests," *FiveThirtyEight*, June 5, 2020, https://fivethirtyeight.com/features /how-americans-feel-about-george-floyds-death-and-the-protests/.

164. "Most Americans Sympathize with Protests, Disapprove of Trump's Response," Thomson Reuters Foundations, June 2, 2020, https://news.trust.org/item/202006 02213748-a24t2/; Morning Consult, *National Tracking Poll #2005131: Crosstabulation Results*, May 31–June 1, 2020, https://assets.morningconsult.com/wp-uploads/2020 /06/01190233/2005131_crosstabs_POLICE_Adults_FINAL_LM.pdf.

165. Morning Consult, *National Tracking Poll #2005131*, 59–60.

166. Monica Chon, "Religious Leaders across the Country React to the Killing of George Floyd," *O, The Oprah Magazine*, June 2, 2020, https://www.oprahmag.com /entertainment/a32746371/religious-leaders-george-floyd/.

167. Chon, "Religious Leaders across the Country React."

168. Chon, "Religious Leaders across the Country React."

169. Becca Most, "Faith Groups Respond to George Floyd's Death," *Southwest Journal*, June 11, 2020, https://www.southwestjournal.com/news/2020/06/faith -groups-respond-to-george-floyds-death/.

170. Rev. Dr. William J. Barber II, "Sunday Sermon," Washington National Cathedral, June 14, 2020, https://cathedral.org/sermons/sermon-the-rev-dr-william -j-barber-ii-2/.

171. Gayatri Spivak, "Criticism, Feminism and the Institution," interview by Elizabeth Gross, *Thesis Eleven* 10/11 (November–March 1984–1985): 175–187.

172. J. Peter Euben, *Platonic Noise* (Princeton, NJ: Princeton University Press, 2003), 86.

Acknowledgments

The archival research required for this project would not have been possible without the patience and erudition of many research librarians at collections across the country. Of particular note are Suzanne Estelle Holmes of Yale Divinity School as well as Joan Clarke and Lucy Maziar of the United States Coast Guard Academy. They were each tireless in their efforts to help me find overlooked and long-forgotten sermons. Other librarians at the Dr. Martin Luther King Archive at Boston University, the Martin Luther King, Jr., Research and Education Institute at Stanford University, the Woodruff Library Historical Collections at Emory University, the Dr. Martin Luther King, Jr., Archives at Morehouse College, and the King Center in Atlanta, Georgia, were also pivotal to the development of each chapter. The staff at the JFK Presidential Library was also accommodating and helpful with the tedious work of copying and cataloguing the 850 sermons. Over the years of my writing this book, many ministers have also shared their sermons, especially those from the week of September 11, 2001. I am grateful to all those who were interested in this project and shared both their work and insights. Finally, this project would not have been completed without the intellectual generosity and patience of Heather Hughes, associate editor at Harvard University Press. Her demanding erudition and aspirational vision for this work enabled me to write a better book. And two anonymous reviewers were of infinite value to the completion of the manuscript. This research clearly belongs to many.

I have been fortunate to have both fabulous mentors as well as engaging colleagues and friends. As always, Wendy Brown remains my intellectual north star. While at Yale Divinity School, both Skip Stout and Nora Tubbs Tisdale were pivotal to the development of this project. Charles Butterworth, Kate DeGroot, Jose Gonzalez, Michael Mac-Donald, Jillian McLeod, Sarah Morgan Smith, Mo Sila, Dan Theriault, Emily Townes, Mary Warner, Karen Wink, Erik Wingrove Haugland, and Mark Yellin have all been the kind of interlocutors one hopes to have when pursuing a scholar's life. I cherish the friendship—both scholarly and otherwise—that they have each provided.

For a decade now, I have been teaching at the United States Coast Guard Academy. It has been both a challenging and rewarding experience. The students at the academy are bright, disciplined (of course!), and engaging. They remind me every week why the classroom remains my favorite place for a lively exchange and a thoughtful development of ideas.

Most working mothers know that balance is usually elusive, and that patience and flexibility are mandatory. My four children—Olivia, Sophia, Renny, and Colin—have shown both patience and flexibility with their often late, sometimes absentminded, but profoundly devoted mother. There has never been anything more important to me than trying, and then trying again, to be a good mother to these gifted and amazing four young adults.

INDEX

Abernathy, Reverend Ralph, 139–140, 143–147, 148, 149, 160; eulogy to King in Abernathy's church, 151; on King's funeral, 163

abolitionist movement, 180

Abrams, Reverend Cooper, 240

Adams, Ansel, 68

Afghanistan war, 255, 269

African Americans, 18, 30, 87–88; as conscientious objectors (COs), 53; internment of Japanese Americans and, 72; Kennedy's death mourned by, 100–102; Korean Americans' relations with, 192–195; Los Angeles clergy and the White imagination, 189–197; Los Angeles uprising and, 170, 178–179, 186–187; 9/11 and, 234, 235; Protestant majority among, 9; Rodney King verdict and, 173; World War II and, 44–45. *See also* Blacks/Black Americans

African Methodist Episcopal Church, 125, 169, 174, 178, 189, 305, 321

agency, 30, 95, 113, 124, 222

"Alert When He Comes" (Carpenter sermon), 256

Alexander, Elizabeth, 172

Alexander, Reverend Scott W., 256

Alfred P. Murrah Federal Building (Oklahoma City), 1, 22, 44–45, 197, 339n6; government workers in, 201; spontaneous memorial on site of, 212, 232; transcendent status in sermons, 208–209. *See also* Oklahoma City bombing (1995)

Allen, Ivan, 145, 153

Almon, Baylee, 226, 231

American Council of Christian Churches, 51, 348n85

American Mourning (Stow), 226

Anderson, Benedict, 274

Anderson, Michael, 220

Antigone (Sophocles), 2, 5, 17, 264–265, 326, 333–334; as analytic touchstone, 14–17; "Choral Ode to Man," 15–16; contemporary politics and, 18; mourning for George Floyd and, 336; Obama's role of pastor and, 286; unmourned loss in, 114

anti-Semitism, 224, 331

apocalypse, 56, 132

Arab Americans, 204, 233, 237, 240

Arbery, Ahmaud, 18, 335

Arendt, Hannah, 21

Aristotle, 5

Arlington National Cemetery, 19

Arnold, Reverend O. Carroll, 111, 113

"Assassination of JFK and the Crucifixion of Jesus, The" (Holliday sermon), 88